A taste of the messages in this book,
quotes from Jesus...

"Love has no opposites."

"Most conflict is self-generated by rejections of life and denial of existence as it really is."

"Kindness is the heart of living. It is what makes life bearable, meaningful, and delicious."

"There are no structures that cannot be superseded and rearranged by love."

"Any prayer asked in love, or honoring love will be answered, although your Father has no covenant to answer the prayers of your ego, to solve its self-made problems, or to make its fictions result in happiness. Your Creator is one with reality, so how can He answer a prayer that seeks further separation from the love and the reality that He is?"

"Beauty is a choir of singers, a chorus of dreamers, a concert of aspirations, an orchestration of goals, a symphony of ambitions, and a ballet of productions."

"Reality is a living, responsive flow of life which continues forever on many levels of existence. Reality honors each being, and responds to its love. You are invited and encouraged always to shape reality to your needs and purposes. However, there is a significant difference between shaping reality and inventing it. You would be wise to learn the difference and to know that the fictional self is the creator of fictional realities which have undone you."

*"Future is the promise of completion which you remember and seek again. In that pursuit, infinite potential will supply your needs, yearnings, lessons, and alignments, until at last you realize that **true completion has always been**, and is reattained through liberation of desire as well as attachment."*

"Being in the Heart is prayer. When you enter the Sacred Heart, you are restored in your life and you are made whole again."

"Everything was created in innocence. Behold this if you would see the face of God."

"Anything sent forth to deceive you will be directed exactly to your ego, or to your mind. The reason is that a person's ego considers anything to be true which supports its survival, just as the mind considers anything to be true which supports the supremacy of logic. As a matter of fact, the mind cannot discern fact from fiction if both are presented with equal logic!"

"Through judgment, a man reveals what he still needs to confront and to learn. Through discernment, one reveals what he has mastered!"

"It is not the mind's province to create reality, but rather to observe, integrate, understand, and implement reality. When you surrender to the fact that existence does not require invention--that it simply is--you will be on the threshold of looking into the face of God."

"Your heart is one with the love of God, and God is one with reality. You might define truth as a triangle of God, love, and reality. Truth is the point where love and reality are one in God. This is why truth is the universal solvent for all blockages, limitations, conflicts, and problems of mortal existence."

"The original sin was judgment ... Judgment is actually the only sin of which a pure and perfect child of God is capable."

"The long era of judgment has been man's darkest night, but that will end soon when the last judgment has been made. The last judgment will be the judgment against judgment itself."

"Morality is change for the better."

"External motivation will eventually destroy a person's ability to honor his own purposes."

"History repeats itself generation after generation because of judgment and denial which create ruptures in the flow of life. The universe fills the

ruptures quickly with the very thing your objections denied."

"In organic life, DNA is constructed to conduct the complex and mysterious function of love."

"Love is your true self, which springs forth from God, the indefinable everlasting fountain of existence. The fictional self is who you thought you were when you forgot that you were love."

"Everything and everyone belong. Bless them, respect them, and forgive if necessary. "

"The highest unity is one which respects differences as well as sameness, and regards both with equal respect."

"When you are being the love that you are, you realize that the secret of success already exists in the nature of your beingness. Solutions to problems, answers to prayers, and revelations of purpose already exist. It is your duty and challenge to make yourself available to receive them."

"The most important person to forgive is yourself."

"God's will abides in truth. Know the truth, and you will know the will of God. The heart knows truth as that which sets it free."

"As a man loves, so he is. As he believes, so he becomes."

"Love commands the universe. Man only resorts to control when love is missing. In a world obsessed with control, it is difficult to find even a moment's peace."

"In releasing, you let go of the clinging, and you are made whole again. In releasing and honoring what has been, there may be tears, but there will also be doors opening to future possibilities."

"The Sacred Heart is truly your higher intelligence and the source of an inspired life."

"Unity is the instrument of all goodness. Division is the instrument of all evil."

"A being who is far from home will attract others who are equally detached or lost. Demons are only lost souls."

"The universe is implicitly and explicitly of one piece. At the point of perfect stasis between the implicit and explicit, there is a condition of hypersynchronicity, where matter, energy, space and time move into a 'no-resistance' mode of infinite potential. This is the synchronizing of matter to a 'zero point' of perfect synchronicity."

"The mind has no power to change your life. That privilege belongs to the heart alone."

"A problem can never be solved at the level of its creation and existence."

"Your immortality is not imprisoned within a wheel of life, or pathway of cause and effect."

"You are not alone. As you suspect, there are younger and older brothers elsewhere. Those civilizations which are equal or behind yours cannot reach you anymore than you can reach them."

"A being's greatness is measured by his outreach, not by his containment. Not by how much he can hold but by how much he can give."

"The greatest mystery of the universe is that Love is the sacred aspect of beingness. Be it to the fullest, and the rest of your life will fall into place. Love is who you are!"

"Everyone has a covenant and a purpose which is special, and if you do not fulfill it, there is no one else who will."

"Ethics might be summarized as cause and effect in balance and applied for the greatest good."

"The mind only solves problems of logic and balance, never problems of life."

"When you change your heart, you change your life."

Acknowledgments

In 1996, the original audio tapes revealing my conversations with the Master were first released publicly. From that time forward, a ground swell of devotion and teaching has developed around the world. We now have a fellowship, whose love and common purpose have truly provided the strength, courage, support and momentum for me to complete the years-long task of preparing myself for the task and honor of putting these words of Jesus into print. Eternal thanks and endless love are given to each of you who led in this mission. There is nothing of value that has been done alone... Without you, my sky would have been without stars!

I will forever be grateful to Brian Bibb, my husband in the years of this story, whose vision, tenacity, courage, and tireless efforts propelled me into the winds of destiny. Endless thanks belong to Lila Lear, whose initiative and lightening fingers presented me with a transcription of the audio tapes in 1997 along with a gentle directive to "get to work." My editor extraordinaire, Wanda Evans, provided a living instruction that "less is more." Her firm hand, cool head, and professional savvy gave me strength where it was needed and freedom where nothing less would do. Most of all, she helped me to find that point of synchronicity between myself and Jesus' words where his presence was the most visible and mine was the least intrusive. Her masterful editing is a gift to the world.

My constant companions through the many months of writing, were my devoted readers, John Ryan, Mary Cole, and Nancy French, who lovingly gave hundreds of hours of their life and energy to help ensure that Jesus' message would reach the reader with clarity, vitality, and freshness. They have my deepest appreciation, gratitude and love forever.

Special thanks are given to three others. Dr. Robert Applegate of Christ Truth League was the light in my window on many occasions when I needed spiritual encouragement and penetrating simplicity on points of theological concern. Dr. Harold Puthoff, physicist and Director for Advanced Studies at The University of Texas, gave me added confidence to share the Master's scientific revelations, along with invaluable points of clarification and understanding. I am privileged also to count among my friends Dr. Don Slanina, whose knowledge of physics provided helpful guidelines for me with regard to scientific material.

Dedication

Our Father who is innocent and pure,
Holy is your name.
May love be seen as all that is.
May earth be seen as heaven is.
Nourish this day with your bountiful supply,
And allow us to receive as we give that right to others.
Restore us from the perils of illusion,
And renew our perception of truth.
For truth is the kingdom, and love is the power,
And Yours is the glory forever.

Love
Without End™

Jesus Speaks...

Glenda Green

Spiritis

Published by: Spiritis Publishing
P.O. Box 239
Sedona, AZ 86339

Cover design: Robert Howard Designs
Front cover painting: *First Light*, a spiritual portrait of Jesus Christ.
©Glenda Green, 1998.
Back cover painting: *The Lamb and The Lion*, a portrait of Jesus Christ.
©Glenda Green, 1992.

A Spiritis Book

Eighth printing, December 2001

Publisher's Cataloging-in-Publication Data

Green, Glenda
      Love Without End: Jesus Speaks..., by Glenda Green.-1st ed.
      p.cm
      Preassigned LCCN: 98-73963
      ISBN: 0-9666623-1-8

      1. Jesus Christ-Apparitions and miracles. 2. Jesus Christ-Art
      3. Green, Glenda. 4. Love-Religious aspects-Christianity. I.
      Title

BT580.A2U6 1999   232.9'7
                                              QB198-1410

TABLE OF CONTENTS

Part One

Chapter 1
The Way it Was 1
Chapter 2
The Lamb and the Lion 5
Chapter 3
A Miracle for Breakfast 21
Chapter 4
Life Goes On 27

Part Two

Chapter 1
He Spoke 43
Chapter 2
The Wondrous Universe 61
Chapter 3
The Love That You Are 79
Chapter 4
The Adamantine Particles 105
Chapter 5
The One Spirit 129
Chapter 6
The Heart Is Your Higher Intelligence 155
Chapter 7
Bridges 179
Chapter 8
The Blessed Life 197
Chapter 9
The Ten Commandments Of Love 215
Chapter 10
Your Rights and Freedoms 237
Chapter 11
God and Reality 253
Chapter 12
Jesus on Science 281
Chapter 13
Pathways to Success 305
Chapter 14
The Beloved 323

Part One

The Journey to Acceptance

All manner of thing shall be well
By the purification of the motive
In the ground of our beseeching.

T.S. Eliot

Chapter 1
The Way it Was

This is the use of memory:
For liberation—not less of love but expanding
Of love beyond desire, and so liberation
From the future as well as the past.[1]

T. S. Eliot

I look forward to the day when we can share our love through common consciousness, and when all the messages which the Master has given to humanity are so well known that none require a preface. Until that time, however, the reality of context is inescapable. Many of you will surely ask, who is this woman who has spoken to Jesus and how did it happen? The conversations presented in this book are more important by far than the nature of their occurrence, and yet for the sake of clarity and history, they are inseparable from the process.

The special quality of His truth is that there is a sacred resonance and harmony within it which clarifies, integrates, and focuses the truth of all men. His presence is recognizable without introduction. Mine, however, is not.

By profession I am an artist, and by grace I am a woman whose greatest truth was found in the Master's presence. Nevertheless, this book is not about religion, and I am not a theologian. Were it not for events which were nothing short of sacred phenomena, I would in no way be equipped to deliver these messages to you, nor would I possess the wellspring of substance which you are about to receive. These messages were not derived from reading, research, religious preparation, or human mentors. The tapestry of this missive and the loom which wove it were my experience of painting the Master's portrait. The originator of this dialogue was the Master Himself, and I was the participant. Therefore, certain aspects of my story are relevant to the reader's larger understanding. This is not because I have any special importance, for certainly I am one with the rest of humanity. The purpose in telling you about myself is to build immunity for you against subtle intrusions of my character upon your own viewpoint. Thus, I may become translucent or even invisible to the Master's message. It is also my fervent hope to share with you a precious miracle, an insertion of divinity into the predictable order of life. By presenting the picture of an ordinary person in fellowship with His Holiness, perhaps I can give you a reference point of comfort from which to receive a similar communion.

In a presence as real as life, but manifested from realms divine, Jesus appeared to me and was with me for almost four months between November 1991 and March 1992. During this time we spoke . . . as friends do . . . of matters large and small. Our conversations were not about idealistic worlds or visions of things to come. His messages were about life as we live it, and the potential for Heaven that lies within each of us now. His words are immensely practical, universally timeless, and refreshingly relevant to our most advanced level of knowledge. There is a clarity in them which needs no extra support or explanation. Therefore, if moved to do so, you may go directly to His messages in Part Two and begin.

To assist the reader's study, I have presented the Master's words in italics. That way, they may be isolated from the dialogue and savored independently. At the same time, I have made every effort to remember and to reconstruct the anecdotal aspects of His visitation, revealing the queries, motives, and emotions which I brought to the situation. The friendly nature of our exchange was always directed to things that were of mutual interest or relevant to our relationship. Our topics of conversation ranged from the practical to the miraculous, with pleasant interludes of chitchat.

Every day that we spoke I took voluminous notes, sometimes during the conversation, but most often in the evening when I was alone. My sole intent in taking notes was to preserve the wisdom presented for my own future reference. During the process of transcription it never occurred to me that I would ever share my conversations publicly, and most certainly I did not proceed with academic diligence to cover all aspects of theological concern.

This was a deeply personal experience, yet it was also external to myself. Not only was there a sacred presence before me, visible to my eyes, but also there was a beautiful voice, and I responded to it with my own. The words you are about to read are not the result of automatic writing or channeling. We are all channels for God. Nevertheless, the practice of channeling as an intentional process was not used. Channeling, as a way of directing communication from other realms into this one, is a very ancient practice currently revived in its popularity. My reason for mentioning it, however, is neither to commend nor to disparage—merely to distinguish. The words Jesus spoke to me were audible, and I responded in full consciousness.

As for existential explanations of it all, my perspective is not yet grand enough to encompass the many possibilities. What happened between November 23, 1991, and March 12, 1992, was nothing short of miraculous. However, it is not necessary that it be explained or regarded in any particular way. I simply hope that the reader will receive the story about to be told as the enlightenment of a woman who found her place within the Master's truth.

Regardless of whether you call Him Friend, Teacher, Master, Lord, or God Incarnate, it still remains a historical fact that no single individual has had more influence upon the course of human events in the last two thousand years. Regardless of one's beliefs or even disbelief, His impact belongs to us all. Well beyond the countless numbers who center their religious convictions around Him, there are other millions who behold His influence, wisdom, love, and virtue despite their disinterest in the religions built in His name. This is a reality which exceeds the varieties of private or collective faith.

In respect of that reality, while honoring the sacred aspects as well, I have chosen to refer to Him as either the Master or simply, Jesus. While some readers might prefer more sacred protocol, I feel that the term, "Master," is suitably honorable without establishing a religious viewpoint which might exclude others from the study of these messages.

What you get from the messages is a direct result of what you HEAR! Basic to all of Jesus' teaching to me was that of innocent perception: *"Open your eyes that you may see and your ears that you may hear. For there is nothing hidden that will not be revealed, nor has anything been kept secret that it should not come to light."*[2] In the end, we will all draw conclusions about what we have heard, yet little will be seen or heard if we enter the listening without an openness to receive or without a yearning heart.

Chapter 2
The Lamb and the Lion

When the short day is brightest, with frost and fire,
The brief sun flames the ice, on pond and ditches,
In windless cold that is the heart's heat,
Reflecting in a watery mirror
A glare that is blindness in the early afternoon.
And glow more intense than blaze of branch, or brazier,
Stirs the dumb spirit: no wind, but Pentecostal fire
In the dark time of the year. [3]

T. S. Eliot

The winter of 1989 brought to north Texas a wave of bitter cold. Though it would not be a white Christmas, the arctic air would keep us close to the hearth on Christmas Eve, warming our hands and hearts by the fire. Midnight passed, and dawn would soon be arriving. Except, for us, there was a different light about to burst on the horizon. At two o'clock in the morning, Gunner, my Himalayan cat, tore me from the depths of slumber with a siren-like scream. It was not, however, to announce the landing of Donner and Blitzen on the roof. He was warning me that something far more sinister had arrived through a construction flaw in the chimney of our wood-burning stove. Fortunately, Gunner became the smoke alarm that was missing in our country home. By that time, fire had consumed most of the living room, and every normal exit from the split-level structure was blocked by flames and billowing smoke. Our only chance for survival was to jump out of a second floor window with a few clothes and Gunner in hand. From the yard we watched as most of our worldly possessions went up in flames, including most of my art.

In utter exhaustion and despair, my husband and I fell asleep late on Christmas afternoon in my mother's house, with Gunner at our feet. We had been sleeping for several hours when I was startled from my dreams with a gentle nudge in the ribs.

"Wake up, Honey!" Less than twenty-four hours ago I had suddenly been awakened on the brink of disaster.

"What now?!"

His voice was brimming with excitement. "I just had a dream that you are going to paint a great portrait of Jesus Christ, and somehow the fire was necessary for that to occur."

"You're delirious," I mumbled, "Go back to sleep." Not impressed that his dream could be a divine message, I told myself that he was feeling the prayers and sympathies of our friends. I pulled up the covers and returned to my private retreat.

Neither my rebuff nor his return to slumber diminished any enthusiasm for the dream. As we sat down for breakfast the next morning he mentioned it again. I explained how there must surely be synchronicity between our vulnerability and the concern of others for our plight. "As they hold us in their thoughts and prayers, we could become the recipients of many spiritual blessings. Let's be grateful, and acknowledge. But for Heaven's sake, don't project beyond that!"

I thought about giving him a lesson in art history; detailing how, since the rise of literacy and the mass availability of Bibles, religious art had become a secondary medium for delivering God's messages to the earth. Consequently, artists of creative power had gone on to more expressive fields of endeavor where creative liberties were permitted.

Before having my morning coffee, however, I did not feel like explaining all that, so the short version would have to do. My whole career had revolved around secular art, and I was not about to jeopardize the name recognition I had worked so hard to attain among my peers and collectors by painting "Jesus pictures." Besides, I just wanted to put the pieces of my life back together--and that meant putting them **back the way they were!**

Without a place to work, my painting career would be suspended anyway. Therefore, it seemed to be a priority to work full-time rebuilding the basics of life. Through an odd serendipity, we found a charming old stone house with an acre of land at the north edge of Fort Worth. The ranch style home needed extensive renovation, yet we were strangely drawn to the additional bonus that it was still zoned for agriculture.

Anyone who has ever remodeled a house knows how consuming it can be. For six months we ate, slept, and literally breathed the reconstruction of our new home. My husband Brian helped on weekends, but it was my full-time job. Actually, it was good therapy, putting back what had been destroyed, and by the time the house was finished, I felt somewhat restored myself and ready to paint again.

Yet something had changed in my heart. Perhaps the magnitude of our recent loss had generated a sense of practical anxiety in me. For the first time in my life as an artist, I didn't just set up my easel and paint from the depths of my inner vision. Instead, I studied the market-- analyzing patterns of supply, demand, and success. Although my new work lacked the power of the lost masterpieces, it did have a lovely appeal, technical strength, and an excellent chance of competing successfully in the marketplace.

With that hope in mind, we packed the car and trekked to a major dealers' show in Los Angeles in the fall of 1991. During the five day show I picked up some nice orders, and made a number of promising gallery affiliations, but the show had not been an overwhelming success by any means. However, something of much greater importance happened in that huge convention center. I saw myself for the first time conforming to a segment of the artistic world primarily devoted to establishing name recognition by volume production and commercial success.

Many an artist would have danced with glee to have the level of success which I had achieved by other standards. After all, I had produced portraits for many prominent Americans, including the President pro tempore of the U.S. Senate. My portrait of Dr. Paul Peck was hanging in the Smithsonian Institution, while another of my paintings was hanging in the Museum of the City of New York. I had a New York publisher and many of my paintings were in prominent collections around the country. Altogether, my resume reflected talent, success, and real acceptance by the "keepers of excellence" within the art community. So what was this nagging recrimination I had about achieving commercial success as well?

The flavor of external pursuit was leaving a bitter aftertaste. With a sense of surrender, I resolved to use the rest of my traveling time for personal renewal. If possible, I would locate a "still point" of peace within myself where true motives could be examined and reestablished.

On a whim, we detoured from the Interstate in Arizona, traveling to Sedona and the beautiful red rock country south of Flagstaff. Though there was no obvious event, something happened amidst those ancient sandstone spires, because the next morning I felt revitalized and confident to handle whatever was to come. There was a sense that things would be different. Just how different was still to be revealed.

Homeward bound, it seemed as if we flew through New Mexico. As I listened to the music of Mozart and allowed its beauty to give my soul wings, it was easy to review my life and highlight the things I considered most important. Eventually a silence flooded me, and nothing seemed to be of value except the need to arrive at a new beginning. Without consideration of its impact, I turned to Brian and said, "If I dropped my career, would you mind?"

"No," he said, "You do whatever you need to do."

What were thirty plus years of hard work, after all? There was an inner confidence that something else would come along. If I had known what it was to be, I might have been less relaxed about the whole matter.

As we drove across the high mesa, my sense of relief matched the expansive horizon. In that desert quietness, there was a peaceful reverie which brought to mind impressions of incredible beauty. Though I am accustomed to receiving and playing with visual images, these stood out as extraordinary. Just as I relaxed into my inner sanctuary, Brian asked for the first time in several months, "Have you thought about that painting of Jesus lately?"

I started to bristle at his intrusion. Of all things to talk about, why did he mention **that** subject again? He had brought it up at regular intervals since his dream, and I had never responded in any way to make him think that my original position had changed even a smidgen. With my eyes still closed, I tried to suggest that I was half asleep by mumbling, "No more than you'll let me forget."

With gentle persistence, he encouraged me to consider all possibilities now that I stood on the threshold of a new opportunity. Immediately a beautiful landscape emerged on my mental screen—fields leading down to a lush green river valley and, on its banks, a tree with a split trunk under an azure sky with billowing clouds. This was quite unusual, as my self-generated imaginings rarely took the form of landscapes. Its beauty resonated profoundly through my whole being.

Brian must have sensed what I was experiencing, for right at that moment he asked, "What are you thinking about?"

"I'm not thinking about anything. I'm looking at a beautiful landscape in my mind's eye."

"Oh." A minute or so passed, then, "If you were to paint Jesus," he said sweetly, "how would you do it?"

"That's a pointless question, because I'm not going to take on the project . . . for all the following reasons."

My hope was that if I itemized every objection, then at last the whole proposition could be dismissed.

I had a Masters Degree in Art History from Tulane University, and my area of specialization was medieval European art which, by and large, is Christian. So I was well equipped to explain that the history of Christian art had derived its formulas from theology. It had its own symbolic language which served as a teaching tool and theological reinforcement. This had been necessary because historical facts were scanty, and creative inspiration too often exceeded the boundaries of Church doctrine. A case in point occurred when Michelangelo almost lost his life by taking liberties with the ceiling of the Sistine Chapel. The Pope was a man of theological protocol, and the artist was a man whose vision into eternal realms was untouched by formula.

I knew of no historical descriptions of Jesus, and certainly there were none in the New Testament. For a portraitist, that alone was enough to stop the project in its tracks. Moreover, I knew enough about the art of portrayal from my years as a portraitist to respect the intimate relationship between body and soul. In other words, no other man could pose for Jesus and project the right feelings into a painting.

Now, if those objections were not enough, I was adamant that I would not invent a portrayal of the Master. In the world of imagination, I felt that everyone had an equal right to see Him in his own way. Therefore, I was certainly not going to impose my private preferences upon the consciousness of others. With a sense of finality I presented my closing consideration, in hopes of barring the door to any further discussion. "I'll tell you what. **If He shows up for a sitting, I'll paint Him.**"

Brian diplomatically backed off for a moment, but he wasn't finished. All too soon he asked, "If you were going to paint Him, what would you call the painting?"

Too exasperated to protest any more, I started to say, "I don't know," when the strangest thing happened. A visual arrow shot through my mind with a trailing banner on which appeared the words *The Lamb and The Lion.* Momentarily stunned, I couldn't think or edit my perceptions, so I just repeated the words aloud in a distant voice. Brian said something, but

I didn't hear him. I was too absorbed in the realization that I would, indeed, be doing the painting that his dream had foretold.

But how? Had I not established all the impossible conditions? All I could do was consent to give it my best effort.

When we got home I gave myself three months to research any available material which might support the project. As a start, I re-read the New Testament, which was of little help since it does not contain a physical description of Jesus, although there are some clues which suggested physical attributes. For example, that He was born into the house of David, that He was a carpenter and fisherman, and that He was physically strong enough to carry a massive cross after enduring brutal torture.

Focusing on His livelihood as a carpenter, my study revealed that carpenters of that time were not just skilled in measuring and joining wood together for the construction of buildings. They were also required to go into the forest, fell the tree, and transform it into the lumber they would use. Clearly, carpentry of two thousand years ago was a job for a veritable Paul Bunyan of a man.

Knowing that the Master's family belonged to the house of David, within the tribe of Judah, I studied the recorded attributes of those people. Each of the twelve tribes of Israel had its own character, appearance and domain. Then, as now, genetic potential in Israel was greater than limiting stereotypes might tend to suggest. Ten of the twelve tribes had disappeared when the Babylonians scattered the Jewish people in the Diaspora (the "lost tribes of Israel " that we often read about). Only the lines of David and Benjamin, the Levites, and remnants of other tribes returned home. From David came the rulers, aristocrats, and military elite of Jewish society, a fact which made them the target of conquerors. When the Romans took control of the Holy Land, they decimated the line of David, leaving the others to carry on.

Centuries later, as medieval Europeans returned from pilgrimages to the Holy Land, they would bring home descriptions of that limited sample of Jewish potential, co-mingled with memories of Arab and other Middle East people costumed in typical desert attire. These reports were often biased, and formed the backbone of oversimplified pictorial descriptions which persist even into modern times, most especially in Christian art.

Within the few surviving descriptions of ancient Jews, there can be found references to the Tribe of Judah as often being taller and the "fairest of the fair." When asking my Semitic friends as to the meaning of "fair" in their world, I was cautioned not to assume that it would likely mean blond in the Nordic sense. However, it could include light olive to fair skin with hair ranging from light golden brown to red-brown, and eyes from hazel to blue green.

Although He might have appeared in different ways to different people, the charisma which drew strangers and crowds to Him tends to suggest that He was exceptionally appealing by some measure—at least when He chose to be! What form that might have taken, I could only guess, and guessing is something that a true portraitist is loath to do. The earliest paintings of Him, from the first and second centuries, show a handsome youth, but those portrayals reflected the influence of Roman fascination with Apollo rather than any true likeness of the Nazarene. Often those symbolic parallels came to be exploited and confused as the church was Romanized.

For this reason early church leaders prohibited artists from portraying Jesus in any manner which was physically strong or beautiful. They supported their position by emphasizing a 700 B.C. prophecy in the Old Testament book of Isaiah 53:2, regarding the future coming of their Messiah: "(H)e had no form or comeliness that we should look at him, and no beauty that we should desire him." Most scholars today agree that this prophecy cast a forward glance upon the Messiah's **role and social demeanor** rather than His physical appearance. In other words, the coming Messiah would not be a worldly prince, rich and well arrayed, from whom one would seek political favors, privilege, and financial advantage. In every way that interpretation was true. But would it not be odd if the Lord of Life who could raise the dead were, Himself, anything less than a picture of health and physical well being? To me that logic is inescapable, but to church authority, concerned only with establishing His spiritual supremacy, that passage from Isaiah was useful in diminishing any focus on His physical form. Most portrayals of Him in the last seventeen hundred years are a legacy from that decision.

The power of tradition was ominous, and the more I knew, the less capable I felt. All the conditions that I stipulated were based on points of integrity about which I felt strongly, therefore it was an impossible scenario. How could I ever do this painting? The many tidbits were interesting, but if I just pieced them together I would have a quilt, not a whole image with character and strength. After three months, every road

I traveled led me to a dead end, and the contradictions before me were more than I could deal with intellectually.

Now, what was I to do with what I had learned? By itself it had no power or application.

The answer came on November 23, 1991. The lovely autumn day portended nothing but its own beauty. Little did I know what was about to happen, or that it would bring into focus the discordant affairs of previous years, opening windows to an inconceivable future.

Clear morning light spread its fingers across the lawn, brightening everything in its path as it brought into focus a few bright red leaves still clinging to the trees of our large city lot. Such times are made for dwelling in thought, when everything external is in perfect order. I would be alone all day, so there would be nothing to interrupt my peace of mind. As steam from the coffee warmed my face, the hammock rocked slowly, stirring the cool November air.

Sorting through memories, I rather enjoyed the panoramic flashbacks of personal history. The recurring pattern was clearly one of new beginnings, yet with unmistakable irony the most critical event was the one of uncommon destruction on Christmas, 1989. If I had understood paradox then as well as I do now, perhaps I would have looked for prophecy in the reversals which had driven my life since that time. However, as I reviewed my thoughts in that clear November light, the only peace I found was in the hammock's rhythmic swing. It seemed to be gently suggesting . . . surrender . . . surrender . . . surrender.

Despite my pleasant reveries, the awesome glow of nature was distracting me from the inner simplicity I needed. Besides, it was time for lunch. After a quick sandwich, I decided to linger in the dining room for meditation and prayer. This room was central to the house, and so when the chandelier was off there was a pleasant half darkness even at midday.

It was a great room in which to be alone with God. This issue was between me and my Holy Source, and it truly needed to be resolved. My prayer began with protests, pleas, and conditions, which I hoped would bring resolution. Then I expressed my emotions, my doubts, and my fears. Yet there was no peace forthcoming. Finally, asking forgiveness for ever considering anything so far beyond my capacity, I confessed that I had no passion for this project—or at least not yet. Still no result. Last of all, I considered that my engagement in this process was a stepping stone to some other more feasible undertaking which Divine Will envisioned for me. Exhausting myself through exploring all the possibilities of what that might be, I finally rested my head in folded arms on the table. For more than an hour I slept.

What aroused me was a brilliant glow in the room. At first I thought that Brian had come home and flipped on the lights. Glancing upward, I observed the chandelier was still off. This did not surprise me, because I sensed there was nothing artificial about this light. It was a soft white radiance which suffused the room like a cloud which had descended from Heaven. The whole house possessed the stillness and silence of new fallen snow.

Though the room was still, the air rippled like heat expanding air over a flame, except the ripples flowed in all directions instead of just vertically. I traced the silvery, radiant patterns back to their source in the arched doorway and saw that they emanated from a spot of hyper-luminescence which was almost blinding. This resplendence was not flame like, however, since the whole room possessed the same quality of light. The difference was in the intensity of the brilliance itself and the dazzling patterns of silver and gold with opalescent white and sparkles of lavender, blue and rose.

I could look toward the center for only a second before the brilliance caused my eyes to fill with tears. Stunned, I had to look away, and at that moment I heard sounds which formed the pattern and cadence of language, although it was not a language with which I was familiar. As the "words" formed a meaning in my mind, He said, *"Greetings,"* and called my name.

There was an unmistakable Holiness in this Presence. I turned to look again, but the radiance was just too intense. Closing my eyes, I protected them from the glow and wept at the same time. No sooner had I escaped within myself than the Presence shot a beam of energy from Itself to a point between my eyebrows. I felt a sensation of pressure between my eyebrows which caused me to open my eyes and verify. What I saw was a stream of energy pouring in. Returning to the comfort of my inner vision, I watched as a picture was being etched into my awareness. It took about five seconds for the rendering to be completed. The vision seemed to be implanted in my optic nerve. It was stationary and available for me to look at whenever I chose.

Mesmerized by its beauty, I directed my attention inward for another fifteen or twenty minutes to gaze upon the vision of Jesus Christ which was complete, three-dimensional, and holographic. He was majestically standing on the top of a hill overlooking a green river valley. Unmistakably, it was the same landscape I had seen while driving through the New Mexico desert. Now it was complete with the Master, grazing sheep, and a billowing cloud forming the shape of a lion. I couldn't have asked for a more vivid or realistic picture from which to paint. It was the next best thing to having Him actually present.

When my awareness finally externalized, I found that the radiant Presence had gone and everything was back to normal. Nevertheless, I knew that I would never be the same again. That intuition proved to be true, for everything in my life changed after that Holy Moment.

For three days following the visitation I spoke very little, not wanting to risk the loss of holiness which still lingered. I was afraid my voice would reflect my state of continuing awe. Then I would have to speak about that exceptional event. On the fourth day at breakfast Brian caught my glance, and I couldn't hold back any longer. I described it all in vivid detail, as he looked at me with peaceful amazement.

Graciously holding back the, "I told you so," which must have been on his mind, he offered to help me with the project in any way he could. Overcoming my insecurity was the help that I needed most. That felt like an overwhelming task for anyone.

As I described the vision in detail, mentioning the sheep in the pasture and the lamb which Jesus was holding, I saw a burst of inspiration in Brian's eyes. "I know what I'll do! I'll call some sheep ranches and locate some lambs for you to study."

By that afternoon, he had canvassed every sheep ranch within three counties. We were disappointed to find that late November was an unlikely season for lambs. Undaunted, Brian suggested a Saturday visit to my hometown farmer's market. Starting at the crack of dawn, with camera in hand, we were off to hunt for lambs. At least if I could hold a lamb and get a souvenir photo, then some progress would have been made.

On arriving, we made a quick dash to the livestock area, only to meet with disappointment. There had been two lambs, which had already sold by 8:30 that morning. Feeling out of luck, and unsupported by Heaven, I was ready to go home, but Brian was not.

"Let's go up this lane," he suggested.

In a distant corner we found a grizzled old dealer from south Texas with a scraggly flock of different breeds. It was an unimpressive assortment of dirty, lumpy, wool-bearing creatures. I started to turn away when, suddenly, one sparkling white ewe emerged from behind the flock and made her way over to me. I had never seen anything like her short pristine wool, long neck, and regal face. Her stately appearance was only enhanced by her obvious pregnancy.

All I could think to call her was Mary, from the nursery rhyme. For her fleece *was* "white as snow." We bonded within minutes, and I wanted to take her home. Realizing there would soon be a lamb, it occurred to me that purchasing Mary would make them both available for study. The greater coincidence was that our restored farm house was zoned for agriculture even though it was nestled within the city.

There we were, two rookie city shepherds loading Mary in the back seat of our Cadillac. She still sparkled, even outside her natural environment, which prompted me to ask the dealer about her breed. "She's a mouflon," he answered, as I handed him my check. That meant nothing to me, and so without further conversation we drove away.

We felt a little "sheepish " as people gawked and laughed at our back-seat passenger. But what did they know? To distract ourselves from the embarrassment, we cooed to Mary and made plans for her housing. Then, Brian inquired, "What's a mouflon?" Neither of us knew, but we were suddenly frozen with anxiety that maybe we had just purchased one of those new hybrids which were not yet on the earth when Jesus walked it. I had visited my uncle's sheep ranch many times as a girl, and I had never seen anything like her. The more I thought about it, the more it became an issue, for any modern element would surely compromise the painting's integrity.

After Mary was settled in her quarters, I headed off to the library to get my question answered. I found what I was looking for very quickly as I opened the pages of an encyclopedia. In amazement and disbelief I looked for confirmation from two other sources. The mouflon was recognized as the oldest domesticated breed of sheep in Europe, and is considered to be the ancestor of all domesticated varieties. **Moreover, it was commonly herded in the Middle East 2,000 years ago.**

I re-read those passages until they were committed to memory, and with private elation I pondered the miracle of how many parts of the puzzle had to have already been in place for such an amazing act of perfection to occur. Short of traveling to the Middle East and bartering with a Bedouin, I could not have obtained a more suitable sheep to model for the painting. The odds of finding Mary in my home town were staggering to the imagination. As a child I had played on the very ground where I found Mary. How long ago, I wondered, was this painting committed to destiny?

With all our plans for the holidays, we agreed that it would be better to start the painting early in January. Besides, this would give me time to make some preparatory decisions and get the canvas ready. The first thing I needed to establish was the scale. So, I cast my attention on the vision and asked for guidance from Jesus. This was the first time it ever occurred to me to regard the vision as a means through which to dialogue. The answer was clearly given to me in a telepathic mode, though no words were spoken. The canvas was to be forty-eight inches square.

That was a restless December. I felt like a race horse waiting for the gate to open. Reassuring myself frequently with inward glances, the vision remained crystal clear and seemed to intimate that a whole new world was being born. It was clearly living, and I beheld it in wonder. Even more incredibly, as I looked upon the vision over the next few days and weeks, details began to take shape. It was growing by collecting Its Life Force and then manifesting all that It was. The vision became more and more alive! The energy pulled to Itself so much of His Life Force that what started out as only a visual phenomenon gave witness to a feeling that "He was there!"

Miraculously, He found ways to make me comfortable during those weeks before I began the painting, although I can't say that I ever got used to it.

Finally, there I was in my studio on January 2nd, a Friday, beholding the emptiness of that large blank canvas. I could not stop smiling as I picked up my pencil and began to transcribe His presence onto the pure white surface. The only thing which troubled me at all was the awkwardness of looking inward to see Him and then looking outwardly to transcribe the vision. No sooner had I considered that to be a difficulty than the most startling thing happened! The inner vision was transformed to occupy its own space within the room. After that, whenever I worked at my easel, He would appear as a presence of three-dimensional reality before me. From then on, it was more than a vision. He was there, and we would become a team for creating the painting.

It took two or three days to complete the drawing, so I didn't start painting until the following week. After applying the first layer of paint, I expected to be taking some time off. Such is the way it is with oil paint, which has a lengthy drying time. That is one of the time consuming aspects of the medium. Fortunately, some of the colors dry a little faster than others, so there's usually some part of the canvas upon which I could work. Nevertheless, waiting at least one day is typical. The next morning I entered the studio to check on the canvas and *everything* was dry. Absolutely everything! I was shocked. I never use dryers or thinners because the constitution and longevity of the paint could be compromised. So how was this happening? It was a mystery to me, but the fact was, the paint **always** dried within hours (not days) for the duration of the project. This had a tremendous impact on its estimated date of completion.

Working together with the Son of God had a lot of advantages. For one thing, the relationship occurred in a synchronous realm which might be called "the miracle zone." My greatest difficulty was in getting used to it. Accepting the idea that there were not going to be problems was a greater adjustment than one might think. In this world we have come to regard problems as "normal." The timing of everything was flawless, and all my needs were provided.

Except for Sundays, the painting unfolded without interruption until February 6th. I had gone as far as possible without the lamb, and expected to get some time off. That new agenda, however, was shot down precisely at four o'clock the next morning. Brian got up in the middle of the night to get a glass of milk and check on Mary. When he cast his flashlight back toward the barn, instead of seeing one pair of eyes, he saw **two**! He woke me up, and we ran out to catch our first glimpse of the baby . . . wobbly and wet.

"He's so precious," I said, and that became his name. I did get some time off though, because Precious was so tiny and vulnerable. At first he would just fall asleep in our arms. So we celebrated his birth and played with him for the first two days. He posed for the painting when he was three days old.

An element typical to most creative projects is something artists call "jungle time." That's the process of getting lost in all the options and problems in order to find the "answers" through instinct, ingenuity and creative resourcefulness. Jungle time is part of the allure of any creative pursuit, because in it the artist explores his uniqueness and emerges from it with a signatory resolution. For the first time in my life, that process had no attraction or relevance for me. I was content to proceed with neither problems nor expectation. Despite that surrender, however, there was no feeling of being an illustrator, because a higher form of creation was constantly surprising me with its own dynamic unfolding.

Nevertheless, I began to wonder if there might be some small, appropriate contribution I could make to proclaim, if only to myself, that "I was here." As I surveyed the whole composition, it occurred to me that it contained no symbolic recognition of the Trinity. Or at least I did not see it at the time. I had just painted the little boat that floats on the river, and with a flash of ingenuity I got the idea of adding two more boats to create a flotilla of three. They would be so tiny as to be hardly noticeable, except that **I** would know.

I promptly went to work on the miniature fleet, with poised confidence that it would be suitably respectful and discreet. The first boat was a simple construction, hardly more than six or seven brush strokes. However, the other two just would not manifest. No matter where I placed them, they could not integrate with the vision or fit into the landscape. After spending the bulk of a day stressing over two stick-figure boats, I finally realized the only difficulty I had encountered with the painting was of my own doing. With peaceful resignation and deeper understanding, I turned to Jesus and remarked, "I guess there's just one boat."

He grinned and replied, "*I guess there is.*"

There was only one other occasion when I interjected my own will into the process. That was prompted by a sense of doubt about the vision, or perhaps by a subtle premonition of things to come. There's an oak tree to the left of center in the painting. In the vision its trunk was split, and I questioned Jesus about that. "The oak tree is often a symbol of strength," I pointed out. "Are you sure you want it split?"

He looked at me, accepting my reasoning, but not agreeing with it. With quiet authority, He turned the question back to me: *"How is it in the vision?"*

"Well, it's split," I replied.

"Then that's the way it must be." It would be some months before I could know and appreciate the full implication of His answer.

Work proceeded without a hitch after that. However, there was a startling revelation about two weeks before its completion. When I got up to leave the room for my afternoon coffee break, I looked back to check on my work as I always did. This time **it looked back**, **as if to check on me**! With holographic projection, the whole painting turned to face me. I stopped short in my tracks and gasped, then ran back to the other side of the painting. It continued to face me from **every angle!** (Three-dimensional rendition is a standard of excellence in the art of realistic painting.

However, there is a difference between holographic projection and three dimensional illusion. Old master paintings are renowned for their convincing illusions projecting in all directions. In such portraits, eyes may often "follow the viewer." That doesn't mean, however, that the illusions will leap **in front of** the canvas with full compositions projecting absently. In holographic projection, complex forms will realign, and reproject according to changing angles of perception.) It was quite phenomenal to see this happening in the painting.

It is my standard procedure to paint in privacy, showing the works only when they are finished. Brian knew that, and was respectful of my wishes. At that moment, therefore, I did not share my discovery with him. Only our cat Gunner had seen the painting in progress. There was no way of keeping Gunner out of my studio, for that was his bedroom. I presumed he could see Jesus, for he sat perched on my drawing board facing the vision, staring hours upon end every day. Jesus had spoken to him several times, and petted him once. That evening he watched in quiet amazement, wondering what all the commotion was about.

From that day forward, the painting took on a life of its own. Its integrity was complete unto itself and true to the vision. Without embellishment I followed the inspiration before me and found it a joy to surrender to higher creation. The painting has remained holographic, and today viewers find the variable projections of imagery and expression to be an empowering enhancement to their communion with the painting.

Even the best of things must eventually end, and in the case of this project I was certainly glad that I was not the one to decide when that would be. From the beginning, I had recognized that the vision had such power, I could see myself twenty years hence still trying to perfect it. Therefore, I was actually relieved when Heaven decided to "wrap it up."

That was March 12, 1992. On that day, there was so little left to do that I was down to polishing particulars. There were a few strokes I wanted to add to Jesus' hair. It was blowing in the wind, and I wanted to separate the strands to show a lightness of air passing through it. One after another, I put these final touches in place. When I looked up I was startled to see the vision dissolving into a cloud of sparkling light. Almost in panic, I looked inward to the point where it had been joined to my consciousness, but the "cord " had been severed. Setting my brush down, I smiled, then smiled bigger, unable to suppress the joy I felt. As I beheld the vision departing, I also witnessed a beginning. For as the visual image faded, the love and energy of its essence settled in upon the canvas. The painting was finished, but its life had only begun.

Many who have seen the painting feel a living presence within it. *The Lamb and The Lion* is more than just linen and paint. It is now a conduit for the life force of the original vision, and those who view the painting may continue to enjoy it as an extension of the Master's power and love. After Jesus left, I visited with Him many times through the painting. Most especially I wanted to know, "What next? What am I to do with this artifact you have left in my custody?"

Chapter 3
A Miracle for Breakfast

And what you thought you came for
Is only a shell, a husk of meaning
From which the purpose breaks only when it is fulfilled
If at all. Either you had no purpose
Or the purpose is beyond the end you figured
And is altered in fulfillment.[4]

T. S. Eliot

The search for purpose is a powerful, driving force in everyone's life. This is especially true with regard to our central motivating purposes, although it is equally gratifying to discover meaning within the propelling events of life. We ardently want to know whether the coincidences which occur in our lives happen by random chance or by divine orchestration. The key to understanding purpose, however, lies not in anticipating events, seeking them, or avoiding them. For, indeed, if our lives are divinely guided to do a particular work, then the events are destined to find us regardless of our expectations or explanations. I have discovered that peace of mind comes from surrendering to such points of destiny. If and when there is enough insight to see the interwoven threads of life, then an integrated whole may be revealed to us. When that happens, life makes satisfying sense and brings into focus a fulfilling recognition of vital purpose.

No sooner had the finished painting provided me with feelings of contentment and sufficiency than it plunged me into a greater unknown. As I sat before it, reverently remembering the pleasure of His company, a mixture of tears and smiles filled my countenance. Mainly, however, I felt confusion and concern—old familiar feelings I had not known since before the visitation. "Why? For what purpose has this come to be?" These

were questions I directed toward the Master's portrayal which was now on
our living room wall.

I missed Him deeply, though His love was lingering everywhere like
the fragrance of clean mountain air. Within a few days, however, my heart
was filled again with the soothing resonance which I recognized as His
Presence. A new dimension of our relationship had begun, along with a
new and deeper means of communing. Though no words were spoken, my
questions could now be answered.

I **felt** Him say with unmistakable grace, *"Give it to my people."*

He had answered my question, but with no clues of how to proceed.
Moreover, His request was more easily made than done. His people are
everywhere! They come in every color, nationality, and heritage. Within
the Christian community there are countless creeds and hundreds of church
denominations. Many of His most devoted students and disciples do not
participate in any religious structure at all. And well beyond the
boundaries of what we call Christianity, His teachings are an influence
around the world.

Where was I to begin? The obvious answer was anywhere. With
simple, contagious enthusiasm, word began to spread—from us to others.
Soon strangers from across the country would be arriving on our doorstep,
unannounced, asking to view this painting of Jesus! It is staggering to
imagine how many barriers had to come down, and how many inhibitions
had to be suspended in order for such a thing to happen. People became a
living miracle as they sought and experienced His presence in the painting.

As visitors carried back reports of excitement to their groups and
churches, invitations began to pour in for us to share the painting through
outreach. As with people, so too the denominational walls came tumbling
down. In the next two years, we gave our best effort by traveling across
five states to more than eighty churches and most denominations . . .
Protestant, Catholic, Charismatic, Episcopal, even Cowboys for Christ!
Reaching well beyond the walls of church dominion, we went wherever we
were called.

As we shared the painting, miracles followed upon miracles. That was
a new dimension of growth and life experience for me. There was no way
of explaining or expecting the miracles that might occur. They came
simply as gifts to those who received or witnessed them. If there is
anything more elusive than the subject of purpose, it would be the one of
miracles, that special realm of higher purpose which laces our life with

golden thread. Moreover, it seems as if there is no order of importance in the realm of miracles, for each one represents a moment of consummate grace upon the Earth. So, how does one comprehend the miraculous or recognize its approach?

Rarely do we anticipate the miracles which change our lives, for they simply arrive as the most marvelous of surprises. It is easy for me now to cast a backward glance upon the trail of miracles left by the Master through His painting and feel the tranquil pleasure that such memories bring. However, the birthing of a miracle is often as painful as the birthing of a child, for new life must rip the veil of existing structure if it would declare its presence.

Though love, life, and growth are like the mighty forces of an ocean, even they could be more easily harnessed than the power of love at the Master's command. Complacency, reservation, and conservatism are not words that leap to mind when I think of His influence on my life! In those days of discovery and growth after the painting's completion, my relationship with Him continued to emerge with transforming grace, like tulips pushing through the Earth in spring. Along with that came greater attainments of truth more fully integrated with life and more applicable to it.

Eventually I came to realize that miracles are just the power of growth as love and life push through the veils of illusion that hold them back. If one focuses on the impact of love and its capacity to bring miracles into being, then they become an expected part of life. If one focuses on the structures that deny the greater power of love and life, then an emerging miracle may erupt with startling surprise!

So accustomed are we to smiling in the face of a miracle that we often fail to consider that it might have been prefaced by elements of danger or trauma. Events of those two years should have taught me something about the bittersweet flavor of miracles. It seems, however, that a full understanding of that reality never seems to come until one is at peace with the holistic nature of life. In the summer of 1992, I was given further instruction in that school of thought.

What I would have given for a higher level of understanding on that morning of July 20th! I could have enjoyed my breakfast with peaceful anticipation instead of dwelling in a state of frozen turbulence, stunned by a terrible surprise which offered no promise of resolution. Little did I know that I was enduring the labor pains of a new birthing miracle—the most significant one for me since the Master's entry into my life. My ordeal had begun the day before.

July 19, 1992, began as a typical Sunday for us. As soon as breakfast was over, Brian loaded the painting in our station wagon while I dressed and reviewed the notes for my morning presentation. This time we were traveling to St. Francis of Assisi Episcopal Church in Willow Park, Texas. Father Hermann, the pastor, had heard of *The Lamb and The Lion* and asked us to present it to his congregation, and to tell the story of how it had come to be.

On our arrival, Father Hermann and several of the parishioners were waiting to help us install the painting in the fellowship hall. No sooner had we set it up than tragedy struck—a floodlight fell from its tall tripod, crashing into the canvas!! Several people watched helplessly as the light plummeted to the floor. One woman, Judy Huber, dove to the floor to deflect the heavy fixture, but she failed to reach it in time. The light crashed into the left side of the painting, landing right in the split trunk of the old oak tree.

As we straightened the painting and re-balanced it on the easel, everyone present observed the extent of its damage: a four-inch dent in the canvas with a one-inch tear at its center. I passed my finger **completely through** the incision! Being an art historian and past museum professional, I knew what options existed for repairing a painting damaged to that degree. The dent would always protrude, and though the tear could be patched and inpainted, its presence still would be noticeable to anyone who looked for it. Unfortunately, there's not much difference between a torn canvas and Humpty Dumpty. You can put the pieces together, but they'll never be whole again.

From where does the strength come to continue, when everything inside says, "quit!"? Fortunately, there are more dimensions to our strength than we normally use, and that Sunday I discovered my extra reserves. The painting would be far enough away from the congregation that I would not have to discuss the tragedy with anyone who did not already know about it. With trembling hands and shallow breath, I began to speak. I was scheduled for a morning presentation before Mass and then an afternoon discussion with open house. Somehow I got through the day. Benevolently, one of the blessings of shock is the anesthesia it brings.

Late that afternoon we carefully placed the painting in its case, hoping to avoid any further damage, and silently drove home. I wanted to pray, but for the life of me, there were no words for what I felt.

The next morning I woke up with a sense of dread. Every moment that I forestalled the inevitable was a salve to my nerves. That morning required a full pot of coffee. Sitting alone, I tried not to look at the large picture case leaning against the living room wall. Memories washed across my consciousness as I recalled the events and miracles all leading to this morning.

Between tears, I found myself asking, "Why?" The answer came quickly enough.

As soon as I could muster the strength, my first duty was to examine the painting and estimate its damage. My second duty was to contact a conservation studio. The canvas could never be made whole by any human means, but it could be made cosmetically presentable, and professional restoration would prevent further deterioration at the point of rupture.

As I carefully glided the painting from its case, there was no way of preparing myself for what was about to be revealed. **The injury was gone!** I cautiously ran my fingers across the surface, carefully examining the area that had been torn only yesterday. **There was only perfection; no dent, no cut, no loss of paint**. Flipping the painting over to its back side, the weave of canvas presented itself with a countenance as tight and strong as the day it was stretched.

Holding it up to the window, I could see no pinholes of light, nor even a fleck of paint missing. Examination of the back side through high magnification revealed that not so much as a fiber was torn. What happened to me at that moment was almost as disturbing as the original injury. My expectations had been completely dismantled. As structure revealed its illusional nature, I was shaken to the core. With a mixture of emotions impossible to describe, I looked at the split oak tree in humbled amazement, and remembered the day I asked Jesus if it had to be that way.

Soon shock gave way to thrill, and my urge to share was overwhelming. Brian was gone for the day, so the first person I telephoned was Judy Huber. Together we went over the events of the last two days, time and again, confirming the experience we had shared. As soon as we could break away from our choruses of praise and squeals, Judy relayed the news to Father Hermann. In a calm, expectant voice he remarked, "I'm not surprised. I prayed for it all night."

About a week later, everyone who had witnessed the incident met at the church to examine the painting and celebrate its healing. Each brought his own written account of the damage he had seen. St. Francis Church retained their letters—unmitigated testaments to what happened there on July 19th. It's a good thing that confirmation exists, for the painting itself shows no sign, even under intense magnification, of ever being dented, abraded, or torn in any way—and most certainly not repaired!

In the following weeks and months, I had to clarify this experience through seeking greater understanding, for inquiries about it would not cease. Even so, the miraculous cannot be "figured out" in the normal way, because the logic we use to explain our reality is endlessly conditioned by predictable patterns of cause and effect. Such thinking could never comprehend a miracle, much less explain one.

There is a strange aspect to the way I remember the event—almost as if there were two sets of experiences symmetrically connected on different dimensions of reality, delicately separated by the thinnest veil. On one side of the veil—the one supported by physical perception—I can recount in vivid detail every moment of the shocking event on that Sunday. No doubt my recollections would closely agree with those of the other witnesses. On the other side of the veil, however, there exists an expanded consciousness which retained a perception of the **painting's wholeness** despite the assault!

It seems as though my normal perceptions of reality which extend horizontally had been intersected by a vertical insertion of a higher truth and power. Such thoughts caused me to wonder if perhaps the whole of universal reality performs its endless creation around the intersection of timeless moments where horizontal plausibilities cross in perfect harmony with the vertical possibilities for ascending or descending consciousness.

Is it possible that the duality around which we build our lives is like the split oak tree? Could it be that Jesus' whole mission on Earth was to show us that while duality exists, there is a greater wholeness which reduces it to mere illusion? In our lives there are crowning moments, but there is also hardship. We know pain all too well, and yet there is perfection coexisting with it. As I look back over my life there is this kind of complexity through it all, yet simplicity as well.

Will there suddenly be a moment when we finally decide to disallow imperfection the dominant influence it has now? Or could it be that nothing but wholeness ever does prevail once we are willing to perceive it? Perhaps that is the key to His message . . . and the mystery.

Chapter 4
Life Goes On

If you came this way,
Taking any route, starting from anywhere,
At any time or at any season,
It would always be the same: you would have to put off
Sense and notion. You are not here to verify,
Instruct yourself, or inform curiosity
Or carry report. You are here to kneel
Where prayer has been valid. And prayer is more
Than an order of words, the conscious occupation
Of the praying mind, or the sound of the voice praying.[5]

T. S. Eliot

There is a time for outreach and discovery, and there is a time for sanctuary. For a while it seemed as though I had achieved both through the same process. The public debut for *The Lamb and The Lion* was on Palm Sunday immediately after its completion. Again, the order of events was perfect. Just as Jesus entered Jerusalem on Palm Sunday, so did this painting enter its ministry on that day. It was shown again on Easter and virtually every Sunday thereafter. So meaningful and graceful were the course of events that I did not look for sanctuary in any other way.

By the fall of 1993, however, I was road-weary and eager for a bit of rest and relaxation. The last eighteen months had been a whirlwind of activity, travel, challenge, and personal growth. Moreover, when we were not on the road we were usually receiving visitors from far and wide in our living room. We especially enjoyed the children who came to our home. Their candid and innocent recognitions of the Master were always delightful and often profoundly inspirational. In return, they got to stroke Gunnar or at least catch glimpses of the cat who saw Christ. So enthralled were we in the process of sharing that we forgot about our own needs. As

I realized the extent of my exhaustion, I sought communion with The Master about it. In my reverie, I was flooded with nostalgia for the peaceful harmonies I had formerly experienced in the studio. I had painted only once since *The Lamb and the Lion*, and nine months had passed since that one exception. Willingly, I had chosen two years previously to retire my brushes as I sought a higher pathway, and I could have lived with that decision if the hand of destiny had not intervened. Ironically, as that destiny unfolded, the brush was brought back into my hand. Now, two years later, I was not using those abilities, and that was the cause of my nostalgia.

The duties I felt toward *The Lamb and The Lion* held an importance which cast a shadow on everything else, and besides, what other subject could provide me with such passion and peace? In short, it was a tough act to follow! Until the fall of 1992, my love of painting had been dismissed as an aspect of personal history.

I was frequently asked to create other paintings of Jesus, the most popular request being to paint Him with His Mother in a traditional Madonna pose. With as much diplomacy as I could summon, I tactfully declined all persuasions, reminding everyone who inquired that any subsequent portrayals of Him would have to be as specially ordained as the first one. If He wanted another painting enough to arrange for its creation, then it would be my pleasure and privilege to consent. Aside from special circumstances, however, the common rhetoric of religious art still held little attraction for my creative heart. With such considerations in place, I really believed that further portrayals were unlikely—and that was true for more than six months.

In the fall of 1992, much to my surprise, those special circumstances were arranged and another vision was brought to me. It happened in a little country church where I had given the evening presentation. During the closing prayer, I noticed the rare fragrance I always sensed when Jesus was in my studio. Lifting my head and opening my eyes brought confirmation of what I suspected. **He was there!** Without a word to startle the others, I quietly beheld a fascinating process. With every passing second He regressed in age until He became an infant in His mother's arms. Mary was young and classically Hebrew in appearance. In her loveliness, she was the image of innocence and barely more than a child herself. After a few minutes, the vision stabilized and remained unchanged for the two months required to paint it. *The Flame of Love,* as the painting came to be called, was completed on the twelfth day of the twelfth month at twelve noon, **exactly nine months** from the day *The Lamb and The Lion* saw its completion. The final touches were barely made in time for a formal reception in its honor that afternoon. More than two hundred people attended. Eyes filled with tears and mouths fell agape at the youthful authenticity of Mary. Others were stunned at the undeniable resemblance of the child to His manly fulfillment in *The Lamb and The Lion.* From that moment on, our life became a flurry of activity, and my brushes gathered dust.

I virtually forgot that painting was still in my heart until September 1993. Finally, on that bright, autumn morning, I wanted to create art again. What's more, I wanted to do it in a home that did not belong to the rest of the world. As I recognized my personal yearnings, I recalled the serenity of being in His presence. It was so different from the hectic pace Brian and I had been maintaining. Looking across the living room, I focused upon His countenance in the painting, hoping to join Him in that place of special peace. Just then a very interesting thing happened. Instead of seeing His face, I saw hundreds of other faces—people who had been blessed by the painting. One by one, layers of faces peeled away until I saw only His. That communication had special significance for me. It was about simplicity, reverence, and sanctity. I knew that a turning point had arrived in the life of the painting. Just as I wanted the solitude and sanctuary of my studio again, I was being told that the painting required sanctuary as well. It needed to be in a reverent and quiet place where the hearts, lives, and beliefs of everyone approaching it could be equally respected.

One of the first decisions I ever made about the painting was that its life and service should be ecumenical, belonging to no denomination, and preferably to no religious doctrine whatsoever. Perhaps the most distinguishing characteristic of *The Lamb and The Lion,* in contrast to thousands of other portrayals of Him, is the uniquely personal and gracious welcome it extends to everyone. I wanted to keep it that way. My hesitation in regard to housing the painting in a church stemmed from those considerations as well as the fact that most churches are open to the public for only a few hours, one day a week. These things were both a reality and a concern to me. I did not have the answers, although I was certain He did. Through prayer and meditation I released my anxieties to a higher guidance.

Sometimes, however, release is more easily desired than attained. For several weeks, no logical solutions were presented, and worries mounted. I didn't have a clue where to look. Tense days led to restless nights as we continued our outreach and kept up our normal routine. I should have expected a miracle, but as usual, I let it catch me by surprise.

For the second time in my life I was about to be awakened by a Holy Light in my home. This time it happened at three o'clock in the morning. Startled from my sleep, I looked for rational explanations, but there were none. It became evident that the light was supernatural, just as the first one had been. So, I propped up my pillows and waited. Within minutes the light had become focused in the corner of the room, taking the form of an angel.

That was a startling phenomenon! As a child I had believed in angels, although I never thought about them except at Christmas, and certainly I never expected to see one during my years on earth. What was before me was a rare perception, for I am not a psychic visionary or gifted with extra perceptual abilities. Until recently, my perceptions had never exceeded the normal fabric of human experience. Therefore, as an artist I was also not inclined toward the subject of angels. My lifetime of involvement with the visual arts had assisted me in developing a strong and vivid imagination capable of recalling or redesigning whatever I have seen. However, if anyone had asked me to paint an angel, I would probably have responded in the manner of Courbet, the great French realist, who said more than a century earlier, "If you show me an angel, I'll paint an angel." Altogether, my lack of expectancy left me unprepared for what was before me.

I sat up bewildered and stunned as the angel said, "Be not afraid. I have come to let you know that your prayers have been heard. Arrangements are being made for the painting's home."

I was delighted with **what** he said, but I was even more fascinated with **how** he said it. The sound that my **ears heard** was lovely celestial music, while at the same time the sound that **my mind heard** was the spoken English language. It left me with the distinct impression that the music he "spoke" was a universal language which would have translated into whatever word-based language anyone hearing it might be accustomed to using. In days to come, as I reflected back upon this event, it occurred to me that even the visual apparition might have been a translation of realities from a universal presence to a form more suitable to being perceived.

His stay felt like twenty minutes, but it was probably shorter than that.

No less than the angels of legend, he was the bearer of good news as well as the bringer of answers. Despite my repeated requests, however, he would give me no specific details on Heaven's plan for the paintings. Before leaving, he placed his "hand" on my heart and said "I leave you with this seed of consciousness from which you will be given further insights and instructions."

I waited passively under the supposition that any instructions or answers I needed would come forth spontaneously. After a week or so, however, curiosity overtook my patience. Waiting has never been my favorite pose, and certainly not with matters of destiny. I thought of a thousand prayers, but quietly surrendered to silent meditation, hoping to fall into that special place in my heart where the angel had left "the seed of consciousness." I dwelt in peace for the longest time, then looked, knocked and prodded. Nothing came. Just as I was about to leave that contemplative state I heard the music again. I focused in as I had done before, and the words were made manifest.

"What?" I shook my head in disbelief. The one thing he said made no sense in relation to my concerns. He told me to "build a prayer screen."

What was a prayer screen, and why did I need to build one? I had sought an answer and received a work order! For the rest of the day I searched for justifications, but none of them made any real sense. The only rational conclusion I could draw was that a prayer screen might foster a place of greater reverence in which to pray and meditate more effectively.

Nevertheless, who am I to argue with an angel? Off I went to our local home improvement warehouse to search for ideas of what to build and how to do it. I spent considerable time there walking the aisles, looking for sparks of inspiration and clues of how to proceed. After the many months of renovating our house, I knew my way around rather well and was on a first name basis with most of the salesmen. In spite of that, my search there seemed to be in vain. All of the materials were rough and heavy, and required power tools. On my way out, I passed through the display of doors when suddenly I tripped on a solid object and almost tumbled to the floor. Someone had left a door lying flat in the aisle. I reached down to pick it up, expecting it to be heavy. Much to my surprise it was very lightweight. It was a hollow ash door, and as I held it I noticed how lovely the wood grains were. Moreover, it was only twenty-four inches across—a suitable width for what I needed. Within minutes I was integrating the possibilities. I could hinge three of these panels together and have a lovely screen! A bit of decoration, some varnish, and then it could be a prayer screen—whatever that might be.

The motif of synchronicity and purposeful coincidence was only just beginning. The doors needed to be shortened, but I had learned how to do that from the men who had renovated our home. Once the panels were ready to be assembled I took them into my studio. Looking them over carefully I noticed that the grains on one side were beautiful and suitable for varnish as they were. However, all three doors were plain on the other side. Clearly, they needed some enhancement. But what? Before I knew it, I was standing before one of the ash panels with brush in hand, spontaneously painting an angel.

It seemed to be an appropriate reflection of responsibility back to the one who had ordered the screen. Little did I know that the door in front of me was more than a painting— it would become a threshold for my own greater unfolding! By 1993, angels had become a popular subject for artists and decorators. However, I did not see myself as part of that domain, which seemed rightly to belong to artists with visionary perceptions of the angelic realm, or else to those with antiquarian love for Classical and Victorian concepts. My realist style and one-time angelic visitation hardly qualified me for either. On that day in the studio, the only intent or purpose of which I was aware was that of decorating a "prayer screen" and completing a work order! For my reward, I hoped to find an answer on the finished side of that project. The answer took its time in arriving, but the reward which accompanied it was greater than anything I expected.

From the beginning, there was a noticeable upsurge of energy and personal joy as I painted the angels on those doors, and the completed screen was much more beautiful than I envisioned. It was finished just in time to be shown at our annual Christmas party, although it was not for sale. It had been nine months since I had presented any new work, so that fact alone made it the talk of the party. There also was something refreshing and candid about the response it elicited. One woman, in particular, fell in love with it and persistently tried to buy it. Uninterested by her proposition, I explained the best I could, that the screen had a special inspirational value to me and that it was not for sale. Disregarding my "No," she telephoned daily until I finally consented to her wishes. Her persuading argument was that I could make another one for myself. With that plan in mind, I agreed that she could have it.

As soon as she arrived home with her angel screen she noticed that it was too large to fit comfortably with the floor plan of her house. Unthwarted by small issues, however, she took an imaginative look at another possibility and then telephoned me to gain support for her idea. She wanted to dismantle the screen and hang the separate panels on her wall. In the final analysis, she loved the angels more than the screen. As a result of her influence, new perceptions and possibilities would open for me as well.

Meanwhile, other synchronicities were accumulating around her which could hardly be regarded as accidental. Two days later she telephoned again, asking me if I would be willing to replace the angel panels she had purchased. "Why," I asked? "Have they been stolen or damaged?"

With a bit of timidness, she admitted that she had sold them, and proceeded to explain why. A prayer group to which she belonged had met in her home the night before, and two members of the group wanted to purchase the panels for their church. With a persistence reminiscent of her own, they apparently had refused to take "no" for an answer.

This project was beginning to reveal a noticeable pattern of "will" far greater than my own, like wind blowing through the trees. I was curious to know what was blowing in. So I quickly assembled the materials and began to create her replacement panels. Although it began as a duty, before I knew what was happening I was immersed in a delightful process of discovery, with the rarest expressions and freedoms I had ever felt. By instinct or anticipation I must have known this might occur, because I had already made a crucial decision. I had selected wider doors and had reduced the height considerably so that the proportion would be more suitable for paintings with design, expression, and development. As I brought them to fruition I found depths of intuition, creative confidence, and instinctive beauty that would have been blocked in the past by my classical work habits and expectations of effort. Moreover, it all happened very quickly. In less than two weeks I had her new paintings ready for delivery.

No sooner had she hung them on her wall than she called me again. "Glenda, could you paint one more panel for me? I sold another one." The wind through my trees was moving up to gale force! This was just the beginning of a phenomenon. For almost two years from that moment I painted angels on doors, and always within days of completion someone arrived at my studio to behold and declare, "That's **my** angel!"

What never ceases to amaze me is the perfect synchronicity in the angel's choice of ash doors for a medium. In addition to being a door, it provided a **doorway** for expanding my awareness, and a metaphorical expression of the angelic presence in the universe. After all, do they not stand as guardians of the doorway to higher consciousness? One thing is certain, as a classically trained artist, I would never have selected such a medium without external intervention. Most certainly, I would not have accepted it as a catalyst for stylistic evolution.

That's getting ahead of the story, however. The cornerstone and pivotal reason behind the unfolding events was about to be revealed in February of 1994. My client's friends from the church (which had purchased the first two panels) wanted more angels and wanted to meet with me personally. We met in our home where they saw *The Lamb and The Lion* for the first time. It was a warm and moving experience for us all and the beginning of a deep and meaningful friendship. In addition, they commissioned me to paint seven archangels for their chapel.

That project consumed most of the approaching spring and gave us a chance to become better acquainted. This was a Christian organization which was more than simply a church. At the time of its founding in 1939, this non-denominational fellowship declared that it would remain open to all people and open to all aspects of Christian truth, hence its name, "Christ Truth League." Since that time it has taught and served quietly on its beautiful fourteen acres in Fort Worth. In keeping with the ecumenical ideal, its outreach has largely been through publishing and through generous support of other Christian fellowships. The chapel, which is a charming mix of traditional and modern motifs, is situated in the midst of an exquisitely landscaped garden. Altogether, this lovely environment has a serenity and spirit of sanctuary which can refresh the weariest soul. It certainly has that effect on me.

Dr. Applegate, the minister, was deeply inspired by *The Lamb and The Lion,* and asked me if I would display it in the chapel and provide a Sunday service. As it turned out, the day we chose was also the first day all of the new angel paintings would be in place on the walls.

When that day arrived, it was a dazzling spring morning without a cloud in the sky. I was happy about the good weather, although it did not seem to matter as far as the painting was concerned. Regardless of inclement weather preceding or following a presentation, at the time of our arrival, conditions would always clear and be fine. More than once, rain would be pouring through gusts of wind until the moment we needed to expose the painting to the elements. Then, a spontaneous clearing would occur! These were common and predictable miracles which I had come to take for granted. Nevertheless, I was glad that the birds were singing and the sun was shining that Sunday. It was just one more thing I would not have to worry about . . . or so I thought!

Just as the benediction was being said, the sky darkened and the elements clapped a loud *amen* with thunder and lightning. In just moments, rain was pouring in sheets. In every other instance where weather had presented some obstacles, a little patience always provided safe passage. But it would not happen on that day, nor for three days. Day and night, it rained continuously. The only thing that was clear was the fact that the painting had to remain.

For the first time in the life of the painting, it would be transferred to someone else's care. The painting was not insured outside of our custody (not that I had any real worries), therefore the church accepted its new responsibility with a bit of insecurity as well as reverence. To that end, the members and ministry of the church brought sleeping bags and maintained a seventy-two hour vigil around the painting which proved to be as much for their benefit as for the painting. Many dreams and visions were brought to consciousness as well as soul-deep bondings with the love and natural grace of the Master's portrayal. The most important dream was brought to Debbie, the church member who had purchased the first angels. She was told that *The Lamb and The Lion* was home.

Had this dream not been divinely inspired, that would have been an audacious presumption. For never had I mentioned to anyone except Brian that any home other than our own was being considered! It was actually several weeks before she worked up the courage to mention her dream, and even then, only when I first remarked that our visit to the church with the painting was the highlight of our spring. Her message caught me by surprise, as did the whole proposition. Having had no knowledge of Christ Truth League prior to February, I had once more been brought to face the unexpected. However, as I surveyed the possibility, it became obvious that housing in their chapel met every criterion I had wanted, including the fact that it was open seven days a week to all people for prayer and meditation. It was easy to find, reverent, and beautiful.

Arrangements were finalized, and by June *The Lamb and The Lion* and *The Flame of Love* were happily situated in their new home.[6] It was a wonderful conclusion to a long journey. Every part of the journey had been facilitated by miracles, but only then, as I beheld the two paintings hanging contentedly with their escort of angels did I begin to realize how important the patterns of synchronicity had been as they moved through my life and brought the will of God into clear view. Synchronicity must surely be the dynamic process of miracles unfolding, if only we would listen and respond.

Every day the paintings continue to receive new visitors, often from around the world. People of every age, creed, and color come to behold, pray, meditate or quietly receive the blessings of the Master through His portrayal. What the symbolic contents of the paintings mean I cannot say, since they were neither the invention nor the choice of my own consciousness. For many people, the elements of the painting have become catalysts for personal messages. I am equally limited to explain or justify the way He chose to be presented. The vision was by His initiation and arrangement. However, I would like to think that He looked that way when He walked upon the earth two thousand years ago. Many people who have had near-death experiences have written or called me to confirm this hope by sharing their experiences of Him from a higher plane. One minister, whose friendship I now cherish, offered the following passage from one of her seminary books as additional support for the hope that these portrayals may be realistically authentic. This is a description of Jesus by Publius Lentulus, Governor of Judea, addressed to Tiberius Caesar, Emperor of Rome.[7] It was found in an excavated city, written in Aramaic on stone:

> There lives, at this time, in Judea, a man of singular virtue whose name is Jesus Christ, whom the barbarians esteem as a prophet, but his followers love and adore him as the offspring of the immortal God. He calls back the dead from the graves, and heals all sorts of diseases with a word or a touch.
>
> He is a tall man, and well shaped, of an amiable and reverent aspect; his hair of a color that can hardly be matched, the color of chestnut full ripe, falling in waves about his shoulders. His forehead high, large and imposing; his cheeks without spot or wrinkle, beautiful with a lovely red; his nose and mouth formed with exquisite symmetry; his beard thick and of a color suitable to his hair reaching below his chin. His eyes bright blue,

clear and serene, look innocent, dignified, manly, and mature. In proportion of body, most perfect and captivating, his hands and arms most delectable to behold.

He rebukes with majesty, counsels with mildness, his whole address, whether in word or deed, being eloquent and grave. No man has seen him laugh, yet his manner is exceedingly pleasant; but he has wept in the presence of men. He is temperate, modest and wise; a man, for his extraordinary beauty and divine perfections, surpassing the children of men in every sense.

The most remarkable aspect about that passage is that it was written **about a Jew by a Roman,** and **about a man by a man** in a day and age when such tender and reverent compliments were most unlikely except under conditions of extreme respect!

The paintings now had a life of their own. As for myself, I continued to paint angels on ash doors until early 1996. Perhaps that was the length of time needed for me to pass through **my** next doorway to greater understanding and personal unfoldment. I must add, however, that I did not "see" every angel I painted. I sense their love in a powerful and moving way. Every now and then I caught a glimpse of some passing light out of the corner of my eye or an unusual fragrance that appeared out of context. Nevertheless, my perceptual field was still grounded in the common dimension we call "normal"—whatever that means. I painted them because a hunger in my soul had been aroused to know and to behold the higher life. Even more than that, the act of surrender which had been so painful in the beginning was now becoming a submission to joy as I allowed the forces of higher consciousness to pour through me and bring to fruition the beauty of its presence.

I no longer needed a sitter in front of me or a vision to behold. The "vision" now was the beseeching of my heart which desired nothing less than a chance to honor and serve a higher guidance, as well as the privilege of connecting with my fellow man, soul to soul. The threshold had been crossed, and a new world of creative expression welcomed me. As that realization was attained, I made the artistic transition from doors back to material more suitable to fine painting. The ash doors, as a tangible metaphor, were no longer needed because now **my heart** was the doorway.

As my new work evolved, so did my own awareness. I continued to paint angels, and they were more beautiful than ever. Yet more importantly, an extra dimension was developing in the expression. This was a dimension which included and revealed the human soul. After more than one hundred paintings of angels, one thing I noticed about them all was an unmistakable presence of the persons for whom they were painted. This does not mean there was a physical portrait, for that rarely happened. Nevertheless, there was clearly a signatory presence which sometimes expressed itself through a choice of colors, symbols, or settings, or more likely through the nature of the communication itself. It would be far from the truth to say that I understand the nature of angels or their relationship with us, although I do know that it is not their duty or right to interfere with our lives. Apparently, as companions from other dimensions, they sometimes steer us from danger and seek always to elevate our understanding. This is done through a soul connection. That soul connection became more and more obvious to me. When I first began painting angels, my emphasis was upon the angel as a unique manifestation from the higher realms of existence. However, by 1995, a significant change of priorities had occurred. The higher part of the human soul, which **touches the angels**, became at least as important in my new paintings as the presentation of angelic motifs. No doubt, this parallels and reflects the pattern of my own spiritual growth in those days.

As life progressed, there was another significant change . . . learning to proceed without *The Lamb and The Lion* as my constant companion and inspiration for both living and painting. At first it was like having good friends move away, yet still feeling the ghost of their presence in all the familiar places. Then I spilled into a reverie of treasured memories. Yet as time passed, I realized that nothing important had been lost. The Master was still with me in spirit, and the richness of my personal growth was more than my hopes had envisioned.

Each day while I painted I would look for His presence, and usually I would find reminders of His influence. However, a peculiar change of emphasis was happening in my relationship with Him, just as it had occurred with the angels. Our connection through the soul was becoming more important than any physical manifestation. I found myself remembering the original sacred visitation more vividly than the vision which came from it. On that special day, November 23, 1991, I had no idea who was standing before me in the white light of pure spiritual form. All I was certain of was His Holiness. In recent years, as I savored the memory and clung to it for guidance, I came to realize that it was Jesus as a pure and eternal soul. This greater understanding has had a profound effect on my own self-awareness. Now it has become a beacon for everything I seek to become. In honor of that memory and the growing awareness of its purity, I have created a painting of the original encounter which I call, "First Light." It represents for me the beginning and ending of my search. For in the perfect peace of Love, Truth and Serenity is our ultimate sanctuary. This is the Sacred Heart, the Kingdom of Heaven which dwells within.

No longer do I seek my inspiration from the external. Daily, my sanctuary is being attained, not as a passive retreat, but as a dynamic, living process which guides my life and my work. At last I know that the Sacred Heart is humanity's church, the inner sanctum where the soul is forever in communion with God and in brotherhood with all life.

> *We shall not cease from exploration*
>
> *And the end of all our exploring*
> *Will be to arrive where we started*
> *And know the place for the first time.*
> *Through the unknown, remembered gate*
> *When the last of earth left to discover*
> *Is that which was the beginning;*
> *At the source of the longest river*
> *The voice of the hidden waterfall*
> *And the children in the apple-tree*
> *Not known, because not looked for*
> *But heard, half-heard, in the stillness*
> *Between the two waves of the sea.*
> *Quick now, here, now, always—*
> *A condition of complete simplicity*
> *(Costing not less than everything)*
> *And all shall be well and*
> *All manner of thing shall be well*
> *When the tongues of flame are in-folded*
> *Into the crowned knot of fire*
> *And the fire and the rose are one.*
>
> T.S. Eliot[8]

Part Two

The Master's Message

"The wonder that I feel is easy,
Yet ease is cause of wonder. Therefore speak:"

T.S. Eliot

Chapter 1
He Spoke

As anyone might expect, The Master's presence is awesome. I was also privileged to know how human, warm, caring, and even humorous He can be. Until recently, however, that was an untold aspect of my experience with Him, even though it was the best part for me. The unique and wonderful aspect about a visitation which lasted for more than four months is that there was enough time to be personal, to share, and to become acquainted in the way friends do. In this conscious and caring communion, we had many conversations about topics large and small.

Altogether, it was more than I could share with others for more than four years. So I regarded our communion as simply His private gift to me. When anyone would ask me for deeper insights about the visitation, I would just say, "Love is what it's all about."

From time to time, I would mention to my husband, Brian, and others, that Jesus and I had exchanged some bits of communication. That seemed to fit within the scope of their expectations, for after all, if a vision could be so alive and so enduring as to "sit for a portrait," then why wouldn't there also be some measure of communion which could be translated into words? That was their logic, and so I left well enough alone, preferring to let a blanket of silence conceal the fact that we had **extensive conversations** during our time together. Once the flood gate was open, I knew there would be no stopping the questions that would pour through it, most especially, "What did He say?" However, in the spring of 1996, Jesus appeared to me again and asked me to speak.

There is a staggering responsibility that goes along with relaying His words. There are a number of good reasons why I had been reluctant to bring His messages into a public forum. In the first place, they were presented as a subjective response to my inquiries, issues, and pursuits. The questions I asked were, in many ways, a mirror of **my** soul and His answers were often directed to the core of **my** being. It has taken four years of distance from the point of subjective impact for me to think upon His words with any objective detachment.

It is also not my desire to filter His presence for you, or to tell you what to think about Him. I am certainly not a theologian. It is my hope that I can clearly relay His messages as if they were spoken to you in the first person. Then you can interpret them as you will. They can touch your heart and mind in a manner appropriate to your understanding of Him or your relationship to Him. For this reason, I have chosen to present all of His words in italics. That way you may understand them in their original context or separate them, if you wish, from any nuance or meaning cast upon them from my side of the equation.

Above all, I recommend that you receive these messages through the heart, and remember always, this was a conversation, not a dissertation. He was not composing a new scripture; neither was He delivering a new Sermon On The Mount. He was simply talking to a friend. Like any normal conversation, ours would have many ramifications. One thing would lead to several other related topics without prescribed agenda as the drift carried it, and as our hearts directed. The conversations grew in power, length, and intensity as our relationship developed over that period of time. I have harvested the jewels from it and, hopefully, if I have strung the pearls together well, His words will provide you a personal message which is greater than the sum of its parts.

It was only with respectful restraint that I ever asked anything at all. I did not want to take advantage of His position. He had honored me enough by just being present, and I did not want to assume rights that might not exist, to pry into subjects or areas of knowledge that were not mine to pursue. As a measure of that respect, I waited for Him to initiate all conversations in the beginning.

The first thing He ever said to me was "*Glenda, love is who you are.*" At that moment, I had no idea how important His statement was or how central it would be to everything He would say. For the time being I was just content to hear His voice. It was baritone, rich and melodious, full and manly. The sound of His voice was so deeply nurturing and satisfying that I felt like the Biblical "woman at the well." It was like clear water that quenched my thirst. Hearing it was enough. How often do we read and seek, only to find ourselves even more thirsty? Not with Him. He could speak one word and I was quite content. There was no need to supplement His words with other readings, or to ask endless questions. Even though I often felt like a child in His presence, the feeling never extended to the point of regarding him as a "Daddy" whose patience could be tried with childish curiosities. You might be thinking, "Glenda, you could have asked the secrets of the universe." Eventually I did, but for the most part it was enough to know the One who had **mastered** the universe. Why did I need to ask anything? His presence brought with it a wonderful serenity and contentment that kept me always at peace.

At first I was afraid that I would not be able to work in His presence and still be absorbed in my typical studio routine. Art is a process which goes best when the artist surrenders to random and unpredictable possibilities. Frankly, the physical side of an artist's environment is often less than tidy, although stronger adjectives than that may appropriately describe my work space! How could I "roll out the red carpet" and still be my usual, creative, sloppy self?

Miraculously, Jesus made that possible. I suppose He considered it His first task to make me comfortable enough to do my job, which was to produce the painting. It was necessary that I be able to paint in my normal way and He assumed responsibility for that.

He took pleasure in the things I enjoyed, was patient with my coffee breaks, amused Himself with my procedures, and often made polite suggestions as to how I might do it better. He made me feel pretty, even though I usually wore blue jeans and sweat shirts, often had smears of oil paint on my face instead of make up, and smelled of turpentine instead of roses. A perfect gentleman, He was kind, thoughtful, and relaxed. Never, in His presence, did I feel deficient. At the same time, He led me to heights of perception, understanding, and inspiration which would have been inconceivable only days before, all with a grace and ease that made it seem so natural.

From the very beginning, I was in awe of how well He mastered the small as well as the large. The least thing, the simplest courtesy, the tiniest observation were all important to Him.

Actually, our conversations began with one small observation which was quite humbling to me. That first day, as I was drawing my initial sketch, I was sitting very close to the canvas, perhaps a foot away, because my eyesight was less than optimum. In the last few years I had become near-sighted, but I did not want to admit it. It was a condition I had decided to tolerate as long as possible, because my love for visual beauty was too pure to have it filtered through ground glass. If I could have persuaded the highway department to renew my driver's license, then I would have had the problem well in hand. But Jesus saw me straining, and said, *"Glenda, are you having some trouble with your eyes?"*

I deflected the question, not wanting to answer it fully. So I remarked, "I've just been having some eye strain lately from my nervousness. And I didn't get much sleep last night . . . the excitement and all." It bothered me, however, as I wasn't being completely truthful.

Later that night, Brian asked me how the day went, and I said, "Oh, it was wonderful. I don't have the words to describe it, but I have to confess I feel a little guilty about one thing. He asked me a question which I didn't answer honestly." I explained what happened, and despite all consolations, there was no containing my nervousness about still having the same problem the next day when I would see Jesus again.

"I can't face Him," I told myself. So I went out to be fitted for glasses, and the subject was never mentioned again. When I first donned my new glasses the next week, I noticed He gently and courteously looked at me, just smiling as we got on with the day's work.

It was not until a couple of weeks after the painting was finished that I discovered a miracle had happened. As I straightened my desk, there were those glasses, abandoned beneath layers of clutter. It's possible that I wore them once or twice, but somewhere in the course of being in His presence the affliction was healed. The reason I hadn't noticed it until that moment was that in His presence, everything was always perfect. There were no negative standards for measuring or exposing deficiencies!

A few weeks later, when I went to get my driver's license, my eye test revealed that I had 20/20 vision without the glasses. I never wore them again.

If I had to regard anything as the crowning jewel of His message it would be the rulership of the heart. So many times He would say, *"Remember, Glenda, you are love."* He would then proceed to give me greater understanding of the heart's importance. His first comment to me about the heart triggered another response of embarrassment.

We were only two or three days into the painting and I was trying to make small talk with Him, mostly to put myself at ease. In my years as a portraitist, I had learned the importance of creating a comfort zone by directing attention away from the sitting. In relation to my esteemed guest, however, the pursuit of trivia seemed utterly inappropriate. So I nervously rebounded to the opposite mode of trying to impress Him. I shared with Him a color wheel which is my own original design. During my college years, I had expanded my curriculum to include physics as well as art in order to pursue the subject of optics, and to understand color more fully as light. From that pursuit, I developed an advanced color theory which had given me a nice little professional edge. This was a formula which had served me well and has given a unique flavor to my paintings. Most people who knew about it were impressed, and those who didn't understand it just got quiet, or a little defensive. He simply looked at me—a bit sad. I was stunned with His silence. How could I respond to a feather wall . . . a point of no resistance?

After a while, He asked, *"Glenda, what is it about color that frightens you?"* It was like an arrow that went straight through the veil, right into my heart. No one had ever seen through me in that area about which I felt so confident. No one had ever seen through my defenses. He had **burst my bubble**! I sat there almost in tears because I had been seen so clearly. I groped for words: "Why did you say that?"

"Well, your mind is working overtime to compensate for something with which you are clearly uncomfortable. You do not have to know in order to love, for love is the power."

Exposed in my vulnerability, I struggled to explain, "It's just that I love light and color so much, I never felt I could do them justice. The beauties of the universe thrill me to the core, and I feel inadequate in their presence."

He assured me I had accomplished more by expressing the passions of my heart and releasing my fear, than I could ever have done through mental comprehension. He went on to say how the mind will look for troubles of the heart as fertile ground for dominating it. *"The mind will actively seek to compensate or to exploit the heart's troubles, but it will never seek to remove or to cure them. For the heart's despair is the mind's option for power."*

"Is the mind always that way?" I queried.

"Well, often. But actually the mind can be a very good servant, if you allow it to be just that. You must realize and hold firmly to an understanding that the mind has no power of its own. The mind either integrates and projects from experience, or else it develops a logical matrix to serve, to explain, and to implement the powers of the heart and the soul. The

problem arises when the heart is oriented negatively in some way toward life, because when the heart gives the mind a negative impulse such as insufficiency, insecurity, fear, or anger, the mind operates with reverse logic."

We have all seen that work. But at the moment I couldn't think of any examples, so I asked him for one.

"The most obvious example is simply the absence of data or experience—a tangible mystery—which the mind fills with its own inventions for fear of losing control.

"But now, let's look at this. When a man's heart has become attuned to scarcity, his mind will work overtime to generate ways and means of making money. There's a certain logic to this in relation to survival pressures, but it never solves the problem or changes the basic belief. The man just copes, or grows rich, to finance and perpetuate poverty consciousness in himself or others. And so he overworks to support a kind of material wealth which dominates his life but never results in a deep and true sense of prosperity. There is only compensation for lack, for the mind only solves problems of logic or balance—never problems of life.

"The man's poverty consciousness resulted from wearing so many blinders to the abundance of life that he eventually believed in scarcity and then invested in it. Now by comparison, there was another man who beheld the wondrous universe with awe as he expressed his gratitude for the infinite supply. This man has given his mind a positive impulse, and so his mind will seek ways to make that abundance real in his life.

"With less effort, greater prosperity is attained. The same is true of physical well being. A man who believes in illness will struggle all of his life to be well. And his mind will provide him many ways to prevent or to remedy the ailments without ever removing the source of trouble. Yet a man who believes in health and wholeness will set his mind to the positive service of making it true. Given any negative belief or impulse the mind will operate dysfunctionally. There may be perfect logic, but applied in reverse mode (as if reflected by a mirror) to compensate for—not solve—the problem."

Then with a sense of wonder, He looked around and out and said, *"My Father's universe is infinite and infinitely abundant. By beholding and believing in this the mind can then work in a direct and proper way to bring abundance. If given a positive impulse the mind works properly. If given a negative impulse, the mind works in reverse. That is its logic.*

Just behold infinity. Behold, and be in awe of the infinite everlasting creation."

Then He recited one of my favorite passages from the New Testament. *"Consider the lilies of the field. They do not labor or spin, yet I tell you not even Solomon in all his splendor was arrayed like one of these. Behold infinity every day and all that you seek shall be given you."* Never before had I seen such beauty in that passage.

He had been extremely generous with His information, but I needed to ask one more thing in order to make better sense out of what He had already said. So, I ventured to inquire, "How does the mind relate to the soul?"

"The soul is the totality of your love, awareness, experience, ability, memory, emotions, and potential which comprise your immortality. Your mind is the recorder and administrator. In this capacity the mind is a useful and important asset to your existence. But it was never built to be the commander. The mind has no power of its own, and it can't alter basic conditions.

"At the center of your soul is the Sacred Heart. This is the point at which you are one with God. The heart sees infinity within and without. It can behold perfection. It can ascertain the origin of conditions and change them. The heart is your higher intelligence. It is centered in a viewpoint of infinity established by your Creator. Thus the heart honors your individuality, the oneness of God, and the integrated unity of all that is.

"Would you like to know something fun to do at sunrise and sunset?"
"Sure."

"Find a place where you can watch the sun rise or set. Be careful not to look straight into the sun until it hits the cusp of the horizon or is filtered by the atmospheric densities at the Earth's edge. But once it is orange and comfortable to watch, you will find in its center an infinity point which will resonate with the infinity point in your own soul, and this will give you much nourishment and positive awareness even to the point of biological nourishment. It will actually assist in the manufacture of vitamins and the utilization of minerals."

This reminded me that primitive man revered the sun, even to the point of deifying it. His response was to the point. *"Primitive man recognized the life-giving powers of the sun, although he did not know how to properly regard it. It is a mistake to worship the sun or any other created thing. However, it is not a mistake to recognize the presence of* *infinity **within** creation. The sun is a powerful display of infinity. Another inspiring display is the starlit sky, or the vastness of an ocean viewed from the high seas."*

Many times He reminded me to *"contemplate infinity every day, inwardly as well as outwardly."*

One day I asked, "How do you contemplate it inwardly?"

"Infinity is not a subject limited to vast spaces—or even to immeasurably small ones. Infinity is not about quantity at all. It's actually about quality. Let me tell you about your heart."

This was early on, and was to be the cornerstone of much that He would teach me. *"The heart of which I speak is not the physical organ, although the physical organ is an appropriate symbol for the true heart, because the physical organ nourishes your body with lifeblood every moment. The heart of which I speak is the central focus point of your very soul. It is the lens through which your soul integrates all of your Earthly emotions and all of your divine awareness into a focused point of infinite integrity. This point is on the threshold of your physical existence, at a point slightly below and behind your physical heart."*

Then He said, *"Locate it."*

When I did, it was as if my whole framework just vibrated and pulsed with energy. There was a sense of life within me, and it required no thought to move into that point. Simply focusing upon it and being aware of its existence was empowering.

*"This is the source of power your Creator has established within **you**, not your mind. Your mind is merely a servant, and it behaves well if it is given positive impulses; it behaves very poorly if it is given negative impulses. The heart generates all of the Earthly emotions as well as the blissful emotions of the higher realms. But it is so much more than just emotion. It is infinite awareness, and the basis of all the higher consciousness you will ever assimilate. It is from this power, within the center of your being, that the entire script of your life is written. Live in your heart—not in your mind—to fulfill the script of your life or to rewrite it. Your mind is powerless to bring that about. But every desire of your heart will be fulfilled."*

He then mentioned something that seemed to be a historical event, although perhaps it was metaphorical. I don't know, and perhaps it doesn't matter. *"There was a time when the heart was so distraught with life that the mind was spinning in upon itself with contradictions and chaos generated by the heart's negative impulses. The servant mind attempted mutiny over the master heart because survival demanded that the servant mind at least be logical. Clearly the heart was in trouble, and the mind was of no help. But, to save itself, the mind accused the heart of betrayal. Then the servant mind set out to get along without the heart by generating its* **own reality.**

"*The mind wanted only to be logical and so it sought for control over circumstances that were incomprehensible to it. From the viewpoint of the mind,* **control and understanding are one and the same.** *The mind assumes that it understands whatever it controls. This is the central problem—the eye of the storm—in a mind-dominated world, and the single most important reason to require that the mind be your servant and not your master.*" He said today even as we speak, this inversion occurs in the lives of many people. "*But mutiny is not the answer, and substituting control for understanding will only deplete your life, leaving it stripped of richness, power, and meaning. The answers to healing your life will be found in the inner strength of your heart. Only correct understanding will accomplish this, and that requires addressing the problem for what it really is* "

He suggested that I earnestly practice this every day. "*I give you three practices: The first is to strengthen all of your positive emotions through daily gratitude and admiration. The second is to disempower your negative emotions daily through forgiveness. The third practice you will have to work at a little more diligently, but, Glenda, I think this will come more easily for you than for some people, because you practice this already as an artist. I'm referring to innocent perception.*"

"What do you mean?"

"*OK, look out the window. Now look back at me and tell me immediately what you saw.*"

"I saw five branches, and there were four birds on the wall. Also there were two little twigs on the window sill along with some bird droppings."

"*Good. That was innocent perception. You simply told me like a child what you saw. This is what children do so well. They just perceive and respond without preconception. This is what you did in your childhood, and you retained the ability a little better than some. Now, if the mind had answered me, the mind would probably have hesitated for just a moment while it gained control. Under the cover of hesitation, you would have blocked out what you saw, and then you might have reported to me something like this: 'Well I think I saw twelve branches, six twigs, three birds, and a clean window sill.' Because the mind feels most comfortable within structure and symmetry, it tends to impose artificial order.*

  "In other words, your mind would have rewritten the script to 'improve' upon it. The mind would have rewritten the script to try and pre-conceive reality, to do its own designing and redesigning of what is. This is what the complex, sophisticated mind tends to do always. It looks for idealized patterns that it can impose on existence and then call them divine when, Glenda, you do not have to do anything to make this universe divine. All you have to do is to perceive and then to regard with honor that which is already here. Behold, be grateful, and forgive that which you did not understand or control. For life is divine, it is perfect, and it naturally manifests the will of its creator."

  How wonderful! That message left me feeling like a child again, alive with expectation. At that moment, in His presence, everything glowed in the innocence of its native state. I could see how the mind, attempting to generate reality had performed a tyranny upon our world. There was one moment when He strongly reinforced a similar realization. *"The mind generates structures as reality, and all of the oppressive structures which you experience in the world are from those mind-generated concepts: attempting to create a perfection that doesn't need to be created because it is already there. In other words, the mind breaks things in order to fix them for a price. This includes breaking lives, breaking hearts, breaking souls, breaking relationships, and breaking wills, just to gain the upper hand through some kind of glorified structure which it presents as 'the answer.' In such a world, dominated by mind and oppressive structures, if life would be bearable at all, the poor sacrificial heart had to become the willing servant. The heart had to compensate for all the loveless barriers and oppressive formulas that man-generated realities had sanctioned. With such concessions by the heart, the inversion was then complete. In a world where the mind is master and the heart is servant, the real powers of the heart have been long forgotten, locked behind a prison door, and forbidden the freedom of exit. In such a world the heart is considered to be feminine, adaptive, and sentimental, a center of awareness which serves a person's emotional and creative needs only . . . a 'wife' to the mind, but nothing more."*

  He explained that this was the tragedy of our upside down world and that it was His gift and chosen task to come and restore the heart to its true power. *"When the heart is in its rightful place, the mind can then be a truly useful servant, and ironically it becomes both brilliant and blissful.*

"Like any servant, the mind works best within established and limited parameters. One of the indelible characteristics of the mind is that it must have at least two points of fixed reference in order to be operable. Thus, it simply cannot deal with infinity. On the other hand, the heart is centered around a viewpoint of infinity, and from this it draws its power to truly deal with life. When the mind serves the heart, anything is possible, although when the heart serves the mind there is nothing but limitation. Emotional energy will seeth and boil into restless liability."

The problem was easy to observe. As I thought about the world I saw the problem everywhere. But there was one more thing I wanted to know. "You have been so clear about the heart, would you mind also giving me a working definition of the mind?"

"The mind is essentially composed of two parts. The first part is an integrating and transmitting instrument which is basically a complex DNA computer. It centers in your brain and nervous system but actually involves every cell of your body. The second part is an electromagnetic field permeating and immediately surrounding your body. This is the primary gathering, storage, and retrieval system for all your sentient experience and thought integrations. All data in the mind is encoded mathematically and is triggered by a (+) or (-) access or entry impulse. This is why the mind will perform dualistically unless supervised by the heart. When the mind dominates, polarity is the order of the day."

He explained that inversions of heart and mind also result in many social difficulties. *"When the mind dominates, then charity has to be an organized pursuit under the governance of structure. When this happens, human brotherhood is in a tragic state of disempowerment. But when the heart is in a proper relationship to God, and the master of one's life, then charity occurs as a natural aspect of sharing."* He paused, reflectively, and then continued: *"I tried so hard to get that point across to Judas, but he was a man of structure and he refused to listen."*

In response to his statement about Judas I dared to ask, "Jesus, please forgive me if I've crossed my boundary, but would you mind telling me why—if you knew that Judas was going to betray you—did you allow him to be in the Sacred Circle?" What follows is one of the warmest, most brotherly stories He ever shared with me.

"Judas' position in the circle was chosen by my Father, not by me. Actually, there is a lot to the story of Judas that was never told, because

after his betrayal and suicide, he was so hated by everyone that he was shunned and their hearts were not ready to forgive. I understood Judas from the very beginning. I did not know how he would betray me, and I didn't know what method he would use, but I knew it was inevitable. I also knew exactly why my Father had placed us together. Actually, Judas and I grew up together. I didn't go out and choose him to be in my circle. He was my best friend as a little boy. Born to a very influential, well-educated family, Judas had all the advantages that wealth and education could bring. His family gave him all the privileges and advantages of structure available in those days, and because of that he was destined to become an obedient servant to structure. Moreover, his mind was reinforced with academic and intellectual pursuits, to the point of overshadowing his heart. Together we flowed as clear and muddy rivers side by side. But I loved him and he loved me. We played together as children. We played 'Cowboys and Indians'—well actually, 'Jews and Romans.' Often we played 'Hide and Seek,' and when we would look for each other I would always find him, but of course, he never found me. It was easy; I'd just look behind the largest structure, and he would be there. But I could be sitting in the middle of an open field and he would walk right by me as if I were invisible. Nevertheless, we enjoyed life together, and because I was young and full of boyish pranks, I enjoyed showing off to Judas. As a little boy, long before anyone else saw the miracles I could perform, I would do disappearing acts for him, and sometimes I would turn dead branches into live ones, just to show off. I guess it was just part of my youthful temperament.

"But Judas was very impressed, and from the beginning he knew I was the Messiah. He believed that with all of his heart. But, of course, his idea of the Messiah was patterned after Moses or King David, a priestly king who would perform miracles of conquest and cause the world to say, 'the King of Kings is here to restore Israel.' The messianic prophesy was largely directed to reclaiming political power. He thought I was going to dazzle Rome with God's power the way Moses went to the Pharaoh and commanded his staff become a serpent. He expected me to bring Rome to her knees so that the armies would move out of Israel, and we would have our land back. You see, Judas never really knew who I was. He just knew as far as the mind and structure would permit, and no further.

"As we grew up he was always my challenge. He always let me know the degree of misunderstanding that was possible in any particular

*situation. That way I could address the degree of misconception that might
exist for anyone else. We were exact opposites, and so he was a very good
sounding board for opposition. This is not a derogatory statement. He
chose his part, and he played it well. I long ago forgave him for the pain
of his actions, for without them the miracle would not have been possible.
And contrary to many accusations, he most certainly did not betray me for
the silver, nor did he even think that he was betraying me. Judas was part
of a proud and affluent family, and without doubt he would have donated
the money to charity or to the synagogue. Judas was as devoted to
structure as I was to God. That was the essence of our drama.*

*"As he departed from our supper room on that fateful night, I did not
know exactly what he would do, but I knew he was off to do his thing. He
was off to manifest his destiny, just as surely as I was prepared to manifest
mine. He was the son of structure, and I was the Son of God . . . we would
surely have a showdown before the evening was over. Up to that point we
had coexisted in complementary fashion, but now the time had come for the
drama to completely unfold. I don't think the way he does, but if I were to
infer his intent I would have to explain it this way: He was impatient with
my non-political teachings, and he wanted to force me into a polarity so
that I would take a stand against Rome. Doubtless, he formulated his plan
to bring me to power—**his idea** of power. When he went to the Roman
soldiers, he knew they would come for me. And he must have impressed
them with reports of my strength, for they arrived in legion force. I
presume that he expected me to show off to them as soon as I was
surrounded. Perhaps I was supposed to disappear or turn the soldiers into
pillars of stone or trees. Perhaps I was supposed to turn into a dove and
fly away. He expected something miraculous to happen, and it did, but the
miracle that happened was far too great for Judas to envision. Because the
miracle that happened is that I simply surrendered.*

*"No one was more shocked than Judas, and I'm sure that he killed
himself not out of guilt, but out of a devastating realization that everything
he had planned had gone wrong! My surrender was the one thing he would
never have expected, because the mind, with its obsession for control,
regards surrender as defeat. On the other hand, the heart knows its
immortality, and so it can dare to surrender. The paradox of the
surrendering heart which retains its mastery is perhaps my finest miracle.
That was my purpose in being here. The rest is history."*

"You said you forgave Judas. Did he ever accept your forgiveness?"

"Not yet. But if he ever awakens to the truth of what happened, his return to God will have a shattering effect on the tyranny of structure in this universe. Do not condemn him, for that will only support the tyrannies which he still defends. Pray for his soul, and perhaps a miracle will happen which will be talked about until the end of time."

I was glad that I had the courage to ask about Judas, for it unraveled a mystery about which I had often wondered. With a certain confidence under my belt, I dared to ask another question, though as I asked it, I realized that I had just been given the answer.

"I have wanted to ask about your suffering on the cross. Did your power surpass the reality of death, or did you receive its full measure and then transcend it? I realize now that you suffered death as we would, and then transcended it because only that submission and triumph could reverse the inversions of our world. You had observed our plight from a higher dimension and knew what was required, but Judas was so immersed in structure he could only project a strategy based upon historical precedents and desperate measures. You brought to us the flame of life from a new dimension, and this was why Judas could not see what you were about to do. No servant of structure could have anticipated the real miracle."

With a warm smile He replied: *"That's right. You learn well. The real miracle of my crucifixion and resurrection is that the Sacred Heart was then restored to its position of sovereignty over structure, and love claimed its victory over death. Once I reinstated the heart's supremacy, all you have to do is to accept and to apply its power in your own life and in your own corner of the world. Your heart does not need to work its way back to God, for it never left God. The heart, in its perfection, is the one connection with your Creator which was never severed. But it must regain its certainty as master over illusion! All miracles happen that way. The heart is the bringer of all miracles.*

"Do not ever underestimate the power of the heart to bring forth a higher intelligence, a higher awareness and greater solutions to existence than you would ever have anticipated. This is why so many times people will experience a miracle of healing in the face of death; because in the face of death, they go ahead and let the structures die. They think, 'I only have six weeks to live,' and then let go of external demands. The mind loses all importance, and loved ones become more dear than ever. All of a sudden the heart-fire burns brightly, whether through grief, joy, contentment, or resignation. Only then, through the fire of the heart is a

miracle possible. Most people facing death go ahead and die to the world of structure, and then at last they really live. That is what I meant when I said you must die first in order to live. Because when you live in the heart, you live immortally, you live eternally."

His enlightenment about the heart and its miracles brought back a special memory which I had not recalled in years. Back in 1981, I was in New York City under contract with my publisher to make fine art prints. In those days Brian and I were wanting to adopt a puppy. And our hearts were set on a wire hair fox terrier. Since there were several excellent kennels for that breed in New York City, we decided that I should proceed with the project while I was there. I interviewed several kennel owners by telephone, and there was one I particularly liked. Best of all, she had some puppies available, so I made plans to go and see them. Being a country girl from Texas, I knew very little about the neighborhoods of New York City. So when she gave me her address in the Bronx, nothing triggered in the way of an internal alarm system.

I was living downtown and would be traveling cross-town during the afternoon rush hour. Considering the time of day, I thought it best not to take a taxi all the way to the Bronx. The subway would probably be quicker. Besides, I always enjoyed the democratic assortment of humanity on the train.

The station I entered was near Wall Street, and in that neighborhood the train was characteristically full of well-dressed brokers traveling back to their uptown apartments. I, too, was nicely dressed and so I comfortably burrowed into my newspaper as I affirmed my smart decision to take the train. At every station the dress code and demographics would change somewhat. It was fascinating to notice the transformation as the train progressed from one neighborhood to the next. Finally, when we went through the Bronx tunnel the scenery changed significantly. There were no more Bally shoes and three-piece suits. Instead there were open-toed sandals, black leather pants, and tattoos. As the train stopped I saw a sign which read "Bronx: Next Two Stops." Just at that moment everybody got off the train, and even more strangely, no one entered. As the train took off, there I was, the only person left on the three cars which I could see through. It was an eerie feeling, being so alone when only a moment before we had been packed like sardines. As we squealed to a stop in the first Bronx station, the doors opened and six boys sauntered in, ranging in age from about twelve to sixteen. As they stepped aboard they dumped some empty wallets onto the tracks. I presume they were ditching evidence of their day's work. A cold panic filled me, but something deeper told me to keep still. There was nothing I could do but pray that someone else would board the train, or that they would ignore me and sit at the other end. But neither happened. Instead they sat surrounding me, two on each side and the others facing me. We sat there in silence for a minute that felt like an hour, until finally I couldn't contain myself. Oh, what the heck, I thought, this may be my last day on Earth, so I might as well enjoy it. I just looked up and said, "Hi!"

It broke the ice, and one of them asked in a macho tone, "Where you from?" Somehow managing to squeeze some words out, I surprised even myself with the deep southern drawl: "Aah'm from Texas."

"You're from T-e-xxx-i-s!?" he mocked. "What are you doing up here?"

I cheerfully responded, "I came to get my puppy."

Whether it was my enthusiasm or the magic of puppies which relaxed the "tough guys" into being regular boys, I'll never know. Whatever it was, the whole tone changed from that moment. Of one thing I am sure: Without the command of my heart and the suspension of my mind, the whole event would have resulted in some kind of pain instead of a treasured memory. This would have been a no-win scenario for mental maneuvering, for I was on their turf. If I had shown even the slightest sense of judgment through emotional reaction or fear, they would have noticed and used it to justify some kind of hostile action toward me. On the obvious level of our encounter, I was clearly at a disadvantage. The mind could not have penetrated that problem, for any mental projection I might have made would have been seized by them for their benefit. Fortunately, the heart is not confined to the dramas and deadlocks of mortal conflict.

As Jesus said, *"The heart always brings new life to any situation and opens up possibilities that would have been impossible without it. Sometimes a 1 percent change is enough to make all the difference, because that's all it takes to reposition a situation which seems to be absolute and to demonstrate that it actually is a relativity. Only God is absolute. All else is relative. That's why a man who judges becomes imprisoned within the deadlocks of his mind. The blind spot which generates this self-destruct mechanism is that the mind formulates its control around the factors it considers to be absolute, and yet it cannot comprehend the One and Only Absolute there is. This is why I stress to you that the mind is a brilliant servant, but a fatal master. Before you build it you must know how to unplug it."*

Fortunately, on that day I unplugged it. Without conscious intention, I shifted into some kind of "over drive" which placed higher faculties and resources in command. The boys and I proceeded to make small talk about puppies, and soon one of them became curious about why I would come all the way to New York to get a puppy. "Well, I'm an artist, and I'm up here to do some work." The eyes of one boy lit up brightly as he said, "I'm an artist!" And two others responded in unison, "He's good, too!" "What kind of art do you do?" I asked. He pointed out the window at all the graffiti and thumped his chest like Tarzan. "I did that!"

For the first time in my life I had a positive response to graffiti. It was an amazing feat of self expression. More than that, I cannot begin to express the relief I felt in discovering a second subject which we had in common. All I could think to say was, "Do you know how many artists would give their right arm to have that much work on display in New York City?" He beamed.

We were becoming friends, and they were relaxing into being boys. They wanted to know where my studio was, where I was staying, and Manuel asked me to give him art lessons. I agreed, "If I'm here long enough, I'd be happy to. Actually, I think you could teach me a thing or two about getting public exposure." Then one of them asked me if I had any pictures of my art. Before I could catch myself, I had opened my purse and pulled out my wallet. I started to flinch when I realized what I had done. Oh, what the heck. I just pulled the pictures out and passed them around. They were impressed, and I felt a sense of ease amongst us. We were like a bunch of kids at summer camp, talking about kid stuff, puppies, and art. Then suddenly one of them blurted out, "Don't you know it's not safe for you to be down here?" I replied innocently that, "Where I came from in Texas, most everywhere is safe." One of the oldest boys scolded, "Well, somebody had better take care of you up here! We'll walk you to your taxi." When we got off, I felt like Guinevere escorted by her Knights of the Round Table.

The taxi driver, who seemed to know the group of boys, grimaced when he saw us coming. Once I was in the car, he asked, "Are you all right, lady?"

"Yes, I'm just fine." Then he proceeded to chastise me, stressing in several different ways and languages, "Don't you ever do that again!" As

I sat there reviewing the events of the afternoon I silently agreed that I should not be so naive in the future. I also thought that, if by accident, I ever did find myself in a similar situation, I hoped I would handle it in just the same way. I never saw the boys again, but there will always be a place for them in my heart.

When I got through telling this story to Jesus, His eyes were welled with tears. I said, "I didn't mean to make you sad." He replied, *"You didn't make me sad. I remember the event very well, and I was extremely proud of you and the boys. I'm very sentimental about moments when people's lives are changed."*

Chapter 2
The Wondrous Universe

There were days when little was said, and then there were other days when our conversations were like a salad bar, providing a rich assortment of variety with the only consistency being the input of His greater wisdom. In the beginning it was mostly that way. As time passed, He infused my consciousness with a broader viewpoint, capable of assimilating larger patterns of thought and meaning.

The growth of my consciousness might be compared to a teenager enrolled in ballroom dancing. An instructor's first task might be to get the student's "two left feet" untangled, synchronized with the music, and off his own toes. At first, it was hard enough to keep from tripping myself, although He adroitly kept His own balance. Then one day, by a touch of grace, I began "waltzing to the music."

That acceleration of harmony was expedited most dramatically one morning when He observed me assembling pieces of understanding like a jigsaw puzzle. Offering to help me make sense of it, He suggested that I reach for my drawing pad and felt tip marker. *"You're trying to erect a building out of bricks and mortar without a plan. Let me provide you with some key factors which you're groping to find."*

On the large white sheet of paper, He had me draw an equilateral triangle with the base at the bottom, so that it rested stably with its apex pointing upward. He described the components of the universe as being basically three. The first is love, the second is spirit, and the third is a substance which is **finer than anything** that has yet been isolated by science! It is finer than the atom or any of its component parts. As the ultimate simple particle, **it is the irreducible building block of the universe**. Comprehending this particle is currently a major objective in physics research. It is variously called by several names, including the

Higgs boson, and some have even called it the "God Particle." There is, however, an ironic truth in that sarcasm. This particle is prior to the existing family tree of particles, which accounts for its difficulty in being studied. Apparently it **creates mass**, whereas other particles are the **result of mass**. *"There is a particle substance, which is the matrix of all energy mass. Its particle units are utterly generic in nature, and are the basic, irreducible components of physical existence."* He called them *"adamantine particles."*

At the top of the triangle He placed Love. *"The Source of Love is the Father, the Creator Himself, who is to all of existence like the sun is to life on Earth. Yet, the light of His Love is so brilliant, only its halo can be perceived. The Source of Pure Love is the ultimate source of all love. From that Love you are emanated, or created.* **Like a ray of light, you are an entity of His Love.** *Love is the name of God, and Love is your name as well. In that, you are created in His likeness. You are known and shall always be known by the nature of your love.*

"Beyond the recognition of love, the presence and nature of God can simply not be described, for Holy Presence is the definer, not the defined." No sooner had He said that than He anticipated my next question by adding, *"The Holy Trinity is also a sacred mystery which precedes and determines the tri-part universe. Like God, it cannot be defined, but is manifested everywhere in the very presence of all that exists. In the dimension of knowable reality, you might say that the one spirit is Holy whenever it manifests the presence of God, and the adamantine particles are literally the Body of God whenever they bring form to His will."*

Whenever He would direct His attention to the Father, his eyes would well. Perhaps it was partly because He was looking into a blinding light. However, the love and reverence He felt for the Holy Source was more than even He could express in words. The emotions which poured from Him were message enough. *"The name of your Father is Love. And so, too, is that your immortal name. Love is the essence of true beingness. Love is not something that you do or don't do, give or don't give, receive or don't receive. In other words it is not a commodity, not a derivative substance. Love is not something which is subject to the laws of abundance or scarcity. Love is WHO you are."*

"For that reason, love is ultimately unconditional, because it is not subject to any of the conditions of existence. I am glad to hear people talking more about unconditional love today, but they need to understand

*more fully how and why it is that way. Love is unconditional because it is our Origin, and who you are . . . not something that is **done** unconditionally. Actions are always conditional to some degree, because relationships have conditions, because existence has conditions. And if love were something you do, there would be no escaping that fact."*

There was a sense of relief, as I settled down in my chair. I wanted to understand and practice unconditional love, but I had not wanted to be an unconditional doormat.

*"The true nature of love is the answer to the riddle. The greatest mystery of the universe is that love is the **sacred aspect of beingness**. Be it to the fullest, and the rest of your life will fall into place.*

"The second great element of existence is spirit. All things are of spirit." Pointing to the left corner of the triangle, He instructed me to write 'spirit.' *"There is but one spirit. Spirit is in all things, around all things, with all things, and of all things. There is no such thing as spirit being isolated to a pure zone, apart from manifest creation."* He cautioned that there have been many theories of matter versus spirit. *"Such theories reflect an absence of real understanding and an obsession with the dualities of structured thinking. Inseparable and indivisible spirit is in all things. There is no place where spirit is not. Spirit is one.*

"Spirit must be understood as whole, continuous, and unbroken. Whenever a person views spirit as the opposite of matter he has entered the world of misconception and duality. It is not true that Earth is material and Heaven is of the spirit. Spirit is the unity of us all, and of Heaven and Earth. It is through the oneness of spirit that the miracle of prayer can work. It is through the oneness of spirit that the power of dreams, of visions, and of prophecies can work. In the spirit we are one. Therefore in spirit we live one life, unified in a state of brotherhood, in a state of common awareness and seeking—either enlightenment and uplifting, or darkness and down pulling—whichever way one chooses it to be. Regardless of how your experience unfolds, we are of one spirit, and your experience is shared by all.

"As a matter of fact, the greatest breakthrough of modern physics, the one that every other discovery hinges on, was the discovery of the unified field. Every development in modern physics would have been impossible had that breakthrough in consciousness not occurred. Scientists just have not realized yet that what was discovered is the physical presence of spirit." He explained that our science is on the threshold of its next greatest

leap, which will provide a basis for discovering the adamantine particles.

The third corner on the triangle represents the element of particularized reality, through which differences of potential and separate configurations are made possible. This third element manifests as particles. Sometimes He referred to them as particles of infinity, but usually He called them adamantine particles. The first time I heard the word "adamantine" it had an unfamiliar ring to my ears. I just assumed that it was a word unique to Him, or perhaps to Heaven, or to some other dimension of reality of which I was not aware. So I just accepted it as an exotic word.

Later on, when He used the term "adamantine particles" interchangeably with "particles of infinity," I asked for some clarification. Explaining His choice of words, He indicated that *"'adamantine' comes from the root word 'adamant' which means, unsubmitting, impenetrable, unyielding. This is a particle so small that it is irreducible, non-negotiable, fundamental, and utterly elemental. It is from this particle that all complex forms are built. This describes the character of the particle, and the term 'particle of infinity' refers to its function, for it is basic to all physical existence without dimensional limitation. This is the particle that the ancient Greek philosophers postulated when they first named the atom."*

Of course, what science calls an atom today is a very complex particle, and not at all what the Greeks envisioned. With His usual affirmative tone, Jesus encouraged me to consider that the search for smaller and smaller particles has been a necessary process for "peeling the onion" of our scientific understanding. He assured me that the ultimate particle discovery is on the horizon, and that it will unlock a door to many current mysteries about the way things work.

Returning to the diagram, He said, *"Look at the triangle again and take note of its arrangement. Love is at the top. Then spirit resonates to love and love commands the adamantine particles. From this, all creation has occurred."*

Before I could proceed with that lesson, however, I had to clarify an issue that was now bothering me. "In this world we talk about each other's spirit as an aspect of individuality. You know . . . your spirit, my spirit, Brian's spirit, my cat's spirit, and so forth. Are there separate parts within the one?"

With tranquil firmness, He assured me, *"There is just one spirit."*

"Well," I persisted, "I always know when you enter the room, because your spirit feels different."

"No, it is my LOVE that feels different. We are each known by our love. Spirit resonates to our love. It's just like a lake with many fish, where every fish sets off a different vibration within the water. So, too, your love resonates with the spirit differently than anyone else's, like a fingerprint. You may say, this is what another's spirit feels like. But actually, this is how the spirit, the one and only spirit **resonates to him***. If you want the one and only spirit to resonate with you more affirmatively and distinctly, then truly* **be the love that you are***.*

"What you have learned to recognize, Glenda, is my love. My love feels like no one else's. Brian's love feels like no one else's. And so it is. Each person's love feels like no one else's. So the spirit responds and honors each one's love as a unique imprint, and that love, in turn, commands the adamantine particles. It is love which defines your individuality, not spirit. Spirit is the indivisible element, and adamantine particles are the building blocks for complex existence. They are utterly generic in nature. Only love has the capacity for singularity and individuality. Without love you would be as indistinguishable as a grain of sand on the shore."

Building upon this introduction to love, one day He asked, *"Glenda, would you like to know the best way to discover and to prove that you are love and that love is not an external commodity?"*

"Sure!" I rushed to reply.

"Love your enemies."

It wasn't the answer I had hoped for, and I was not exactly comfortable with the recommendation, although I was all ears to hear more.

"When you are in the presence of your enemies, you know for a fact that any love you are able to feel is not because of external factors. You are not loving your adversary because of his kindness, or because you like the color of his eyes, or because you stand to profit by the encounter.

"In the presence of your enemies, you know that you **are** *love . . . and the source of your love. That is the most important reason I told you to love your enemies—not for you to become weak or passive, not for you to be walked on, not for you to suffer, not for you to yield advantages to those who oppose you—but for you to learn that you are love.* **In knowing this, you gain command***.*

"External conditions do not have the ability to teach you who you are.

However, as long as you believe that they can, you will always be seeking permission from the external world to exist. That obsession is your real enemy."

Directing my attention back to the chart, He reiterated, *"Love commands the adamantine particles. Between you and anyone opposing you there are many shared particles. Now, of the two of you, which one is going to command them?"*

"The one who loves!"

"That's the first point. But there's more.

"Such experiences will give you an opportunity to learn the most important thing you can ever know about yourself, as well as the subject of love. The world would have you think that love is the consummating emotion of desired and pleasurable effects. In other words, that love is created. Nothing could be further from the truth, for love is the universal instrument of cause and command.

"Last, but certainly not least, you might just find out that the person in opposition to you was not really your enemy!

"And let's not limit this to human opponents. Let's talk about a storm that is approaching. How could you turn a storm around?"

"I never thought that I could," I said, sitting there in amazement to think He would ask me such a question.

"You would look for the motivating force of the storm, and then be the love in its presence. You can command the storm, for the adamantine particles are commanded by love. Love is the Source of everything. It is the commander and that command has been delegated to you as a child of love. This is why, in any situation, you can win by the power of love. Not by DOING LOVE. This is where you trip up. You have to BE LOVE! Love that is a burning fire at the heart of any situation. You can literally quell the storm by loving the forces that comprise it."

After a quiet moment, He continued. *"Behold the beauty of the storm. Behold the beauty of the forces that make it up. Love it to its very core. Find the necessity of it until you are one with it. Several things could happen, depending upon your degree of assurance. The storm could just dissipate into thin air. Or possibly, it would turn into gentle rain. Maybe it would be redirected to another place. Or, at the very least, it would bring no harm to you. For love does not hurt love!*

"If you want to get varmints out of your house, love them into another position. Many people already know this, and don't use chemicals. They

just love the bugs elsewhere. I can't begin to tell you how many changes you can make in your life, by using love to command the adamantine particles."

In all the days I spent with Jesus, I do not recall His using the word "control " as part of His instructions of life. Several times, however, He made reference to the tragic state of people locked into obsessions for control. He said, *"Control is a ploy for achieving dominance within a dualistic situation. When people are operating within polarities, control is what they use to reinforce their preferred position. What makes it even worse is that after control is established, the polarities will be maintained in order to perpetuate the control."*

By contrast, command was a very positive topic for Him. He seemed to imply by tone and gesture that it is part of our covenant, and that exercising command is central to our dignity. The sole authority of it is love. BEING love.

"All the particles you have ever commanded with love are yours to have forever."

That was a mind-boggling thought, far too great to take in all at once, but I composed myself enough to inquire, "Is that how you resurrected your body?"

"Of course. It was the love that gave me total command of all the particles that had ever composed my body, and they were reconstructed by the laws of love instead of by the laws of structure. Thereby, I was a prisoner of structure no more."

Then He mentioned the new Earth with the new bodies we will have, which will be under the conscious direction of love. He did not say when, but He assured me that *"the transformation will be brought about by knowing the truth of what love is. In this new state of existence, love will literally cause the pulse beat of your heart and the cells of your body. Love will propel the blood through your veins. Love will spark your thoughts, and all the energies around you, and all that you magnetize to yourselves."*

"Is that how you multiplied the fishes?"

"Well, yes," He modestly admitted.

"You really did multiply the fishes, didn't you? It wasn't just a metaphor, was it?"

"No, it wasn't a metaphor. I really did multiply the fishes. You know, all I had to do was love one fish enough."

How simple He made it sound. All I could do was look at Him in wonder and whisper, "That must have been some kind of love!"

His understanding of everything was whole. He bore no witness of duality or opposition, and there was no stress anywhere in His presence.

He had profound respect for technology when it was based upon truth and understanding, and when it was used to implement a democratized consciousness of reality. He seemed to have a great respect for science, for scientific thinking, and for higher pursuits of competence. However, He did not favor support for artificially created structures of the mind. He wanted to see our understanding based on simple truths of existence, and applied to support our actual needs. There was a sense of disregard for excess technology which exists only to create monopolies of power, to leverage the compliance of people, or to create dependencies on artificial environments and situations. Aside from that, He had a tremendous reverence for workability, because He knew it drew its power from the laws of God. *"Workability is the harmony of God, manifest upon the Earth,"* He proclaimed.

Too often we regard the tenets of structure as the cause of orderliness and workability in life. This is a grand illusion on which structure has momentarily secured a franchise. He frequently reminded me of our right, as loving beings, to innocently perceive all that is. Then we can make it work by commanding the love which joins us to it.

"Your mind prefers to structure your involvement with reality, and to justify that obsession, it wants to pre-guess and predetermine what life represents. The structural models which the mind projects then become the great trap. Such formulas condition your perceptions to honor their designs as 'sacred' and even more basic than innocent reality. That is the lie."

In no uncertain terms, He made it clear that intelligence is not limited to the mind. *"Mind is the meeting ground of structure and intelligence. If your intelligence were limited to the barriers and mortality of structure, then your potential to have a transcendent comprehension of the universe would be hopelessly impossible.*

"Innocent perception is the great revealer." He would encourage me to sit quietly and perceive . . . look out a window, and just say what is. You don't need a formula or a formal education to approach life.

Sometimes I would talk about the painting in relation to structural composition, and He would help me to see the process more directly, to see more innocently just what was there in front of me. Anytime I would start to make a mental formula out of it, He would redirect the flow, saying,

"Glenda, you don't need this. You don't need these mental formulas through which to view life or to explain what you're doing. Just be here and perceive. Relax and just be." His constant encouragement was just "to be."

Once, when we were talking about innocent perception, it triggered an old question I had from the book of Genesis. It was about man's expulsion from the garden of innocence, because of our ancestor's inquiry into the subject of good and evil. I wanted to know why man was forbidden to study good and evil.

"Because study is a pursuit of the mind, and the mind is endlessly polarized. Therefore, when the mind pursues the subject of good and evil there is no escaping duality. It will only use its perceptions to judge and to condemn." Then He added, *"The heart already knows the paths to right living. The heart does not need to study a subject which is native to it. The mind, however, can never know true goodness.*

"The real basis for goodness is love, then honoring life through innocent perception and compassionate service, according to one's purpose. You cannot intellectually comprehend the subject of good and evil. It falls into place only when you are being the love that you are. No amount of good deeds can compensate for an inadequacy of love. It is love which the spirit cherishes, and the spirit will not be cheated from that love. Love is above ethics and always will be. Otherwise how could there be grace? True ethics are shaped out of the patterns of love."

When we try to mentally comprehend the subject of right and wrong, apparently all we do is fall into judgment, condemnation, barriers, and the exiling of those with whom we don't agree.

"Conscience is native to your heart. What you call 'guilt' is a built-in alarm system which signals your departures from the heart. A man who follows his heart will never feel guilt, even if he steps a little outside the bounds of what society deems proper. But, on the other hand, a man who lives only in his mind will bear a secret guilt, even if he tries logically to 'do the right thing.' There will be no inner satisfaction in it, and so he will soon lose his ability to know what the right thing is. Eventually he will cease trying, leaving hidden guilt which imbeds as a recurring distress. He may spend fortunes on therapy or alcohol to anesthetize or remove it. But the eventual result is that a mind-dominated person will destroy his immune system. This is the end product of a mind-dominated world. But you can reverse it very simply, with total grace."

"How?"

"Follow your heart!"

I chuckled with the thought that rolled into my consciousness, "The mind follows the bucks, doesn't it?"

"Unfortunately, that's true."

One thought led quickly to another, and then I was face to face with my next question. "In the New Testament, Paul teaches, 'The love of money is the root of all evil.' Did you say that?"

"Close, but those were not my exact words. As Aramaic was transposed to Greek, some of the practical simplicity of my message was absorbed into the more abstract nature of Greek thinking. Aramaic was a people's language, not a scholar's language. That's why I chose it. In addition to that, Paul had his own way of carrying the message of love, according to the needs and understanding of those he served.

"GREED is the root of all evil. In the presence of greed, people go to extremes, and in the presence of extremes, the idea of scarcity is invented. When scarcity is invented, fear sprouts up like weeds in a garden. Every negative emotion known to man is born from fear.

"So this is the notorious family tree, from the roots to the branches. The extremes produced by greed beget scarcity, scarcity begets fear, and fear is the root of all destructive emotion and action."

"Well, I feel relieved! I would like to have a little more money."

"That's okay. You can have money. Money is just a certificate of exchange. Actually, people are economically healthier when they are doing a lot of exchanging. I like to see people actively exchanging goods and services. When economies are fluid, the structures have trouble dominating. When people exchange freely, no one goes hungry, no one goes unemployed, and no worthy idea goes unproduced."

"Jesus, some people say that **hate** is the opposite of love, and recently, I read a book which suggested that **fear** is the opposite of love. What do you say?" A wry grin began to take shape on His face as He focused a quizzical look at me.

*"I thought you would have realized by now that **love has no opposites**! Love is the solvent which ends all polarity."* His eyes were like clear pools of water, as I gazed into them, and beheld the simplicity of His succinct reply. But, He also knew that I still needed to dialogue on the subject, so He offered the following considerations: *"Fear abounds in the absence of love, and hatred is fear of love itself. Greed is an obsessive desire, which*

attempts to nourish and supply the needs of life without love. You might say greed is an attempt to counterfeit and to subvert the power of love. This is why it is the root of all evil. And it is not limited to material possessions or money. There can be greed for attention, influence, fame, education, therapy, dependency, even misery . . . anything which can establish bonds of attachment without love. So you are not wrong to consider that the absence of love brings problems. These are the greatest problems a person can have!"

"Why greed?"

"If you were trying to replace love utterly, how much would you need?"

"I get the point."

"Without love, a man has lost all basis for command. The best he can hope for is control, but that requires leverage . . . lots of it!

"I have said before, the meek shall inherit the Earth. But what you need to know is that this instruction has also received a poor translation, for in your language 'meek' implies humility and servitude. This is not what I meant. The word 'moderate' would more accurately convey my message. Those who live in moderation, will form the basis of the new Earth economy, and thus inherit the Earth."

"I'm not disagreeing with you, for it sounds great in principle, but why is it that greedy people seem to get ahead, and moderate people are held back?"

"That's because many people who practice moderation today are doing so only to be self-contained and to defend themselves against dreaded scarcities. The ideal reason for moderation is to share and to collectively participate in a spirit of abundance.

"As for greed, the initial advantages of it are quite deceptive. Greed has a built-in 'therapy' which at first generates a sense of elation. Prior to the pursuit of excess, a person might have reduced himself to a belief in scarcity and then wearied himself with countless decisions of, 'do I have this or do I have that?' Then one day he declares, 'I think I'll have it all!' An incredible thing has happened at that moment. He has removed his belief in scarcity and ended the duality of endless decisions! In doing so, he has released a great force of creativity within himself. Now if he could seize the quality of that force and apply it to the connectedness of all life, he would have fulfilling prosperity instead of a destructive addiction. But too often, a person applies it to himself alone, and recreates a new scarcity

called *'only for me.' Abundance applied to the 'self alone' is a betrayal of the perception!*

"I suggested that you contemplate infinity and the abundance of the universe so that you can strengthen your connections to the rest of life, not that you would possess it all for yourself. There's a simple guideline which will give you unlimited potential for expansion without the perils of greed: **Do not take more than you can truly love."**

This led to a question of ownership. "Some people believe that nobody owns anything. What do you say about that?"

"That is a very good question," He remarked. *"Let me put it this way. It has to do with what you are trying to own. Striving to own structure is a futile and thankless labor for it is all transitory and illusional. This is why the Creator rested on the seventh day. The effort to own and to manage structure simply is not worth it. Besides, all that your love has commanded is yours to keep anyway.*

"If nobody ever owned anything, there would not be a commandment against stealing. So, yes, you do own. But your ownership is based upon your love, and the influence it has had on the adamantine particles of your very existence. These you take with you forever. Ownership is a responsibility issue, not a title of purchase. No amount of money can give you true title to that which you have not loved. That is the law of sacred allotment. That which you have purchased with money, but for which you have no love, will own you until the time when one or more forces of the universe rip it from your hands, and mercifully set you free.

"You own your life. You own the things that the Father has given you, the fruits of your creation, the fruits of your labor. You own the effects of all your cherished imaginings, dreams, and aspirations. You own the fruits of it all, and all the memories. **Wealth is the harvest of love.** *Remember, love commands the adamantine particles. All that you have ever loved is what draws to you . . . the affairs of your life, the friends of your life, the family that expands your life, the dreams that extend your life. These things are yours, and this is to be honored."*

He cautioned, *"Don't try to own structure for its own sake. All structure is mortal. All structure fades away. I recommend that you store up your wealth in Heaven where the memory of your love will recreate all that is yours, leaving behind the structures which deceived you.*

"Actually, this is the true blessing of the Sabbath. The day in which you release from your life the dominance of the structure. You behold the

laws of God, the infinity of the cosmos, and rest. In so doing, you have suspended the artificialities and illusions which would seek to possess you, so that you may return to the love that you are."

"I thought the commandment said to remember the Sabbath and to keep it Holy."

He said, *"Go get your Bible, there's more to it than that."*

I had not realized before that the commandment also includes the sons, servants, cattle, and strangers in town . . . everyone and everything. The image which came to mind was a picture of total relaxation from all the rigidity of our lives.

"You cannot take a Sabbath by yourself," He pointed out. *"The Sabbath is a blessing you extend to everyone universally as a gift of freedom. It is a gift of amnesty from structured existence, which reveals for a moment the power and sacredness of **just being!**"*

"The seventh day has been greatly misinterpreted to mean that the Creator retired. Nothing could be further from the truth. The true meaning is that He creates, maintains, loves, and assists by BEING, not by DOING. Resting, not retiring! If you would be like your Father, you will learn the secret of commanding life through BEING LOVE. As you attain that ability you will rise above structure. The seventh day is a celebration of your Creator's supremacy over structure. Whenever you take it unto yourself, you harmonize with that principle. Whenever you extend it to others, you are liberating the world from its prison."

"Why has this principle been so difficult to perceive?"

*"When structure interprets the Bible, it does so to perpetuate its illusions. When love reads the Bible, it does so to **penetrate** illusion and arrive at the truth."*

"When you speak of structure, certain ideas come to mind, but my understanding may be too limited. Would you mind clarifying for me exactly what you mean by structure?"

"Structure is an organizational factor in the universe, although a secondary and derivative one. It is love which first brings order out of chaos, but structure implements the durable patterns of orderly arrangement. Love built your home; structure holds the walls in place. Love built your nation, structure administers it. Love determines the parameters of right conduct, structure formulates the laws which enforce it. Like the mind, structure is good if it serves, and tyrannical if it dominates inflexibly, never submitting to the revisions of love.

"Structure represents the predictable, agreed upon patterns of existence which start with simple forms and build to complex ones. It is the patterning which causes the differences of potential, and holds organizational formulas in place. For example, structure is what makes the difference between steam, water, and ice even though the ingredients are the same. But structure is not the 'will' which determines whether H_2O will become steam or ice. That is determined by harmonic adaptations to the environment (love).

"All structure is derivative summarization, and is subject to revision, suspension, or development. You might say that structure is the conservational imprint which allows desirable creations to be stabilized, retained, and combined into larger aggregates of form and matter. Structure is what holds things in place.

*"Laid upon this gridwork are many mind-generated patterns and structural models used by man for control. There are no 'sacred designs' which **preceded** reality. This idea has been invented to make you afraid to revise or to dispense with unworkable structures, and to give structures dominance over you."*

Occasionally, when I think about structure, I compare it to the "Save" button on a computer, which lets us retain and integrate one formulation into another, or to bring up a program again in another time and place. It's comforting to know that structure is only as important as it serves the ongoing creations of love. It's reassuring to also remember there's a "Delete" button which restores life back to innocent potential!

"In society, structure is most protected by those who have attained what they want. Ironically, it is also blindly obeyed by those who have so little they fear any and all change, thinking that change will only bring more loss. This is the harmony between the rich and the poor. By contrast, those who establish and implement values based on moderation and mobility use enough structure to make life work without inhibiting growth.

"You experience the structures of life as blocking attachments, and they actually rob you of your true wealth. Your true wealth is on a much higher level. It is the harvest of love. You have to experience letting go in order to receive. Learn the power of letting go. This lesson is as important as loving your enemies, because when you let go of structure, the real wealth that is there will multiply many times.

"The first thing you will learn is that you simply cannot lose your true wealth. The only thing you ever need to diminish is structure. With that

realization, you will make real steps toward overcoming your enslavement by structure and move into the greater reality of brotherhood."

He gave me a few practical examples which were relevant at the time.

"Just consider this house which you bought to renovate. By changing the deteriorating structure, you increased the value, but you are not going to put that monetary gain in the bank unless you sell the house and release it. See, that is your choice. You can keep the structure of these four walls or you can sell it and get your money. That is true of everything. Wealth is acquired as structure is released. Structure establishes order, and this is good. You build it, then in letting go, you receive your wealth. So this is what the Father did on the seventh day. He said, 'This is good, but beingness is far better. I shall be in receivership of my true wealth which is the harvest of love'."

Through twinkling eyes He concluded His teaching that day with a gentle smile and a powerful summation. *"The children of God were created to harvest His true wealth, which is love. You are both His harvest and the instrument of His harvest. You are the children of His love. So the same is true for you, and this is how you build your material wealth as well. You deal with structure; you build it. You say, this is good. You sell it, and make your profit to use for something else. If you never become attached to structure, the wealth will continue to build. Structure is the illusion that blocks your attainment of ultimate wealth—spiritually, intellectually, and physically. You must release the illusion to attain the truth."*

I had time that night to wonder how this principle could be applied to the crucial issue of human relationships. How would we discern between the reality of a relationship and the structure of it? What is the element in relationships which needs to be released?

He must have wanted me to figure that one out for myself, because with the fullest intention of bringing it up the next morning, I would simply think upon it, instead of asking. The way I see it, in any relationship there's a lot of role playing, and sometimes we forget that role playing is not the heart of a relationship. The heart of a relationship is the reason for being together, the love that binds, and the honor that makes it worth pursuing. The truth of who you are, and the truth of the other person, can be so much greater than the roles are capable of defining. Often we forget that roles are like rooms in a home that can always be redecorated, but the people who live there are the constant.

Sometimes I think it may be good to let go of the role playing and just be; or maybe exchange some roles to better understand the other person's part in a relationship. That may bring in a little fresh air to expand mutual understanding, to recognize love beyond the boundaries. I do not think the harvest of love in relationships comes about by ending them. I think it happens when we release our mental preconceptions and the restrictions we've placed upon them. Perhaps only then can we have the wealth of a true relationship.

At another time, He added an extra dimension to that understanding when He described the experience of death as releasing the complex structure of physical form. *"The soul witnesses an incredible energy release of that which was only on loan, and an even more wonderful homecoming of all that has been given you by the Father. That which is commanded by your love is yours to hold forever. All who have shared your love will remain in union with you. That is your ultimate harvest."*

While we were on the subject of how our wealth continues, I asked Him about life continuance. That was an item of particular interest to me, and so I inquired about it several times, whenever it seemed appropriate. He said, *"Life as you know it here is too structured for you to perceive your greater continuity. All that is you continues. Life just leaves its complex form. Nothing that is you ever goes away. All of the adamantine particles that make up your body remain with you. You are remembered in the spirit forever, and the love that you are will always carry your name. As you are remembered and cherished by spirit, your re-creation occurs again and again throughout eternity, whether it be in heaven, on Earth, or anywhere else in your Father's infinite domain."*

Eventually, I had the courage to use the word "reincarnation." "What do you have to say about the subject of past and future lives?"

His reply was to the point. *"Your immortality is a simple thing, and so your understanding will be more accurate if you keep it simple as well. By the will of God, life creates a place for you infinitely again and again, according to your love and in relation to your loved ones."*

He cautioned, *"The philosophy of reincarnation is not that simple. It does affirm your continuity, and that is good. However, there's a twist in it which defers your immortality back to structure and linearity, which is not true. Your immortality is not imprisoned within a wheel of life, or pathway of cause and effect. Neither are you the product of linear evolvement. You were created in perfection, and perfect love, and you do continue to re-manifest infinitely, but it is according to the will of the*

Father, and according to your own purposes, your own love, and your own place of service and learning." He added, with a touch of humor, *"You actually have only one life! It's just a very long one, with many chapters."* I laughed, and all seriousness disappeared.

As I digested that infusion of understanding, I saw how some people are searching for cause and effect reasons to explain their lives, so they extend their search even into ancient history, looking for an origination point. **The origination point is love** . . . God's, theirs, and others'. There is cause and effect in the way matter, energy, time, and space integrate and combine to become physical substance, in addition to the structures which conserve and limit those creations. Nevertheless, love is the real source and is the commander of even structure—not the **result** of it. For the first time in my life I saw that love is a **cause**, not a creation! I was pleased with my realization, and He watched serenely while I painted.

Before the day was over, He spoke again. *"All too often people who look to the subject of reincarnation for answers are actually trying to find themselves. That is a misdirection. There is **no other** time or place to find yourself. **Now** is your only context! The past is gone! Only the ego would cling to an identity out of context. You will rarely find anyone talking about a past life as a pauper, a leper, or a thief. Typically, one boasts about lives lived as a king, a hero, or a saint. That is the ego talking out of turn, trying to enslave the soul in its structure. Your immortality has no need of structure. The source of your identity does not lie in any kind of linear path. The source of your identity lies only in your love."*

He looked at me and asked, *"Who are you?"*

"Love," I confidently replied.

"In truly knowing that, you do not need to know anything else about yourself. That will bring the other answers you seek. It will bring to you an assurance of your immortality and faith in the immortal love which you share with others. As you become strengthened in that understanding it will also bring into focus your own true purpose, for your purpose is rooted in love."

"There are many therapies having to do with hypnotic regressions into past lives. Do they work, and are they of any value?"

"It all depends on the honesty of those facilitating and receiving the remembrance. As to the value, that lies entirely in letting go, in releasing that which is no longer useful. Sincere and thorough forgiveness will accomplish the same thing."

"Is there anything forgotten in our collective past that we need to know about?" I asked.

"There is the original birth trauma, which most people are still working through.

"There was a time before which you were, but there will never be a time after which you are not. There was a time when you were one and complete within the Source of Love. Love, however, decided to give you immortality **as yourself** *and to grant you an identity of your own. It was a great and glorious gift that you were given, full of promise, opportunity, and responsibility. But the children of God, having no point of reference other than the simplicity of a common light, experienced it as shock and interpreted the gift of life as separation. Many deeply wounded themselves by viewing it as rejection.*

"That was a tragic misconception, and many of the problems and pains that have been suffered by humanity are the result of this birth trauma. Some people can relate to this directly, because the trauma of physical birth also has left them with emotional scars of rejection and isolation. After years of dysfunctional relationships, a recognition of the problem and correct therapy has often proven to be healing.

"How much more significant it will be when the soul recognizes its duress and awakens to its magnificent endowment."

"What is preventing the realization?"

"People are torn between wanting to go Home and fearing the loss of personal freedom . . . wanting to stay apart and fearing the perils of becoming lost. It must be realized that even though you are one with the Father, you will never be resorbed into collective anonymity. Each person is honored by having his own place within the one spirit, and there will never be a time after which you are not.

"You have been given eternal life in your own name. When you are able to comprehend the grandeur of that gift, you will be able to experience your birth anew with ecstasy.

"You viewed it as separation the first time and have dramatized and structured it as separation ever since. Herein is man's dependency upon structure and his obsession with it. For structure has become a substitute source of security. The great healing that is soon to take place on the Earth will lift mankind above the trauma of his original birth, revealing the truth of his being, and establishing his place of honor within the wondrous universe."

Chapter 3
The Love That You Are

The question of your life, and everyone's eternal petition is, "Who am I?" Without an answer to that, everything else is to some degree a mystery. Shakespeare's Hamlet spoke the immortal line, "To be, or not to be . . . ." The greater question is, "**Who** are you"?

Are you merely human, a child of your race and nation? Are you an immortal soul, a child of God . . . a spirit, a purpose, a source of ability, a ray of light? All of the above are true, and yet the question remains, what is the **ultimate** core of your being?

Jesus said, "*You are love.*"

For lack of understanding, I thought at first that He was affirming His love for me and others by encouraging me to have a higher regard for myself. Only after days of instruction and reinforcement, did I begin to realize that He was talking about the power given to us from the beginning of time, the very basis of our kinship to God.

Without meaning to sound critical, I had to share with Him my private opinion that some people don't appear to be gushing fountains of love and happiness. If I were to generalize upon the horror stories reported by network news, then it would be hard to accept His instruction at all. With a bit of remorse at seeming so judgmental, I asked Jesus how my perceptions could be reconciled to His teaching.

His response was, *"Everyone was created **as love**. Current conditions are a reflection of each person's wellness and his ability to deal with life. Often the love has been neglected, disbelieved, abused, or denied. A rose in the garden is still a rose, even if it is wilted and covered with mildew. The weary and troubled faces you see around you are the faces of those whose love is broken.*

"Once a man's sense of self has been separated from his true nature,

then love can be understood only as an action or a feeling. In that state, everyone will surely will fall short. On Earth, that is the current belief about the subject of love."

It's not easy to restore a truth, especially if it means diving headlong into ancient wounds which were the causes of our misunderstanding. In this, as in everything else, He was masterful. (Any slowness I might have experienced was just my own inertia resisting a greater comprehension.)

Once He began to talk about love, His emphasis was on the nature of **being** love versus **doing** love. This is the whole key to unconditional love. Many people are seeking to practice unconditional love today . . . truly wanting to be there, but finding their way blocked by merciless obstacles. After all, who wants to be an unconditional doormat? Or to be unconditionally stupid? No sooner do I think I have transcended a condition and loved beyond it than it snaps me back in the face! How does one love unconditionally and also take into account the fact that life has conditions to it? He helped me find the answer to that riddle.

His comments were, *"As long as you consider love to be an external force, it will always be subject to the conditions of life. **Life does have its conditions.** Nature has its conditions. For example, winter is necessary that spring may bring forth new life. Man has also established many conditions within society. Some of them are wise and others are not. Most of these conditions need relaxing, for man has built them into walls and prisons. You can ease conditions by broadening your tolerance, widening your viewpoints, increasing your forgiveness and expanding your curiosity for life. Yes, the conditions need to be loosened and returned to a greater compatibility with natural order, but the fact still remains there will always be **some** conditions to life. For example, you may enjoy helping a man by giving him twenty dollars, yet feel a certain reluctance about giving him the keys to your house. If you loved him enough you could give him the world. Nevertheless, there will be an inevitable point where you encounter external resistance and feel personal resentment. At that moment you would be facing conditions. In the management of life, a line must always be drawn somewhere in order that balance and fair play may **also** be practiced. Balance is an eternally recurring condition in life. Often it is the deciding factor between war and peace.*

"Therefore, expanding and looking outward does not provide the ultimate answer about unconditional love. So let's just drop that line of reasoning for a moment, and look at love from another viewpoint. Let's

*return to the truth and consider that you **are love**, that love is not an action, and not a commodity that you give or trade. You don't leverage it, you don't barter it, and you don't exchange it as currency. You don't possess it or brag about how much more you have than another. When you truly understand love you will be unable to view it as an external factor."*

After a while it became easier for me to see the wisdom in His answer. When we think of love as an external thing we run into conflict with external conditions. These conditions vanish, however, with the realization that love is who we are. Despite our many external limitations, or the predatory forces that would seek to take advantage of them, the miracle is, **love works!**

As I assimilated that understanding it became easier for me to see how an enemy is reversed to a friend. By recognizing our enemy's potential for love, we have made contact with his heart and he is less likely to continue his hostility. **Love does not attack love.** Your secret sign to all your brothers is love. If you have ever wondered who you are—a human being, a spiritual being, a lighted being, a child of God—the answer is, all of the above. As love you are a radiant sun, and what do suns do? They give off light. As love, spirit resonates to you, honors you, and gives you a place within it. As love, you are a child of God. Above all, **you are love!** Each person is love in his own special way. Perhaps the greatest obstacle in getting this point understood is that we are still confused about love as affection and attachment. In a world that is so dominated by structure, we have the idea that attachments and affections are scarce and so we cling to the few that we have. We cling to our favorite people, our favorite belongings, and our favorite pleasures.

Jesus said, *"Love can also mean letting go. The pain of this realization might be unbearable if it were not fully understood that the power of love lies in the depth of your being. Releasing attachments, as an act of love, is the most difficult expression for anyone. Second to that is the releasing of hatred and fear through forgiveness. Forgiveness could take on a more positive meaning if it were observed as an act of perfecting the love that you are. Last, but not least, love may require that you release your compulsive urge to do something when there is nothing for you to do. Like the Holy Father, who rested in order to command by love, so too is that an option for you. There are times when doing nothing is the greater expression of love, and the ultimate expression of being. All leverage over you ceases when you understand these things."*

Our discussion of those ideas stimulated a curiosity about the Scriptural reference to God as "The I Am that I Am." He replied, *"That means that **beingness is supreme**, and that God is the Source of all Being. The name of that Beingness, however, is Love! In you, too, beingness is above doing, and the name of your beingness is Love.*

*"The Creator **is** love, the Source of love, and the origin of your own beingness. In that image you were created."*

"What does it mean to be created in the image of God?"

*"It means that you are a child of the Creator. Not a created thing. The mystery of the Creator is beyond any knowledge which can be projected into form or image. However, the knowable aspect of your Holy Source is Love. That love extends throughout creation. Humanity has a very special place in that regard, for it has been given the privilege of recognizing itself **as love also** and of activating that power for further creation.*

*"This does not mean that the Holy Father has then diffracted into an infinity of little gods. There is but **One God** which provides an enduring unity to all that is. What it means to be created in the image of God is that Holy Will pours through all mankind generation after generation by way of a **common essence**. That essence is love.*

"An instructive analogy which you might consider is the role of DNA in your own body as a language base for the body's integrated performance. You could take tissue samples from different parts of your body and DNA analysis would identify them all as being uniquely yours. However, not one of these samples is equal to the whole body, nor could any one of them function alone. Yet the fact of a common DNA code allows all facets of the body to cohere and to work together in a coordinated fashion. You might say that love is the common DNA you share with your Heavenly Creator which allows you to act in coordinated service to the Source of Life as well as to all the manifestations of it.

*"Love is the imprint of your beingness. In knowing that, you will understand why lesser actions fall short. But more importantly, you will begin unfolding that special nature which you were really created to be. Think not of love as an action, however, nor as a magnitude of effectiveness. If you compared yourself to the Creator in magnitude you would collapse into helpless despair. Love is not a quantity, **but a quality of beingness** which brings forth rightness of action.*

"Love is a quality, unbounded by fences and magnitudes, which derives its power from God, the ultimate Source of Love. As such, love has

some inalienable rights. First of all, you have the simple right to honor within yourself all that love has brought you, and to assimilate those things into your character. For your character is the summarization of your love. No one can ever take that from you.

"Love is universally free. Thus, in being love, so are you. Your body may be imprisoned, but your love has no boundaries.

"Love commands the adamantine particles, thus in being love you take command of your life.

"Love is the master of conditions, not the servant of them. Thus in being love you are no man's slave.

"Love is the law, and any law is only as valid as it is rooted in love. By this, all men shall know the law, and be equal under it. This is why I left you with only two commandments: To love God with all your heart, and your neighbor as yourself.

"Love is universally resonant with all of life, and in being love you are also resonant with life. There are no conditions to the truth of who you are. It is your sacred right to be the love that you are, and that is unconditional."

There were a few times in my life when I had already experienced examples of these teachings. As I recalled such moments in His presence, they stood out with greater clarity and insight. It was a privilege to share them with Him and to distill their deeper meanings.

One particular story is extremely relevant to His message. It took place in New Orleans when I was working on my Masters Degree at Tulane University. I had the good fortune to live in the Garden District in the renovated slave quarters of a home built in 1836. The magnificent old mansion was like a picture from "Gone With the Wind"—its garden surrounded by a ten foot brick wall and lined with fragrant magnolias. There were only two entrances to the estate, which sat on the corner of Washington Avenue and Carondelet. One was through the front gate, and the other was through the massive carriage gates which led under a portico and on to my quarters. My little house had two stories and its own balcony from which I could gaze across the garden toward the mansion with its lacy French wrought iron. There was a sprawling live oak tree outside my window, with a long sculptural branch extending to the ledge of an upstairs window. Without air conditioning or window screens on the second floor, my cat enjoyed an open and charmed access to the house day and night. It almost seemed like paradise.

The one drawback to this place, and the reason I was able to afford it on my student budget, was that it was right on the fringe of the most dangerous ghetto in New Orleans. St. Charles Avenue, only a block away, was the demarcation line between the rich and poor in that part of town. Unfortunately, the beautiful mansion in which I lived was on the wrong side of the trolley tracks. As prudence directed, I cautiously exited through the front gate and avoided the Carondelet carriage entrance. However, one of my more fascinating pleasures was to sit on my shaded balcony and watch the neighborhood children playing outside the carriage gates. I wasn't familiar with their games or what they did, but some of them were very young children. Some looked quite like urchins, clearly neglected, and all of them unsupervised. Often I wondered if there was something I might do, in the way of "big sister" contributions. Instead, I chose just to remember them in my prayers and hold them in my heart. As I watched the children play, I felt incredible love for them and deeply hoped that goodness would prevail in their lives and provide them with opportunities for an upward way. Perhaps I could have responded with fear, or locked my windows and avoided late night departures. Yet, in all my days and nights of coming and going there were never any problems. Although I watched the children from a distance I never approached them in any way. All the same, my love for them grew. This was actually the first time in my life when I fully experienced the greater power of being love versus doing it. It was also the first time I ever realized how judgmental it can be to **do** love before you have **been** it!

Easter morning came, and I was sound asleep. Someone had left the carriage gate open, or perhaps the children had pushed through it, for as the sun rose over the mansion roof I was awakened with choruses of music as a group of little boys sang below my window. I waved from the balcony, and they presented me with a little basket of flowers which they had probably picked from someone's yard. That was our only meeting, and after a few minutes they left with Easter wishes, having given me one of the loveliest Easter presents of my life. We never met again.

I can only conclude that the children must have felt my love and responded to it. The greater realization, which I cherish now more than ever, is that the children were able to reveal their **own love** instead of being sheltered by mine. When I shared the story with Jesus, His eyes twinkled with pleasure. He said, _"There is no greater gift you can give to another than that of self-realization. That is The Father's intent for everyone!"_

To this day, whenever I feel tempted to extend my love as a gesture of "know-best" interference, I am reminded of the greater power of loving acceptance. This does not mean that we are to turn our heads in blind disregard for the plight of others, because we are a brotherhood. On the other hand, when we set out to **do love** before we have **been it** we have simply judged a condition and failed to honor the person within it. Until we can walk in another man's shoes, what right have we to tell him what kind of shoes to wear?

With even the best of intentions, when love is offered **as an action** it is often rejected or responded to with hostility. This is because it was received as a judgment from the other person's viewpoint . . . not as love. Jesus said that when you are being the love that you are, you will be led to right action.

You might ask, do I have to **direct** love toward people, consciously pray, or focus it in a special way? I am not sure that you have to do anything more than **earnestly be** the love that you are. The rest will follow. There's another story from my childhood which illustrates the power of love within a man's character. This, too, I shared with Jesus who helped me find even greater meaning within it.

I was born in the 1940s in a small Texas town. In its population of fewer than 10,000 people there was quite a montage of realities. Against a backdrop of Victorian mansions with gingerbread spires there was rapid growth and modernization with lingering remnants of depression era life scattered here and there. The "star" of this recollection is Mat, a man who hauled trash in his mule-drawn, buckboard wagon. Trash collection was not the industry it is now, and a man with entrepreneurial spirit and available equipment could always find work. Mat did a number of other chores around the neighborhood, and one of them, which I fondly anticipated, was springtime cultivation when he would bring his plow and mules onto our large acre lot and "turn the soil" of our back garden. His wife Viola, who was my mother's housekeeper, was a warm and gracious lady. She was partly responsible for my upbringing, and sometimes I played with their children in the afternoon.

Every day Mat would pass by our house with his wagon and mules on his way to one or more jobs. As a little child, no more than four years old, I would wait and listen for the clip-clop of his mules. The fascinating thing is that I could feel his presence for blocks away before the sounds foretold his approach. Mat had a certain light about him and a way of being that was uniquely his own. I don't remember anyone in my childhood who was more radiant than Mat. He had a rare ability just to "be there," to be with anyone. Although he lived a simple life, he was a noble man. I know now that he had accepted his limitations in life as an opportunity to perfect the love that he was. You didn't have to know Mat to feel his light or interact with him to receive it. He just glowed with contentment and peace. Mat's bountiful character was a springboard for my early, gregarious love of life. Every day when weather permitted he would give me a ride to the town square which was only about five blocks from home. After waving goodbye, I would proceed with my agenda which included a visit to the shopkeepers and then a long hike back home through vacant lots, stables, grandmother's garden, and secret hiding places. That was my daily route. You see, those were "Little Rascals" days, and I was one of them. Mat gave me my earliest lesson in being love . . . it isn't something you do . . . it's who you are! As a way of being, love is amazingly contagious!!

After finishing my story, I looked to Jesus for embellishment or contribution. He just glowed, shrugged His shoulders and commented, *"How can I add to perfection? That's the way life should be."*

The way He said that, honoring life at its best on Earth, was like a splash of refreshing water on my face, waking me up. Until that moment I must have been lulled to sleep under the comfortable blanket of assuming that perfection happens only in Heaven. Related to that was my other supposition that His instruction of "love is who you are" was an idea that could be fulfilled only in Heaven (with the possible exception of saints). For the first time it struck me that we are love not only in relation to God and to our ultimate attainment, **but also here and now in relation to life**. It was not an easy concept to grasp in the practical sense, however. So I asked, "Can you give me more examples of being love in real life? Is it like the wide-eyed bliss of a child?"

*"I don't think I need to remind you of all the sweet and obvious ways of love. You know them by heart. Would you like to understand more about **being love** in the trenches of life?"*

"That's really what I meant. It's just that I don't **feel** the trenches of life when I'm with you."

He smiled.

"In the trenches, love is knowing that your very presence makes a difference. It means being true to your own calling and capacity for service, refusing other calls to riches and fame which could diminish the

glory of your real character. It often means standing firm in the midst of chaos, with patient conviction that you hold a piece of the unfolding puzzle. Love is a businessman who persists with dedication and clarity through many sleepless nights of high demands upon low budgets until a solution appears. Love is a devoted and patient mother who never ceases in her vigilance to heal and redirect her restless, troubled child. There was such a mother who tried attention, affection, scolding, corrective education, and counseling. But nothing external worked. Never giving up, she went so far as to consider placing the child in her brother's family, giving her son a new start. Then one night, as she prayed and meditated upon that final possibility, a startling realization came to her. She saw that she was part of both the problem and the solution. To separate herself out would be to deny a vital connection they both needed. Refreshed from her realization and a good night's sleep she awakened her son the next morning with a 'soul to soul' hug unlike anything they had shared since his infancy. The healing began.

*"You see, being the love that you are means **to accept and to connect** with the situations of your life. Too often people skateboard on the surface of life, seeking sensation, driven by desire, and propelled by dissatisfaction. The irony for them is that life works only when one steps off the skateboard and makes contact with the pavement. The first step in realizing the love that you are is to honor and to accept your inevitable connection to life.*

"This is not a somber pursuit, I promise you. The more you move into contact with life and harvest its revelations, the more you will develop a sense of humor. Actually, it's the superficial, politically correct actions and attitudes which strip away from life its fabulous moments of laughter. Laughter is good for the soul, especially when you can laugh about your own issues.

"Never underestimate the power of your connection to life —the center of self in contact with the Reality of God. It will humble you. It may also ennoble you, enlighten you, or bring you to tears. Aside from everything else, it surely will lift you above the problems which have been oppressing you.

"A woman in childbirth could hardly endure the pain were it not for her connection with the miracle in progress. An athlete would not persist through the pain of a dislocated shoulder were it not for the collective spirit he shares with his team members.

"Life is an adventure in connecting. The connections you make affirm

and strengthen your character. The ones you make in love are the ones you will hang your garlands on. All the rest are consumable experiences. They may entertain you or challenge you, but in the end they will leave you hungry and thirsty for the real meaning of life.

"The soul is crying for a reality experience which only physical life can give to it. The body is crying for an immortality experience which only the soul can give to it. As you permit this union to fulfill itself, you will directly know what it feels like to be the love that you are.

*"Man was created through progressions of unity —first with God, then with life, and last but not least by marriage of body and soul. As a child of God, man was given a sense of self, with a secondary covenant **to accept it**. The body needs to acknowledge the soul in order to have a higher life. The soul needs to honor the body in order to fulfill its physical experience. The body and soul have much to offer each other. The soul brings to the body visions of a higher life, higher consciousness, and higher principles, along with the courage to pursue them. The body gives to the soul many experiences, along with the greatest experience of all—compassion. The body also provides a field of focus for application and service to life. In their mutual connection and integration the body and soul magnify and direct the heart's purposes.*

*"Your first duty is to accept the union of body, soul, and love that exists within and **as** yourself. How can a woman find her place in the world or a man make peace with his brother when neither have successfully made the most critical integration of their lives?*

*"Many descriptions of body and soul are inadequate to explain their vital relationship to each other or to account for the struggles that are part of their union. It is the body that usually wants peace, quiet, and protection. Without the soul and the motivating forces of love, the body would pursue a life of least resistance. Its major sins are related to a resistance toward change, preferring comfort and convenience. The body is not a risk taker! By contrast, the sins of adventure are usually traceable to the soul. It is the soul that has come to the Earth for experience. The soul already knows the sweet sound of harps and the fragrance of Heavenly roses. What it doesn't know without physical experience is what a rose **thorn** feels like, or how exhilarating the 'G-force' of a jet plane can be. It is the soul which enjoys the excitement of a World Series game, or the joy of falling in love and getting married. These are wholesome experiences. The soul, however, in its zeal for experience can also solicit problems and*

trouble. This is most especially true when the soul is not at peace with its Earthly covenant.

"A soul disconnected and willfully uncontained can cause great problems for itself and others. A body ignorant of the soul can be buried alive in the lust or drudgery of self-protection. Neither extreme is good, nor the will of the Creator.

"The marriage of body and soul can be a difficult struggle without an understanding of love. As you find that power of love within yourself, balance and resolution occur. Many a man has fallen into a life of crime or self-destruction before this could happen. Crime is the result of a soul which has lost its connection with love as well as the focus and service of its physical life. Human foibles are to be expected, but not crime. If you help a man restore within himself these three cornerstones of existence —soul, body, and love —you will help him find his life again.

"Where would you draw the line between foibles and crime?"

"Crime is a destructive action against the workable, creative, and synchronous tendencies of existence. Therefore, crime is an action set against everything the Creator has put in motion. The consequence of crime is that it will destroy the integrated wholeness of its perpetrator. This is not to say that the Creator will not use destruction for some good, or that the perpetrator will not be forgiven. The point is that crime destroys wholeness. Your understanding of crime should be kept simple and to the point, which is why Moses condensed it to ten laws. This gave his people an easy guideline while avoiding endless lists of misdemeanors and judgments. Most debates on the subject of right and wrong are divisive to the stream of life, and may greatly inhibit the soul's ability to navigate it. Judgment concealed as righteousness will produce endless lists of right and wrong. It is not the will of God that you obsess on these issues, for they will inhibit your progress toward fulfilling the union of body and soul.

*"It is far more important that you learn to work things out and to forgive. You are a brotherhood, and who among you is not struggling with the imbalances of body and soul? That is the nature of a foible —a body and soul struggling with its union, experiencing disharmony and strife in the process. This is no different than a child learning to walk who falls and wails in despair while trying to hide the vase he accidentally broke. Such things are annoying and frustrating to all concerned. But they were failures in **pursuit of wholeness**, unlike crime which is a **violation of wholeness**.*

"I was often asked why I chose my disciples from the fringes of

society, men who had not always followed the guidelines of propriety. The answer is that they were vital living men in full display of their covenant with God to unite body and soul. I gave them the greater understanding that through the presence of love that process can rise above human instability and be filled with transcendent grace.

*"In accepting the covenant of unity you will find moments of laughter, moments of sadness, and moments which beg your forgiveness. In resolving those issues you will find the compassion to understand others. And last but not least, you will know that love is **who you are**. For only by the power of love could the vital connections be made and the condition of oneness be achieved."*

Jesus said that man's greatest misdirection has been to spend his years making connections with structure instead of making connections with God, with life, and with his own nature. Therefore our problem has become one of serving two masters, love and structure.

Structure was a big subject about which we spoke frequently and in great depth. He said that structure is our greatest challenge in understanding the way life works. Until we gain that understanding we are likely to suffer much needless pain and external discouragement. For it is our willingness to be dominated by structure that has blinded us to the ways and greater powers of love. For example, He said that from the viewpoint of structure, a storm is just the product of cause and effect. Once it is set in motion with a particular set of conditions and vectors, it is going to strike in a fairly predictable way. However, love commands the universe and motivates everything into action. Therefore, a senior factor is at work when you have included love in the program.

"It is very difficult to be a storm when you are being loved. Even if a man waits until he's desperate before adding the love, it's better than not at all. Of course, that's a little like baking cookies without sugar and then just sprinkling some on top. You'll like the results better if you use sugar ***in*** *the recipe!"*

Our dilemma between love and structure usually costs us the clear perception of how to **include love as we go**. Structure would deceive us into postponing love or dispensing with it altogether—usually under the pretense of waiting until it can "make a difference."

When you are being the love that you are, you bypass that issue altogether, for you are **living** the solution. Jesus said that was enough. *"That which is for you to have and to do will find you. There is no* *difference between loving what's before you and loving something else which might be preferred.* **The blessing lies not in the object of loving, but in the opportunity for loving."**

I asked, "What should I love first?"

He replied, *"Whatever is in front of you."*

"What do I do first?"

"Whatever is facing you."

"Who do I help now?"

"The next person with whom you speak."

What do I learn next?

"The solution to your problems. You do not have to seek your lessons. They find you. Too often people seek a lesson or a purpose elsewhere because they think the one in front of them is not good enough. Often they are hard on themselves by seeking difficult lessons while failing to respect the power of a simple lesson staring them in the face. You have quite enough before you. When you have mastered that, your next lesson will appear."

My response to that was, "I think we search outside ourselves because we feel so lost and so disconnected from our Source." He smiled compassionately, and reminded me that our connection to Source is within the Sacred Heart, **not elsewhere**. Then He proceeded to explain the divisive nature of structure and its many illusions.

"If you consider that everything in physical existence is made of the same adamantine particles, then structure can be seen as providing the separate and complex arrangements which distinguish one form from another. Such differences in patterning are characteristic to the special nature of trees versus birds, or iron versus mercury. Within the context of larger patterns, such physical forms are stable for long durations, but even so, they are still mortal. Therefore being mortal, they are not qualified to command your life."

He said that it is the will of the Holy Spirit to see you whole. Structure is the great deceiver that has made you feel that you are compartmentalized and that you have been separated into many parts. Not only are you fundamentally love, but you are cumulatively all that you have ever loved and all that has loved you. So your love is held in memory as well as potentiality. He made it very clear to me that love is not only a Divine Energy that exists in the present, but it also is memory and future potential. In other words, *"Love is a Source of Life that has no end. Your name is love, and your character is composed of all that you have loved, all who have loved you, all who have shared your life, and everything you have brought into existence through your love. That is who you are. You will never be separated from that love. Love is your immortality. Structure creates the illusion that your life has been cut into segments of time and space or suspended elsewhere in improbable situations. Only the dominance of structure can ever separate you from the totality of who you are. The power of the Holy Spirit is that it can shatter the illusion of separation and restore the soul to its simple wholeness. In the presence of the Holy Spirit, you are one with your Creator, and all that you are is rejoined in personal integrity. Wholeness is Holy, wholeness is healing. That is the essence of all miracles —physical, mental, financial, and social. Whatever has been torn apart comes back together into a state of wholeness. Love supports wholeness, and wholeness supports love. Through that common bond, love can heal anything."*

I commented about the Biblical incident where a woman touched His garment and was healed. He replied, *"She touched my love and was healed."*

"On the other hand, it is the nature of structure to cut your life into pieces and then set one part against another. Would you have that for your master?"

My immediate response was one of complete revulsion, and without hesitation I asked, "Is that the source of human suffering?" His answer was firm and to the point.

"The source of human suffering is separation from God, from the love that you are, and from an understanding of how love commands the universe. In a state of separation, however, the most grievous mistake is the one of serving structure. As a master, structure is cruel, divisive, and treasonous. In a state of separation, structure will always seek to master you, but ironically when wholeness is restored structure becomes a humble and willing servant.

*"You see, the reason for this is the universal law of command. Love commands the universe, the adamantine particles, the one spirit, the heart, and all of life. Therefore, when you have separated from that power you resort to ploys for control. Therein is the leverage that structure has over you. As long as you seek to control life or think that you can, you will grovel for structure, and it will hold you by 'the short hairs.' The tragedy of such pursuit is that you will **never control life**, but as a child of God,*

*you do have the greater power to **command it!***"

That comment triggered a flashback for me to a time when I was a teenager. In those days, rodeos and horses were my sport, and barrel racing was my specialty. One day I was practicing at the arena when an old cowboy noticed some trouble I was having with my mare. Her timing was slow, and the circles she was cutting were much too large. I was struggling with all my options for control, having no success. The old man motioned for me to come over to the fence, and I was hopeful that he would have some training tips for me. He did, though it was nothing I had expected. In a Texas drawl, between puffs of a cigarette, he asked, "Honey, how much do you weigh?" I had a "Twiggy" sort of figure in those days, and I blushed to admit that I only weighed 102 pounds. Then pointing to my mare, he asked, "What makes you think you can throw around a thousand pounds of horse flesh like you're trying to do?" I was stumped! What kind of question was that? I started to shrug it off and walk away when something inside told me that he was leading up to a point I needed to hear. This was a man who had trained champions for almost fifty years, but I couldn't tell yet whether he was about to put me down or give me the benefit of his experience. Nevertheless, I was curious enough to take my chances. He continued. "If you make that mare choose between doing it your way or hers, she'll probably compromise and fall short somewhere in the middle. Then you'll try to make up the difference with persuasion or force. You'll never get real performance like that. The secret is to become one with the horse, so that your way **is her way!** Then you'll **outweigh** her by 102 pounds . . . and be the one in charge." I was all ears after that, and he proceeded to teach me some secrets of "oneness."

As I told the story to Jesus, His presence helped me to gain a deeper understanding of that riding lesson. We exchanged glances through penetrating eyes, and He knew that I had grasped a very special truth. **Control is an instrument of separation. Command is an instrument of oneness!** Even in a situation as harsh as war, every good general knows that the secret to effective command is esprit de corps and common purpose. God gave His children **the power** which love can bring, but in combination with control it diminishes. In combination with command it is magnified.

That realization was amazingly relevant to the problems of structure He had been teaching me. As He had just said, structure is an instrument of separation and the establishment of control agendas.

Jesus told me that structure causes illness and depletion. Deteriorating structures tax us endlessly to repair them. The body is a complex form, comprised of both love and structure. This paradox of complementary forces is integrated around the pivotal unity of the spiritual heart and its higher intelligence. *"When structure is out of balance or in conflict with itself you are going to feel pain."* He added, *"Even greater pain comes when structure is in conflict with love, and you do not know how to resolve the conflict. The answer lies in knowing the correct priority and in understanding the greater dimensions of the heart to master any situation. Structure is no match for the heart except to make the heart strong.*

"Nurture the heart," He often reminded me. *"Strengthen the positive impulses of the heart through admiration and gratitude. Begin each day by canceling the negative impulses of your body, your existence, and your surroundings through expressions of forgiveness. Remember that any negative impulse can throw the mind into a reverse logic, and this is how you begin to create the contradictions of your life. When you want a problem solved, the mind actually begins to create further aspects of the problem **as the solution**. The mind does not work toward solutions. It works toward perpetuating the problem itself. A man who believes in scarcity will program his mind to believe that scarcity is a reality. Therefore, he has to make a lot of money to compensate for scarcity. Consequently, He will make his money in a way that will allow scarcity **also to persist**. He will continue to invest in scarcity. He will align his values to items in limited or controlled supply. 'There are only a few diamonds,' he will say, 'so of course they will remain costly.' Or 'there is a fixed amount of prime real estate, so naturally the investment will be sound even though the cost is high.' He will empower his thinking with the economics of leverage, and then the leverage will begin to cause problems in his own life. He is forever working for more money to secure more leverage for himself, until eventually he is out-leveraged by life. In such a state of mind, he will never solve the riddle of abundance at all, but merely defend himself against the consequences of believing in scarcity! Scarcity is an aspect of structure, and so it is a self-perpetuating problem with no solutions. No matter how large or complex, all structures are deteriorating. The principles of thermodynamics demonstrate the self-consuming nature of structure. At the same time, the universe is infinitely expanding. There is just no end to its abundance. This seeming paradox is explainable only by the power of love."*

Another practice to strengthen the heart is innocent perception. Don't be obsessed with figuring out life before you live it. He reminded me often *"to live, experience, and enjoy."* How wonderful it can feel sometimes just to "take off" for a weekend trip, having no itinerary except for a willingness to be surprised by new perceptions and adventures. Sure, it's important to plan business trips and formal vacations where the guidelines of structure can be of service. Nevertheless, those are rarely the vacations that refresh and restore.

Many times He helped me with artistic problems by simply getting me to look at what I was doing without judgment or preconception. Often, He would gently nudge me out of "thinking again"

"Just set your considerations aside and do it,"

He would say. Whenever I followed His advice, I would accomplish the task in a fraction of the time it would take to **think and do**. It seems to me now that we often procrastinate under the influence of a mind that is looking for an easier way. In the long run, such maneuvers just cost us time, energy, and most importantly our position of command. He said, *"By moving straight into action without reservation you build positive momentum which saves time and energy, and strengthens your position of command. Be there with what you are doing and innocently enjoy the process. This is what children do. This is the key to heaven. This is the key to being here now and cherishing this time and place in your life. Whatever you are doing, savor it. Sit on the grass and savor its moisture and coolness, the refreshing breeze that hits you, or just the warmth of a human conversation, by looking into someone's eyes and really being alive."*

He would have me do things like look out the window and count the leaves on a bush. Then, before I would have a chance to calculate with my mind, He would retrieve my attention saying, *"Look back at me and tell me how many leaves you saw."* I would start to say I didn't have time to count them all, but instead I would just answer and it would always be correct. He would stop me before my mind would get involved. *"There is a simplicity to life which brings joy, if you would only receive it **as it is**."*

I remarked how enlightening it can be to contemplate the different layers of meaning that may be present in a simple occurrence. He agreed, but at the same time He cautioned that everything has a right to be **only itself** without having to be a symbol for something else, or food for thought. *"Beingness is sovereign,"* He remarked, *"and need not justify itself."* When He mentioned that, I released an old feeling of defensiveness which I used to experience when people would "read" symbolic meanings into my paintings, inferring that some additional significance might give added value. I felt rather unsophisticated to have painted only a tree and nothing more. He replied, *"What's wrong with a tree being a tree? Symbolic communication can be interesting and meaningful, but there is nothing more powerful that **just being**. One thing does not have to mean something else in order to be. By denying even the smallest things the right to be, you are undermining that right for yourself. More than likely, those who do this don't even realize they have the right **just to be themselves**! By habitually assigning extra meaning and significance to everything, a person is stealing power from life to give to the mind. What do you think will happen if such tendencies become an obsession?*

*"All things manifest by the power of love, not to serve agendas of external meaning. A little weed which comes up in your garden springs to life because its parent left a seed, the conditions were hospitable, and the Holy Source of all being embraced even the 'I Am' presence of a weed. Don't jump to conclusions that it is a symbol of opposition, or a confirmation of dark destiny. It's just a weed that came up in your garden because it wanted to live there. And if you don't want the weed, express your feelings, and bless it on its way. The best way to get rid of anything you don't want is to bless it, because love honors love. Blessings honor blessings. **Much of life will take care of itself if you simply employ that as a dynamic guideline for living**. This is the **supremacy of being**.*

"From the beginning there have been three holy elements —the three pillars of Being. The first and the Ultimate is the I AM presence which is the Source of Divinity. After that is Innocence, which is the spiritual presence of Divinity. And third, there is Love which is the manifest presence of Divinity and its power of creation. All three aspects of being are extended to man for his blessing and fulfillment.

*"In the 'acts of creation' the purpose of the seventh day was **to cease doing and rest**. This was **not an end to creation** or the Creator's retirement. It was to set in place the Ultimate Plan, which is to command by Sovereignty of Being . . . and that Beingness manifested is Love."*

He explained that in our awareness of existence we perceive a natural correlation between beingness, doingness, and havingness. In its true priority, our beingness is our love, from which come our abilities, from which come our attainments in life. The world of structure, however, leads us to believe that we must **have** before we can do, and **do** before we can

be. In the case of professional competence, this priority has some relevance. When it dominates exclusively, however, it results in licensed professionals who are not motivated by love and thus are lacking in true ability. Such an inversion of priorities will result in material possessions for leverage and the use of that leverage as a substitute for honest performance. The end product will be "image creation" instead of true beingness.

According to Jesus, our experience of self-esteem, pride, confidence, and well being is not attributable to ego, but to love. *"Ego is the empowerment of false or transitory images **which have replaced your love**. False images of glory have nothing to do with your well-being, but actually deplete it."*

He said this will happen whenever we begin the pathways of our life with havingness. Self images will accumulate, layer upon layer, and there is no way to have peace among them or to resolve them into a simplicity of being. But He assured me that when we reverse that direction and establish our self understanding upon the love that we are, all the derivative images will lose their power to dominate us. The world is full of lost people seeking to explain their existence with identities which have come from something or somewhere. Even a negative something or somewhere is better than nowhere! In other words, when you do not know who you are, anything is better than nothing.

"The truth is, YOU ARE LOVE, and you are derived from nothing except your Father, the Source of Love. This can be an uncomfortable realization, for it exposes the responsibilities you have for your life.

"Love is the primal power of your beingness. Goodness is the wise, dutiful, and devoted management of love as the power of life.

"To this end, some order and guidelines are helpful, but the obsessive and vested dependency upon structure, its requirements, and the identities it invents for you can bring much pain and suffering.

"All complex forms are mortal. They must break down and change in order for life to continue her work. Clinging to structures and complex attachments as they are breaking down can be an agonizing experience, regardless of whether it is bodily attachment, social, or business."

"Then what can we do?"

"From the viewpoint of love, you can redirect the inevitable changes to the betterment of yourself and others. However, you can only do that when you have made structure your servant.

"You must be vigilant in your observations of structure, for it is an organizational component found throughout existence. For example, it is simply the complex arrangement of physical forms which come and go. It is also an aspect of mind-generated formulas which are used to understand or manage life. There are many layers of existence formulated through structure to which man has added many factors of mental programming. Structure can serve you if you remember its limitations, or oppress you if you allow it to get out of hand."

So I inquired, "When has the influence of structure gone too far?" With a touch of whimsy, He replied, *"Well, it has gone too far when it perpetuates a belief in the world being flat after evidence proves it's not. It has gone too far when holidays have lost their meaning but persist as ritual. Structure has gone too far when government seeks to survive only for its own power and not to serve its people. Enough is enough when any bureaucracy ceases to serve, and begins to be self-protective and self-enriching. Enough is enough when business is all paperwork and has lost its sense of values and production. Enough is enough when school teaches only theory and little about the way life really works. **When structure becomes the master—the determining factor—it has gone too far**. In the end, structure will always betray you, **because it has to. Structure is mortal**. Even the natural structures of the universe are mortal, not to mention all the mind-generated formulas which support only passing agendas."*

He continued, *"The structure of scientific theory needs to be relaxed if innovative thinking is to occur. Business structures need to be relaxed if new values are to emerge. People need to have a sense of governing themselves so that responsibility can grow. If respect for ethics is to exist upon the Earth there has to be a sense of joy in doing the right thing, rather than fear of punitive action for doing the wrong thing. Enough is enough when you can no longer feel the heart's command, and the heart cannot empower your life. Structure seeks dominance because its mortality begets an insatiable fear."*

"Are mind-generated structures just as treacherous," I asked?

"Even more so," He answered, *"because most of the time, you confuse them with reality. The mind loves structure because structure represents logic, and at the same time it gives the mind many movable parts which it can weave into its own complexity. Through collective agreement, the mind affirms its own inventions as reality Much of what you call reality is not*

reality at all, but just mind-generated structures upon which you have agreed! Once the heart is ruling your life, you will probably choose to live without most of the mind-generated structures, or at least you will know how to discern which ones to keep and which ones to dismiss. The mind has an endless love for structure, and is blind to its perilous liabilities."

He added, *"The most dangerous structures are the ones you internalize in the form of identities. 'I am this, I am that, I have this position in the community, I have that heritage.' You have been 'had' when you internalize structure, because what you internalize becomes invisible to you. Internalized structure is the main interference with your perception of infinity and your awareness of immortality. It is bad enough that you are obedient to structure **externally**. But you will suffer much loss of awareness if you **internalize** it. When this happens you will think you are a product of structure. Nothing could be further from the truth.*

"If you knew yourself only as love, you would have no fear. But all other identities are rooted in structure, and so they are mortal. Mortality lives in fear of death and survives by instilling fear in all of its willing participants. With this fear comes pain and suffering.

"Once you internalize structure, your life will be driven by two powers: Love and fear! But you can't serve both . . . although most people try."

"Does this mean that love and fear are opposites?"

"As I have told you before, love has no opposites, for it is the divine solvent which ends duality. Love can be a choice, however, and so it has alternatives."

"What's the difference between an opposite and an alternative?"

*"An alternative is just another possibility upon which you have chosen not to focus. Therefore, its effect on your life is minimal or nonexistent. The children of God extend creation through their choices and by their viewpoints of reality. Thus **alternatives are inevitable**.*

"You see, fasting is an alternative to eating. Both can be experienced, but not simultaneously. You might have viewed them as opposites, because they are the product of choices. They do not oppose each other or empower a polarity. Actually, one erases the other. Alternatives are the product of free will and the fact that you are given choices to make. Alternatives are life empowering and life changing.

"For example, the life of a man is greatly changed after he marries. His focus in life will be quite different than it was when he was single. To

have or not to have children is another decision that will change the script of his life.

"Some choices are so basic that paradigms are established upon them and the declined alternatives utterly fade from view. These are the choices which are the most difficult to reverse, because the alternative seems to be lost. This is why it is so important that you remember who you really are and that love is your core reality!

"The most important choice you were ever given was to be the Love that you are, or not . . . ." Following that statement there was silence and a vacuum which He chose not to fill with words. After giving me a few moments to contemplate that statement, He continued.

"Most beings responded to that choice in part, and by degrees, with hesitant affirmation. This aspect of indecision brought them face to face with an abyss of mystery filled with fear, structure, invented identities, and a life and death struggle for survival. For many, there have been great bitterness and hatred. Even so, none of this is the opposite of love. All of those negative emotions and experiences are the result of having chosen an alternative to honoring the love that they are . . . which is denial. Love can resolve it all. If love were an opposite to such negativity, then the presence of love would only empower the difference and only ignite a polarity!

"The subject of opposites could not exist without structure. What you perceive as opposites is just an apparency within a limited field of perception. If you saw the whole picture, the polarity would dissolve. Opposites are really just broken circles for which you do not see the connecting link.

"For example, if a child looked at a flat map of the world laid out on a table, he could speak about 'the ends of the Earth.' All you would have to do is pick up the map, make a circle of it, and show him where the land and seas connect. You could speak of day and night as opposites. This might seem especially so, if you lived in a valley where the changes came and went abruptly. If you lived on a mountain top where the transitions were gradual, then you would observe the connection. If you took a ride to the moon, you would look back upon the Earth and see the process even more clearly as an unbroken circle with phases.

"This is true of all 'opposites,' even technical ones." He looked toward my paint pallet and made a reference to the colors I was using. *"Black seems to be the opposite of white because it is the ultimate in absorption while white is the ultimate in reflectance. In actuality, however, this*

*spectrum extends **beyond** black and white. Black proceeds to dark transparency, as white proceeds to light transparency, and both eventually arrive at total clarity. The circle is therefore complete.*

*"All opposites can be resolved by the connecting link which restores their circle. To institute them as a polarity is an agenda of ignorance and self-serving structure. Love is the ultimate connection, and in the presence of love, other connections are easy to find. In its absence, many needed connections may be obscured for eons. **Love ends duality, thus it has no opposites.***

*"Love has no polarity, but when you have chosen **alternatives to it**, the structures which replace love are full of opposites. Fear is a common emotion of those whose lives are driven by structure, for structure is mortal and always in peril. Hatred is a common attitude of those whose lives are vested in structure or conquered by it. Hatred is just a defense against the return of love.*

*"**Love opposes nothing, but conquers all. Love is in the world but not of it!** Fear and hatred, and the evils which come from them, are all derivative. Love is primary. Love existed before the universe, and most certainly before the structures of the world. In the beginning there was no evil, fear, or hatred. There was only One Love, One Body of Potential, and One Spirit. As manifestations began to take shape, free will was extended to every aspect of love, to be life, to experience life, to fulfill its potential, and to know itself as love. There was even the choice to deny its own nature, if that should be desired. From this last choice all the 'weeds' of peril have sprung.*

*"This last choice was a very important gift. For without it you would have been an aspect of love without the power to forward creation. You would have been a creation of God, but not a Child of God. Once love has become your choice as well as your nature, all potential for duality is erased from your life, and you are **given command**.*

"You must understand, however, that when I speak of love in this way, I am not referring to an emotion of sweetness, a feeling of affection, or a sentiment. Often these are simply positive responses to personal attachments. The love of which I speak is a function, a power, a purity of intent, and the core honesty of all that is. Any subject about which you can be utterly honest—including your own involvement—is a subject for which you have great love!

"When love is master, decency and honesty are brought to the world

of structure. Whenever structure dominates, life becomes a theater of smoke and mirrors. In a dominant position, structure is innately dysfunctional, because it can neither cause nor correct, although there is no structural error that cannot be remedied through correcting priorities.

"Structure gives form, facilitates, and conserves. That is all. No one ever would have placed it above him had he not forgotten, denied, or separated in some manner from the love that he is. Structure merely gained seniority by default.

*"Structure has its derivatives, but it created nothing. This is true of all things, but most especially in regard to man. Man is not here because structure formed its patterns in a certain way and evolved man as its consummating product. Structure facilitates production, but it does not cause it. Structure is the mortar and the mortality of the universe, not the grace or the immortality of it. It is a factor of organization, but it has no power of its own. Internalizing structures as an aspect of self-knowledge only extends **your power** to them. There is no point in that, for you will never find yourself, your immortality, or any experience of infinity within structure.*

"The recovery of your immortality and perception of infinity cannot be separated from the knowledge of your true source as love. Structure wants you to know yourself as an identity, not as love. Identities block your immortality. All identities should be regarded as temporal. There is great empowerment in letting them go.

"You will take into your very being whatever you allow to define or to explain your life. When a person believes that his life is the result of history, external conditions, or accumulated identities, then he has internalized structure. Compared to the power of love within each person, it matters not whether he was born a prince or a pauper. Both conditions are equally insignificant! There is no gain in internalizing such structures. There are, however, three great losses that will result if you do. First, you have substituted a false identity for the love that you are. Second, endless conditions will derail your innocent perception. And third, you have become partners in structural mortality."

He explained that our desire to posses structure often accounts for our obsession with it. Structure, He added, is not worth owning. It is very frail and it passes, but the creative imprint your life has left upon the universe will endure. *"This is why I said to store up for yourself riches in Heaven where thieves cannot break in and steal. Structure is innately perishable.*

It is mortal. When you have created anything, your imprint is left upon it forever and, like a cookie cutter, that imprint can be used again and again to recreate the same thing." I can actually relate to that teaching through personal experience. As an artist I put my heart and soul into everything I paint, and sometimes people ask, "How can you sell it, Glenda?" My answer has always been that I sell only the canvas and the paint. I have never sold the imprint of my creativity. Everything I have ever created could be recreated again and again and again. If this is true for an artist, how much more would it be true for our Holy Source? How easy would it be for our Father to create us again and again from the imprint of our love by the Power of His?

The recovery of our immortality is very closely related to regaining a memory of our true name. He said that, ***"Life is love in action,*** *whereas time is just structure in action, attempting to survive!*

"Once you have internalized densities of structure, then death becomes an inevitability as well as a necessary process."

He referred to death as a *"clearing house for useless identities."* The implication was that death and the illusion of time will continue to prevail as long as we are servants of structure.

"You are actually not part of the time stream. It only seems that way because of your involvement with structure."

He explained that everything is actually "in the now," ontologically speaking. (Ontology is the science of naming something, identifying it, or assigning it meaning.) *"Ontologically you are love. Ontologically, time has no beingness. Try to locate it—putting time* ***in*** *space as an actuality. What do you have?"*

I answered, "Now."

"That's right, 'now' really does exist. The enduring 'now' is home to all beingness. Structure has no endurance. Therefore, to structure, time is simply the process required for it to be born, to live, and to die. The process you commonly call time is just structure in action. It is structure's bid for survival. To you time is irrelevant, for life is love in action. Time, as you perceive it, is the start, the progression, and the end of structure performing its pattern of duration. A motor was built, it served a purpose, then it began to wear out, the repair bills mounted up and it was junked. From the scrap yard back to the steel factory, the motor became something else. The cycle of action that describes the life of that motor could be viewed as time, but for you time does not really exist. If you try to pinpoint

*any part of it, all you have is **now**.*

"You will experience a great clarity when you finally know the difference between universal law and the tendencies of structure. You will not abandon structure, but you will at last be able to put structure to your service. You will be able to detach your own destiny from that of structure so that its mortality cannot betray you. Much more importantly, when you are fully certain in the wholeness of your being that you are love, and that structure is your servant, then you will say to the mountain, 'Come' and it will come, and you will say to the winds, 'Be still' and the storm will cease. ***This is the key to everything.***"

Chapter 4
The Adamantine Particles

Whenever Jesus spoke about the adamantine particles, He would always remind me that love commands them. He said emphatically, *"No matter how far we advance our technology, unless we have love, we have nothing."* These particles represent a continuous flow of high frequency potential which manifests into discrete forms and arrangements under the command of love. Unfortunately, humankind is so dominated by sensory perception and structural explanations, that we are virtually unconscious of this powerful moving force of life. This ever present and never-ending river of life so completely eludes our normal perception that I am confounded in the task of explaining it. Only by resorting to the Master's own approach would I have any hopes of being successful.

As I reviewed the various ways in which He addressed the subject, one thing was consistent. His explanations were always simple, relevant, and direct, although I was usually caught by surprise. We would be talking about something quite ordinary, when He would introduce a new consideration to change my viewpoint or to provoke a higher understanding. His original comment might have been as unassuming as, *"Have you ever noticed how well it goes when you love your work?"*

Naturally, I would reply in the affirmative, and then we would be "off to the races," moving toward the larger purpose of His statement. In presenting this subject, it is my intention to focus on its practical application to life as well as its simple adherence to truth. Therefore, in beginning, I would like you to contemplate how a cheerful attitude graces the day with more pleasure. Is it not true that everything around you is transformed when your love radiates its light? Have you noticed how beautiful a pregnant woman can be? The old adage "the world loves a lover" can also be demonstrated in countless ways. A couple in love are glowing and magnetic! Is it not a pleasure to be in the presence of their happiness? Now, just imagine the exchange of energy they will have with each other over the course of a lifetime or just in the space of a few days or weeks. A dramatic example of this mutual energy exchange can be found in the newspaper photos of couples celebrating their fiftieth anniversaries. Over the years they have even grown to look alike! Sometimes you can also enjoy a chuckle at the resemblance between people and their pets! This is quite a phenomenon that leads us to ask, "What is going on?"

Jesus explained that in the presence of love there is an exchange of adamantine particles. Take, for example, the love of a married couple. The man's love has an effect on the adamantine particles of his wife, while the woman's love has a similar effect on her husband's. Love is intermingling their life energies as they grow together in thought, mind, and heart. Over time, even their physical appearances begin to blend. Have you ever noticed how people from common geographical origins often bear subtle resemblances to one another? With the aid of technology, people can even be traced to their birth families by voice tone. It is their love that binds and sets the adamantine particles into harmonious resonance. These things are evident to anyone who cares to look.

The knowledge of adamantine particles is not limited to particle physics, galactic travel, or etheric realms. It is critical to our understanding of life right here and now. From the conscious awareness of this life force, you will begin to understand why the plant you love is the one that blooms. Where love is present, there is a free exchange of adamantine particles which accounts for one's ability to have a positive effect upon life. These tiny particles are the building blocks for all complex forms in the universe. If these tiny irreducible particles are under the command of love, is there any wonder that an immediate improvement results from giving some animate life form, such as a plant or a pet, to a person who is physically challenged? Such a practice of giving love gifts is proving beneficial in many realms of healing. Minimum security prisons and mental hospitals are finding plants and pets to be great therapeutic aids. These living companions provide a new way of interacting freely outside the realm of structure, freely with life.

Almost everyone has gone to nature for healing, or just to "get away from it all." Perhaps one of the **best** reasons to be with nature is to **connect with it all**. It appears not to matter whether one's connection is conscious or intuitive, exchanges still occur according to patterns of synchronicity with the environment. It never ceases to amaze me how the fisherman "feels" where the fish are biting and the woodsman "feels" his path. I shared with Jesus my fond recollection of riding horseback across the hills of North Texas. Never once did my horse step in a gopher hole or trip on a rock, even though she never looked down. He explained that her ongoing exchange with the Earth kept her informed of the terrain. This depth of information and perception is available to anyone who understands the continuous exchange of life energy. We usually refer to this feeling as "intuition" or "sixth sense," but such references tend to suggest the nebulous world of privileged perception. Jesus said, *"This awareness is available to all,"* and that our ancestors were more practiced in these abilities than we are today. Like any true ability, this perception of vital exchange grows with practice, and declines with lack of usage. I began, therefore, to observe as much as I could in everything I did.

Whenever possible, I took special notice of nature and its patterns of vital exchange. One day, just for sheer pleasure, I spent a whole day in our city garden on my favorite bench in the shade of a magnificent old pecan tree. There, in quiet admiration, I bathed in the free flow of adamantine particles. It was not long before I felt complete oneness with the environment in a way that released all barriers. Then suddenly, a flock of crows descended upon the lawn in front of me just as a host of squirrels rushed through the trees. The crows pecked the grass while the squirrels scampered for nuts. There were some mockingbirds and a few little yellow finches that decided to pay a visit. It was almost as if my secret garden had come alive. One by one the crows and squirrels approached, innocently and freely, as if they had never seen a human and had no perception of me as a threat. The sense of peace was remarkable and the sensation was one of "inhaling nature." Then a fascinating thing happened. One of the crows had caught a green garden snake, and held it up proudly for me to see. I remarked, "Oh, isn't that pretty." I'm not sure why I expected the bird to understand my meaning. I simply felt that he would. At that moment he walked over toward me, and stopped about five feet away to demonstrate how proficiently he could devour his dinner. He was quite the showman!

Shortly after that, I noticed a little squirrel gathering and burying pecan nuts. The new pecan crop was still a bit green, so I was curious about his actions. I began to converse with the little creature and asked, "Isn't it a little early to be doing that?" He looked at me intently, tilting his head to show genuine attention. Proceeding to find an older nut, he approached me and held it up for inspection as if to ask, "Is this okay?" As he scurried off to bury it, I affirmed his wisdom with a complementary remark. When he had finished that task, he selected another nut and confidently walked over to me. After peeling it, he dropped it at my feet. I've fed the squirrels many times, but never before had I been fed **by** a squirrel! Through the innocence of nature I had been given a perfect example of the way love brings about an exchange of adamantine particles.

"The sharing of adamantine particles is the breath of life," Jesus said. *"There is an ongoing exchange of these particles throughout existence. They not only comprise organic life, but also the planet, the wind, and every substance that is. Everything breathes for the whole of its duration. Inhaling and exhaling, these particles bring vital balance and connections to life. To one who is attuned, an illness is clearly revealed through irregularities in the breath of life. In the presence of love a natural rebalance occurs. This is how the laying on of hands can help to restore health to another. Such is the power of healing touch or even a simple hug."*

During that discussion I asked, "Can a healing occur even if the touch is indirect? I was thinking about the woman who was healed when she touched your robe."

He replied, *"She touched my love and by that she was healed. As you touch each other, especially the loving essence of each other, you are healed. Living in isolation and living in separation can imbalance your life quickly."*

My curiosity grew with His encouragement, and my thirst for knowledge came alive. I wanted to know in detail, "What are the adamantine particles?" He replied, *"They are the fundamental building blocks of physical existence. They are particularized energy potentials which activate, unify, and give form to infinity. As points, they are irreducible, indivisible, and generic. Their very existence, however, establishes a pattern of dimension. Between one point and another, is there not dimension? Between a series of points, is there not a pattern of dimension? Thus there is space. Through such alignments, energy is activated and conveyed into particularized situations."*

I thought back to my college physics and remembered that light can be both a particle and a wave. In that same way, He described the adamantine particles as both a particle and a form of energy, except that there is nothing smaller or simpler. *"One way of stating it is that they are the ultimate points which unify infinity and activate its potential."*

I was puzzled, however. "How could infinity be unified?" I asked "That seems like an oxymoron."

He further stated, *"I'm sure it does from the point of view you are using to explain the physical plane. Right now, human understanding of energy and matter is limited by the concept of energy as force. Most of science and most thinking interprets energy as force, combustion, and pressure waves. The concept goes something like this. Force results in pressure waves, pressure waves create density, density results in matter, and everything left over is infinity. That is the oxymoron!*

"A leftover cannot be defined and provides no basis for interaction. As long as infinity is regarded as an indefinable leftover, how can its properties be described? How can it be used? How can it be activated?"

There was a natural rightness about everything He said, which caused me to think about life more profoundly than ever. Yet He made me feel as though an indwelling consciousness had always been there, and was now beckoning to be awakened. I awoke more fully with everything He said.

He explained that the idea of "energy as force" has dominated man's thinking about every form of energy from industry to government to life management. Ideas beget performance. What is dominating the world? Force! What is causing many of our problems? Force! He assured me, *"This will all change when the paradigm of understanding shifts from electrical to magnetic performance. As a matter of fact, that shift will be necessary to finally define and understand the adamantine particles. It is magnetic potential which accounts for the unified field, and actually it is magnetic cohesion which unifies physical infinity. Infinity is **not** the leftover. Infinity is the unifying factor which **integrates everything**. When you have made the change in thinking from electrics to magnetics, every aspect of your technology will change as well."*

He explained that much of the difficulty we are having with fuel and crude energy is because mankind has interpreted energy as force. We are using force to generate resistance and from that resistance we get electrical energy. When we have entered the field of magnetics, we will have what He called *"harmonic, non-toxic energy."* We will have the true energy of the universe that can run everything from our lives to our thinking. Only then will we be able to operate in a practical sense with infinity.

"Right now you are dealing with scarcities, forces, and leftovers —

scarcity being that which is subject to control, force being that which is used to control it, and leftover existence being that which is not understood. Looking at infinity as a leftover is not a very productive attitude, but that is about to change," He promised.

"How will we make that transition?"

"It will all begin with a proper respect for the ultimate power. When that understanding is attained and activated by a sufficient number of people, the entire paradigm of humanity will be lifted above the belief in energy as force. In the face of enough love, force loses its power to dominate consciousness. From that point forward, consciousness will awaken at quantum speed. It will be so powerful as to bring answers by the second.

"Until then, remember that adamantine particles respond to a magnetic field. With regard to human potential, the heart is your magnetic center. It is through your heart that you are magnetizing adamantine particles and by your love that you command them."

"Are all the adamantine particles alike?"

"In their native state, yes."

"Can you tell me how they take form? You said they respond to magnetism under the influence of love. Can you describe how the process works?"

He paused for a moment in a state of silent creation, like a stage designer preparing the backdrop for a play. Then He presented this visual scenario: *"I'll give you a very special room to walk into. It's a very low gravity chamber filled with ping pong balls which are all moving at a gentle, chaotic, random rate. Bouncing off the walls, back and forth, they keep going and going. A unique characteristic of the ping pong balls is that each one is laced with iron dust. Your part is to enter the room wearing a magnetic vest. One ping pong ball after another will attach to you. Chains of ping pong balls will form, extending in patterns exactly like the impulse pattern of magnetic attraction which called them into assembly. The ping pong balls connect and extend outwardly according to the patterns of the love that you have introduced into the magnetic field.*

"There is another example I can give you. You may remember the children's magnetic drawing boards. Beneath a clear plastic cover are iron filaments which respond to a magnetic pencil. The magnetic pencil attracts the iron filaments and causes them to group together in lines and patterns to form a drawing on the board. All kinds of patterns can be created by

*guiding the magnet over the iron filaments. Now just imagine that your heart is the magnet and your love is the pencil. That is exactly what your heart is. This is your power of influence, and you are literally impacting every aspect of your life by **just being, being the love that you are**. You are a magnet that writes upon the drawing board of your life. As you enter any situation the adamantine particles inherent to it will adjust to the influence you bring. You don't have to dream up a grand plan and put it on the drawing board. **You are the grand plan!** All you have to be is the love that you are. Everything will line up around that. The greater the love, the greater the influence. Nevertheless, you don't have to **do** anything other than be the love that you are. Your love brings forth the patterns and manifestations which will result."*

He pointed out that all physical existence is comprised of adamantine particles and space —mostly vast amounts of space. These particles cohere magnetically to form the basis of all complex patterns of matter and form. Conglomerations build structure, which are then held together by energetic tension which creates the illusion of solidity. All solidity is structure, and structure accounts for all solidity. If we would penetrate the barriers which stand between us and the infinite supply of life energy we must realize the illusion and look beyond structure.

He cautioned me, however, to be alert for the possibility of a defensive reaction which can happen when a structured arrangement is infused with new properties of love. *"There can be an initial resistance or even rejection! This is because structure often serves force and frequently masks chaos. Structure is a conservation and filing system which houses, distributes, and utilizes particles, but it has no capacity to generate living dynamic order. Therefore, when love enters the picture, generating a true harmony and synchronicity among the particles, a new and living flow of life is begun. This can have a shattering effect on the brittle and inadequate structures which are providing the illusion of solidity. It can actually be 'life-threatening' to any structure which might be restricting the flow of life.*

"Often the introduction of love will cause pre-existing factions to fly apart. When this happens, you must remember that only the brittle inadequate structures were lost in their effort to imitate love and counterfeit order. Recovery, however, brings new and real order. There has never been a time on Earth when this message has been more relevant! There is much love being poured upon the Earth at this moment. So much

that it will have a shattering effect on some of the needless structures now prevailing. They will fall to the Earth, as they must. Yet, from that will spring new life, new hope and new growth."

I realized that when He made that statement, He was referring to complex temporal structures generated by man and not to the natural subatomic structure of atoms and molecules. Nevertheless, it caused me to wonder about the continuity of even natural structures throughout eternity. This idea intrigued me, so I asked Him one day, "Do the particles that make a tree always make a tree, or do they go on to be something else?"

His reply, as always, was simple. *"The life course of adamantine particles is always directed by love. Particles, however, do have memory and retain experience. Therefore love, in directing the flow of life, tends to allow tendencies and preferences to beget further experiences along the same lines. This is further reinforced by the fact that adamantine particles which have already been committed to form, are still locked into the more complex particles of neutrons and electrons, not to mention the atomic arrangement of such elements as hydrogen or oxygen, which still persist even though the tree is now flower bed mulch. When the tree dies, the adamantine particles which comprised its life force, usually go on to be another tree. Actually, this is what life is. A free and unstructured supply of adamantine particles operating under the influence of love. **Life is just love in action**. This is why people need to get away from stagnating routine and obligations. It is important to relax, to go on vacation, or simply to get a hobby. It is healing just to interact freely with life, and to receive a fresh new supply of adamantine particles. Inhale them, enjoy the abundance around you."*

His feelings about life were loving and reverent, and were coupled with great appreciation for its nurturing strength. One day as I admired His love for life, I made an interesting observation. Whenever He referred to life He used the feminine gender. This was particularly fascinating, since He used the masculine gender in reference to our Holy Source. My curiosity resulted in a two-fold question, beginning with the relevance of gender to God at all. The second part was in reference to His preferred usage of it.

"The Holy of Holies is above gender, although It possesses within Itself the potential for manifesting both male and female. Such manifestations are part of the eternal balancing of existence. The most basic manifestation of male presence is that of being Source. The most

basic female manifestation is that of consciousness and love as the dynamic powers of Life and Creation."

"Then, is life the feminine aspect of God?"

He replied, *"I like to think of it that way."*

My preconceived ideas about the subject of gender were beginning to shatter. In Western Culture we usually refer to active influences as male and passive elements as female. He explained that our concepts about gender, *"have been conditioned by the forces of cause and effect which prevail only in the densely formed patterns of physical structure. On higher planes of existence there is only 'cause and cause' in synchronicity."* He emphatically stated more than once that, *"Cause and effect are derivative aspects of the universe, not primal ones."* He reiterated once again that, *"On higher dimensions of awareness, firm and steadfast influences are regarded as masculine, while the active, interactional, and adaptive modes of creation are regarded as feminine."*

While we were on this subject, I seized the opportunity to ask Him for clarification on a few passages in the Bible which sanctioned male dominance and female submission. As a modern woman, I felt very uncomfortable with such concepts. He explained that some of those passages were just historical reflections of the way life was lived in those days. In other cases, however, the message was a metaphorical reference to the principle of universal order. *"It is unfortunate that such passages were used to support destructive patterns of socio-political behavior, and that much greater truths were lost. Universal order is maintained through balance and mutual respect of the male and the female. Nevertheless, there is also a universal mandate that constancy must govern activity, that truth must reside above adaptation, that Source must precede the created, and that command of change is delegated to the immovable. Evidence of this can be found throughout existence."*

He indicated that such a balance exists even within each person. *"There is a male and female aspect to each personality, just as there is a male and female aspect to life. Such indwelling potential can be either 'in balance' or 'out of balance.' For example, a man who cannot easily change may need to consider that he is more than just male. Perhaps one who cannot devote himself to any particular thing may need to return to the constancy of his male strength. The same thing could be said of a woman. When she cannot find a stable purpose or pursuit in life, possibly she has overplayed her feminine tendencies. If she would honor the masculine strength within herself, perhaps she would find a little more direction and steadfastness."*

In my quest for clarity, I asked, "Does this principle relate to something as basic as the adamantine particles?" He replied, *"In their constancy, irreducibility, and utterly basic nature, they are male. In their infinite capacity to conduct life, to adapt to the varieties of form, and to nurture love's creation, they are female."* I was intrigued by His response, and even more so because of His reference to love. I asked Him, "Is love both male and female?" *"Yes, of course. The steadfastness of love is male. The activation of it is female."* I remembered that He had referred to life several times as *"love in action."* That statement now made more sense to me, and I began to understand why He had used the feminine pronoun. It also became clear why He had used the male pronoun in regard to our Source. It was a reference made without social or political innuendo, with the purest philosophical correctness.

Our discussion of the male and female principle seemed almost like a diversion, although it was highly relevant to universal balance. The whole dimension of adamantine particles is one of complex interactive dynamics, of particles that revert into energy and energy that manifests into particles.

The continuous flow of adamantine particles bears no suggestion of scarcity. Nevertheless, my curiosity prompted me to ask, "If there is infinite supply, why do we believe in scarcity? What has conditioned our beliefs so deeply that we cannot see beyond our limitations?"

"That is because you consider all substance to belong to the structure which gives it form, instead of viewing the free-flowing river of life as infinite potential connected to its Source."

"What I am just now realizing, you can see with total clarity. How can I increase **my** awareness?"

He soothed away my impatience with a compassionate look and a little smile. Then He proceeded to explain, *"You must first learn about the Sacred Heart and develop the power to center your life around it more completely. This is your true heart and your Sacred Chamber. Most people have closed its doors by the end of childhood. After that, one's perception of life-creating particles diminishes, and what is left appears to be a fixed supply. Then, literally, a person uses up his life, consuming his life resources for structural investments as well as contradictory patterns of living. The result is depletion and old age.*

"Only the true heart can sense the vital flow and exchange of particle

energy. This is why you are more intuitive in the areas of your greater devotion. When the Sacred Heart comes to life again and its fire lights up, you will begin to magnetize a fresh supply of adamantine particles from an infinitely abundant universe. There is no limit to the adamantine particles that can be drawn to you. These can be used for empowering your life, healing it, and lifting it to a much higher state of performance.

"The Sacred Heart is a Holy Chamber. This is the place where true prayer takes place. It is a place of peace and solitude, a place so powerfully connected with your Source, that all you have to do is enter for prayer to occur. It doesn't matter what you say, or even if you say anything. **Being there with your Father is the prayer,** *and entering the Holy Chamber is a sacred act. This is why I suggested to my apostles that they go into a closet, because an external place of silence and quietness helps to promote an entry to the Holy Chamber. I was reluctant to give words to pray, because the moment a person substitutes words for prayer, the point is lost. The only value of words is for the focusing of thoughts to a higher realm and the preparing of one's soul for a surrender into sacred silence. As you are joined in the Holy Chamber with the Source of all that is, a power will be activated which will attract to you whatever is needed. This is a very special place within your beingness, and you can know when you have entered it by the complete stillness therein. Within it, there is sacredness and purity like a blanket of new fallen snow."*

As He spoke those last words, I was momentarily distracted by another perception which captured my attention. Until that moment I had taken for granted a small blessing which was a by-product of His company. The normal odors of linseed oil and turpentine characteristic of my studio were often swept away and replaced by a lovely fresh aroma which I came to associate with His presence. This fragrance was like clean mountain air after a new fallen snow, rich with ozone and an exhilarating bouquet of evergreen. What a coincidence that He would use that image to describe the Sacred Chamber!

I have always enjoyed the high mountains, and visit them as often as possible. One summer while traveling to New Mexico I was blessed with a powerful experience of the Sacred Heart when I visited the beautiful church of St. Francis of Assisi at Ranchos de Taos. This is the Spanish monument whose magnificent adobe buttresses have attracted artists and photographers from around the world. Aside from being one of the most photographed buildings in America, it has something much more extraordinary to offer. It provides an experience of overwhelming silence which is not of this world! As I proceeded to the altar, not only were all the outside noises eliminated, but even whispers and footsteps were absorbed into the silence, leaving only the beat of my heart. I do not know if the builders had intended this effect, or even by what spiritual direction the church was designed. For me, it was the most magnificent physical edifice in which I have ever been for providing an external equivalent to entering my own Sacred Chamber. An extremely interesting and relevant coincidence is the popular legend that all prayers asked within the sanctity of that church will be answered. I know that mine certainly was.

He stated more than once that, *"What the heart commands, it keeps. All the particles that have been designated for the purpose of your life and commanded by your heart are yours to keep forever."* I thought about those words a great deal, although they were too much for me to fathom by myself. So, one morning I went straight to the point and asked, "If I were to cease living on this Earth today, what would happen to all the adamantine particles that comprise my body, my life, and my living?"

"Uncountable legions of adamantine particles simply belong to the universe, bequeathed by the Father for common use through the forming of such elements as oxygen, nitrogen, carbon, and so forth. Such particles would return to their common matrix. Trillions to the cube root belong to the human race and would recirculate into newborn children according to ways in which their love resembles the pathway of love you left behind. Billions of adamantine particles have come to you through your family line and will return there to support future generations of children, according to similarities of love that you would have shared with them. In the days following your departure, the particles which you had exchanged with others, for the mutual sharing of life, will return to their rightful donors. However, at the moment of your passing, all the particles which you have personally magnetized by your heart and used in the creation of your life will leave with you. They will either attach to your soul, or else travel to a place that you have marked with love, and will wait until your heart calls them forth again. Either way, they are yours forever. Often such points of love are designated collectively by friends and family who wish to continue together in eternity or to return to some plane of existence and work together again."

The responsibility associated with hearing that truth was staggering. Many days were required just to absorb and contemplate that revelation. It was truly an awesome realization to think that we leave behind us the very footprints of our lives, and that our footsteps may be patterns for others even though we take with us our love and the other things that are central to our beingness. All of our experiences we leave for others to share while we carry forth with that which we came to love.

It has been said that the air we breathe has also been breathed by all living entities. That thought was expanded for me through my new understanding of the adamantine particles and their river of living supply. With every answer He provided there came new questions. Ultimately, the greatest question is the one of responsibility, and each person must answer it for himself. Do we leave behind us patterns of love or patterns of struggle, patterns of greatness or patterns of illusion? Do we leave behind us knowledge or mystery, love or forgiveness?

"When I suggested that a person store up his wealth in Heaven, it was with this reality in mind. When your life has been lived with a very clear purpose and when your love had been directed to principles and thoughts which carry your love to higher planes of consciousness, then the treasures of your life will be stored more safely. On the other hand, when a person's love and life have been unclear and confused, peppered with insincerity and betrayal, his life particles can become lost in the lives of those He has hurt. This is not good for anyone concerned. All too often these lost particles are held hostage until debts are paid, which can cause great pain and confusion to all parties. It would be so much easier and healthier to forgive and to release.

"Is this what Eastern philosophy speaks of as Karma? Is what you speak of now the cause of it?"

"In the universe, the process of cause and effect describes the way in which balance is lost and regained. When balance has been lost, it must be regained. That is karma. However, retreading the pathways of cause and effect is not the only way of restoring balance and wholeness. By grace and by love there is a higher way. All that is asked of you is that you fervently seek the restoration of wholeness whenever it has been lost. It is my hope that you find it through a reconnection with your Source, who will cancel your debt by the greater power of love, grace, and synchronicity. Karma is a base level ethics action—a kind of police agenda for the universe. Although it works to rebalance life and is necessary to the universe, it can injure souls. It is my central purpose to raise souls to a higher sense of responsibility, one empowered by the Sacred Heart and by the grace of

God, thereby ending that bitter cycle.

The beauty and completeness of that message gave me much to ponder, although I was more emotionally affected by His compassionate explanation and tolerance of human error. *"So much human error and dysfunction have just been forwarded to future generations as part of the total human memory, or perhaps the memory of a family line."* He went on to explain how, with our limited understanding, we tend to condemn a sin or crime which is only the latest manifestation of some desperate pattern begun long ago. *"Who does not rejoice to inherit the achievements of those who have come before? Yet how much more courage does it take to live and continue in the midst of errors that have preceded one's stay on Earth? There is no avoiding the collective inheritance of both good and bad."* Then He looked deeply with penetrating clarity into my eyes, as if He were looking through my eternity, and pronounced, *"You are innocent and born as perfection, but into a world that has every conceivable legacy. These legacies come to each person, partially by magnetism, yet partially without respect of person, for all men are equally brothers in the human race. Without exemption, each one must accept some part of the collective inheritance. This is the original and true meaning of a greatly abused statement, 'that none is above sin.' The true meaning of that statement is that no one within the brotherhood is above accepting some part of the negative legacy and the responsibility for transmuting it. The next time you see someone living in a way that is upsetting to you, instead of condemning, you may say a silent prayer of thanks that it is not you who had to accept that commission. When you see a handicapped person, instead of seeing disability, perhaps you could look at the great courage and ability it took to receive that destiny. When you see a man living under a bridge, you might think of honoring a soul so noble as to endure loss and abandonment for his charter. When a child is dying of cancer, instead of pitying its loss of life, see instead a soul so assured of immortality that he could receive that legacy.* **Do not view hardship as punishment, but rather as inclusion.**

"This was the great lesson of Job, a wealthy man who lived in ancient Israel. He enjoyed the favor of good fortune and rich blessing until a series of reversals changed his life for the worse. Job tried to interpret his hardship as punishment, yet that made no sense. He tried to interpret the hardship as something he had to work through, and that changed nothing. He tried to interpret it as something he would have to receive as a lesson.

Still nothing changed. He tried penance and supplication to God in the form of prayer, sacrifice, and worship. Nothing in the way of cause and effect brought satisfaction, however, nor any results. In desperation, he pleaded for explanations. 'Why,' he asked God, 'do good people suffer while the evil are left free to exploit with their profits?' When the Almighty answered him from a whirlwind, He brought only more questions to Job. 'Have you ever given orders to the morning, or shown the dawn its place? Can you bind the beautiful Pleiades? Does the hawk take flight by your wisdom and spread its wings toward the south? Does the eagle soar at your command and build his nest on high?' God's message to Job was that the answer lies not in bitterness, or judgment, or even in the search for reasons, but rather in the vastness and grandeur of the universe.*

*"Finally, Job surrendered, accepting the hardship as his new lot in life. At last he understood that his charter within the brotherhood of man was to accept the bad with the good. By the grace of God he was then restored to his original wealth and his original blessing. However, it was not by justifications of cause and effect that this was accomplished, but by the higher power of acceptance and grace. Life is to be shared for better or for worse, as **all men rise together** toward a higher plane on which to live. It is the greater wisdom to realize that often what you might consider to be the worst is just an illusion that will also pass."*

"Must it always be that way?"

"It will be as long as you are under the illusion of separation from each other and separation from God. It will pass when you know that you are love and when you accept your rightful position within the One Spirit. It will also greatly help to seek the river of abundant supply which can transmute or override structures like the surf of an ocean. Once you know this, you will perceive the limitations of structure and cease to be its servant."

Too often, in our human formula we shun or pity those we wish to hold apart from our lives. Honor and inclusion were His answers to that dilemma. This does not mean, however, that we should condone crime, or tolerate conditions which foster disease, or relax into indifference about hardship. The point of His message was that human difficulty **belongs to us all**. Where is there anyone who has the right to stand apart and judge the rest?

On this occasion, and several others, He distinguished between three levels of understanding which have a direct impact upon our well-being in the universe. The lowest level of understanding pertains to one's immediate survival, with little perception or recognition of consequences. While this may satisfy short-run necessity, it can lead to bitter traps and deadly results. The next level of understanding is that of cause and effect, which leads to decent, civilized behavior with significantly more command of life. If one stops at this level, however, life will be dominated by structure, linear logic, control, and judgment. Life will be lived in a box! Fortunately, there is a third and higher level. The highest level of understanding involves surrendering to the power of wholeness which is all inclusive. According to Jesus, this final level requires a great leap of faith and consciousness, **for it is truly where faith and consciousness rule**. Both are required in great measure, as well as love, acceptance, and forgiveness.

When I asked Him if we should focus only on the highest level of understanding, He answered. *"All three levels of understanding are needful and valid. It may surprise you that some people need to be taught how to survive, or helped in doing so. Others need a refresher course in cause and effect! Nevertheless, everyone would be the wiser to understand that infinite wholeness has the power to utterly command life, shatter it, or rebuild it according to patterns of greater good. When one is attuned to that power through love and synchronicity, separation from God and man will cease, and life will be filled with greater blessing, broader understanding, and conscious immortality."*

It is amazing to contemplate the ocean of infinite supply which is always adapting to the commands of love. I have spent countless happy hours since those days of 1992 dreaming about the possibilities and potentialities of understanding adamantine particles, managing them, and creating with them more consciously! For mankind to achieve such an understanding would have a profound effect on everything from health and healing, to maximum-yield, low-resistance fuel, to intergalactic communication and travel. We appear to be progressing toward this goal every day. On November 6, 1997, a newspaper in Beaumont, Texas, reprinted the following New York Associated Press story. **"Scientists achieve 'Star Trek' trick.** In an Austrian laboratory, scientists destroyed bits of light in one place and made perfect replicas appear about three feet away . . . the work is the first to demonstrate 'quantum teleportation,' a bizarre shifting of physical characteristics between (photons) no matter how far apart. Scientists might be able to achieve teleportation between atoms within a few years and molecules within a decade or so, Zeilinger said."

I asked the Master if it could be possible for humankind to abuse such knowledge. His reply was, *"With structural cause and effect that's always a possibility. With adamantine particles it's very unlikely, because man's ability to understand them is dependent upon graduating to a holistic understanding of the universe. As long as man dwells in conflict and manages life only by linear cause and effect, he will never see the bigger picture."*

His response had not totally appeased my concern, so I persisted. "As you have told me, there are always people of different understanding and responsibility levels co-existing. What if new technologies were discovered by scientists of high responsibility and then were stolen by others who would abuse them? That has happened many times in our history."

While nodding to the reality of our history, His countenance remained calm and serene. A comforting smile spread across His face as He gently reminded me that, *"Adamantine particles are commanded by love—only by love. Understanding of them and conscious utilization of them belong to a higher paradigm. Thieves do have their way from time to time. However, the greater law of ownership always prevails, and that law states that ownership belongs to love, to responsible custody, and to the utilization of power for the good of all."*

Although I was privileged to learn about the adamantine particles at the Master's feet, I have to honestly admit that the particles of infinity were not truly real to me until I was given a journey into the cosmos on April 26, 1996. By some strange irony, that sacred journey began in a shopping mall. Brian and I had just finished dinner and were thinking about what to do with our evening. Should we buy a book or go to a movie? First, we went to the book store where I found a book I had been wanting to read. It was a 'best- seller,' and I already liked the author, so I was curious. Noticing my interest, Brian asked, "Do you want that book?" I surprised myself with the sudden answer of, "No." It was not a negative response to the book itself. It was a negative response to my own recent acceleration of curiosity about things external, about other people's truths. At that moment, I felt an absence of desire for any more random clutter. I remembered the "cool, clear water" of Jesus' messages to me, and my mouth felt salty with desires that could not be satisfied. In making that discernment, I must have tripped a switch in my heart. By saying no, I had honored that which was indwelling over and above that which I had been seeking externally.

A total transformation of consciousness began at that moment as a door opened, and I crossed its threshold. What transpired in the physical sense, I do not know. All I know is that I was like Alice in Wonderland. I walked through a door and tumbled into the cosmos. It apparently happened as a parallel reality, while I was standing beside Brian, probably looking quite normal. He accepted my decline of the book and suggested that we go to a movie instead. I said, "Okay."

I would have pacified him with any concession, because all I wanted was to enjoy my private panorama and to keep walking through the corridors that were opening for me. I was going through door after door through a long corridor that was leading upward. With every step, there seemed to be less gravity. Through every door, it seemed as if I were shedding pounds and outer garments of existence. I was becoming lighter and lighter as I walked upward. When the last door opened, I saw the heavens. It was as if I were seeing it for the first time, and for the first time I saw infinity. Like a child, I looked around in wonderment, until my eyes came to rest on an illuminated cloud-like glow in the far distance which looked a little like the Milky Way, except that I knew it was not made of stars. It was sparkling, bright and golden, with no sense of gravity whatsoever—a cloud of particles. Like kites in the breeze, the particles and I began to float together. As we drew closer, I knew that they were **my** adamantine particles preserving in memory and potential the rest of who I am. That experience was like a one-woman homecoming party. It was as if everything that I am had come back to me. I saw Heaven and Earth as one unit, receiving all that I have been, all that I am, and all that I could ever want to be. Beautiful and amazing, it was like walking into the Garden of Eden, and having every delicious fruit I could ever want to taste just for the picking of it. Everything glowed, and there was no sense of heaviness or solidity. This was truly an immortality experience, and I was permitted to savor it with all my senses and consciousness. I could see my body going through the typical motions of Earthly activity that evening, while my soul was elsewhere.

If I could have stayed in both places I would have done so, for I did not wish to leave the heavenly plane. With some degree of reluctance, I returned to the part of me that was still on Earth. I have to say that it felt like I was gone for about three or four months, but in Earth time it was only for the duration of leaving the bookstore, sitting through the movie, and driving home.

That journey gave me many things, among them a firsthand experience of adamantine particles. I am not sure by what means the journey was made possible. However, it reminded me of the days I spent with the Master in my studio. One day when we were discussing adamantine particles, I asked Him about His appearance to me. "Did you arrange adamantine particles in order to be here in three-dimensional space?" He answered in the affirmative, then proceeded to explain that He had taken an assortment of adamantine particles which had a memory of his physical body. He had moved them into my vicinity and activated them with His love. He added that since the particles were not dense enough to reflect light, the one extra factor required was a perceptual adjustment to my optic nerve. He explained that was why the beam of light was projected to my forehead—to facilitate a finer attunement of my sensitivities.

His explanation left me with a sense of disappointment, as if some special part of the mystery had been removed. "But it seems like you are really here!"

Reassuring me of His presence, He confirmed, *"I am here by my love. I just don't have to go through all these mechanics to be with **most** people. You needed sensory information to paint the portrait. Other people need other types of reassurance."*

"Can adamantine particles be directly perceived?"

"Some people can perceive adamantine radiance with the naked eye. It's an ancient perception which most people have allowed to go dormant. That is what people mean when they see auras, or glowing radiance around things. This is a sense which only a few people have in operation today. But like smell, the ability to see adamantine particles was once strong in everyone. Thousands of years ago it was a survival sense pertaining to the selection of food and medicine, as well as friend and foe. Animals still use it today. It is by that sense that a bird knows a poison seed from an herb which can rid him of lice. Upon approaching a benevolent seed which the bird needs, the adamantine particles will glow. In the presence of a harmful situation they will dim."

"What causes that to happen?"

"Life is love in action. It brings light into areas of positive potential and dimness or even darkness to areas of negative potential! Anyone can recultivate this sense with practice and patience. Start with strongly contrasting plus and minus stimuli so that you can see the difference. Then work on the mid-zones. As you gain confidence, start putting it together in

a full spectrum of greater perceptual ability. Give yourself time, and have patience with yourself. Realize it will not come overnight, but the ability is there. It is both natural and normal."

I asked Him if that was mystical perception.

"Actually it's a very practical perception. There is, however, an unsolid dimension of reality where every life form that has ever lived can still be seen happily perpetuating its existence as adamantine memory or adamantine potential. You might regard that as mystical. Although it all depends on how vast one's reality is!"

"Is that Heaven?"

"In a very real sense any vision of immortality touches upon Heaven, although this is not the Heaven of eternal bliss which is found through the Sacred Heart as it reconnects with God. However, this is what many have discovered in their visionary life and called Heaven."

I was not to perceive that dimension consciously until April 26, four years later. At the time, however, His comment made me think of angels. I was curious as to how they fit into the scheme of things. In 1992, angels were not a primary subject of interest for me. Nevertheless, I was curious to know if they had special influence over the adamantine particles through their love.

He confirmed my suspicions. *"Yes, these are beings who do not operate within the world of structure. That is why they can defy the laws of gravity, time, and space, and be in the constant service of God's miracles. They are not restricted by the illusions of structure with which man must deal. Angels have direct influence upon the adamantine particles."*

As we were talking about this, I looked across the room at my cat, Gunnar. Gunnar was the only one else present in the studio while I was painting, and I noticed him often looking over at Jesus. "Can Gunnar see you?"

He said, *"Yes,"* and Gunnar meowed in affirmation. Jesus explained that animals can see adamantine particles much more easily than people can. *"However, if Gunnar did not love my presence, or feel my love for him, there would be no perception. He would have just noticed something in the room that made him uncomfortable, and he would have left. Gunnar is here because he loves my presence and wants to share it with you."*

We both looked affectionately at Gunnar, who expressed his satisfaction with a nibble of lunch. As if by a natural sequence, this led to our next topic. If everything is comprised of adamantine particles which are universally exchanged, then there is a profound implication for the subject of diet and food.

As we opened the subject of physical nourishment, He reminded me that the most important factor is receiving whatever we eat with love. *"Remember, love controls the adamantine particles. Always receive with love, for it is love which instructs the food on how to nourish your body. Bless the food and thank the givers and preparers of it. Your love will be attuned to the energy frequency your heart has set for your body and will properly instruct your body on how to use the nutrients. For better nutrition, strengthen your heart. A strong heart sets the body at a higher frequency, and establishes a lower resistance mode of energy utilization which is not only more efficient, but is also more able to process and manufacture vitamins and minerals."*

Apparently we have the innate ability to manufacture a great many more vitamins and minerals than we are currently doing. It is the lower frequency of our heart that is leaving us under-supplied with self-made nutrients. I asked him about the chemical problems I was encountering with my own diet. *"All of this will take care of itself when your energy frequency is high enough to manufacture what you need. Your body's energy level is too low right now to provide everything for you without support and compensation. Directly receiving sunlight at sunrise or sunset will actually help increase your frequency levels. Whenever you do this, your body chemically responds, and stimulates the manufacture of certain nutrients your energy level is otherwise too low to produce. Chemical resonance equals energy frequencies, and vice versa. Actually, much of the value of hard mineral traces in your bodies is the energetic matrix generated by them. The sun can provide this directly, for it contains both the substance and the fire of every mineral available in your solar system.*

"Diet is relative in very many ways, for it supports the love which precedes and surrounds it. Different seasons, different ages, different health conditions, and different altitudes can affect the whole process. Nevertheless, as your heart grows stronger, it will lead you in this. Just as the birds know which seeds to eat, your heart will attract you to the food you need. Your heart will assist you in processing the food according to what your body needs to receive. Until greater understanding can come into this area, I would recommend that you use moderation in all things, and direct it with gratitude and love."

I wanted to know, "Is it wrong to eat meat?"

"Eventually, mankind will eat little or no meat. However, that will come only when a stronger heart and greater refinement of physical energies can produce hormones and nutrients which cannot be manufactured by most people at this time. It is pointless to feel guilty for eating meat when you need it. Vegetarian ideals should not be prematurely enforced on people who are not ready for them. It is far more important that people awaken in their own hearts and incline in that direction as they look for greater health. In the meantime, you will benefit more by gratitude and appreciation for those who have bestowed the bounties of life on you. For I assure you, it is not by food that you are nourished, but by love. A humble meal that is beautifully prepared with love and shared in loving company is more nourishing than vegetarian cuisine eaten on the run. No combination matters if love is not the central ingredient. The major cause of overweight, malnutrition, and dietary disease is loveless meals from unloved plants and unloved animals, grown on an unloved Earth. There is no coincidence that such problems have increased in proportion to lifestyles of hasty and obsessive eating.

"At this time, most people need some meat to be healthy, and it should never be eaten with a sense of guilt. In the presence of guilt, your love cannot direct and refine the process of nourishment. The food chain is a fact of life upon which all life forms have agreed for the duration of its necessity. Many have chosen that for their loving service. It is a fact to be accepted, to be honored, and never to be abused. In ancient times when man lived closer to the Earth and perceived the one spirit more clearly, this was better understood and more fully honored. Until a deeper understanding is rekindled, all that I can ask is for more kindness, gratitude, and moderation to be shown toward those who share their lives with you. In the western world, far too much meat is being consumed. It is overloading the body with electrical charge and suppressing sensitivity toward the one spirit and the magnetic attractions of the heart. There is no coincidence that excess consumption of meat is having its heaviest consequence in damage to the physical heart. Second to over-consumption, the other great offense against animals is the manner in which they are raised for slaughter in loveless quarters. This is unconscionable and is leaving a bitter legacy in the adamantine particles of nature. Moreover, the food resulting from it is depleted in every conceivable way.

"The entire science of Kosher cooking which Moses taught was based

on an understanding of such factors. For example, one of the rules of Kosher cooking is that veal should never be cooked with milk. Veal is the meat of a calf, and milk is the essence of its mother's love. The substance of the mother's life should never be combined with the slaughtered body of her child. It is a dishonoring of the love. That was the entire reason for it. All the laws of Kosher cooking have their roots in similar concepts of love and nourishment. Unfortunately, much of that wisdom has been lost and replaced with rigid formulas. As with much ancient wisdom, the structures remain and the elixir of truth has evaporated.

"A true understanding of the relationship between food and love could revolutionize health. However, do not forget what I told you about sunlight; to watch the sun in the morning and the evening, because watching the sun can actually set your physical, etheric, and spiritual hearts into a harmonic resonance which will attract what you need and process what you have more perfectly. Doing this will improve your experience of the day, as well as your energy, your nutrition, and your sleep, for adamantine particles are the river of life connecting Heaven and Earth."

Chapter 5
The One Spirit

Our one spirit is a subject of grandeur, impossible to define conclusively. Moreover, if we consider that one spirit connects all things, sustains all things, and is the indivisible oneness of all existence, then from what vantage point can we objectively describe it? Since the very nature of definition is to objectify, contain, and establish that which is and is not, how could we even conceive an absolute definition of our oneness without reducing innocent perception to shaky pretension? It cannot be done. Therefore, we will honor the treasures of awareness which have been given to us, and humbly create with them a mosaic for greater understanding. If this evokes an intuitive connection for us with sacred truth, then we are richly blessed. Regardless, we can marvel at the simplicity of infinite inclusion. There is no place where spirit is not. That is the beauty and the glory of our oneness.

Despite its vast, uncharted extensions, Jesus referred to spirit as one of the great pillars of existence. Love, adamantine particles, and spirit are the landmarks of our consciousness, not because they are three separate entities, but rather because they denote the principle aspects of existence which invariably submit to intelligence and support our understanding with constancy. In referring to spirit, we are referring to all that is. It is that simple.

When Moses left the comfort of palatial life in ancient Egypt to lead the Hebrews out of slavery, he did so on the power of a revolutionary new concept. That concept was the simplistic conviction that there is but one God. What made that idea revolutionary was that it transcended proprietary designations of one god per race, per social group, per tribe, etc. He had also transcended the idea of pantheistic representation of God as the outward thrust of physical existence. The radical idea which changed history was that Moses clearly perceived God to be the **Source** of all that is, though not necessarily the external shape. From a common wellspring of life, endless forms and patterns of existence have come to be. **There is simply God**—the one original essence! Neither Holy Presence nor immortality can be found in outward display. Higher knowledge can only be attained by respect for **ultimate simplicity** which progresses toward unity. Alternately, we lose that understanding as we focus on the chaos of complexity. As we quarrel over whose interpretation is the greater one, we lose the point and the power of Divinity.

Because of that magnificent contribution to the history of mankind, there was created a basis for the integration and unity of human consciousness which would have been impossible if not unthinkable within previous world views. Jesus encouraged me to believe that we are once again at the critical moment of extraordinary soul development, of realizing that there is but one spirit.

"As mankind moves toward that greater awareness, it will leave behind three basic misconceptions about the spirit which are prevalent in the world today. One is that spirit and body are separate. That is not true. The body is a fully integrated unit of love, adamantine particles and spirit. These are inseparable aspects of the whole and yet each is discernible in its own character."

In response I asked, "If these three parts are inseparable, why do we need to have a discernible awareness of them?"

"From the viewpoint of God, there is no difference. However, you were given life, purpose, awareness and continuance as your own special self forever. In order to support that, you were given your own center of awareness and your own special connection to the Father. This connection is what I call the Sacred Heart, which is where your love resides, and your awareness of infinity begins. That extraordinary place is the sanctuary and power given to the sons and daughters of God. You might compare the Sacred Heart to a pure crystal prism through which the light of God enters and then bends in order to establish and manifest unique and particular covenants. In the same way that a prism diffracts a simple ray of white light into a spreading array of rainbow colors, so too the simple truths of God are made applicable to the diversities of life. Therefore, from the viewpoint of your heart, you do experience the Earth and your body as three basic essences. It is right, valid, and intelligent that you do so. Nevertheless, they are all one, and spirit is not separate from the body.

"The second misconception is that the spirit forms a complementary duality with the body. That is also incorrect, for body and spirit are one. The history of western thinking has left you a legacy of dualistic concepts from which you have developed your thinking and operating. Mankind looks at everything in terms of opposites. He measures up by down, north by south, white by black, and dull by clear. Scales of comparison can be helpful in discerning, although such a scale is valid only if both ends of the spectrum are known and available for observation. When the ends reach beyond your consciousness, the scale is irrelevant. For that reason, infinity will be avoided in the presence of dualistic thinking. Science is barred from infinity for the moment, because it is locked into dualistic thinking. For the same reason, materialistic motivation cannot comprehend infinity. When you believe that spirit is opposite the material world, you lose the ability to have an integrated spiritual life. This is a prevalent misconception. How many times have you heard someone say, 'This is of the spirit and not of the world'? The spirit is separate from nothing. Spirit is in all things and of all things. In knowing that, you gain the ability to transmute the world into a better place. Whatever you have denied from the unity of spirit is a thing you have condemned. That is the ultimate judgment—to consider that spirit is absent.

"There is a third misconception which also is a legacy of history. Every race of man, in its tribal days spent close to the Earth, believed in the existence of many spirits. As an observation of natural forces, and the many aspects of life generating an impact upon the environment, such thinking had a rational basis. If such ideas had been left behind with the state of innocence to which they belonged, there would have been no harm. However, that misconception eventually developed into philosophies and religions which centered their beliefs around a multiplicity of spirits, some of them good and some of them bad, with coalitions of spirit competing for dominance of the world. Contrary to that belief, there is but one spirit.

*"There was, however, a positive aspect to that legacy. Those ancient philosophies, with their belief in multiplicity, elicited the beginning insights into human individuality. The recognition that each person is an individual was a major leap forward for mankind. Since man understood spirit before he understood love, spirit formed the basis of his perceptions about individuality. Now, with a greater understanding, you can say more accurately that you are individuals by your love, and the one spirit resonates uniquely with each person **according to his love.** It is by your*

love—or condition thereof—that you are known. It is by the nature of your love that your character is formed. The one spirit is utterly indivisible yet responsive to all."

As we talked about spirit, these were not theological discussions of the Holy Spirit as an aspect of the Holy Trinity. Nor was the impact of that discussion Pentecostal in nature. He was ever so considerate and courteous about maintaining a peaceful and moderate exchange between us where I might feel at ease in my work. Perhaps that is a rare aspect of these messages—that they were so integrated with practical living and so **human**.

On one occasion, I did ask Him about the Holy Spirit and how it related to the one spirit of which He spoke. He gladly explained, *"They are both the same, experienced in two different ways. It is one of the great mysteries of existence that the One Spirit can and does personify the very personality, will and power of God. As such, the Holy Spirit is a mighty vortex of divine energy which pours forth great restorative power. Everything in His path is changed. These are the Pentecostal moments spoken of by those who have experienced them. For most of life, however, the one spirit is experienced as the delegated power of God distributed through all of creation, through every aspect of existence."*

It is the second aspect of spirit which He addressed in depth, because that is the way we know the one spirit for most of our lives, and through most of our existence. Along with that, He stressed the idea of integrated spirituality. Technically, our one spirit is primal matrix in which all things co-exist, forever combining and interacting. As the embracer and defender of our unity, spirit is the undefiled, impenetrable matrix of all existence. The irony of its great pervasion, however, is that spirit can never be observed fully by any sense or instrument, for by definition, an essence can only be perceived through fluctuations and differences of potential.

"If we are one with it, then how can we know it?"

"The place to begin is with understanding rather than perception."

This brings us to a critical discernment. According to Jesus, *"Indivisibility is the domain of spirit, whereas divisibility is the domain of particles. By the very nature of divisibility, particles can be examined and defined, whereas spirit cannot. Particles are separate and divisible manifestations which emerge from the continuous flow of energetic potential. Consider, for example, an atom, which is relatively large and complex compared to adamantine particles. One atom can be viewed as separate from other atoms by the nature of its structural composition.*

Likewise, one rock in a pasture is distinguishable from another. Thus it is that all material substance bears the mark of separateness and divisibility. Its scale is irrelevant."

Adding love to the divisibility of particles and the indivisibility of spirit, we have a grand triangle which is the wonderful majesty of creation. Through the guidance of love, the infinite potential of indivisibility gives rise to divisibility. Then, like waves of the ocean, divisibility surrenders again to oneness. As one person, is that not what we are—the same with many perspectives? As a family, are we not one body with numerous members? As a brotherhood, is that not what we are—one people in a myriad of forms? The Master poetically summarized what my mind could only assemble, *"You might consider the entirety of the universe to be a wonderful ballet of divisibility and indivisibility, choreographed by the Grand Master of Love."*

The love that you are is **who you are**, within this great symphony of divisibility and indivisibility. His explanations were a masterful orchestration of those universal melodies. *"Through the oneness of the spirit, the universe is maintained in unity, and all of creation performs in an interlocking system of relationships where everything belongs and has its place. Spirit is the ultimate medium of communication, for it is indivisible. Through spirit's unbroken essence, all thoughts and intentions are conveyed. As mankind awakens to this, more people will have the gift of prophecy, of vision, of telecommunication, of empathy, of reaching beyond what once was called the void, and knowing there is not a void at all. Where once there was loneliness, there will be comfort in knowing that space is filled with love and continuity.*

"In the grand triangle of existence, love connects and commands the adamantine particles, while spirit resonates to love and connects all substance in perfect unity. In this infinite cycle of creation, each is part of the all and yet there are three discernible functions. Through the joining of spirit and matter, you can observe the delicate and critical point where divisibility becomes indivisibility."

With a look of remarkable clarity He added, *"Defining clearly the point where indivisibility makes its transition into divisibility is the crucial degree of understanding that will launch science into the next millennium. Right now, the greatest hindrance to progress comes from studying the divisible field against a backdrop of impenetrable unknown. The assumption is that the rest will be understood as bridges are built between* *that field and the divisible nature of instrumentation and knowledge. More to the point, it will become understood when its indivisibility is accepted, and study then focuses upon the transitional zone where indivisibility **becomes** divisible. How can you have an indivisible field which functions by laws of separation? New procedures will need to filter down from a larger perspective, however, because a perception of the bridge between divisibility and indivisibility requires an understanding of love."*

That was quite a statement, for clearly it implied that love extends itself even to the point of **technical function** well beyond an impulse to exist and a guidance thereof. I asked for more information about what He had intimated. Later He would reveal a great deal more about the functions of love. However, at that moment He merely offered the following analogy about exchange and communication.

*"Just look at patterns of communication, for example. If it were not for the spirit that binds us we could not communicate at all. The nature of communication requires that what I say, or what I have to offer, has the possibility of becoming a reality to you. Otherwise, my voice would be a meaningless sound, and not communication at all. Now, on the other hand, our communication would have no point if I did not have something to offer which you do not already have. So you see, communication is a delicate resolution between divisibility and indivisibility. The understanding between us occurs at the point where divisibility **becomes** indivisibility. At that point, communication is a vital transmutation of understanding from one to another. What allows that transmutation to happen is the love that we share. If it were not for the love that connects us, I could not give, nor could you receive. The universal facilitator of all communication is the love that we are."*

"Must communication always be direct and explicit, or is the one spirit full of implicit communications directed by love?" He smiled gently with a satisfied look as if to suggest that I had already answered my own question. Of course I had, although at that moment I wanted His affirmation. His expression was more than enough.

Several years later I experienced a touching example of the power of love to expedite a communication between two souls only vaguely aware of each other. This story offers further insight into how the presence of love can establish a basis for mutual response. The incident happened to me on the premises of our art gallery in west Fort Worth. Our little cottage style building was located on a busy boulevard next to Taco Bell, immediately adjacent to the restaurant's drive-up window. The land between us was terraced, so that our gallery sat four feet below the level of their drive way. One day I was replacing some bricks which were missing from the planter box dividing our two properties. As I did my job, suffering the toxic fumes, roar of engines, and boom boxes, I also became the spectacle of everyone placing take-out orders. Though I tried to be inconspicuous, my discomfort was probably obvious to everyone, and certainly I felt an unnerving vulnerability. For the most part, our street served a very elite part of town, yet it was also close to an impoverished area. Therefore, the parade of automobiles beside and above me reflected that range of demographics. It was all in full display, from BMWs wafting classical music to 1965 Chevys with sprung shocks and loud mufflers. Suddenly, I was startled from my work by a strange assortment of noises screeching to a halt above my head. The radio's volume was deafening, and even worse, it was tuned to a hard rock station not particularly to my liking. Quickly ducking back into my work, I decided to lose myself and let it pass. In that scrunched position, I felt like a rabbit in its burrow, and looked for an aspect of love on which I could focus. All I could relate to were the wild rabbits who run for cover when overwhelmed by circumstance. As I joined into a tender coexistence with those little creatures, the most miraculous thing happened. The man in the car stopped revving his engine, switched his radio to a romantic station and lowered the volume! This continued as long as he waited for his order. Then, driving away, he returned to his normal preferences, and with a loud "Varoom" he was gone.

In that experience, I witnessed what the Master had taught me. The One Spirit is in everything and includes **all** of existence. It is the wholeness of all that is, and thus the holiness of our relationship with God and the bond we feel in brotherhood with each other.

I asked Jesus if He could help me to understand the breadth and depth of that concept.

So he suggested, *"Let's take a break for a moment and do this. Get comfortable, stretch and relax. Then take a deep breath and prepare to be at peace with yourself. Imagine yourself as an aspect of God's love—a unit of one. Now, extend your heart, mind, and soul as far as you can, and* **contemplate 'all that is.'** *In this act of beholding, be at peace with yourself, and know yourself as a unit of one. When you have done that, then receive and imagine all that is* **contemplating you!** *Whether you are conscious of* *it or not, this is an eternal dialogue which exists between you, as a unit of one, and the one spirit for the whole of eternity. Envision that for every being. Then consider further that every unit of one in the entirety of existence is in the same eternal dialogue with 'all that is.' The dialogue of the one and the all is an eternal breath, never ending. There is no separation, only rhythms of giving and receiving, speaking and listening, teaching and learning, advancing and receding, appearing and disappearing."*

As I practiced that, I began to experience how the one spirit resonates to different people, different things and different aspects of life —all without separation.

Within this enormous variety, it is natural that we each have our own preferences and orientations, and He said that was only natural and merely a reflection of our individuality. Sometimes we can notice the harmonies between ourselves and others in an energetic way that seems to vibrate. In recent decades, the jargon phrase "good and bad vibes" has come to express that realization. When the children regard something as having "good vibes," they are being very observant. Of course, everything has the right vibrations for itself, although its resonance may not be compatible with everything it touches. *"By the resonance of spirit, you can know the character and intentions of anything. These resonances combine with others in their vicinity to set in motion patterns for melody or cosmic song. This is why music, more than any other art form, can transport the soul directly into spiritual communion. Actually, that is true of beauty in all aspects, for beauty represents a special harmony and synchronicity within the oneness of spirit. Beauty is a landmark along the pathway of spirit. Where you see beauty, a recognition of truth is possible. Beauty is like a message to you that you are walking in harmony as you follow the guidance of spirit through life."*

Naturally, being an artist, that statement intrigued me, and I was particularly interested to hear about His understanding of truth and beauty.

"First, let's look at intuition and beauty. As you already know, art is an intuitive process. Regardless of the art form—painting, writing, music, or sculpture—an artist's primary medium is that of intuitive discovery and expression. In that regard, intuition functions best when it is not overly influenced or restricted by structure. Yet, unguided intuition rarely has meaningful results. Therefore, beauty and intuition are each other's most perfect companion. There is no equal to beauty as a guiding ray for

*intuition, because beauty is an aspect of love which evokes and refines natural order and potential **without dependency upon structure**.*

"As intuition clears a pathway for unfolding consciousness, landmarks of beauty focus the growing consciousness upon constants of reality, and then truth is perceived. Truth and beauty are both constants of the universe, one of revelation and the other of manifestation.

"In every new creation, an artist will grope through a jungle of illusion, confusion, and trial expressions until a pattern of constancy appears before him. This is the image, sound, or concept to which his heart and actions were giving birth. He recognizes the beauty before him, no less than a mother knows her child, even though an indifferent spectator might see nothing special at all. The artist has discovered a constant within the unfolding manifestation, and that is beautiful to him. Later, perhaps, it will be admired by others.

"You have seen this cycle within the history of art. A form of beauty appears and focuses the direction of cultural growth. Eventually it endures past its ability to inspire and excite emulation. Finally, it is perpetuated as an overly sweet, stale formula which decorates surfaces and makes the superficial aspects of life a little prettier or gaudier, as the case may be. Then suddenly, from an unexpected direction, fresh perceptions bring dramatic assertions of new aesthetic awareness. Like chicks hatching in springtime, innovative sensitivity breaks the veil of prevailing ideals, and brings forth life to the subject of beauty. Often, in the beginning, such assertions are not received as beautiful, because they are viewed through old preferences. What many people consider beautiful is the predictable splendor of prior conditions. However, those who guide and nurture the evolution of beauty know that its essence is actually the perception of living truth as an ongoing process of intuition.

"Thinking is also an art form, perhaps man's finest. It, too, functions best when accompanied by intuition and beauty."

As we think, we create ideas and images which allow our consciousness to develop and expand. Most especially, with subjects as vast and nebulous as the one spirit, it is crucial to have corollary concepts which provide alternate viewpoints for unfolding and examining our thoughts. *"Although we cannot define spirit, we can conceive of it and deepen our understanding of it. In that pursuit, infinity is perhaps our closest and most effective corollary to the one spirit. Like spirit, infinity also defies limitation, for it is the ultimate extent of largeness, smallness,*

*quality, and potential. Infinity is an aspect of function and performance
innate to universal potential, rather than an estimation of probable
dimensions. There is no structure that can adequately explain or contain
infinity."*

Until recently, infinity has been set aside by science as a mystical
concept, simply immeasurable and uncontainable in nature. Infinity also
challenges the philosophical structures of analytical, reductionist thinking.
For like the one spirit, infinity is best regarded as an element of integration
rather than separation. Now, however, as philosophy and science turn to
face the more critical issue of integration, the subject of infinity is offering
many intriguing options for exploration and consideration. Establishing
flexibility and adaptability within our consciousness is critical to opening
these new avenues of awareness.

Likewise, in presenting the Master's message about infinity, a
limbering exercise might provide an expanded vision. We'll begin with a
cosmic journey to "the big" then reverse that and explore realms of "the
small." To begin our expedition, let us identify the term googolplex. That
is an extremely large number built up from a googol. So, what's a googol?
That's also a very big number, although it is quite small compared to a
googolplex. The mathematical term of a googol is the number "one,"
followed by a hundred zeros, or 10^{100}. This is the reality of how immense
that is: Over twenty-two centuries ago, Archimedes calculated that 10^{63}
grains of sand (which is quite a bit less than 10^{100}) would fill the universe
as it was then known. The universe as we know it today includes at least
a hundred billion galaxies, each containing an average of a hundred billion
stars. Add to that the mind-boggling number of electrons, protons, and
neutrons and all the other particles of existence which comprise the stars,
planets, dark matter, and every other combination of substance. That
number would equal 10^{86} power, which is still considerably less than a
googol. However, if our entire universe, about fifteen billion light years
across, were packed solid with sub-atomic particles, with zero space
between them, the total amount of particles would rise to 10^{132}. That is just
a little bit more than a googol! Compared to that, how large is a
googolplex? A googolplex is 10^{10}, then raised again to a hundredth power
more! Just to print the number of zeros after the number one, would require
enough paper to solidly fill our entire universe, fifteen billion light years
across. Beyond that, there is a super googolplex, which is a googolplex
raised to an additional one hundredth power. No scale is available for any

conscious mind on Earth to grasp such a number. Now, the reason for this exercise is to explode your mental boundaries, while letting you know that in defining a super googolplex we have just described the postulated dimension of **one gravity unit**. That is **one wave** of gravity. Would it be plausible to expect that where there is one wave, there are more? Then, how big is infinity? The one spirit is the totality of that . . . and more!

Now let's take a ride to the small. Let's just consider how small the nucleus of an atom is. If we enlarged a baseball to the size of Earth, we would see the atoms of that baseball as the size of cherries filling the entire planet. If we were to enlarge one of those atoms to the size of the astrodome, the nucleus would then become visible as the size of a grain of sand. That is very small, and we haven't even begun to consider the smallness of an adamantine particle.

*"Infinity is beyond containment in any direction or by any measure. Therefore, one tends to focus on nearby aspects of reality and then to extrapolate by considering gradient scales of density and other progressions. As you look around, the objects in front of you seem very dense. Then as your perspective broadens to the horizon, it includes a greater percentage of space than objects. As you extend your vision further into the night sky, there is an even stronger impression of expanding space and decreasing density. This of course, is relevant only to viewpoints and distances. For primitive man, however, the natural conclusion to that perception would be that space exists in the distance, and spirit is beyond even that. By contrast, that which was close seemed dense and solid, thus he considered that to be material. Somewhere in the middle, between spirit and materiality, man placed himself. The perception of gradient scales of perceptual density was man's first recognition of infinity, although it was limited by his perspective within it. That **fixation of viewpoint**, existing between two extremes, continues even to this day in man's dualistic thinking.*

*"It is not true that there are layers of density through which you must work as you move upwardly toward a spiritual life. Spirit is not an aspect of dimension, but rather it is an **integrated part** of existence. Within the unity of one spirit, all of your perceptions of density simply become irrelevant and fade into an array of many possibilities. You are not surrounded by rings and levels of density through which you must evolve your life if you are to be with God and return to your true self. Those who hold such beliefs approach life as an endless set of conditions with ever*

more requirements to be met. For them, life is an involvement with structure and the service to it. Ironically, such beliefs are often held most strongly by those who have had the greatest struggle and disagreement with structure. Their viewpoint upon structure and infinity are quite fixed by their failures in commanding it.

"When a person restricts life to his perception of densities, he will regard energy as force. Science is still at the point of considering energy to be primarily force, and such thinking is perfectly compatible with a life orientation based on respect of densities. Energy is viewed as the amount of force necessary to generate a given amount of push and pressure. Force works only against densities, and under such pressure more densities pile up, as they do in a trash compactor. The great fallacy in this explanation of energy, however, is that **the perception of density** is mostly an illusion. Almost 98 percent of physical existence is just space, and space does not respond to force! The limitation of that approach should be obvious.

"Under the influence of love, space responds magnetically to attract and to bring life into focus in a much more effortless way. With that understanding, space becomes more interesting than densities. Force has very little effect upon infinity, therefore as long as thought, science, and acts of human conduct are based on force, infinity will remain elusive. Force and density are companions in performance. One is conditioned by the other. If a society bases its perceptions on force, then it will have a very small range of influence. Force can affect only situations in a very close proximity, within predictable boundaries. The reason is that force generates the very densities which eventually baffle its influence. That is true of both particles and people. At the periphery of a circle of influence, there will always be resistance, and conflict will develop as one circle of influence encounters the density of another. This is a critical issue for planet Earth at this moment, and will continue to be until force and density are no longer the language of conduct and interchange.

"Humankind is standing precariously on the edge of its destiny. It will either rise to a paradigm change or experience decline and possible destruction. This is an unavoidable confrontation. The options will be presented and the choices will be made." He twinkled with expectancy and optimism as he spoke about the changes to come. With an assuring tone, He encouraged me to believe that life would then be more effortless, with a diminishing influence of force in our applications of energy, our industries, and our human conduct.

By comparison, I thought about the kind of images projected by science fiction movies which show our future as a high-tech, heavy-force culture. He replied, *"That's just imagination creating a future out of standards of the present. It is a very common mistake to assume that the 'morning side' of a paradigm mountain gives an accurate forecast of how the 'afternoon side' will be. Those who think in terms of force can only expect more of the same! They cannot comprehend the changes which are about to occur. I assure you that it is impossible to travel across the universe on force-based aeronautical engineering. Within a certain limited range, force works. Force-based mechanics can sustain a space program with aspirations of traveling to the moon, or Mars—maybe throughout the solar system. However, you are not going across the galaxy with force-based thinking and force-based engineering. You will soon enter a world of very advanced technologies, although it will not be based on high-friction, high-resistance engineering upon which your civilization currently relies."*

My response to that, and what ensued was the only reference He ever made about civilizations on other planets. "You spoke of sheep in other pastures, did that include pastures beyond the Earth? Are there elder or younger brothers that we do not know about?" That was the only time I ever sensed any nervousness in Him. It was not a serious discomfort, just a charming little wiggle the likes of which one might see in a father whose four-year-old child had asked, "Where do babies come from?" Clearly, He knew more than He wanted to say, yet He did not want to misrepresent anything either!

"You are not alone. As you suspect, there are younger and older brothers elsewhere. Every brotherhood, however, is an entity unto itself with its own right of familyhood, to come of age together. Looking elsewhere is not the answer at this time. Looking to each other and to God is the answer to becoming all that you can be. In many ways your science fiction movies have misled you to believe that consciousness follows technology. Such movies give the false impression that structured, polarized consciousness can be expanded in outreach across the universe simply by accelerating technology. Then somehow, as if by magic, consciousness can be caused to grow. Nothing could be further from the truth. Technology does not cause an increase in consciousness. **Consciousness causes technology***. First a change of consciousness must occur before a greater technical outreach is possible. Your planet and*

others of its kind are like islands in a great ocean with no easy way of bridging the distance. Mutuality is the law of intergalactic connection. Those civilizations which are equal or behind yours cannot reach you any more than you can reach them. There is enough distance between each one to ensure that this will remain true. Those which **can draw near** have the consciousness to compress great distances. Aside from possible desperation or degeneration, it is not within their consciousness to exploit or to conquer mankind.

"I would be misleading you to imply that the galactic community is without its points of turbulence and misbehavior, for there is **always** free will. However, there is a rule that is generally true, and you can rely upon it to give you comfort. Those who could harm you cannot reach you. Those who can reach you would not likely harm you. In His great wisdom, The Creator saw fit to space all life-bearing planets far enough apart to establish this condition. This is combined with a secondary fact that all truly advanced technologies are based on principles of synchronicity, holistic patterning, and respect for the dynamics of life. The idea of marauders traveling at the speed of light and beyond, **simply for conquest**, is pure fiction. The synchronicity required for that technology simply could not be derived from a consciousness based on conflict.

"Through the one spirit, all beings of love everywhere are exerting an influence on each other. Sometimes this is recognized and felt directly, and most often it is simply received as resonance or harmony which one chooses to accept or ignore."

"I understand communion, but could you explain more about the resonances and how they can help us have a more connected life?"

"To get a better look at connecting resonances, consider a great lake, very still in the early morning. Beside it are two stones. Now Love walks by and picks up the two stones, tossing them in the water—one into the left side of the lake and the other into the right. Although the impact of hitting cool water was exhilarating, the two stones felt momentarily lost. The perception of eddies expanding through the water was most enjoyable, albeit a lonely pursuit. Then all of a sudden, the eddies of one stone crossed paths with the eddies of the other. In a burst of joy, each stone realized that the other had been found. At last, they were in communion once more, although now with greater assurance, for they knew how to know each other in spirit. With that certainty, they can never be lost again."

That story added a whole new dimension to the subject of separation. Perhaps Love walked by and threw the stones in separate directions so as to demonstrate the impossibility of spiritual separation. The splashes that we make in the waters of life will surely resonate with the love that we are, and reaching out to infinity will continue until our eddies cross in patterns of recognition. People often ask me how I dealt with my sense of loss after Jesus left. That answer is easy. If there's one lasting thing I gained from the experience we shared, I would have to say it is the ability to recognize His presence anywhere. He said, *"You will know me by my love, for the spirit resonates to my love."* Of course, He can be many places simultaneously, because the physical barriers are only illusion. Often I feel His presence, just as you must surely be feeling it now, along with mine. From this awareness, I have also learned to feel the presence of my departed loved ones. Now I have them more than ever, because I am free from the attachment of physical dependency. The two stones thrown into the lake wound up truly finding each other, because they found each other in spirit. Perhaps as we awaken to the one spirit, our concept of friendship will take on new and greater meaning. There are so many connections to be made and re-made—perhaps even across the universe! This can happen in prayer, in meditation, or spontaneously in empathic moments.

"Connection and reconnection will flower like blossoms in spring — from the gray of winter, they will spring forth in a blaze of glory. The infinity of spirit is like an ocean of potential which resonates with us all. Through this great medium, anyone who removes the walls and barriers of structure can commune without considerations of time or distance. Therein lies the power of prayer, empathy and prophecy. However, it should always be remembered that the one spirit is of God and of us all. One keeps it holy by keeping it whole. To use the spirit for selfish purposes (within self-protected circles) may cause great harm to oneself, for this will eventually cause separation from God. When a being has forgotten the power of love, and has abused or ignored the whole spirit, he has lost his compass and forgotten the name of his home. Closed circles of spirit tend to grow around those who have uncharitable or even harmful wishes toward others. Those who wish to exclude you from their love will have theirs cut short. And those who would seek to disconnect you from spirit will experience separation and disconnection for their lot. Most people live within circles of spirit which provide them with a brotherhood and a comfort zone. There is no harm in that if the totality of spirit is honored as well, and if the

circle of spirit does not become an attempt to project structure and division within the realm of the indivisible."

I considered that to mean it is all right to have a close circle of friends with which we share our pleasures and preferences in life, as long as we do not use those friendships as a basis for considering that we are the privileged and chosen ones, while all the rest have been rejected.

"Never divide the spirit, for it cannot be done. You will waste your energy, and the result is that you will divide yourself. There are no set formulas for negotiating the difference between your close circle of friends and the infinity of spirit. I merely ask that you keep the spirit holy. This is done in two ways. One is to honor the Holy Spirit's divinity as a personification of the Father, and the other is to keep the spirit whole in all your daily living. Behold the oneness of all that is. None are rejected from the whole spirit, and none are unchosen by the Father. However, many have become so comfortable within their own circles of spirit that the whole spirit is rejected. By their own rejection, they are separated out from communion. And by their own unchoosing they are unchosen to have a greater and purer awareness. This is what I meant when I said, 'Judge not, that you be not judged.' For in judging, you have actually separated yourself from the one spirit, and have rendered your own judgment. **The original sin was simply judgment.** *By judging, every being initiated his own consequence of separation. That is the only way a pure and innocent soul, created in the image of God, could ever have turned away from the community of love. The direct consequence of judgment is separation. Whether you know it or not, you are in an eternal dialogue of 'the one and the all.' Whatsoever you cast off, in that same way you will be cast off from it. No inner circle of spirit can protect you from the consequences of the eternal dialogue."*

"Is that what you meant when you said, *"As you sow, so shall you reap?"* I asked.

"It is the same concept, simply larger. Most people interpret that historical message to have only the most direct linear relevance, meaning: if you water the grass it will grow; if you make friends, you will not dine alone; if you constantly borrow, you will always be in debt. These things are true, although the point of my message was not limited to linear cause and effect. Expand the idea of cause and effect until it becomes three hundred and sixty degrees, spherically. Then you have a greater understanding that the large shall nourish the small, and the small shall

empower the large. If you would wish to have peace in your own life, then pray and work for peace on Earth. If you would have prosperity in life, then live by and support principles that can bring prosperity to others. In doing this, you will inform the one spirit of your heart's truest desires, and in turn the one spirit shall honor you with that which you seek for others. Such is the eternal dialogue."

I saw the goodness in it all, and strangely enough, it prompted me to ask, "Is evil the opposite of goodness?"

"No more than illness is the opposite of health. Illness is the absence of health. However, illness is not a condition which exists independently of health with the power to oppose it. Like illness, evil has been misconceived to have power of its own. Far too much attention and regard have been given to the concept of evil tempters, disrupters, and fallen angels under the misguided consideration that they have any power of their own. If my gift to the Earth was only to oppose evil, the gift would have been wasted. All gifts of love and goodness are given so that wellness may prevail in such abundance that evil is nothing more than a flyspeck which is ignored, if seen at all."

Because of the nature of that answer, I never felt it necessary to discuss the cast of "dark beings" which have played such prominent roles in the literature of conflict. I concluded from His reply that they do exist, although powers ascribed to them have been exaggerated by misconceptions of duality.

*"**Evil is not innate to existence**. Good and evil were not established as equal and opposite forces belonging to an eternal drama. **Evil is simply disconnection from God and denial of the love that you are!** Goodness is the other choice. Such a choice has to exist, otherwise the granting of individuality would have been a meaningless gesture. A choice has consequences. So it is with the choice of love or the denial of it. Avoidance of a choice also has consequences, and that is the **perpetual dialogue of indecision** which results in dualistic thinking.*

"However, when you consider the impact of evil, you must be careful not to judge the hearts of others, simply because you don't agree, or because their actions seem destructive. Much of what the world calls evil is really the struggle between oppressive structures and hostile retaliations. Many other actions that might be condemned are just the working out of some ancient disturbances of life by someone courageous enough to finally see it finished. Some situations embody the lessons which spirit is bringing

to a person from the great dialogue of interactive living and teaching. All these things can be viewed with tolerance, once their place in divine order is understood.

"Evil is derivative, not primal. **Evil created nothing.** Through love, God created everything, and **there are no other causes**—dualistic or otherwise. In the beginning there was not good **and** evil. There was **only good**! There is a difference between creation and derivation. **God is the source of all creation. Derivation is the result of choices!**

"The source of **all evil** is the denial of love which results in the ill-fated chaos of life unsupervised by love. When a person has denied the love that he is, he loses the power to command the affairs of his life. In its place he will use force or deception. Love commands. It does not control. When any person, situation, or element of the universe denies the love that it is, it loses command, and so it snatches control. The result is a heartless momentum of debased values, implemented by deception and controlled by force. Once a man has lost that deep indwelling power of love, when desperation strikes, he will strike back! No one, however, can initiate evil without a long term progression toward it, for there is no evil at the core of any child of God. Only through denying love and empowering one's life with attitudes of hatred, jealousy, and greed could one ever bring about situations which are ripe with evil. This is what I mean when I tell you that evil is derivative and not original."

So then I asked him, "Is evil just an illusion?"

"No, the consequences of denying love are very real. However, you must be careful not to judge what you see, **for your judgment will be illusion!**"

Then He explained: "Judgments are the mental mechanics of separation, therefore they could be nothing but illusion. By comparison, the mental mechanics of involvement result in discernments based on reality. There is a reality to evil, and I gave you the definition and the reason for it.

"Consummate evil is the intent or action of turning love against itself. That is a presence which most beings, being love, never understand or magnetize. There is no basis of coherence between evil and love, unless love has been denied. The greatest protection you have is to simply be the love that you are. In the two commandments which I gave to humanity—to love God with all your heart and one another as yourself—I gave the antidote for evil! If evil approached, you could simply say, 'be gone,' and *it would leave. The only reason evil is present at all is that the one spirit includes even that. God is greater than any rejection that can be made of Him, and He will not allow assaults of evil to disturb the oneness of spirit.*

"There are among you some great beings, strong in their love, who have been given the ability to actually see evil, that they may minister to the Holy Spirit and keep it whole. These great beings are in the ministry of the Holy Spirit." Although I did not ask, I seemed to know in my heart that this special group included His mother Mary, her many followers and the many legions of angels who maintain wholeness at every point.

Evil is a reality, but He added that it is not relevant for us to think about it or use it as a pretext to turn our lives into a paradox of dualistic situations. *"There is no learning in that, for compared to the Holy Spirit, evil has no power. Moreover, what most people call evil is an illusion generated by their own misconception or judgment. Once you have made the decision to love, evil has no more hold over you. Your only necessary involvement with evil is to make a decision. Without that option, without the right of choice, there would be no freedom for you and the declaration of your individuality would have been a mockery rather than a truth. The right of choice is your freedom. You can stay lost as long as you want, and you can come home when you're ready. In the meantime, you may experience all the lessons that the denial of love can bring you!*

*"There are no decisions that cannot be changed, and none have to last forever. This is why the Holy Spirit is always anointing its ministers with a higher understanding, so that the freedom of choice may be honored with a minimum disturbance to the one spirit. You might even consider the possibility that those beings who have denied God and love have made the ultimate sacrifice to prove that such freedom **does exist**. From a certain viewpoint this might even be viewed as a courageous act **of love**. For how can a being of love ever really be anything else? A thorough perception of that might end your dualistic thinking forever. There is no division of spirit."*

He said the spiritual exercise we need to focus on is the eternal dialogue of the one and the all. In so doing, life will unfold with growing pleasures amongst a few growing pains, but it will unfold holistically, not dualistically. *"A being's greatness is measured by his outreach, not by his containment. Not by how much you can hold, but by how much you can give. Containment is the way of structure, whereas outreach leads to freedom and the overflowing of life and basic goodness. One knows this in communion with the one spirit. Knowing and practicing this will end separation forever. You will at last break the walls that have reduced your awareness from the infinite scope of life's potential. If you want to have more influence, then be in communion with the one spirit. In so doing, you will be able to replace force as your survival mechanism, with grace and intuition. You will be able to reach out to the allness of infinity with your thoughts and magnetize the supply and joy of your life."*

In relation to this, there was an interesting comment He made about ethics. *"Ethics is the interactive rhythm between individuals and their collective matrix. A collective which does not support and elicit the true and greater ability of its individuals is ethically depleted. On the other hand, an individual who advances himself in a manner irrelevant to the greater well- being is ethically irresponsible."*

While we were on the subject of good and evil, it seemed an appropriate occasion to ask about Heaven and Hell. "Are Heaven and Hell places, or are they qualities of existence?"

*"If you consider that a quality of existence **is** the essence of a place, then the answer would have to be, 'both.' Like good and evil, however, Heaven is primary, while Hell is derivative. Heaven draws its power from the basic goodness in all existence and the willingness of life to obey the commands of Love. Heaven is anywhere that love prevails in the manifesting of existence. Let it begin in your heart. There is also a place close to the Heart of The Father where souls are made new again and healed from all illusion and suffering. This is the sacred experience of afterlife so lovingly sought. Even so, Heaven need not be confined only to that precious domain. Nothing would please The Father more if **all were Heaven!** Heaven can exist in your heart at this moment if you let it. Then, with equal grace you can extend it outwardly into your life. Eventually, as the universe moves toward its fulfillment, Heaven will be everywhere!*

"Hell, on the other hand, is the torment of a soul at war with itself, with God and with existence. You have heard that 'war is hell.' Well, I tell you that Hell is war. When a being of love has chosen evil for his direction, how could there be anything other than war?"

"How do we deal with that?"

"Forgive, forgive, and forgive again. What good will it do to add more conflict? Moreover, if you deny love, then where have you placed yourself? Man has created the societal nightmares you call Hell, through denials of love and forgiveness. There is a great fear and misconception about

forgiveness. You must understand that a man is not forgiven that he may return to mischief, but that he may return to God!"

"Are we not to fight for what is right?" I asked. There seemed to be a certain reflective pause upon His countenance as He selected the words for His answer.

"Let's begin by establishing some priorities. Instead of rushing out to fight for your judgments and presumptions, find out first **what is right!** *Then declare it, and establish your position in that regard. If there is to be war, let it begin by the hand of your adversary. If you are attacked, then command with love and fight only as necessary* **to end the war.**

"A son of God does not seek to make war, for war is societal cancer and a blight upon the Earth. War will eventually reside in the souls of its every perpetrator. Even the petty wars of social and business aggressions, and mental disputes will be visited upon the souls of its perpetrators. You are not here to disagree, but rather to find your commonality —your commonality with God, which is love, and your commonality with each other, which is love!

"A being at war with himself thinks nothing of starting wars in other places. That is an interesting aspect of evil. Once a person has denied the power of love, life opens very few doors for him except for those he breaks down with force or deception. War is often a desperate attempt to generate opportunities which no longer exist for those who have denied love.

"Receive this with understanding. However, be careful not to judge. The practice of judgment greatly restricts anyone's perception of life. There are only two mistakes of knowledge, and both of them are activated by judgment. One is knowing wrongly. And the other is assuming that reality is limited to what you know. As you grow and live, you are daily increasing your awareness of what God has put before you."

"In the practical sense of daily management, how can we apply the ways of spirit?"

"Through simplification of life, under the command of love. By way of the great spirit, you will magnetize to your life that which you need, and your love will shape it into that which you need and desire. Spiritual management, in the 'mop and bucket department' of everyday life, is the work of attraction and compression. That is just the right application of effort for a being of love. Consequently, you will enjoy it in the process, and you will have enough time left over for rest, recreation, and inspiration.

"Compression is the power of simplification applied to complex potential. The results are both commanding and instantaneous. Have you ever noticed that the most important actions or changes in your life began in a split second, in the twinkling of an eye? It might have been the recognition of an opportunity, the moment you knew an answer, the recognition of a purpose, the moment when you knew you were in love, or the time when everything came together. The instant of compression is a potent catalytic moment. It is a compelling recognition of personal rightness in the presence of its reason for being.

"You are accustomed to causing effects with force and action, rather than magnetism, attraction, and compression, therefore you must be patient with yourself as you learn a new direction. As you progress in your learning, never underestimate the power of baby steps. Compression is very potent! If you don't think so, just consider the power of one atom. How many adamantine particles do you think are compressed into one atom that its decompression can blow up a city?

"Here's a little story which demonstrates the effectiveness of compression on a practical level. There was a country gentleman with an acre to clear. That acre was overgrown with scrubby trees, weeds, and knee-high grass amid scattered outcroppings of rock. Not wanting to do the job himself, he drove to the back roads, where he hoped to find a strong country youth who would work cheaply. After visiting with a few neighbors, he found just the one he was looking for, and drove the young man back to his acreage. The owner had privately figured the job to be about twenty hours of work, so he offered him a flat hundred dollars, which sounded better than five dollars an hour. After examining the project, the young man was not very excited about working for such a small wage, although he didn't say that. He just considered the problems and answered, 'Yeah, I'll take the job. But do you mind if I work on it for two weeks?' The owner was delighted with the possibility of getting more work for his money. The key to the young man's plan was that he owned a flock of weed-eating geese and twenty goats. Placed on that acre for two weeks, the results would be transformative. Moreover, the youth had other resources. He had a neighbor near to him who owed him a favor. That neighbor owned a front end loader and a riding lawn mower. So, with the neighbor's consent, he borrowed that equipment to cancel the debt. After two hours of moving rocks and mowing grass, the acreage sparkled. The beauty of the young man's plan is that he coordinated and compressed all of his resources, to *which he added two hours work. The job was completed in two weeks as promised. The owner, who had kept an eye on the process, exclaimed with amazement and admiration, 'It's beautiful, but son, you only worked two hours. Don't you think you are a little pricey?' The young man reminded him that he had set the price! His employer admitted that the boy was right and gave him the hundred dollars."*

The point of the story is that through effective use of compression, the country boy figured out how to make some profit. What he **did not do** was as important as what he did. Namely, **he did not sell himself**. Instead, he sold the job! Rather than put a wage on his efforts, he placed a value on the results. He practiced attraction, magnetism, and compression under the guidance of value. His indebted neighbor had little ability to pay, so he figured that a loan of the neighbor's front end loader and riding lawn mower would handle that. The young man already had the goats and geese, which needed to contribute to their upkeep. He placed them on the land for two weeks, invested two hours of his own time, and the job was done. What an ingenious way of thinking and compressing! By integrating a series of options and combining them for focused production, the young man realized a profit. In the process, he exceeded the owner's expectations. The owner had no quarrels, although he was shocked, because he had a preconception that the youth was worth only five dollars an hour. By not agreeing with that judgment, the young man vindicated his own worth and also gave the man more value for his money.

In more ways than one, Jesus encouraged us to take the price off our heads, for indeed we each are priceless. Moreover, by submitting to hourly wages, we are usually working below capacity. His emphasis was on pricing the job, not the man or woman. Within that concept, I saw an incredible new landscape for economics. The new understanding revealed that true profit is not derived at the expense of others. A force-based economy actually yields no true profit to anyone. It just recirculates net gains while competing for advantages in an ever ascending, inflationary momentum which simply moves fast enough to conceal its debts.

In response to my realization, He gave me this additional understanding. *"Inflation is caused by counterfeiting profits. This is done through escalating the forward momentum of monetary exchange faster than debts can appear. Thus there is an **illusion of profit**. As long as technology, production, expansion, and human energy can sustain the momentum, the illusion can be maintained. This is why inflation takes a* *nose-dive very quickly in poor nations and conceals itself so well in the rich ones. Inflation is the economic freight train of a force-based culture. On the other hand, compression-based economies do not generate inflation, and do not consume lives. Eventually that will be the way of the Earth. Until then, anyone can start his own compression-based way of earning. Others will follow your success."*

"How do we do that?" I asked.

"Begin by finding in your life an ability, product, or service which has a value to others. Don't assign yourself an hourly wage. Even though you will be accountable for the quality and value of your work, you need the freedom to compress your own time and space in performing it. Every job has a realistic value on the competitive market place. However, working for hourly wages leaves you no room for true profit and gives a person no choice except to forcefully compete for illusionary advantages. Besides, there is no hourly wage that can match the potential of a child of God. Hourly wages are ultimately demeaning, although in the workplaces of today they are inevitable for most people. When that reality is unavoidable, accept it with grace and gratitude, though you do not have be limited by it, or allow it to make less of your potential. There are many salaried jobs which can be converted to contract employment, payable as tasks are completed. Other situations are suitable to bonus programs and production scales. Most creative employers welcome ideas which increase both production and employee morale. There are heavy structures and control agendas in the workplace which will not change quickly or on a whim. However, the change is coming. It will be mandated by circumstance! In the meantime, ingenuity and perseverance can make a dramatic difference through demonstrations of workability.

"Whenever you do something easier and better, you will inspire others to do the same. As you discover more effective ways for living and working, you will also have more time for play, study, prayer, meditation, and living! Everything you do is being watched and replicated. Through the one spirit, nothing goes unnoticed and the effect is very, very contagious."

He reminded me of a story I heard once in zoology class which is a very good illustration of the power within our shared lives. This story, which takes us into the animal kingdom, centers around an observation called the "hundredth monkey" phenomenon. The principle discovered in the following observations have since been studied extensively. According to the story, some anthropologists were studying a community of monkeys on an island somewhere in the south seas. The monkeys on that island had a primary diet of sweet potatoes. Their daily ritual involved digging a sweet potato, breaking it in half, and then eating it. Typically, they would eat out the center to avoid the sand, discard the rest, and then go back to dig for more. One day, by ingenuity or impulse, one monkey decided to wash his sweet potato. By washing the potato, it became entirely edible. That meant, of course, that there was less waste and he didn't have to dig as many sweet potatoes. For every single potato he consumed, the others would have to dig three. An added bonus was that he didn't have to spit sand, and I like to think he also had time for splash and play. His advantages must have been conspicuous. Nevertheless, his strange behavior labeled him as a weirdo among his fellow monkeys. He had broken tradition! Despite this simian heresy, intelligence and workability eventually won out. Shortly, his family and buddies began to wash their sweet potatoes, also. The number of monkeys who washed their potatoes slowly grew, although hundreds who kept to the old ways remained at a distance, viewing the beach parties with suspicion. The comfort and familiarity of digging sweet potatoes, spitting sand, and wasting most of what was found still outweighed the prospects for innovation. Therefore, change continued slowly. The anthropologist patiently counted each monkey, and noted little progress. Then one day a remarkable thing happened. When the hundredth monkey changed his ways, so did all the rest! There had been a roll-over phenomenon which transformed the mass consciousness of the whole monkey community. From that point on, all the monkeys on the island washed their sweet potatoes! Amazingly, an **even more remarkable thing happened**. This little island was only one of a chain of islands on which the dietary habits of monkeys were virtually the same. As soon as the paradigm changed on the first island, it changed **on all the other islands as well!**

Spontaneous synchronicity is the tangible, pragmatic result of spiritual dialogue. Consciously or unconsciously, communion between the one and the all goes on forever. Through responding to it with love we have our "Wow!" moments in life, those powerful spontaneous insights for which we do not labor. Another, even greater blessing comes from our spiritual oneness when we participate willingly and consciously with it from the depths of our being. Such communion will bring rare and exalted moments where inner and outer reality strike a perfect harmony.

Through our one spirit we touch one another and are blessed with friendship; we touch God and are blessed with peace; we touch a need and are blessed with opportunity; we touch a hope and are given a vision; we touch a feeling and are given expression; we touch a truth and are given a voice. Through childlike simplicity, we behold the spirit in wonderment. However, we do not find it by looking outwardly to the horizon, to the highest mountain, or to the North Star. The spirit is in our midst unseen, as it was so profoundly written in Luke 17: 20-21. *"The Kingdom of God does not come with observation; nor will they say, 'Look here! or see it there!' For indeed, the kingdom of God is within you."*

Chapter 6
The Heart Is
Your Higher Intelligence

The heart was the Master's favorite subject. He dwelt on it the longest, and frequently made mention of it to enhance the value of other subjects. For Him the heart was sacred, and most certainly it seemed to be His home ground. *"The heart is your connecting link to God and the universe, which integrates your own unique center of experience, awareness, and character with that which is beyond your comprehension."* Acceptance of that statement can only lead to the conclusion that the heart is our home ground as well, the point from which we burst forth into life and by which our immortal continuance is sustained. *"The heart is magnetic, silent, and still. The feeling of being there is like one of resting in a peaceful Heavenly lake, or floating in a vacuous space. As a magnetic center, your heart is the great generator of all your life energy, and whenever you empower your heart you raise your energy level physically, mentally, emotionally, and spiritually. Within the heart you will also find clarity, resolve, steadfastness, intent, stillness, respect, justice, kindness, and perceptions of greatness."*

One day as we were speaking about the heart, He requested that I refer to the chart I had drawn to illustrate the Grand Triangle. He indicated that there was one more element necessary to complete the diagram. His instruction was, *"Draw a circle in the center, leaving the circle empty inside, then extend rays of light outwardly from its circumference. This will add a focal point and also suggest an outreach into infinity."* It looked right, and the triangle felt complete. He proceeded to explain, *"If I were going to tell you where the heart fits within the pattern of existence, this would be a visual way of illustrating it for you. The heart is essentially the center point of stillness and peace from which one views infinity. As a being views infinity, he is activating all levels of potential within and around himself. The love that he is, the one spirit, and the adamantine particles assemble their patterns of existence under the heart's guidance. A person's soul is the integrated oneness of love, spirit, adamantine particles, experience, deeds, hopes, and dreams which comprise his life. The heart is the soul's gateway, both into life and beyond into eternity. The heart is the timeless and indestructible source of all higher knowledge. It is the one point within each person where the inner and outer forces are the same. Within the heart, the will of God and your own may be brought into harmony."*

Clearly, the "heart" which He was describing was something far more powerful and all encompassing than anything our common ideas would suggest. Therefore, one day I asked why He chose to refer to something so awesome and important by the name of a physical organ, even if the organ was of critical importance to our lives and an object of legend and story. He replied, *"The symbol is an important one with powerful life-giving connotations. You just need to expand your understanding of it. Like the relative stillness at the hub of a wheel or the eye of a storm, there is a point within your very existence where the physical, mental, emotional, and spiritual components of your life reside in a common purpose, in simple harmony. At that point there is no difference in space, time, or substance. The body's heart expresses that presence physically. The quality of life it generates can be seen in the vitality and strength of your blood. Blood is not an accidental symbol for life. Future discoveries in medicine will confirm that fact."*

As He proceeded to give me an expanded understanding of the heart, His words glowed in splendor against a backdrop of my own limited conditioning on the subject. What amazed me is how little of that prior conditioning had amounted to true knowledge. Even if it is not fully understood, there is probably no subject more talked about in our culture than the heart. We have a holiday in celebration of the heart, and then there's Christmas, Mother's Day, Father's Day, Memorial Day, and numerous other events which celebrate some aspect of our heart's devotion. Country music plays songs for the broken heart, and counselors seek to fix them. The heart's power is invoked on billboards, in magazine ads, and television commercials for purposes of selling everything from dog food to automobiles. Yet how little we know about its fullest and truest meaning. Concerning our bodily heart, physicians report that the physical organ has never been stronger, which accounts for our larger bodies and greater longevity. Yet, at the same time, heart disease is still on the best seller list of tickets to Heaven! The physical heart is a life giving organ, with deep and wonderful resources, most of which have yet to be discovered. Oriental medicine and philosophy have informed us about an important and wonderful energy field which surrounds both our bodies and our physical hearts, and every day more evidence is surfacing that this complex and intricate field of electrical energy is a life enhancing source to the physical heart. The study of acupuncture delves more deeply into this subject matter and is readily available to anyone who is interested in knowing more about the meridians in and around the body. That fascinating subject opens a whole new world of complementary knowledge to western science and medicine. There are also references to the heart which draw their meanings from popular psychology. There are many studies, references, and counseling therapies which address the differences between right- and left- brained approaches to life. One of the assumptions is that right-brained people are "heart people." In other words, they are emotional, intuitive, empathic, and responsive people while, in contrast, left-brained people are logical, analytical, competitive, and initiatory. This dichotomy is often carried to the extreme of referring to "heart people" as feminine and "logical people" as masculine. Considering the bicameral nature of the brain, there is a certain amount of truth to such observations. Nevertheless, the real truth is the reflection such limited assumptions cast upon the culture in which we live. One of the things which such ideas bring to light is the fact that in our culture, the heart has generally been considered the emotional, empathic, intuitive, and feminine side of our being. **The complete spectrum of the heart's power has been missed by most people**. All of the above considerations about the heart are important and valid, yet each alone is incomplete. Even taken collectively, they do not equal the Sacred Heart of which Jesus spoke.

This following statement is worth repeating, and He said it more than once to me: *"There is a point within each person where the physical, spiritual, emotional, intellectual, and intentional components of one's existence are in perfect synchronicity. At that point, there is no difference in elements, time, space, or condition. This is a personal 'zero point' which is known prior to birth, immediately after death, and anytime in between when a person's will has been perfectly reconciled with the will of God. A person is forever able to connect with his Creator in that sacred place, regardless of how far he has strayed through the process of living. At the point of true simplicity, you may enter into perfect communion with the Father. Whenever you do, your life will be renewed or even transformed.*

"The heart is a magnetic vortex through which the blessings of all essences and potentialities are received, integrated, and focused into living. Through the laws of electromagnetism, that power is converted into life energy. The heart, being essentially magnetic, functions best through innocent awareness which attracts and receives. Acts of judgment, which divide and repel, will shut the door of the heart behind you. If you would make the heart strong, you must first learn to perceive with innocence, accept, and forgive. As you empower the heart it will open to you. At first, you may simply notice this change as more passion for living, more peaceful sleep, or better digestion of food. The heart is the center of your health and quality of living, therefore those things will be addressed first. As you progress in your affirmations of the heart, however, your life will begin to have more abundant fruits, and you will have the energy needed to make more dramatic changes. Eventually, what you gain from your heart visitations will surpass your wildest dreams. There will be levels of energy which are transformational and transmutational."

In a world so preoccupied with power, is it not ironic that the heart is so little understood. For Jesus said, *"The heart center is the true source of human power."*

In response to that comment I felt impelled to ask Him about an issue that was now of great concern to me. "You have made it clear that Love is the power of the Universe, and now you have stated that the Sacred Heart is the center of power given to humanity. With such a positive foundation, why then is power such a difficult and corrupting problem for planet Earth?"

*"The problem exists not with power, but with **surrogate power!**"*

I immediately responded, sensing where He was leading. Nevertheless, I did not want to presume, so I asked, "What is surrogate power?"

As usual, He began His teaching by establishing the standards of perfect understanding. *"True power resides with God, and is indigenous thereto. Through enduring connections with the Creator, that power is transmitted to individual beings and all living things, to be held **indigenously within each life**. Such power can be lost or corrupted only through denials of love and separations from God, because all power from*

God is essentially pure. **Surrogate power is delegated by man to structure, authority, and forces external to himself.** *Surrogate power can extend man's influence over the environment. However, when delegated power assumes the rights of indigenous power, it corrupts very quickly. For example, when two men form a business together, they create a surrogate power. If it is understood as such and supervised equally by both, the structure they created can be useful. If one man should usurp the other and assume the delegated power only for himself, it will surely corrupt. Education of children is a surrogate power, delegated by their parents. As long as it reflects the values and wishes of the parents, that power is held in proper custody. Should it be used to undermine the indigenous power which exists between parents and children, there will be problems. A government is surrogate power, delegated by the governed. As long as it serves the needs of the governed and respects the indigenous power from which it was formed, that surrogate power can be useful.* **The moment surrogate power assumes the rights of indigenous power, corruption will begin.** *Usually this is implemented by the use of force, mandatory conformity, suppression of rights, and dishonesty. Surrogate power always draws its energy from indigenous power. When this is respected and openly acknowledged, surrogate power can be an effective extension of authority. Although, if force and dishonesty have* **reversed priorities** *to give the false impression that surrogate power is* **real power**, *you then have a situation where the flea is trying to own the dog, and enforcing its claim with threats and punishment.*

"Under such oppressive conditions nothing works better than a declaration of sovereign rights held by **indigenous power**. *This is the power of all true liberators. It's what the Founding Fathers of your nation did in 1776. It's what occurred with the abolition of slavery. It has happened within communities, families, careers, and personal lives. This is what happens when a person returns to the heart and activates the indigenous power established there by the Creator. Sometimes surrogate power fights back, although it never wins. For it has no authority of its own!*

"For each individual there is a responsibility to know and to honor the difference between indigenous and surrogate power. Your indigenous power lies in being a child of God, in the love that you are, and in your eternal covenant with the Father through the Sacred Heart. In the course of living you also delegate authority to many self-created identities, most

especially social, career, and achievement identities. Whenever such identities command and own your life, assuming the rights of indigenous power, then problems will arise. The term 'ego' has various meanings in your language. Nevertheless, the dysfunctional problems associated with ego might best be explained as the result of surrogate identities displacing the soul's true self.

"In the depths of your being is your own sacred center. It is the still, quiet chamber deep within where you are one with the Father. Through this connection is your own indigenous power. Therefore, you cannot underestimate the value of this knowledge to your life. Priceless to your life is knowledge of the heart itself. This is a place you must go alone, for it is your sacred ground. The very act of being there is the essence of prayer. When I told my disciples to go into a closet to pray, I was being quite literal in two regards. Any quiet secluded place will do. The main thing is to select a place which is appropriate to the sacred chamber you are about to enter within your being.

"The Sacred Heart has an exact location in the body which can vary slightly in every person, but it is approximately the same. It is located in the space between the spine and the physical heart, anywhere from an inch above the physical heart to three inches below it. Although the physical heart is slightly to left of center, the true axis is centrally located. People who are living very physical lives, such as athletes and manual workers, often have a lower position of the heart vortex due to their need for physical balance. Scholars and musicians might need to look a bit higher."

He suggested that I look a little higher because of my receptivity to aesthetic inspirations and frequencies.

"As you enter, you must release your attention into silence, letting it fall until it comes to rest. This is the way of quiet contemplation in which you may behold the oneness of all that is. This is your sacred place, for it is the pivotal link between the body and soul, the physical and the immortal, between yourself and God.

*"When the heart is healthy and fully alive, it is the most natural place to be. But when it has been forgotten and abandoned, certain difficulties will accumulate around the prospect of re-entry. **The most critical issue is that the heart carries an imprint of your true character and the love that you are.** That is its **only** recognition of you. Therefore, when you attempt to enter with false identities, spurious agendas, impure thoughts, or excess baggage of any kind, you may not present a workable entry key. You are*

*most worthy to be in the heart, for indeed it is your home, the center of your being. Nevertheless, as the defender of your immortal soul, its security system is formidable. By the will of God, that which is **not you** will not be recognized. All illusion, pretense, and judgment must be shed at the portal. Is this not also how you must enter the Kingdom of Heaven . . . as a little child?*

"There are two ways to enter. The easiest way is to quiet your mind through surrender and resolve, allowing your attention to become like a pebble cast into a great, still lake. Then float away into the stillness and vacuity until you come to rest. The other way is more difficult, although each attempt will bring you closer. The process itself is cleansing and transforming. It involves opening and reentering the heart directly, and re-anointing it as the sacred center which it truly is. In this approach, you will locate the doorway through which the heart communes with infinity, the one spirit and the Father.

"To begin, you need to be aware that a circle of energy surrounds your body. It is much like a protective cocoon. Then establish within your mind's eye a perceptual viewpoint on the back side of that circle, facing your spine. From that viewpoint, facing your back, scan the extent of your spine as if you were looking for the doorway to a cave. In looking for the heart's doorway, you may at first find the opening very small, but as you enter, it will dilate and you may see infinity laid out before you. For some people the door may be sealed so tightly that its presence will only be sensed, and a large stone, figuratively speaking, will have to be rolled away before the opening becomes evident. Never despair . . . the opening is there. You will find it if you continue to look and it will open when you knock. Do not be shocked with your first perception. You may sense the cold, dark air of the cosmos. Often there is a chilling effect, for spirit is cooler than the body. Some may see a burning bush at the entrance; others may see the door encircled with flame. Others will see, or sense, a mighty angel with a sword guarding the entrance. You may hesitate to enter because of your perceptions of holiness and want to take off your shoes, symbolically speaking, or rinse off in baptismal water. Those who are not ready for this perception will deny it or run, for the holiness they perceive is their connection to God. By entering the portals of the heart in this way, you will inherit the wisdom which was placed there for you from the beginning. Your unfolding consciousness of the Sacred Heart will begin to revive many dimensions of intelligence that have been lost to you. At the

very least, you will experience true relaxation."

He explained that the heart is always guiding our lives regardless of whether or not we call upon it or even acknowledge it. It is our sacred link to the Father, and it is always working as our higher intelligence. *"The Father is with you always through your heart, yet every visit to the inner sanctuary strengthens your relationship to it and your Creator. Just being there is prayer. It matters not what you say, for the Father knows your every need and desire. The prayer I taught my disciples was worded especially to facilitate a strengthening of that bond between Father and child, Heaven and Earth. It is the heart's function to honor the sacred bond."*

The Lord's Prayer is perhaps the best known prayer in human history. It has been translated in virtually every language of man, and has been paraphrased in numerous ways. Originally it was spoken in Aramaic, and a careful study of those ancient words can add greater strength and clarity to the familiar English translations.[10] The following is one of several renditions I have known since my childhood.

"Our Father in heaven,
Hallowed be Your name.
Your kingdom come.
Your will be done
On Earth as it is in heaven.
Give us this day our daily bread.
And forgive us our debts
As we forgive our debtors.
Lead us not into temptation,
But deliver us from evil.
For Yours is the kingdom and the power
   and the glory forever.
Amen."

*"When the bond is strong, words are insignificant. The words you pray are less important than **being** in the Sacred Heart. The special quality of the prayer I gave my apostles is that it was designed to take them directly into the Sacred Heart. It will do that for anyone who reverently contemplates the meanings contained within the words. The wording is exact, although unfortunately some translations have replaced the word*

'debt' with 'sin.' That is incorrect. You do not bring even so much as the word or the concept of sin to the Father within the sacred chamber, although it is both right and appropriate that you ask for your debts to be canceled at the door. Your Father desires for you to reside in completeness and abundance, provided you also wish it for others.

"Your Father resides in oneness and perfection, knowing nothing of sin. It is from each other that you need to be asking forgiveness. This is why I said that if a man has offended his brother, he first needs to go to his brother and ask forgiveness. Then he will be pure of heart and may enter the temple. When you are pure of heart in that way, you are one with the Father. This is what I meant when I said, 'Blessed are the pure in heart, for they shall see God.'

"Most often when I spoke of the temple, I was referring to the Sacred Heart and not to an architectural edifice. Just as surely when I referred to the Kingdom of Heaven, I was referring to the zone of perfection which is the bond between God and man, and is found within the Sacred Heart. God is the author of perfection. **Wherever that perfection dwells, Heaven unfolds. Man's doorway to that perfection is the Sacred Heart. Seek it first, and all else shall be given to you.**

"Inside the sacred silence, you may experience bliss and quietness, and receive a healing, or nurturing. Or you may see infinity unfolding before you. This viewpoint of infinity is the source of your higher awareness. It honors you, the love that you are, as a unit of one in the eternal expanse of all that is. There in that center of priceless wisdom, you will find dimensions of specific intelligence which are ever guiding your life into pathways of right action. There are seven dimensions of intelligence which resonate outwardly from the center of your heart. You may at first regard them as principles for living, but as you master them more fully, you will see them as dimensions of greater knowledge and ability. They are: unity, love, life, respect, honesty, justice, and kindness. Through these dimensions of understanding the heart can restore wholeness in an infinity of ways, to achieve an infinity of results, from an infinity of starting points. This is the capacity of the heart.

"All reality including material existence arises from infinity, not the other way around. Infinity stands with God as prior cause. As a child of God, you stand with infinity also. **Infinity is the unlimited potential of God, which first manifested as awareness, then as love, next as spirit, and finally as an infinite supply of adamantine particles which can be**

arranged in an infinity of ways. Now remember that as an aspect of God, you are part of infinity, not part of the resulting structure. This position, in the order of things, allows you to have a viewpoint of infinity and to look upon the vastness of physical existence without being overwhelmed by it. This is how you can be an individual, utterly unique in a universe which thrives on duplication, replication, and similarity. You remain enduringly yourself, for you are part of infinity and thus incomprehensible to the physical universe. You are an expansion point of God's infinity, and the viewpoint from which you perceive infinity is your heart. The heart is your gift from God. It is your eternal bond with the Father."

I thought for a moment and then asked, "Were we not originally one? From the viewpoint of the One, is there not already infinity? Why was anything more needed?"

And the Master replied, *"If you had a radio with one speaker and mono-dimensional sound, even though it was perfect and infinite sound, would you not prefer it to be stereophonic? The Holy Father, the Source of Infinity, is indeed One and the One Infinity. Nevertheless, His greatness extends beyond that to generate what might be called **stereophonic infinity**!*

*"That was accomplished through His children! You see, the singular infinity of the Father precedes the children, but together with His children is the living essence of a stereophonic universe. Without the children, there could not be stereophonic existence—a phenomenon which is created by attaching the principle of infinity to an infinite number of viewpoints! **You are thus the richness of the universe, the depth and completion of it all**. It is so important that you respect your individuality and the self-awareness that you possess. From that self-awareness, you derive your capacity for thought and imagination. Contained within it is your right to be an additional source for infinity and creation. Without self-awareness, you would merely be a conduit, unconsciously responding to preordained conditions. Self-awareness is the ignition which sparks your ability to be a secondary source of infinity. Within that infinity, you will provide dimensions for expanded existence. The universe is a partnership, wherein the Creator may have rest and the Created may have freedom! It is a relationship which you also can experience symphonically with others by seeing the eyes of the Father when you look into the eyes of your brother. As you do that, you are extending the symphonic richness of infinity."*

In my experience, it seems that we fall short of recognizing this symphonic relationship through indifference and disregard. All too often we overlook our fellow man out of disrespect, dislike, jealousy, or simple unawareness of his value to life. There is a piece of rural humor which captures the essence of that omission. It's about a farmer who had a beautiful piece of property and a wonderful farm. Though the work had been hard, his crop was abundant. Close to harvest time he was standing alongside the tractor appreciating the bountiful yield when his minister drove up and parked beside him. The kind reverend gestured and remarked, "Son, God surely has blessed you with a beautiful farm." The farmer replied, "Well, Pastor, He has indeed, and I can't tell you how many times I have given thanks for it all. But you know what? You should have seen it when He had it all to himself!"

Jesus said, *"You are indispensable to the continuing expansion of infinity. You **are** the extra dimension! The heart is your gateway to performing in this extra dimension. It is the beginning of your higher intelligence."*

Jesus explained that in the course of living, several levels and qualities of intelligence are involved in the creation of consciousness and the manifesting of solutions about the problems of life. The highest intelligence is love itself. For love alone holds the ultimate secrets and solutions for existence. The lowest intelligence, relevant for man, is bio-genetic, which takes care of bodily functions as well as providing impulses for survival. Bio-genetic intelligence is unfit, however, to formulate policies for living due to its extreme fear of death and its adversarial approach to the environment. When bio-genetic intelligence attempts to create philosophy, it views morality as the product of punishment and guilt, while power is seen as a territorial imperative. Racial, political, and social similarity become the bases for social inclusion or exclusion, and God is viewed as a partisan ally in the struggles of life, provided one has been obedient, of course. Fortunately, above this level of intelligence is a mind capable of gathering and assimilating much wider perceptions and information about life. As a man becomes more consciously aware, the narrow viewpoints of bio-genetic intelligence are supplanted by a broader spectrum of mental abilities and capabilities. Jesus explained that the mind is a vast memory bank which assimilates information and integrates experience into logical patterns for practical application. Its greatest product is rationality; its greatest limitation is a dependency upon structural concepts. *"The mind is an integrational facility of alternating functions which are electrically encoded in binary mathematics, much like a mechanical computer. Mental intelligence is a system of knowledge created by the environment which it serves. An environment may be as small as one's daily life or as vast as the cosmos. The semblance of expansion in the mind comes from the simple fact that within the smallest systems are patterns which connect and eventually lead to larger ones. Nevertheless, it matters not what size the mind is. A mind is still a servant. Therefore it does not have the intelligence of mastery."*

When the mind attempts to create philosophy it does so in concepts of idealized form. Consequently, its formulas often fall short of the actual realities of life. Propriety, correctness, and reform are the mind's concept of morality. Power is viewed as proprietary control of knowledge, and society is based on management hierarchies. To the mind, law is an issue of correctness rather than fairness. If mental intelligence considers the reality of God at all, it is through idealized concepts designed to separate perfection from imperfection in order to pass judgment upon it.

Despite its limitations, the mind is a valuable servant which above all has lifted man to a place of dignity within his environment and given him dominion over the forces of nature. The mind has given man a vast array of information about the universe, and the leisure in which to contemplate it. In gratitude for this service, there is much to honor. Nevertheless, considering the mind's inadequacy to **compassionately** explain life, is there any wonder that legions of humanity have reluctantly preferred the explanations of life provided by bio-genetic intelligence? At least bio-genetic intelligence is pro-life and ally-supportive within small circles of familiarity! These considerations were the basis of a discussion I was having with the Master when He made the following critical statement.

"It is imperative that man acknowledge the heart's higher intelligence, for the mind alone cannot tell him who he is, and genetic intelligence is a lethal weapon when combined with the technological potentials in the world today. By comparison to the mind, the heart is a function of intelligence based on the ultimate in simplicity and synchronicity. Its matrix is a synergistic center of awareness which perceives a unified relationship with all that is.

"The levels of intelligence available to man could be summarized as survival, logic, synchronicity, and love. All four are present in the lives of each person, although a man will focus on the one which assists him the

most. If he knows little about the heart's intelligence or the greater intelligence of love, he will emphasize one of the other possibilities. Genetic intelligence is well equipped to sustain physical life and to interact emotionally with the environment. Mental intelligence can formulate reports and engineer rocket ships. Neither, however, is equipped to give meaning to life nor to establish a connection with Divinity. Attempts to apply them beyond their means has led to destructive misconceptions.

"Ultimately there is one infinite and connected intelligence. That is the one spirit. Perhaps this could be referred to as the great Cosmic Mind, although the term 'intelligence' would more accurately describe its function and availability to all of life. A mind, precisely speaking, is composed of at least minimal structure due to circuitry, self-contained integrations, and proprietary applications.

"Only the heart's simplicity can comprehend infinity and connect Heaven with Earth in a meaningful way. From a center of equilibrium, quite like the hub of a wheel, the heart unfolds its awareness in seven concentric rings of understanding. Each succeeding dimension of intelligence builds upon and completes the one or ones coming before."

The first dimension of intelligence is Unity.

This is the primary awareness that there is but one God, one power, which is the unifying force in all of life. This awareness affirms the oneness of spirit, reveals the wisdom of the ages, and provides insight into the larger order of things. Through respect for unity, one comes to understand the patterns of cause and effect which permeate all of existence. The intelligence of the heart reveals cause and effect to be a great deal more than linear consequence. An action which is good for the whole may be repaid in an entirely different manner, yet in a way which is also good for the receiver. *"Where unity is supreme, there is nothing more adaptable than goodness. Just as water seeks its level, so too, goodness seeks its application. Due to the power of unity, even actions which were intended for harm can be redirected by God into some form of goodness.*

"Unity is also the source of intelligence, for it grants the ability to integrate knowledge and to correctly define priorities. That is the beginning of wisdom. Integration is the principle of successful thinking and living. Without priorities, there can be no focus in life and no values. This translates into higher intelligence when you understand that there are core issues in everyone's life relating to dominance. Dominance is always an issue in the world. Competition hinges on the problem of dominance,

ranging from business to military conflict. In personal lives there are endless battles for position. These things are easy to see, but unfortunately competition for dominance does not end with the obvious. Food cravings and other addictive compulsions are simply competing with natural functions and striving for dominance. The list is endless. Until one allows God to be the unifying force in life, there is nothing else capable of ending the chaos of competition. All addiction and compulsions are the result of false dominances and surrogate powers. Perhaps the greatest dominance of all is that of manufactured identities to which a person, himself, has suspended his rights. Such identities are very addictive. It is false dominance that has led you astray, burned your time, your hopes, your dreams, and your love. Without false dominance, you would have infinite wisdom at your fingertips and the time in which to use it. In the presence of unity, which is God, the One, the Supreme, you have all the power you need to fulfill your life and existence."

He suggested that we meditate on the principle of unity when we are in the heart, and declare that God is the one and only power that may determine our lives. The more we open ourselves to this awareness, the less other things will have the ability to control us. God's power will then translate to us through the heart, that we may have command of our lives.

The second dimension of intelligence within the heart is Love.

*"Love is the power of the universe. Therefore, your greatest defense in life is to protect, honor, and respect love in its many forms. When you maintain this principle with clarity, your life purposes will come into view. This is because all of your purposes are etched in love. Love is beyond just a feeling or an orientation. It is a dimension of intelligence and purposeful living. Above all, it is the **essence of beingness**. A person who is operating with a commitment to purpose has higher intelligence than one who is not. A person who is operating on his true purpose is then able to assign values to life. The heart's intelligence is cumulative. Through perceptions of unity, priorities are established. Then love assigns the purposes. Furthermore, love heightens a person's instinct to nourish, enhance, and apply those purposes. Love is both a way of being and also a pathway for becoming. Love ignites life. Love savors life and sustains faith and hope. Even though life often brings lessons in hard packages, learning happens only when forgiveness has occurred and love is restored. It is love that ignites the learning. Only with love can learning occur. That is how you take something from the school of hard knocks and transmute it into a*

permanent gain for yourself. You can then say, 'I don't have to do this again. I have completed the lesson. I know the meaning.' Love brings certainty to life, and when your love is clear and unpolluted with regrets or false desires, you will have the confidence to live your life with passion. When you are certain of your love, there will be fuel for passion. With passion, there will be fuel for life. Meditate upon love as the power of your beingness and the essence of who you really are. Earnestly apply its principles and you will be successful in love and life."

The third dimension of intelligence within the heart is Life.

"Life is love in action. The hope of life is meaningful experience, happiness, fulfillment, and continuity. Life has indwelling intelligence. Follow life, serve the living, and fulfill your love by following the pathways that life is revealing to you. There is great wisdom in that simple process. This is why I told my disciples to follow life and let the dead bury the dead. Dwelling on old mistakes is very costly. Life and the living will light your way and unfold your future. Instead of watching life through a rear-view mirror, look before you and behold the current possibilities with innocent perception. In practicing this, you will cultivate the inborn intelligence of how life works and how the love that you are can foster better involvements with it. Forgive yourself and others, for yesterday has already been lived. That is what I meant by 'the dead.' Be here now and face the path in front of you, for that is where life is.

"Regard the present moment as sacred. In this, you will find answers to many problems which have baffled you. Respect life in all its ways as an unfolding of experience. Life is not behind you—it's in front of you. It is not history or a memory. Life is that which is birthing before your very eyes. Know that, and your intelligence will become a dynamic force rather than a stagnating body of knowledge with formulas for mortal structure."

The fourth dimension of intelligence within the heart is Respect.

This is a word that has lost a great deal of meaning in our world today, although in the Orient, respect is still a very important dimension of honor. I had always considered respect to be an aspect of protocol. Therefore, I was very curious when He referred to it as a dimension of intelligence. *"It begins with respect for God, respect for yourself, respect for your brothers, and for all life forms. Respect is a point of honor, although it is a great deal more than that. Though we are one in spirit, each being is unique in love, purpose, and life. Unique qualities belong to each person and endow him with abilities, freedoms, and responsibilities that may not be present for another. Each person, and every aspect of life, is irreplaceable. What you do not bring to the Earth, no one else will. Respect begins with knowing that you and your Creator have a covenant, and in that covenant are all the answers and resources you need to make your life work. Then you extend that right to others. This ultimately leads to respect for Divine Order, which is the highest intelligence. Knowing this will give you strength to release your worries. Most of what you worry about never happens. A certain part of your trials must be accepted. The remaining part that you might wish to change will require focus and resolve, which you will not possess if you spend all your time worrying. Composure comes from respect for Divine Order. Do not complain, for that is disrespect. Do not wallow in self-pity, for that is disrespect of self. Why should a child of God feel sorry for himself? That is the essence of denial. And in so denying, do you see how you disempower?*

"Through respect for Divine Order, patience is cultivated. This brings knowledge of proper timing. In that is great intelligence. Often other issues and other needs have to be worked out before your plans can unfold, before your place can be set at the table. By respecting all things, and most especially Divine Order, you will attain peace and patience. Through this, you will be directed to the most efficient use of your life, so that you can experience self-respect to the fullest. The greatest act of self-respect is to honor the Sacred Heart as the seat of your covenant with God and your access to higher intelligence."

The fifth dimension of intelligence is Honesty.

"The practice of honesty will reveal the power of innocent perception." Innocent perception was the sweetest part of all of His teaching because it required nothing more than being alert, with eyes wide open, like a child watching a caterpillar. He said that innocent perception was a crucial factor in all new findings, because we must set aside our filtering concepts in order to discover what has not yet been revealed. It is also through innocent perception that we come into the presence of God. *"This is why I said you must become as little children to enter the Kingdom of Heaven.'*

"Without honesty, there is no such thing as higher intelligence. In many ways, honesty is the summation of other dimensions of intelligence, for how can one even access intelligence except through the practice of honesty? How can intelligence be applied to life unless a situation is honestly evaluated? It is unfortunate that honesty is regarded primarily as a guideline for morality rather than an aspect of intelligence. Honesty

*brings solutions to every problem of life, as well as science, law, and social management. Honesty begins with the most simple question, 'what is it?' followed by a direct uncensored answer of **what is**.*

"The most dangerous person ever to deceive is yourself, for in doing so you destroy your basis for honesty. Honesty is the foundation of intelligence, while dishonesty is the foundation of stupidity. Therefore, the first step for any science, study, or project is to establish the basis for honesty and honest progression. Compared to that, theories are secondary. If researchers had spent as much time establishing foundations for honesty as they have in proving theories, learning would have advanced a great deal further. The same is true for social management. For example, honesty is the critical ingredient in formulating workable budgets, ventures, and productions.

"Many doors are shut to a dishonest person. Even if he could enter, he could not walk through the maze of his own self-deceptions. This includes honesty about habits, relationships, ideas, careers, and plans. You are not going to go any further than honesty will carry you. Contemplation of honesty will open the chambers of your heart and opportunities in life which have been hidden from you."

The sixth dimension of intelligence is Justice.

Justice is the foundation of all civilization and all cultural intelligence. When justice ceases, civilization crumbles. Justice is a great deal more than morality and the execution of law. It is also fair play. Justice is the golden rule of fair exchange.

"Exchange is the basis of life in the universe, from the most elemental particles to the most complex human situations. Justice is the intelligence of exchange and balance. When balance is maintained, health prevails. This is true in all things, from a healthy person to a healthy planet.

"Through practicing balance and fair exchange, you will develop wisdom in your discourses with life and with others. Your instincts will alert you to the validity of ideas, as to whether a project will be fruitful, or whether a job is right for you. You will also know how to determine fairness in wages and pricing. All things return to balance eventually. Being a wise and effective custodian of those balances is the hallmark of justice. There is a special dimension of intelligence in the heart which allows this to happen."

He explained that our common practice of competitive pricing, confirmed by a consumer's willingness to pay, does not necessarily mean that a correct value has been determined. *"There is a fair price for everything, and that derives its justice from an exact ratio of displacement. How much energy, time, effort, and ability was spent in producing the product and service? Paying too little and paying too much are equally damaging to the act of exchange and both will inhibit a return to equilibrium."*

I thought about the many countries where price haggling is still a way of life. With a sense of whimsy, I asked, "Are we supposed to challenge all prices?"

With an equal sense of whimsy, adorned by a smile spreading across His face, He replied, *"Only if you're willing to challenge the low ones as well as the high ones! Challenging prices or any other exchange only for your own profit is less than true justice and will weaken the intelligence of your heart. Justice is the principle of fairness, and it works both ways!"*

A few years after my conversation with the Master, I was reading a very interesting book in which I saw a corollary to His statement. The writer of that book mentioned that to bargain was to "bar gain." I took this as confirmation of what the Master had taught me, and decided at that moment that I was going to arrest my love of bargains, and earnestly apply the principle. Until that moment, I had rationalized that sales, happy findings, flea markets, and garage sales were exceptions to the rule. After all, what someone else had devalued seemed to be fair game. That very day, however, I had a chance to discover the real power of fairness. I was starting a new painting and needed to purchase some canvas. The canvas I use is very fine Belgium linen, which costs somewhere between sixty and ninety dollars a yard. Due to the price, I don't usually store a lot of extra footage, and neither does our local art supplier. Therefore, I'm always pleased when an extra roll has been stocked by the store so that I may purchase it by the yard. The morning when I called, there happened to be an open roll. Gratefully, I promised to "be right there, so hold two yards for me."

On arriving at the shop, I exchanged greetings with the manager, and he proceeded to cut the two yards I had requested. I had not asked the price because I knew the probable range, and besides, this was my only chance among local stores to find such quality material. When he handed me the ticket, I saw that I had been charged thirty dollars for two yards. Without hesitation I said, "That's not right." He was startled with my remark and asked, "Did I overcharge you?"

"No, no, you have **undercharged** me. This isn't even close to being right! Get out your catalog, and you'll see." As his finger ran down the column of numbers in his wholesale catalog, I could see that my bill should have been one hundred and ninety dollars, instead of the mere thirty for which he was willing to settle. Assuring him that the correct price was what I wanted to pay, I stressed that I wanted him to feel justified in selling canvas by the yard! I'm not sure if he was shocked, embarrassed by his mistake, or amazed that a customer would care about his interests.

Nevertheless, he protested my offer and said, "No, you can have it for thirty dollars."

I continued to argue, "Figure the fair price."

He scribbled on some paper then gestured with an open hand, "What the heck, let's just say I'm closing out the roll for fifteen dollars!"

What really happened that day was a mutual gesture of friendship which was more important to both of us than the price of canvas. I tried to pay him the whole amount, and he would not take it. So, instead, I proceeded on a shopping spree to give him the business he deserved. That way, I was able to reciprocate on some level which was acceptable to him. After that, we were especially good buddies, and he was always delighted to point out the sale items and volume discounts. This was such a gratifying experience that I began applying the same principle everywhere. Now, when I see something on sale, I ask first, "Are you really sure you can afford to sell it for that price?" What this expresses is a genuine desire to be fair. What happens is often amazing. There is a corollary to this also, which is the other side of justice. By giving justice, I receive it.

The greater lesson in that experience was a confirmation of what the Master had told me about love and exchange. *"In every exchange, love is the element, energy, and willingness which allows it to happen. Stealing, invasion, or trespassing may be brought about with force or deception. There is no true exchange, without love. You may think you are exchanging merchandise for money, but what you are really exchanging is love. You are exchanging friendship, rapport, confidence, trust, and values that build justice. When justice is gone, trust is gone. When trust is gone, civilization is gone.*

"Don't think you are going to disadvantage yourself by practicing justice. You see, everyone has special advantages in life, according to his covenant with the Father. By not pursuing unfair advantages, you are blessed with greater clarity about your own opportunities and advantages.

Everyone has advantages. In order to find them, a person has to first surrender his pursuit of unfairness. In self-pity, a person may protest and say, 'I don't have any advantages.' Who would have thought Helen Keller — both blind and deaf—had any advantage? It may seem that she had every disadvantage in the world. You see, this is the law of the meek who inherit the Earth. When you forfeit and surrender all pursuit of unfair advantages, you find that you are sitting in a gold mine of advantages that have been given to you. That gold mine can only be found in the innocence of your heart."

This brought to mind an example. There was a man who had pursued a life of crime until he was arrested and sentenced to prison. Actually, he was a repeat offender. Finally, the judge barred any more options for parole until he made some really major changes in his life. While in prison he began studying law, and other subjects, which he began teaching to other inmates. Before long, he became one of the strongest motivational forces in the prison. To make a long story short, he is now a prominent member of the New York Bar Association, and author of many books on the human decline into criminality and prison rehabilitation. He is now a very respected man. His recovery could not have happened, though, until he reached "the bottom" and ceased his pursuit of unfair advantages.

That example caused me to pause and reflect before asking the Master this question. "Most often when justice is mentioned, it is in regard to retribution or law enforcement. I can see now that the subject is far more extensive than that."

He replied pertinently, *"If containment of criminality were the only reason for justice, it could hardly be regarded as higher intelligence. **The true purpose of justice is not about containment of anything! Rather, it is about adjustments and resolutions. Justice is a way of life which nourishes goodness and stewards the never ending flow of exchange!** Nevertheless, criminality flourishes when there is widespread **injustice**. To make a comparison with personal health, you may relate the disease of criminality to the onset of serious heart trouble after years of stress and unhealthy living. Justice is like water. It finds its own true level if there is enough fairness and exchange to accommodate the flow. When adjustments cannot be made, desperate measures will often be attempted. There are many possible causes of criminal action. Yet, when a society practices justice, there is no fertile ground to permit its cultivation."*

"What about the typical person," I asked? "Most people I know play by the rules but do not think much about justice. Most people are just looking for opportunities to get ahead in a way that does not break the rules. How does the average man find his advantages in life?"

"Instead of imitating or resenting each other, be like unto the Father. You are a child of God. Restore the connection, for there is a unique and special reason that each person was created. In that truth, you will discover both your advantage and your justice."

The intelligence of justice brings us to understand and care for the natural balance in all things. Considering the vastness of the universe, and the complexity with which our involvements are intertwined, how can we always know the greater forces of equilibrium? Therefore, giving and forgiving become essential elements of intelligent living.

This is where kindness enters, not only as an expression of grace, but also as intelligence . . . perhaps the greatest of all.

The seventh dimension of intelligence is kindness.

"Kindness is not just an act of charity to the young, the vulnerable, or the needy. It is the will of God for everyone. Your goodness is strengthened through kindness. It is the will of the Father that you know and use that power to be a wise custodian of what you have been given. Through acts of kindness your own abundance increases, for you have multiplied the ways in which your giving may be returned to you.

*"Kindness is not often mentioned in the world today, and few have any understanding of what it really is. There is even a disregard for kindness as an act of propitiation made by the strong to the weak—a compensation for their dominance. Thus, many are embarrassed to accept kindness. If you contemplate kindness in your heart, however, you will find it to be a far more interesting subject than that. The world regards kindness as a compensation for life, or a gentle protection from its harsher realities. Actually, kindness is the **heart of living**. It is what makes life bearable, meaningful, and delicious. You may begin by asking yourself this question, 'What would be the greatest kindness I could do for another? Then what is the kindest thing I could do for myself?' Be specific. That is the key to unlocking the intelligence of kindness. Generalities about kindness may lead to lovely sentiments which are inapplicable to your circumstance. You may be surprised with the answers you are given to direct and probing questions."*

As I paused to think, I realized how many false perceptions we have about kindness. How conveniently we settle for social courtesy and consideration as the limit of kindness. How readily we show concern while avoiding true involvement. How many children have been indulged, when a warm hug and a firm "no" would have been the greater kindness? How easily have we indulged ourselves, when restraint would have been the greater kindness? How often have we worried all night, pacing the floor, when going to sleep would have been the greater kindness? How frequently have we contemplated revenge, when we should have forgiven and released?

"In order to develop the intelligence of kindness, you must discover the joy of truly giving and forgiving —no strings attached, not even so much as for glory or recognition. A man who reserves his offerings only for exchange or control will soon lose the intelligence of kindness. Next, you must learn how to be kind to yourself. Some people are afraid of being kind to themselves for fear that it represents weakness, or that it may lead to indulgence. Others eat chocolate and watch TV all day. That is avoidance of life; not kindness. Such disabling habits exist because they do not know what kindness is. In tapping into kindness, you are literally tapping into the intelligence of God. In understanding kindness for yourself, you also understand it for others. It is the will of God that you be kind to yourself and others."

Until that moment, I did not realize the degree to which I had equated kindness only with gentleness and tenderness. With a startling realization of how much more it is than that, I felt impelled to ask, "What **is** kindness?"

*"**Kindness is the right use of will.** Kindness is GOOD WILL — expressed as caring, helping, refraining from hurtful actions, sharing, making life work, and consideration of others. Kindness is strength in action. The confidence that comes from showing kindness is a masterful influence over any situation. Think about how much strength it takes to honor your true potential instead of diminishing it. Consider how much strength it takes to show good will to someone who is hurting you!"*

Brian had given me a good example of that several years before. There was a lady who worked above him in a supervisory position. She terrified everyone with her pushy, angry, aggressive, and domineering personality. Brian privately called her "Hell on Wheels." Then one day he collected himself, and said to her, "You know, you are actually a very sweet lady." From that point on, she was kind to Brian. He saw the real truth behind the facade of horrors, and with an act of kindness, their whole relationship changed. This was one of many assaults which had been stopped with a kind word.

"Kindness builds strength, and strength builds greater kindness." As I thought upon that statement, I recalled another situation in which His truth had been illustrated.

I once observed a little dog as it was being struck by a car. I had been told by others not to touch an injured animal, for its pain might stimulate very aggressive behavior. At that moment, however, such considerations had no relevance in my heart. I just picked up the animal and took him to the clinic. Actually, he growled and snapped a bit, but it wasn't frightening compared to the confidence I had about helping the little creature. That act of kindness saved his life and enriched mine.

From this larger perspective, kindness can and should be seen as a guiding light in every part of our lives. Sometimes it involves eliminating the unworkable. Such a kindness was required of me toward a painting I was creating in 1978. The subject was a girl running along in bare feet, wearing a bright green dress, and carrying a bouquet of balloons. Behind her was a stone wall, with a carnival in the distance. It was a very complex painting with a number of problems I could not seem to solve. In those years, I had unbridled energy for painting and sometimes would paint all night. That particular evening was different. I was wearing thin as the painting went from bad to worse. With honest evaluation, I realized that nothing could be resolved in the top part of the composition. For hours I worried over why it had fallen apart. Then I caught myself. **Why** it happened was irrelevant. With mat knife in hand, I walked over to the canvas and sliced off the top half. It was a mercy killing! All that remained were the skirt and the running feet. Strangely enough, it was dazzling and fresh, and my agony was over. It was the kindest thing I could have done that night, both for myself and the painting. Little did I know, at the time, that it was also one of the kindest things I had done for my future. Prior to *The Lamb and The Lion,* that newly downsized painting entitled *The Flight of Spring* was to be the most successful painting of my career. Through it, I acquired a contract with one of the leading publishers in the world. As a fine art poster in 1980, it became one of the best sellers in the world, and placed my name in commercial marquee lights for six months! Clearly, this demonstrates that kindness can come in strange packages. Often it comes as a surprise to both giver and receiver!

As I look around in our culture, there is evidence of an awakening to kindness in ways that were not present a decade earlier. The marketing concept of "consumer friendly" and "user friendly" gives some evidence that business is now paying attention to the power of kindness. Let's be realistic. Whose merchandise would you rather purchase—that of an unkindly business or a friendly one? For whom do you desire to work—a supportive company or an abusive one? Who tends to generate more personal empowerment? Whose products will serve you better? Would you want an automobile that was engineered by a company with hostile management practices?

Jesus compared the universe to a fine piece of equipment which works beautifully when operated sensitively and intelligently. Kindness is not just the caring we give to the helpless and the vulnerable. *"Kindness is the consummating dimension of the heart's intelligence, the will of God for life itself. When I use the word intelligence, do not confuse it with the dry detachment of mental reasoning. True intelligence is merely certainty and understanding, which bring both clarity and passion to life. Another way of saying the same thing is that within the Sacred Heart are seven passions: Unity, Love, Life, Respect, Honesty, Justice, and Kindness, which bring understanding and focus to living. Together they generate COMPASSION, which is the soul's true knowing."*

Chapter 7
Bridges

"You are not alone, if only you would cross the shortest bridge to rediscover the love of your Father and the love of your fellow man."

A bridge is a feat of engineering, a thought, or a power which provides a connection or transition from one space to another, or perhaps from one dimension of understanding to another. In the course of experiencing and living our lives we traverse many bridges. These bridges may appear as the structures that span rivers, or as thoughts that convey meaning, and indeed as expressions that bring confirmation of understanding. According to the Master, there is no bridge greater in its connecting power than Love itself.

In the most beautiful possible way, the Master brought that realization into my heart. As *The Lamb and The Lion* neared its completion, I looked at the pasture full of sheep and remarked how peacefully they were grazing in the valley. The painting had a striking quality which captivated my heart and stirred memories of the Twenty-third Psalm. No sooner had I mentioned my observations, than He began reciting the words of that Psalm. **Except there was one difference** . . . He placed Love in the commanding position of each phrase.

"Love is my shepherd, I shall not want.
Love makes me to lie down in green pastures.
Love leads me beside the still waters.
Love restores my soul.
Though I may walk through the valley of the shadow of death,
I will fear no evil,
For my rod and my staff is Love.
Love prepares a table before me in the presence of my enemies,
And fills my cup to overflowing.

*Surely goodness and mercy shall follow me all the days of my life
And I will dwell in the house of Love forever."*

He was fond of reminding me that God is Love, and the totality of what we experience is essentially love in one form or another. Love is the ultimate bridge to recognizing the presence of God in our lives. Then one day, He added a new element to that teaching. *"Your life is determined by love and directed by your thoughts and actions. According to the nature of your thoughts and actions, your love either will grow in strength, or else become reduced, altered, misconstrued, or even inverted."*

Jesus was reluctant to speak about conceptualizations, ideas, and thought processes until He was confident of my greater appreciation for Love's power and the Sacred Heart's higher intelligence. Therefore, in revealing His messages to you I have respected His preferred sequence of presentation. According to Jesus, *"The mind is not a good starting point, for it is entirely derivative and has no primal energy or power. In searching for primal essence, the mind does not have a clue."*

Once He felt that I was able to discern between mental activity and higher intelligence, He began to discuss the realm of thought. As a university teacher, my greatest challenge and satisfaction had been to assist students in thinking more clearly and effectively. Obviously, thinking is a crucial part of our nature and a powerful aspect of intelligent and focused living. Consequently, once He was willing to discuss the subject of thought, my curiosity blossomed as I sought to understand where it fit into the spectrum of intelligence and ability.

*"The place to begin is with simple awareness. Awareness is primal. Awareness belongs to the Father, to the one spirit, and to every particle of infinity. Everything in existence is aware. Just consider the particles and sub-particles within an atom —how the patterns of exchange are exact and predictable. By what knowledge does that occur? How do roses know when to bloom? How do birds know where to migrate? How do herds of wild sheep know where to find water? How do the Monarch butterflies find their way from Canada to Mexico City every year? Everything in existence is aware. Awareness is where intelligence begins. Yet, the simple presence of awareness does not imply that any thought is necessarily occurring, nor that consciousness as you know it has been created. Concepts, ideas, and thoughts are **crystallizations of awareness** which implement and stabilize awareness or else hold the promise of doing so. Thoughts develop from a*

sequence of useful probabilities."

"Could you please tell me more about that?"

*"Let's take, for example, a Paleolithic hunting party. Life is proceeding by instinct, experience, and necessity as hunters trek homeward after a bountiful expedition. Due to unexpected weather conditions, and their long distance from camp, it becomes necessary to pause along the way for smoking the meat and preparing the hides, or else their harvest may be lost. As they look around for favorable locations, one man sees a large, flat rock which can provide a good working surface. In that situation, the rock's usefulness is nothing more than momentary convenience, and a perception that would be remembered. They did, indeed, remember that rock. On the next hunting trip they planned to find it. Then, season after season it became a ritual stopping place. After many years, due to weather changes and herd migrations, the hunters took other directions where there were no similar rocks. On one occasion, they set up camp in a forest. There, one man notices a large split log and makes a connection. Remembering the flat rock, he has **an idea**. He proposes to split some other trees and arrange them to make a flat surface like the rock. **Now there was thought!** That culminating action represented a direct progression from the rock's functional service to a connection which resulted in the creation of a table. Once a table existed, then further thoughts could give it meaning and multiply its application. The table was "created" through focused awareness and associative linking. Thought was the vital connection—the bridge to creation! Something that had been a useful convenience finally crystallized into a point of conscious functionality and thereafter would be a mental furnishing as well as a practical item in the life of the tribe."*

He explained that the development of symbols occurred through a very similar process of conscious connections. *"For example, ancient man was a stargazer. From these observations, primitive maps were drawn which represented both locations and directions. At first, such maps were nothing more than pictographs of stars or land formations arranged so as to establish a language of associations and connections. With simple observations and associations of mountain peaks, stars, rivers, hunting grounds, camps, and ceremonial areas, a pictographic language was developed. From where did this incentive come?*

"The desire to connect is strong in mankind. It is a desire which has propelled him to his greatest achievements throughout the ages. Included

*in this desire is a primary urge to connect experiences, feelings, reflections, and aspirations in such a way as to add a responsibility factor to native awareness, thus transforming it into integrated consciousness. Conscious-ness is developed both within each individual and among the many, **for consciousness is the direct result of establishing useful connections. Love ignites the desire for unity, and thought manifests that desire through making the connection.***

"History is full of such realizations. Just consider how, in ancient times, heavy objects may have been moved on rolling logs until one day someone made a connection and 'invented' the wheel and axle. The difficulty of maneuvering whole logs was an unnecessary burden, con-sidering that two large wooden disks could be threaded by a smaller log which would freely turn as the disks rolled along. Through focusing awareness, first there is consciousness, and then a development of thoughts, concepts, and ideas. Awareness is the primary condition. Thought is the connecting link."

Jesus explained that mankind periodically enjoys long passages of simple awareness in which consciousness is developed before there can be sudden realizations of conceptual clarity, such as the realization that rock surfaces can be replicated with split logs, or that rolling logs can be more effectively replaced with larger disks and axles.

*"Thought is a connecting link within consciousness, within experi-ences, and within all manner of relationships from social to spiritual. Without 'thoughtfulness,' human relationships would have little quality or meaning. **As you think, so you connect. As you connect, so you think!***

"Once there is a connection, there is also a direction, a sequence. This is where thought acquires its meaning, for in its application to life thought acquires direction—a reason for being. Thought is like an arrow placed in the bowstring of life and propelled by love. Inherent to thought is a vector."

"What do you mean by a vector?"

*"A vector is a direction implicit to the arrangement of two or more elements. For example, if you told someone that you were born forty miles from where you now live, you could be referring to a number of places. However, if you clarified that your birthplace was forty miles **west** of here on Interstate 20, then your hometown could be located on a map."*

"I understand in the physical realm how vectors determine directional orientation. What is unclear to me is how thought can have a vector."

"Let's consider a simple instance in which you purchased a bouquet of flowers. Perhaps you saw it and bought it on impulse without a thought at all. Or perhaps you planned to brighten your dining room with it, give it to a friend, or use it for an artistic composition. A concept by itself is just a focusing of awareness. Thought involves the directing of awareness with intention. **Power is applied to a thought through the directions you place upon it.** *Ideas have little value unless you apply them and allow their impact to continue making connections for the building of life. "*

He then proceeded to elaborate that a vector is comprised of two or more points which constitute a direction or intent. *"Where this concept takes on immense importance for affecting life is that the **first point creating any vector is always love.** Love is the beginning of all things and is the basic power behind all of your thoughts. The second point is the way your love is directed by your thoughts. How are you applying love to life and what are you doing with it? The very tapestry of your life is woven from your love and the vectors you have used to extend it. Trouble arises when your mind uses thought to control, reduce, or subterfuge your love instead of allowing your thoughts to be **outwardly** directed into life. A mind will attempt to control thoughts until it owns them, and then turn them back upon you to influence your behavior. In visualizing the power of thought, the most compelling metaphor is that of a bow and arrow—**thought functions best as an arrow drawn in the bow of love and pointed away from the sender!***

*"Let me give you a real life example of how thoughts can be used to undermine the power of love and diminish the quality of life. There was a postman who hated dogs. Therefore, he naturally magnetized their hostility and was often attacked. Though he took precautions and was armed with physical defenses, the problem was a constant source of stress in his work. So he enrolled in a mind control seminar in hopes of developing a better 'mind set,' which could redirect existing patterns or at least produce some better defenses. A degree of improvement was attained, but only in so far as a thicker veneer now existed between the man and the problem, which gave him some relief from the daily worry. **Nothing had really changed, however, because the mind has no power to change one's life.** That privilege is reserved for your heart alone. The postman discovered how powerful that truth is when a close friend suggested one day that he forgive the dogs which had attacked him. In a sudden burst of unexpected grief, the postman's hatred finally melted away as he realized how the problem*

began. As a child his fondest plea was for a puppy. Unfortunately, his parents lived in an apartment which was barely large enough for the human occupants. Christmas after Christmas the child wrote Santa to ask for a puppy, although sadly there was never a puppy in his stocking on Christmas morning. When the boy was ten years old he saw a stray dog on the street and reached out to pet him. The dog lunged at his face and bit the boy's cheek. While the doctor was putting stitches in the little torn face, the child was formulating thoughts which would reverse his original desire for a puppy. These new thoughts brought 'explanations' as to why he should **not** *have one. Although his desire for a dog was gone, he had not removed the original love.* **He had only buried it beneath a change of thoughts.** *From that moment there would be a problem, because thereafter his thoughts would be turned* **against** *the original love instead of projecting it outwardly into life. Relief and healing came only when he was able to forgive the first dog that bit him, and more importantly to forgive his parents for not allowing him to have a puppy!*

  "Love is the only power in life, and it is the original point to which all vectors of thought are connected. *Where there are contradictory thoughts, there also will be difficulties. Until one's relationship to love is changed in the heart, nothing fundamental will change in life. What is perceived as negative emotion is not the absence of love, but merely reversals of thought which are undermining love's power and goodness. Love disabled by negative thoughts can be a dangerous thing, for there is no greater power than love, and nothing closer to the soul."*

  Our conversations also touched upon the connection between love and purpose, for that is also a relationship based on vectors. *"That vital connection begins with the love that you are, and extends outwardly into life through covenants with the Father and others with whom you share life. In other words, your true purpose is simply a practical extension of the love that you are which has been established by the Father and given to you within the patterns of Divine Order. It is your duty to be yourself, to love the Father with all of your heart, and to utilize the abilities which spring from that connection.*

  "The world would have you see your duties and priorities differently. From the time you were a child you were taught to perform, not according to personal incentive but rather according to instructions and conditioning. Certainly every child needs to accept the needs of others above his personal will. However, that is not the real reason for such conditioning.

The world wants you to prove yourself! Thus you can be owned by your
willingness to earn an identity! There are many qualifying conditions
established by the world. For example, before you can do, you must have!
Money is required to purchase education, equipment and materials for
producing. Although professions do, indeed, have the right to establish
standards of performance and excellence, those entrusted with that
guardianship would be wise to remember that all vectors of thought and
action attach to the primary power of love and beingness. Material
advantage and competitive achievement alone cannot produce quality
performance. Love and the beingness thereof determine all quality. If
priorities used to manage life do not reflect that reality, there will be
problems. When structural considerations dominate and control life, there
will be many dysfunctional relationships, and the ensuing demands will be
contrary to natural life patterns.

"There is great potential within each soul which is ignited by the
*willingness **to be**. To unburden the world's false conditioning, it is*
necessary to know and to honor that truth. From time to time, it is
necessary to go to the mountain, to be alone with yourself and one with
your Father. In such moments you will discover how much you have been
given. If you want to find out what your true potential is, you must consider
its Source. Rediscover your own love, which will bring light to everything
else you have been given by the Father. As you do that, your life will begin
to make sense."

I took a deep breath as I noticed that the Master's posture had
straightened and His eyes were focused with great intensity and power
upon me. He then declared in a voice that was little above a whisper yet
which sounded like thunder in my heart, *"Will is the Father's bridge to*
you. It is the Father's will that you be with Him always in love and service.
In accepting His will, you become the Father's bridge to bring Heaven to
Earth and Earth to Heaven."

I sat in quietness for a few minutes, savoring the magnificent Presence
in front of me. Then I responded with curiosity. "You have said many
times that we have been given free will to pursue the nature of our love and
our need for experience. I am awed and thrilled by your revelation, yet I
can't help but wonder how the free will that has been given to us can still
exist and also be resolved with the Father's greater will."

"Will is not just a strong thought or the projection of intent and
persistence. Too often, the concept of will is misused to suggest an act of

stubbornness or self pursuit. **Will is the activation of wholeness.** *Will is the unity of impulse and focus which ignites individual potential and directs its performance for the good of all. How could that power and privilege truly belong to anyone but the Father? Nevertheless, it is your right and duty to* **discover the function of will** *within yourself and within all of life. In this exploration you have free pursuit. In your own life, you will discover the harmony of your own will with the Father's by realizing and empowering your higher purpose. Now just listen quietly to a few words from the prayer I taught you to pray. 'Thy kingdom come, Thy will be done on Earth* **as it is** *in Heaven.' It is the Father's will that heaven and Earth* **exist in harmony.** *In affirming that, you bring yourself into alignment with your Father's will. I did not tell you to pray, 'Father, your will be done and disregard mine.' Nor did I tell you to pray, 'Father, may I have everything I want?'* **True will**—*the Father's will—is the power of activation within a synergistic whole. Because of this, I assure you there is a point to be found where your will and the Father's are one. It is your duty to diligently search for that point. That is the covenant you have as a child of God. It begins by knowing that you* **are** *the living bridge. The prayer I gave my disciples is a timeless affirmation of the bridges between Heaven and Earth, between brother and brother, between man and God. In fulfilling your covenant to bring connections to life, your perception of will can be in harmony with the will of God."*

"Is this what you meant when you said in the scriptures, 'I and My Father are one'?"[11]

"Essentially, yes. Our Father is the source of all love. I am love, and you are love as well. In that respect we bear the same name. Insofar as anyone fully becomes the love that he is, then there is oneness with the Father. My Father and I are one, for I am the bridge. So too is humanity a bridge between Heaven and Earth. Everyone has a covenant and a purpose which is special, and if you do not fulfill it there is no one else who will. This is the greater truth of wholeness. You might compare the universe to an immense puzzle which will not be completed until every piece is in place, and there are no substitute pieces. Each person is a piece in this magnificent puzzle, and every purpose must be fulfilled. When I said that my Father and I are one, I meant that no one is going around me and no one will replace me. I have surrendered utterly to the will of my Father. The same right has been extended to you in relation to your covenant with your Father."

That insight was further developed a few days later as we enjoyed a more casual interchange of words. Although His presence was enormously elevating to my experience of life, He also graciously joined me on my reality level and often amused Himself as I exercised my creative freedoms and even trivial pursuits. With never-ending courtesy and caring, He understood my need for a little distraction from the overwhelming power of His splendid truth. One day I rolled in the TV and we watched *Bonanza*! As always, there was great synchronicity to the events which happened in His presence. He would insightfully expose the lessons contained even within common occurrences and highlight them with creative parables. As we watched *Bonanza*, the fictional story became a background for exposing a number of higher truths. To briefly summarize, Adam Cartwright had been entrusted by his father to deliver and sell their cattle in a distant market. In order to consummate the business transaction, his father had given Adam a letter of authorization to sell at a certain price. Upon arriving at his destination, Adam met with resistance from the buyer who did not want to pay the agreed price. Although the buyer insisted on re-negotiating and demanded to speak with his father, Adam was very firm. He assured the buyer that in speaking to the son, he was speaking to the father. Jesus said, *"That is what I mean by covenant. You have a letter of authorization to do what you are here to do and no one has the right to refuse that letter if you offer it in good faith according to the Father's will. No one has the right to dismiss you or to use the greater glory of your Father to dim your light, virtue, or worth. You have been given that degree of respect by your Father, and your courage in accepting it will be honored. Regarding your covenant, no one is going to replace you or bypass you. The power of authorization is the privilege of our Father and cannot be assumed by another, simply because of desires and aspirations, or because of the belief that another has failed."*

That statement reflected His enormous respect for everyone. As I absorbed the clarity and directness of His message I became more comfortable with the truth that "will" belongs only to the One who sees the wholeness of existence and is a power which humankind may only **discover and exercise.** Within our relationship to Divine Will, there is freedom, respect, and fulfillment. His revelation about "will" was expressed as a simple holistic assurance that the grand design would not be complete until every piece was in place. *"This is what I meant when I said every letter of the law will be fulfilled, because the law is you and me and all that* *is. The law is reality. It will be fulfilled completely, and nothing will be left undone."*

As He spoke those words, His eyes were radiant. In their glow, I could see His love for even the tiniest butterfly, and I could appreciate the possibility that a butterfly which fluttered its wings in Japan could effect a storm in Africa. Nothing was insignificant to the Master. *"Where there is love there is power in the least of creatures, and there is no order of importance, because existence is seamless."*

Among the many bridges we discussed, the subject of belief was immensely revealing. Never before had I realized that beliefs are only bridges to that which we consider to be beyond our grasp. While beliefs are indispensable to our confidence in living and our spiritual well-being, the fact remains that beliefs are bridges and not an end in themselves. In realizing this, I wanted to know more about the relative importance of **what** an individual believes, versus the simple power **of believing**. "Is there an order of importance to the subject of beliefs?"

*"There is, and it has nothing to do with belief systems. Each person's true beliefs derive from his covenant with the Father. These are the only beliefs with power. All the rest are the result of conditioning or speculation. For you to know what to truly believe you are going to have to enter the Sacred Heart and in quietness behold your eternal connection with the Father. This is because your true beliefs lie on the altar of your heart. I can tell you **to** believe. I can even tell you **how** to believe. **What** you are going to believe, will stem from one of three causes: your covenant with the Father, conformities to the world, or extravagant self-pursuit. The choice is freely given to every man. What you believe is an outward manifestation of your own state of being, magnified by your expectations, purposes, and experiences. It is not for one to judge the beliefs of another, but rather to help him honor the belief which is in his heart according to the love that is there. The purest belief is that everyone should have his own relationship with the Creator. This should not be overshadowed by belief systems. Belief systems are the outgrowth of conformity among people concerning the nature of their common aspirations. It is important that you know the difference between belief systems and the power of pure belief. As you have greater clarity about yourself, about life, and the rest of existence, you can strengthen your beliefs and use them to build the bridges of your life."*

"Isn't it through beliefs that we are connected with the one spirit?" I questioned. His answer, as always, was very much to the point.

"There is no place where you are not connected with the one spirit. Yet, belief is like a thought cast into that oneness. There is direction and intent within all beliefs. If you were to examine your beliefs you might ask, 'What vector am I establishing with that belief? How does it connect with my truest self and where is it going?' Surely the arrow of belief is as swift and true as the arrow of thought, and it will find its mark. There is nothing more vulnerable and formative than spirit. As you interweave your love, thoughts, and beliefs with spirit, your life is formed. You would be wise to respect that truth in all its applications."

As He was completing that idea, I began to wonder about the subject of beauty. It had been the nature of my experience as an artist to first believe in the painting and then see it appear! The first sign of realization always came in the form of beauty. We had not talked about beauty very much. Perhaps it was that I was more interested in things I understood least, rather than things I understood most. At that point, I sensed there was more to beauty than I had suspected. I was not quite sure what that might be, so I began by asking, "Is beauty a bridge, too?"

"Actually, beauty is the result of many bridges from numerous points of origination forming exquisite patterns of harmony. Beauty is a choir of singers, a chorus of dreamers, a concert of aspirations, an orchestration of goals, a symphony of ambitions, and a ballet of production. The presence of beauty is evoked by coordinated vectors emerging with delight and perfection. This is true regardless of whether the beauty lies within a flower, a song, a sunset, or a magnificent painting. Beauty is an affirming and uplifting signal of positive surroundings. Often beauty is a living indicator of rightness on your pathway. Unfortunately, structure can counterfeit beauty in a multitude of ways. This is why distrust of beauty has arisen in some people. Those who can discern between appealing structure and the light of inner beauty, will be guided in their pathways by beauty. In the presence of true beauty, you will sense the presence of God and your oneness within His will. This is why there is such desire for beauty in life, because it brings with it affirmations of harmony and well being."

He then proceeded to expand His instruction concerning life's bridges into greater application and depth. I came to understand that the predictable correlation of cause and effect is one of the finest bridges we could ever know. We all want to know where we are going and hopefully to have some degree of choice and determination over those directions. Much of the mystery and stress of life could be relieved if we would only observe the predictable patterns of cause and effect. **In so many ways He made it clear that whatever we have done will be done unto us.** Whatever we have given will be returned in similar ways. I questioned His assurance. "If cause and effect represent a reliable bridge to connect the present and future, then why do the virtuous often go unrewarded and the villains gain such riches?"

"This is less true than you would think. The superficial appearance of inequity is due simply to insufficient consciousness of how balance occurs in the universe. There are two aspects of cause and effect which behave somewhat differently. One is the linear, predictable aspect of feeding a hunger and seeing it disappear. This immediate response factor has no respect of persons or agendas. With total reliability, it works for both the ruthless and the meek. The disadvantage lies in the fact that opportunists eagerly seek to master such predictable factors for the extra benefits which control can bring, while humble and virtuous souls often consider that cultivating predictable effects may be cheating! Such considerations are tragic for they disconnect more vulnerable souls from the laws of God. The laws of God were established to arm and protect the virtuous—if only those laws would be acknowledged and consciously affirmed. The law of cause and effect works with or without consent or deliberate knowledge, although conscious participation and readiness greatly enhance the built-in rewards.

*"There is a second and greater dimension to cause and effect, which is holistic completion and balance. Due to the oneness of spirit our universe is seamless. There is within this oneness a common heart which feels and knows the rightness of all things, which balances and heals in ways that exceed normal understanding. This Holy Center of existence responds to the **cause and effect of love** rather than the cause and effect of action. Thus, a man may give to one and receive from another. He may toil in a factory and be rewarded by the love of his children. He may selflessly give of his time to conserve nature and be rewarded by the teachings of life. He may visit the sick and be healed of his own self-pity. He may forgive one man and be forgiven by others.*

"This is a dimension of cause and effect which cannot be manipulated in selfish ways, for it is activated only by the nature of each person's love. As you express the love that you are, there is no limit to the blessings which can unfold before you."

As He said that, I recalled His beautiful rendition of the Twenty-third

Psalm in which He expressed the power of love to guide our lives even through the shadows and darkness. I sat in reverent silence for a while, too moved to speak. Then my thoughts returned to practical considerations and current affairs. "There are many people today making predictions. Are they simply reading the patterns of cause and effect and projecting them into the distant future, or is there a greater knowing?"

"A person can know a great deal about future possibilities by examining the patterns of cause and effect. An intelligent person, armed with information, can observe the patterns of cause and effect and logically predict the consequences of long-range tendencies. Nevertheless, if you really want to know where your life is going, look in your heart. Any prediction is only as valid as the heart's support of it. The minute the heart changes there is a whole new scenario. Remember the example I gave you earlier of the postman who finally forgave the biting dogs. After that there were no more dog bites. Therefore the future was changed. Every time the heart truly changes, the future is going to change. The heart is where the inner and the outer are in perfect fusion and perfect oneness. The minute that changes, everything else changes as well. This is why I say that any prediction is only valid for as long as the heart does not change.

"There has always been too much emphasis on external change. There is nothing wrong with making external improvements. Cleaning house is a constructive pursuit. However, a clean house does not make a home. Many people are in a state of burn-out today because they are trying frantically to change life by do, do, doing, or think, think, thinking, and it is not work, work, working! A simple change of heart would handle the problem.

"A powerful change of heart, especially when it is experienced by many, can alter all former predictions. When I walked on the Earth two thousand years ago, the existing conditions were such that a great cataclysm could reasonably be predicted to happen within the following five hundred years. However, that did not occur."

He smiled and radiated pleasure, and a few minutes passed before He continued. *"Why do you think it didn't happen?"*

Instantly, His broad smile was reflected upon my own countenance, as a sense of elation enhanced my inner certainty. "Because a whole lot of hearts changed after you were here!"

He smiled. *"There was a time, two to five hundred years after that when there should have been another great cataclysm. Again, it did not happen. As long as hearts are changing, external predictions are subject to continual revision.*

*"The major forces which invest in prophecy are the forces of structure. Structure requires predictable momentum. Structure invests in prophecy in order to hold itself in place and to keep from being changed. Such prophecy can range from probability analysis, to yearly planning, all the way to long-range investments. You see, prophecy is not merely an esoteric perception. It is also a reality-based observation and a bridge to predictable living. The art and science of prophecy can be abused, however, if it focuses upon emotional and spiritual content designed to penetrate the heart and solicit the heart's support for matters that are only temporal. **Structure invests heavily in keeping the hearts of men from changing so that prophecies will not be undone.** The heart is your true source of prophecy, for it commands the point where the internal and the external are one. It is a far more accurate diagnostic tool than anything the external can provide. All you have to do is enter your heart in order to know your future. The Sacred Heart and its seven layers of higher intelligence will tell you everything you need to know about how your life is unfolding."*

I hesitated for a moment before asking my next question. My sense of reservation disappeared, however, when the corners of His mouth curled a bit and His eyes beckoned me to speak. "If prophecy is simply a reflection of temporal possibilities which can fade or crumble behind the greater power of the Heart's truth, then could you reveal to me the continuing validity of the Book of Revelations?"

"The Book of Revelations is a great deal more than a book of prophecy. It is a timeless revelation about the soul's fulfillment in its return to the Father, along with the perilous demise of all that is false as that alternate potential falls away in the light of truth. This book is not subject to the normal pitfalls of prophecy because it does not center its meanings around the temporal probabilities of life, nor is that the intent of its message. This sacred document has been greatly misunderstood to be an unfolding drama of external events. Certainly a profound transmutation of the human soul would be impossible without correlations and manifestations within outer forms of reality. Therefore, some physical phenomena will accompany the drama, especially considering that the very elements which fall to dust will be the structures of worldly dominance.
"Man cannot realize his sonship with the Father until first he has released all that was created through unconsciousness and disconnection. False

identities, false meanings, and unworthy structures will fall away as the soul is empowered to manifest its true covenant. This is a glorious event to be approached in love rather than fear. Many hearts are changing today before the moment of critical mass and as hearts change toward love, so too will external consequences be reduced. What is to unfold is crucial and inevitable to the destiny of man. No one is exempt. However, there is a choice in how one receives the unfoldment. Those who approach it with love will find it the ultimate bridge to fulfillment."

There is a great deal of concern among many people today about impending cataclysmic events foretold by prophecy. It is rather amazing to think that in His presence, when I could have asked so much, my attention was never directed toward the ominous or to the thought of possible disaster. As He completed the above-mentioned thought, however, I made the one and only inquiry in all our conversations about the possibility of impending catastrophe. His answer was firm, positive, and contained no fear.

*"The structures which dominate the lives of man today were all created in a state of disconnection and unconsciousness. The powerful momentum of these structures carries with it the seed of continuing oppression. In order to survive, such creations must suppress the soul of man and perpetuate his enslavement to them. As the time of man's fulfillment arrives, there will be a simultaneous collapse and retaliation of that which wishes to survive **against the good of man**. This exposure will, nevertheless, assist in the elevation of man's consciousness and bring about a new era of brotherhood on Earth where structures are re-established from a state of **consciousness** and **connection** with Divine Order."*

I then inquired, "Will there be great suffering?"

"Suffering is never the will of the Father, although none will be exempt from the experience. Many will feel little suffering except for the compassion extended to those who do experience pain and sorrow. At the other extreme there will be many others who are so attached to that which must fall that there will be no reprieve from their agony. Even this is a blessing, that lives full of anguish may bleed the venom and thereby have a chance to heal. How the event is experienced will be due in large part to individual choice, and also to the accumulated necessity of fulfilling choices made long ago. Regardless of how each individual receives the impact of change, it remains enduringly true that all mankind will be

blessed with the results of that human transfiguration."

Until the day that such a complete transformation of human potential arrives, there are many bridges which may convey our lives to higher levels of consciousness and ability. According to the Master, it is imperative that we seek always for higher ground because, *"A problem can never be solved at the level of its creation and existence. Every problem has to be solved from at least one level of awareness or ability above it. One of the greatest mistakes mankind is making in regard to life's problems is to address them on the level which caused them to occur and supports their persistence. This leads only to struggle, fighting, and perpetual frustration.*

"To solve a problem it is first necessary to view it from a higher level. This is especially easy to observe in the area of physical healing. A physician or any medical facility can only arrest an illness, keep it from progressing, or reduce infection, thus providing conditions in which healing may occur. The actuality of healing is always a miracle that happens on a higher level through the restoration of wholeness. No matter what the problem, healing always comes from a higher level."

I thought about the many people in America today who have weight problems. They are forever seeking the ultimate cure-all, from diet pills and programs to exercise and hypnotism, in hopes of finding the silver bullet which can solve the problem with one timely application. In response to this and other similar problems the Master recommended that we search for a higher viewpoint which encompasses the problem rather than directly seeking a confrontational encounter. He suggested that we *"Find out for what you are really hungry, and from what you really need to purge. What grief is causing you to bury your life in distress? With those answers, put your life in order and seek to bring more wholeness into the way you live it. It is always wise to seek higher counsel, both Divine and human, to discover ways of implementing a solution to any physical problem. As that solution appears you will know it by the wholeness it brings to your life."*

In regard to improving the quality of our lives, He used the parable of a ship going through a canal, such as the one in Panama, which connects two different elevations of water. This teaching was in reference to an ongoing process which can elevate our lives to higher levels of completeness and fulfillment. *"Upon entering the first lock you will see only the high walls surrounding and containing the water. Accepting this is essential to confronting the limitations you are currently experiencing. It is a matter of faith to confront one's sense of lack and restricted vision* *knowing that when the water level rises, there will be a miraculous change of circumstance. As the gate opens and your ship is ushered into the next lock, the power of greater wholeness will reveal itself. Then unfolding before you, there will be a **new set** of high walls obstructing your vision beyond that level of attainment. Again faith and consciousness will be required to bring the water level up to the newly desired plane. Through every lock the process will be the same. Then suddenly one day the last gate will open and reveal the ocean's magnificent horizon. There will be the new Earth, the dream come true. Until then it would be well to remember, as with the parable of the canal, that no matter what your attainment level, you must have the faith to look around your life and ask, 'How can I make the most of what I have?' Begin with simple possibilities such as making friends with a new neighbor, forgiving your brother, or paying a debt. Remove thorns from your side, such as finding someone else to mow the lawn. Perhaps some remedial help is needed for a child having study difficulty. At times a second job can be useful, or possibly a vacation is even more needed. Wholeness is not invoked by the search for one shot solutions. The search for specialized answers to complex situations yields very little bene-fit. A never-ending pursuit of greater wholeness is the answer to ascending the levels of your life."*

He emphasized that a little bit here and a little bit there works beautifully. Soon enough there will be new vantage points, greater insight, and the quality of life will have risen. A simple example, common to us all, is the frustration we can experience working late into the night with unresolvable problems. Finally, there is a surrender into sleep which brings peace and refreshment. What seemed so difficult the evening before, then appears in the morning as an obvious answer. During that time of rest, the degree of energy, awareness, and wholeness were elevated **above** the problem. If we allow ourselves to be limited by the walls which define and create our problems, we are denying ourselves the vantage point of higher intelligence.

He iterated, *"As you look for solutions, seek for wholeness. The bridge to wholeness is an increasingly broader perspective and an increasingly greater inclusion of life. The world of structure would have you believe that reality is that which is permanent and illusion is that which is changeable. It would have you believe that when a thing is changeable, it is just illusion. If it is permanent, then it is real. According to the Creator, anything is real that is composed of love, spirit, and adamantine particles.*

These three aspects of reality can be shaped and reshaped in an infinity of ways or perceived from an infinity of directions without diminishing their reality. Life is a veritable river in the fluidity of its possibilities."

Through the understanding that He bestowed upon me concerning the fluidity of reality, I can now appreciate the critical role of free will in the life of each individual. If infinite potentialities can exist simultaneously within reality, then there are important choices to be made. Those choices will affect the way iɩ which reality encompasses our lives. With that realization, I can now remember and gain special insights about the great miracle when the torn painting was healed. When I look back upon the day it was damaged, I can recall the tear in great detail as my finger gently touched the gaping hole and felt its raveled threads. In casting my memory toward the following day, I saw the painting whole as if nothing had ever happened. Its wholeness struck me as a luminous glow of impenetrable force and integrity. Now, when I contemplate those two divergent perceptions, the visual image is like an endless curtain extending through infinity. On one side of that curtain was the apparency of damage, while on the other side was a condition of wholeness which had never been altered. That twofold perception demonstrates to me how many potentials for manifestation may coexist in such a way that **both** are possible. Either one could have persisted according to choices made about them. However, *The Lamb and The Lion* was painted so completely out of truth and love that the reality of damage found no place in which to survive. This exposes a critical point about life. In the many possibilities that may coexist in any given situation, do we not create persistence for the one we choose? There is a great responsibility in knowing that we do indeed choose the direction and quality of our lives. This concept would certainly correlate with the Master's teaching about the heart and its power to **change** our lives. Because when our heart changes, our preferences are likely to change also. Perhaps this is the bridge itself—the bridge of choice and responsibility, supported and made whole through faith and consciousness.

Chapter 8
The Blessed Life

Is it possible to enjoy Heaven on Earth? This would seem to be unimaginable when we think of Heaven as being a place only of bliss, in bright contrast to the background of struggles encountered in this world. Under the relentless pressures of mortal existence we would rather seek an escape to kinder, gentler places. During the time I was with the Master, however, I experienced a sense of peace and freedom from conflict unlike any I had ever known on this Earth. Perhaps Heaven really exists wherever God's peace prevails.

The greatest difference I noticed about myself was in the area of dealing with problems. As an artist I have always enjoyed challenges, and often I have received very pleasant adrenaline rushes from successfully rising to an occasion. I am convinced that we attract many, if not most, of the difficulties in our lives because of the experience and accomplishment they can provide. The fascinating difference about being with the Master, however, was the ease with which I could learn, achieve, and grow **without the need of obstacles** to overcome. In retrospect, I have to admit that, on other occasions, problem solving often provided a basis for my ego to claim victory on some illusionary level! By contrast, I now have learned that the real "overcoming" is returning to the bliss of who I truly am, knowing that I can attain repose **independently** of external conditions. Along with that, I have found many trying conditions simply to be unnecessary.

It would seem that somewhere in our personal and collective histories there must have been points when we made decisions about the value of confrontations and difficulties. Since problems seem to be necessary, if not inevitable, perhaps we have chosen a creative approach, looking upon them as adventure and education. Or to the contrary, perhaps we have viewed them as punishment and retribution. In recalling the Master's teaching, there is an even greater consideration that could be examined, and that is the possibility that love embraces problems only to demonstrate their ultimate illusion.

More than once I asked Jesus how to attract blessings instead of struggles. "How do we receive, and can there be a truly blessed life? Can you give me a formula for it?"

With a gentle smile, He replied, *"I already have."*

"Where?" I quickly responded.

"All that I have taught you is about the good life, although you might refer in particular to "The Beatitudes."

"Oh," I remarked, with a crestfallen tone. Despite their inspirational beauty, I found "The Beatitudes" difficult to understand, and frankly they seemed more like a recipe for sainthood rather than human fulfillment. The well-known "Beatitudes" are a pronouncement of blessings contained within His "Sermon on The Mount,"[12] which was perhaps His greatest oration in the New Testament.

After hearing His reply, the only comment with which I felt comfortable to mention was how much I would have enjoyed being there as a bird on a limb to observe the excitement and expectation of those people sitting on a hillside by the Sea of Galilee! How wonderful to have seen Him multiply the fishes! How blessed I would have been to hear the message in His own words!

That sermon has always deeply moved me, and has inspired the deepest longing both to see its fulfillment and also to comprehend more fully what He really meant. Although His metaphors are rich with many layers of meaning, some of the scriptural words and phrases have caused me to feel a certain discomfort. Because of my concern, He helped me to understand the staggering problem of translating His language into other more structured and formal dialects. He explained that Aramaic was a very practical, Earthy, and colorful language of Israel's "man on the street." As with casual languages of any time or place, any particular word or phrase may have had several possible meanings depending on the nuances of expression or the context of delivery.

Jesus compared the range of possible meanings in Aramaic to the unstructured nature of our own colloquial jargon. For example, in our English language we have the expression, "I'm cool." If I were to make that statement, there are several different ways listeners might respond.

One person might think I was referring to the temperature, while another might infer that I was expressing indifference. Someone else might conclude that I was at peace with myself. Still another person might think that I was a very "hip" person. All these possibilities exist within the same phrase. Therefore, the problem in translating His words has been a great deal more complicated than merely finding equivalent expressions in Latin, Greek, and modern languages. Difficult as that has been in itself, the greater obstacle has been in recovering lost contexts for determining exactly what His statements really meant.

Beatitude literally means blessings and great happiness, which was the central meaning of His promise. Yet the Beatitudes also made reference to limitation, sorrow, and suffering as an insurmountable part of the human experience. More than anything else, I wanted to understand why that was so. No sooner had I expressed that desire than He began to recite the blessings that I might hear them for myself and take their meanings to heart.

In His resonant, baritone voice, He began: *"Blessed are the poor in spirit, for theirs is the kingdom of heaven."*

Then He waited for my response.

"I have stumbled over that one since I first heard it as a child," I replied. To me, the kingdom of Heaven means the richness of everything that is. So how does being poor relate to having all the riches of the kingdom? I was also confused by the connection between poverty and Heaven. What did you really mean when you said that?"

"If you had listened with your heart you would have heard the truth, despite the losses in translation. However, since you have now focused on your misunderstanding, let me help you through the difficulty. You're stumbling over the word 'poor.' In Aramaic, the word 'poor' has a number of possible meanings, which can only be determined by the context and thoughts being conveyed. 'Poor' could mean impoverished, or depleted, as in washed-out soil. It could mean lacking in ability, absent of quality, low in potential, or deficient. These meanings translate easily into the definitions of your language. Yet, there is one more meaning that 'poor' had in Aramaic which is not used in most modern languages. It meant 'simple.' When I made that proclamation, my true reference was to simplicity! Let me recite it now correctly for you, and then you can tell me how you feel. 'Blessed are the simple in spirit for theirs is the kingdom of Heaven.'"

"Perfect, just perfect!" And I felt the nourishment of His blessing very deeply. After a while He proceeded to say more about that blessing.

"Essentially, the great caution is to refrain from introducing complexities and hierarchies into spiritual pursuits. While structure is necessary to physical existence, it results only in isolation, frustration, judgment, and arrogance when given power in the spiritual realm. Do not empower belief systems which limit and control your approach to God. Do not submit to the tyranny of hierarchies which require that you ascend in your spiritual life according to permission or protocol established by man. That was the critical issue surrounding the Tower of Babel. The religion of ancient Babylon was controlled by echelons of priestly authority which assumed all rights to govern a person's ascension to heaven. This has been a recurring problem within organized religion, and many spiritual empires have failed simply because they were based on structures of the mind and human authority. The kingdom of Heaven knows nothing of structure and hierarchy. If you surround your sacred experiences with endless requirements sanctioned by man, then basically what you have done is to shut the doors of Heaven. Keep it simple. There is but one spirit. You do not need to climb a thousand steps before you can be fully connected with your Creator in spirit. **Spirit is within you, spirit is of you, spirit is around you, spirit embraces you, and is with you always.** *You do not need the permission of structure to receive everything that the Spirit of God has in store for you. All the great empires of history crumbled to dust because of hierarchies which governed their spiritual lives. This is why I said, 'Blessed are the simple in spirit, for theirs is the kingdom of Heaven.' When you are simple in spirit, all will be given to you, merely for the asking. You do not need to acquire a new dimensionality before passing on to an even more elite dimensionality. Love and simplicity are the only requirements of a fulfilled spiritual life.*

"Every kingdom divided against itself is brought to its desolation. Every city or house divided against itself will not stand. The reason is that there is but one spirit and it cannot be divided. You cannot say one thing has spirit and another has not. You cannot say that one person belongs to the spirit and another does not. Do not take anything from the spirit. Spirit is in all things, of all things, and with all things. Where spirit is concerned there are no prerequisites and no hierarchies. The spirit is one. If you attempt to break it, the divided house will turn against you, the disrupter. Whenever you attempt to divide the spirit, you have granted it consent to

*'collect its damages' **from you**! Accepting and honoring the one spirit from
the simplicity of your own place in life is the key to Heaven. Accept it
where you are, as you are. You do not need to be like someone else, or be
some-where else. A flea at peace with himself, and in wonderment of
eternity, is more likely to see the face of God than a giant whose ravenous
appetite seeks to acquire everything only for himself. It is not the size or
importance which matters, but rather, acceptance and simplicity. There is
a fulfillment in simplicity that will bring you great happiness."*

Never once did He say, "Blessed are those who build elaborate
structures of the mind, or of the world, to extol their own advantaged
positions." Instead, He emphasized that we are blessed in spirit as we
affirm the love that we are and join with the love of our Father in a realm
above human posturing. *"Hierarchies are part of worldly elitism. Structure
belongs to the Earth. As you ascend to a higher, more loving relationship
with your fellow man and your Creator, the dominance of structure will fall
away. Those who claim to be ascending through layers of structured
perception are only **ascending in their minds**. They have not yet seen the
Kingdom of Heaven. As you ascend in the spirit, structured reality falls
away and has no bearing and little relevance to your awareness. In love
and spirit there are neither hierarchies nor structure. **Love is the source
of your life.***

*"Maintain simplicity in your thoughts as well. Thoughts generate
performance in your life. Therefore, it is very important to guard your
thoughts and direct them properly. You could compare love to a
commander-in-chief and your thoughts to a colonel giving orders to troops
in the field. It is important that orders be relayed to the troops, and that is
the role of thought. So guard your thoughts and instruct them well. If you
misconceive them to be the source of your life, however, you will forget
your real power."*

When He said that, it reminded me of a personal experience I had in
the study and practice of positive thinking. When I was teaching at the
University of Oklahoma, I had enrolled in several seminars which I
believed or hoped would help me to stay focused in my work and to better
direct my intentions. Each of these courses involved positive thought
procedures, and at first each one seemed to work and make a difference.
After I used each method for a while, though, its effectiveness declined
sharply. That was actually the reason why I took several courses instead of
just one. I was looking for a procedure that would **continue** working. As

I remembered that experience, I realized that the Master had touched upon an answer. So I asked if He could tell me more.

"Those procedures worked well for you in the beginning because you started with a lot of pent-up love that needed directing and focusing. Once you applied and ventilated that reserve of love there was nothing more to accomplish. **You must put love behind your thoughts to make them work.** *There are many good courses of thought development and management which would work better and have more lasting results if the power **behind** thought were more fully understood. Compare your love and your thoughts to an archer. If your love is the archer, then your mind is the bow, and your thoughts are the arrows. Without a careful direction of thoughts, you are not going to hit the target. Without love to string the bow and pull it, your motivation will be weak or misdirected. These things are all part of your totality, yet the simplicity of your power is love. It is important to guard and direct your thoughts. Even so, do not assign them a separate power from your love, and do not assign to your mind the keys to Heaven. Your mind cannot open that door. Mental activity invariably results in complexities which must then be contained by structure. Within hierarchies of mental structure, ideas ascend in levels of sophistication. Such complicated standards will always establish some persons as better than others. Love, on the other hand, is simple, and so is the spirit. Stay with simplicity and avoid the pitfalls of complicated living."*

A particular curiosity began to develop as I contemplated His comments about thought and the mind. Though He was composed and peaceful, His welcoming look suggested that He was willing to hear my question. Before I would ask the question, however, I needed to sort out the feelings and thoughts which were rising within my being.

Throughout the ages, there has been much reference concerning the notions of sacred structure, sacred architecture, and sacred geometry. I pondered these concepts in two different ways as I contemplated the essence of simplicity. First, I thought about the contradiction between structure and simplicity, and the futility of seeking perfection through structure. On the other hand, I had feelings of admiration for those who had innocently perceived and distilled innate simplicity even within the domain of structure. Certainly, as an artist, some of my most thrilling moments have been when complexity surrendered to simplicity and there upon a surface of mere paint and canvas a composition glowed with excellence. Most especially in great music, I am moved to tears when I hear glorious simple rhythms recurring within complex arrangements of melody and counter melody. My thoughts gradually turned towards an intense feeling of appreciation and gratitude to the awesome simplicity of love, and I was compelled to ask, "Are any of the beautiful symmetries, patterns, and harmonies in existence sacred?"

He replied, *"Only the Father is sacred, although the beauties and simplicities that you may discover within nature, thought, and artistic expression may certainly **convey** His sacred presence. It is fine to be moved, inspired, and even healed by such perceived perfections. If, however, such patterns and harmonies are codified into fixed ideas which purportedly have a life or power of their own, any potential value which may have been present would be canceled. Moments and manifestations of perfection emerge from the normal harmonies of existence. **Except, there are no structures that cannot be superseded and rearranged by love.** Otherwise, how could there be miracles? How could there be freedom for the soul?*

"Until you understand that any structure can be rearranged by love, you can never understand how I multiplied the fishes. If you would multiply anything, all you need do is take one part or sample, then love it enough. This is why it is so important when giving, that you give with love. In that way, you multiply the gift. You can multiply and expand anything. With enough love, one thing becomes the many."

As He said that, I realized how fragile and defensive structure is.

He continued, *"If structure were the lord and master of existence, wherever there was only one fish, it would remain that way. The reason is that one fish represents the boundaries and molecules which embody one separate entity. **What structure defines is separation! In separation, structure prevails, therefore structure is the lord of scarcity!** If one considers all the adamantine particles, all the spirit, and all the love within one fish, the infinite potential is unfathomable. It cannot be contained, and needs only a propelling force to become the many."*

There are many stories of angels who have interceded for people in dangerous situations. Incredible rescues have been reported which seem to confirm the suspendable nature of structured reality. Such deeds may serve to remind us that while we need order on Earth, it would be a mistake to consider any structural framework as sacred. The simplicity of love, spirit, and adamantine particles supersedes all structure. Those elements are common to all form and possess infinite transformative potential.

As I contemplated the enduring nature of simplicity, it was like rolling waves of the ocean. When He began to recite the second Beatitude, it was almost like a new melody following upon the first. Indeed, there is a natural progression from the first to the second blessing, for in understanding that there is but one spirit, one existence, and one eternity, it becomes easier to accept that **nothing real is ever lost or missing.**

"Blessed are they that mourn, for they shall be comforted." His voice reciting those words was very beautiful. My face must have revealed some discomfort, because in a caring tone He asked about my concern. I was remembering my own sorrows, and frankly they did not feel like blessings.

"Again, there is an issue with words and meanings which has suffered in translation. In Aramaic, 'mourning' could mean sorrow, grief, pain, or regret. Most of these meanings have negative connotations and suggest a clinging to loss. However, there is an even more important meaning that could be expressed only in a context which focused upon the value of mourning. I was referring to the act of purging and releasing. This is quite different from the internalizations of sorrow and loss. When a person first recognizes and experiences grief, he takes it upon himself as an affliction. He is depressed, perhaps shocked, and so he turns within to suffer his emotional and spiritual wounds. This is grief. As the process completes itself in the latter stages of surrender, there is mourning. Mourning is the free flowing of tears as acceptance and releasing are experienced. In that state, the heart can perceive a continuity of life even though certain attachments have been lost. In letting go of that which cannot be retained, one heals. It is through releasing that one is blessed. Grieving is clinging to that which has been lost—mourning is the act of letting go. No one feels blessed at the onset of grief. Never would I suggest such a thing. Yet, in the releasing of grief through purging, relinquishing, and the flowing of tears, healing can occur at last.

"This process is relevant to the loss of anything, not just the loss of a loved one. The loss could have been a dream or a hope. Even sensing childhood slip through your hands could bring on a time of mourning to honor the love that is being released. Such purging opens a space in which to celebrate a newly emerging stage of life. There are also times to acknowledge the end of a career or role in life. In releasing and honoring what has been, there may be tears, but there will also be doors opening to future possibilities.

"Accepting this process is great therapy and can result in many blessings. This is because there are two parts to love—attaching and letting go. Only through living and understanding both phases of love is a being complete. The reaching, connecting, and embracing aspects of love are easy and joyful. Letting go and saying good-bye is a great deal more difficult. There is a time to release everything, and in releasing, you let go of the clinging, and you are made whole again. Thus you are blessed."

In deep resonant tones, He continued, ***"Blessed are the meek, for they shall inherit the Earth."***

I was almost embarrassed to admit that I had trouble understanding this one also. My difficulty in accepting this blessing revolved around the submissive connotations of meekness. While humility is a great human virtue, the concept of "meekness" offers other meanings than just that, especially with regard to relative human worth. Meekness was not an easy concept for me to reconcile with inheriting the Earth! "Does this mean that I am supposed to go through life in a subservient capacity? Or are we again dealing with a translation difficulty?"

He smiled and said, *"Yes, greater clarity of translation would help. The word for meek had several meanings in Aramaic. It could mean humble, poor, subservient, or self-effacing. Yet none of those is what I meant. The closest word in the English language for what I intended is* ***moderation.*** *This is the way it should read. 'Blessed are those who live in moderation, for they shall inherit the Earth.' Moderation is the economy of God, and the economy of blessing! Are you not in balance when you live in moderation? When you live in balance, are you not whole? When you are whole, do you not inherit the Earth?*

"Moderation is a relative concept which derives its power from equilibrium and balance. It cannot be enforced with equality or limitation. Moderation for a person with great responsibilities would require greater supply than moderation for a person with meager responsibilities. ***Moderation is not an invocation of limits or conformity, but rather an invocation of the rationality that a man is more complete when he is in balance. What a man requires is governed by what he can love! Through moderation, under the command of love, everything is provided.***

"Pursue moderation in all things. I recommend moderation not only in the food you eat or in your physical comforts, but also in mental pursuits, habits, and work. As Heaven comes to Earth, the standard of economy will be that of moderation. It will not be necessary for one person

*to hoard and another to starve. Sharing will become a joy as you learn that
everything you share will become the basis of your own receiving."*

There is a beautiful logic to these blessings. Each one flows as a
natural consequence from the one before, for when one knows how the
needs of life are provided there is a natural willingness to release that
which cannot be retained. When a person is willing to release, hoarding
ceases to be a preoccupation. When hoarding ceases, there is plenty for all.

Eager to apply what He said, I took a look through my closet the next
day and found some very nice clothes that had been hanging there unused
because they were unsuitable to my needs or appearance. As I started
thinking about friends who might like them, I noticed a new depth of
responsibility in ownership. I was actually concerned about finding the
person to whom the clothing truly belonged. When I telephoned my
friends, the giving was very comfortable and without attitudes of charity
or condescension. I simply said, "There's a dress hanging in my closet
which I believe really belongs to you. I must have been thinking about you
when I purchased it." Then I did the same thing with books and decorative
items. As I surveyed my shelves and closets, I increased my sensitivity for
sharing through respecting the principle of rightness in ownership. Then the
most amazing thing began to happen. Friends reciprocated with sharing and
gifts, and the items they offered seemed truly to belong to me.

He further explained, *"Money can obtain your possessions, although
it cannot establish your true ownership. Whatever truly belongs to you is
determined by what your heart attracts and your love commands. Only the
properties of your heart can bring fulfillment and nourishment to your life.
In practicing moderation, you will know this. You will be able to shop for
groceries and know what foods you need. You will not have to eat
excessively to compensate for subconscious cravings. Mankind has
destroyed much of his sensitivity about true need and rightful ownership
through practicing excess. Such abuse is not limited to excess of things and
physical pleasures. There is also excess of work, excess of denial, excess
of suffering, excess of punishment, excess of grief, and excess of control.
There are those who live in failure and poverty under some misguided
assumption that sacrifices bring freedom from obsession. Instead, their
excess is denial. Anything can be carried to extremes. There is a point in
every pursuit and every cycle when a return to balance is required. In
balance there is wholeness, fulfillment, and blessing.*

"Blessed are they who hunger and thirst for righteousness for they

shall be filled." This blessing is directly linked to the Sacred Heart, for when a person hungers and thirsts for righteousness, the basic purity and innocence of his heart will be awakened. Jesus reminded me many times that the heart sustains the inner core of our innocence and our goodness. Through the heart's power we are able to be the love that we are. This was manifest by perfect example in His presence.

My cup overflowed daily. One word from Him was enough. I was filled when I was with Him because I was in the presence of His righteousness and rightness. Righteousness is a difficult concept to study in the world, because we see so little which is pure and so much which is employed to support false contentions of rightness. Before I could understand the fullness of that blessing, I needed to have more clarity on the subject of righteousness.

"Righteousness is you being the love that you are. It means that you are right with yourself, right with our Father, and right with the one spirit. Simply be the love that you are. That is discovered and developed through a right relationship with the heart.

"The heart is a powerful magnet which generates life energy for the body and the soul and draws to you all the needs and requirements of your life. Within the Sacred Chamber of the heart you will feel the presence of your Creator and be anointed with His righteousness. From these holy communions, higher principles of intelligence will be revealed to you, and through them rightness will come to your life."

The higher principles of intelligence were presented in depth in Chapter Six. However, it is relevant to reconsider them here from the perspective of being right with life. They are: unity, love, life, respect, honesty, justice, and kindness. Unity is the foundation of all rightness through which all love unfolds. When we are prompted by love, we are given command. Through love we are filled with the higher knowledge of life. Life is the third provider of intelligence. Life begets life and attracts life. As we confront life, we see its indwelling truth. Only with respect can we learn. Through respect, we honor the rightness and the beauties of life, as well as the rightness, goodness, and love of others. Innocent perception is looking at the world as it is and seeing that it is enough. All the answers are in front of us. In knowing that, the principle of honesty is empowered. Then follows justice in which we see the balance of all things and the need for all actions to be balanced. At last there is kindness, which is the will of God. There can be no greater rightness than that.

He then continued, ***"Blessed are the merciful for they shall receive***

mercy." Those who extend mercy, receive mercy. In forgiving, we are forgiven. Jesus gave me one more reason beyond that—only the heart can understand forgiveness. Therefore, in practicing forgiveness every day, the heart will be given pre-eminence in your life.

"Practice forgiveness everyday. It liberates the soul from bondage, and beyond that, forgiveness is an action which your mind can never understand. Your mind's sole intent is to balance the books. In issues of morality it only wants to get even. Therefore, practice forgiveness everyday if only in trivial matters. This is an excellent way of tempering the mind and empowering the heart. Mercy is not just a way of balancing cause and effect, although that is certainly a valid reason to practice it. **The greater reason for practicing forgiveness is that whenever you are merciful, you grow.** *As you grow you become more blessed, and the very things that might harm you or cause you resistance will be given no power.* **Mercy is the flower of growth.** *Those who are restrained in mercy will have limited influence in life.*

"Blessed are the pure in heart for they shall see God." This was the sixth blessing.

"In the sacred center of your heart the Father knows you to be nothing less than perfect. The Father knows nothing of sin, which is why the very act of sin separates you from your Father. In the purity of your heart you are one with the Father."

"Then why do we not enter our heart more easily?" I inquired.

He replied, *"The reason is that you do not see yourself as pure, perfect, and innocent. Until you see yourself in that way, you will not enter the Sacred Chamber of the heart. As long as you try to carry all of your unworthiness and mistakes into the heart with you, you will stay on the threshold of your heart and not enter. My apostles were constantly asking me how to pray, seeking for words and formulas. My reply was always that being in the heart **is** prayer. Finally, I gave them a prayer which would unlock the Heart's door. Praying my prayer, anyone can be restored to his purity and innocence. It is an invocation to the Heart. Therefore, when you say the words be sure and linger for a while in silence, peace, and innocence. In the Sacred Chamber you are one with the Father, and in that oneness your Source knows everything you need, and beholds no imperfection. When you enter the Sacred Heart, you are restored in your life and you are made whole again. How can this happen to you, and the face of God not be revealed?*

"Through innocent perception, you may also perceive the presence of

God in all of existence. This is purity of perception. Through practicing this, you can be at peace with your life and see the beauty of what is before you. Everything was created in innocence. Behold this, if you would see the face of God. It is not the mind's province to create reality, but rather to observe, integrate, understand, and implement reality. It is the province of the heart to accept reality. The pure heart will accept unconditionally. Although the mind strives to understand, it will invent what it cannot understand—or worse still, it will judge. This is a dangerous phenomenon, for the mind will invent realities that lead you away from who you are and the true purposes of your life. When you surrender to the fact that existence does not require invention—that it simply is—you will be on the threshold of actually looking into the face of God.

*"Judgment will separate you from this sacred space. Judgment is actually the only sin of which a pure and perfect child of God is capable. Judgment was the **original** sin, and continual pursuit of it will keep you from the presence of your Father."*

I noted the seriousness of His attitude about judgment and felt compelled to ask, "If judgment is a violation of innocence, and if the Father is the Source of all innocence, then why are there so many references to God's judgment in the Bible?"

"The Hebrew word for judgment, which is 'mishpat,' actually refers to redemption and vindication—not to opinion or condemnation. Man, in his true potential, is innocent and good. No one knows and upholds that more surely than the Father. If you would judge any man, you are opposed to the Father. In any situation, it is the Father who sees and defends His children, despite the transgressions of a false self or a world of inequity. Your Father knows the difference and redeems your basic rightness. The ancient Hebrew meaning of judgment is the pillar of your American judicial system which holds a man to be innocent until proven guilty. It is the judge who protects the defendant's right to be viewed as innocent until all of the accusations are considered. This is the Father's stance, only with more clarity, purity, and forgiveness. It is the world which supports guilt and unworthiness and uses the power of condemnation and punishment to support its destructive agendas. If only the sons of God would learn the futility of accusation, then brotherhood would flower with perceptions of innocence.

"In saying this, I do not mean to imply that acts of destruction should not be intercepted and offenders should not be restrained, for how else can a brotherhood be maintained? Even so, such acts of justice should be applied

*with the intent of **restoring** brotherhood and not dividing or dispersing it.*

"Frequently, I used the metaphor of sheep or fish when speaking with my disciples to describe the nature of collective acceptance without judgment. Fish live in schools, as sheep live in flocks. With both, the acceptance of additional members into the flock or school is without qualification or reservation. There is a simple innocence of the one spirit in the midst of these creatures. I have seen a flock of six sheep grow to ten thousand by adding new flocks driven to grass or market. Never was a sheep rejected. Inclusion was unconditional."

I was so glad that He clarified the reason behind the metaphors of fish and sheep, because I had been less than enthusiastic about the connotations of conformity, mediocrity, and dependency which also seemed to be implied.

As He noticed my relief, He added the following statement, *"I meant that man should live together in mutual support and harmony, although certainly not at the expense of individuality and surely not in a state of clannish conformity."*

He demonstrated daily how innocent perception deflects any possible inclination to reform life according to judgment. When I was in His presence, life was acceptable **as it was**. This does not mean that I did not express my difficulties or objections when I felt them. For such freedom of expression is also an aspect of innocent perception. Nevertheless, I saw how we depleted our life force through endless attempts to make it conform to mental preconceptions and judgments. Jesus said, *"Most conflict is self-generated by rejections of life and denial of existence as it really is."*

With seamless grace, that statement led to the next Beatitude. ***"Blessed are the peacemakers for they shall be called the sons of God.***

"There are many ways to make peace in life. A person does not have to be a diplomat, negotiator, counselor, or minister. Nor is that blessing confined to the settling of arguments and disputes. Its power comes from the grace of ending duality. You will be blessed with wholeness as you end duality and rise above the concept that life must be viewed as a conflict between polar opposites. The critical recognition which humankind most needs to make at this time is that a dualistic approach to living is no longer useful. Our oneness of spirit needs to be recognized and implemented through acceptance."

His concept of peace was more grand, with more pervasive impact, than simply resolving conflicts at the office or discord in the home. Although we focus upon annoying issues and often lose sleep over them, they are for the most part isolated instances of conflict. *"The core of man's duality is that he sets up problems for himself and then uses those same problems to declare, 'How brilliant, we figured it out.' When man creates a problem in the first place, he should be able to figure it out! What would be better to ask is, 'Did we really need the problem?'"*

As He spoke, I considered the many ways in which we are conditioned by the presence of apparent opposites—up/down, in/out, forward/backward, happy/sad—to name only a few. "We are living on a planet where there is day and night. Doesn't this affect our thinking?"

He pleasantly responded, *"Yes, it can. Except, you have the choice to focus on that limited observation or to look beyond to a more complete understanding. Let me show you how such an expanded perception can work. Just imagine that you took a ride on one of the satellites in your stratosphere. Now look back at the Earth and tell me what you see."*

"Well, from this viewpoint, I see the sun shining all over the Earth and there is a little bit of shadow on the far side, although the light and dark are not equal. There is a little bit of light almost everywhere."

*"That is the point. Dark and light are not opposites at all. They represent variable conditions of exposure to light sources. That is not duality. The conceptual model of duality is a simplistic frame of reference created by the mind to satisfy its dependency upon structure and symmetry. The mind seeks to **explain** rather than understand.*

"Day and night will not cease. Yet, you need not continue viewing them as opposites. There is no longer a need to think that night has the same power as day. There is just the power of light, with variations of intensity and interruption. Once the full scope of understanding is attained, duality fades. Higher intelligence is manifested through integrated perceptions of wholeness which restore your recognition of the one spirit. The sons of God are those who do not explain life or manage it with dualistic concepts. The sons of God are those who seek to perceive wholeness in all things."

I wondered, "How did we become so entrenched in such myopic thinking?"

Reading my thoughts, He replied, *"Man has been growing and living on an Earth which was also growing and organizing itself. A limited approach to life begets a limited understanding of it. However, the most critical conditioning has come from the way mankind has perceived, generated, and controlled energy. Energy is a crucial survival commodity, and therefore its management has a profound impact upon consciousness. From the moment it was discovered that fire could be ignited by rubbing two sticks together, mankind has been building cultures upon friction-generated energy. Nuclear power plants are no exception to this. The 'sticks' are more sophisticated, although the energy generated is still the result of a polar resistive, friction-generated process."*

"Is this ever going to change?"

"Yes. Science is on the threshold of moving into a new era of energy that will base its performance on principles of primal magnetism. Magnetism may be viewed as either derivative or primary, depending on one's level of understanding. In its primary condition there are no polarities and no scarcities. Now contemplate a civilization in which energy is not a commodity over which to fight or hoard. Can you see how that would change everything?"

Peacefulness prevailed as I contemplated His teaching. Then the silence was broken as He spoke the final blessing. ***"Blessed are those who are persecuted for righteousness sake for theirs is the kingdom of heaven.***

"There is a great lesson involved in this blessing, not just for heaven but also for Earth. It is the most difficult lesson anyone will ever master, yet in learning it a person rises above the tyranny of hardship and experiences true liberation. This is why it is the last blessing."

I was glad to receive His words of assurance because, frankly, this beatitude had always frightened me a little. I felt comforted and humbled by His great strength, and could only respond by exposing my insecurity and admitting my lack of confidence in being able to understand. Nevertheless, I wanted to hear whatever He was willing to share.

*"The power of this blessing resides in the fact that our Father is the Creator of all things, whose presence is with all things and in all things. There is no place where God is not. There is no experience in which God is not. There is no dimension of understanding or awareness where God is not. A man who has known God only in a state of well-being has just known the smallest portion of his Creator. A man who must place conditions on God in order to receive Him, cannot receive Him. One who can know God exclusively in the blissful and abundant experiences has no power over the rest of life. What is the kingdom of Heaven except the wholeness of everything? How can you have **everything** when you are only willing to know **part** of God? This was the lesson presented in*

the Book of Job, although not many people comprehend its true meaning."

"Well, I am one of them. I not only do not understand it, I never liked it!" I hadn't read the Book of Job since I was in college, and honestly, I thought it was a pretty grim nightmare of one poor soul's terrible hardship on the Earth. To me, it did not represent the God of love about which Jesus had spoken in the New Testament, and so I was unable to reconcile Job's painful experience with my preferred beliefs.

In a comforting tone He asked, *"Would you like to read it again with me?"*

I readily accepted. Then He sat beside me, and we read it together. As His words poured over the lines, I was amazed with the beauty I had missed before. Contained within that book of the Old Testament are some of the most exquisite passages ever written about the wonderment of the cosmos, the majesty of God, the vastness of infinity, and the omnipotent power of the All That Is. To summarize the story briefly, Job was a very wealthy man who was blessed with health, family, land, and position in the community. He respected the Sabbath and worshiped God. Then for reasons known only to God, Job's loyalty to God was tested. Job had been grateful for the material abundance with which he had been blessed, but the question was, "Would he be faithful to his Creator under conditions of extreme hardship?" That was what caused my original reaction. I wanted to know what kind of insecure and cruel God would give a man everything and then take it away.

Actually, I was not ready to comprehend the fullness of that powerful message. The story is much deeper than its superficial drama might suggest. What I did not understand is that God was removing Job's limited attachments and dependencies in order to prepare him for having **everything**. In wealth and comfort, Job had only part of God. Job was content with his "bubble" and was not looking for an expanded relationship with his Creator. Therefore, he was not expecting this twist of destiny, nor was he prepared to accept it gracefully. In the beginning, he tried prayers for redemption and confessions of sin in hopes that God would forgive whatever trespasses he might have committed. Nevertheless, the problems only became worse. Then he pursued understanding in hopes that there possibly could be a lesson in all the hardships. Still the problems became worse. He counseled his friends, yet nothing changed. Finally, in utter dejection, Job surrendered to the omnipotence, beauty, and vastness of the universe. He began to behold in awe and wonder the majesty of everything that is. Through those sublime realizations, he came to accept the love of God in all things. As he stopped his judgments, the dreadful conditions ended. Then, miraculously, the moment he accepted everything, **everything was given to him!**

"In the English language, persecution implies an intentional harassment or punishment. In Aramaic, it typically meant 'suffering.' Our Father never afflicts or badgers His children, although it is His greatest yearning to be known by them in the fullness of existence. It is through challenge and the survival of suffering that a person grows beyond his protective bubble to experience the love of God in a greater way. According to the way conditions work, the one who generates conditions is the dominant party in any relationship. Therefore, as long as a person refuses to allow his Holy Source to expand the conditions of life, there cannot be a truly sacred relationship.

"There is a second meaning to this beatitude which relates to the vanishing of illusion. To attain this additional blessing, you must realize that 'for righteousness sake' means 'for love's sake.' Whenever you stand firmly in the midst of a hardship, holding and expressing the love that you are, you will witness illusions falling away. Through being the love that you are, you are empowered to transcend your sufferings."

Jesus said to me more than once, *"Love your enemies if you would convince yourself that love is a power that comes from within."*

Perhaps there are no enduring enemies, but there are adversarial situations. Life has its trials, and when we are passing through these difficulties it is imperative to be the love that we are. In that special state of being, we gain the assurance that we are not externally controlled or dominated by the world.

*"Only in the presence of your enemy can you really discover that truth. Only when you love beyond all of the external conditions which logically tell you not to do so, can you discover the deeper wellspring of love that you are. In the twenty-third verse of the Book of Psalms, King David asks the Lord to set a table before him in the presence of his enemies and to fill his cup until it overflowed. His cup was filled with love. David knew that only through the power of love could victory be attained. **Through love you have the power over any situation.** Only, you will never truly know this until you have surmounted adversity. The last of the beatitudes is the greatest of all blessings. For in that learning, you are free forever from the illusions that would attempt to conquer you and misdirect your life."*

Chapter 9
The Ten Commandments
Of Love

Two thousand years ago, when Jesus was asked about His regard for the law and the commandments, He replied, *"You shall love the Lord your God with all your heart, with all your soul, and with all your mind. This is the first and greatest commandment. And the second is like it: You shall love your neighbor as yourself. On these two commandments hang all the Law and the Prophets."*[13]

With such clarification and simplification of the existing commandments Jesus mandated a paradigm change upon the Earth which continues to unfold even now. In those very statements He has revealed the purpose of law to be a fulfillment and rectification of character, actions, and life. At the same time He has dismissed the concept that law is the authorization of force to institute and maintain agendas of control. He reminded me many times when we talked about the laws of society and the universe that, *"Love is the only power; therefore all valid law is rooted in love. There is but one other thing you need to consider in relation to the laws of life, and that is the pre-eminence of truth in all things. Truth is the constant element within all of life. Only by the truth shall you find your way to fulfillment and transcend illusion. The certainty of both truth and love is found within the Sacred Heart.*

"The reason is that the Heart takes all emotions, feelings, and awareness of life into itself to perfect and to purify. Through this process, all your life experiences are returned to God for strengthening or re-alignment with your covenant and life purpose. At the very center of your soul is the Sacred Heart. It is not the left or the right side of your being, as your mind would view it—for your mind will divide anything into two parts

for purposes of comparison and examination. Rather, your heart is the burning, fired up, passionate, coordinated center of your life which looks for unity, proceeds with love, and magnifies life with honesty, respect, justice, and kindness. Through that potential is a goodness which is empowered and tough. The Sacred Heart is truly your higher intelligence and the source of an inspired life. It is the heart's intelligence which will prevail upon the Earth as mankind moves into the fullness of self-realization. You cannot find your happiness as a divided or weakened self.

"Compared with the heart, the mind's intelligence is devoted to establishing the perimeters and guidelines for comparison and control. Where the mind is concerned, the pursuit of morality is not so much a way of improving life as a way of controlling it. In the process of developing a brotherhood which is kind and supportive, guidelines of morality can be important. However, hard and fast rules are often instituted not to lift people up, but to put people down. This is the work of the mind intervening and usurping the heart's power, to establish foundations for judgment rather than for living.

"True comprehension of morality and ethics far exceeds the mind's dominion, although there are aspects of ethics which govern the mind. The most important principle of ethics to bear upon the mind is that of correct priority. The mind is a servant and not a master. The second most important factor is the support and enhancement which the mind does or does not give to innocent perception. It is not the right or privilege of the mind to invent or recreate reality in order to support or confirm its own agendas. Ultimately, all guidelines for mental ethics must be governed by standards of 'workability.' This is the function through which any mind integrates with universal law. There is also a strong implication of obedience here, for obedience is application of life and effort to workability. For example, a bridge builder who is obedient to the principles of pragmatic engineering is a successful producer whose bridges withstand the elements and convey travelers safely from one side to the other. Everything has its patterns of workability, and it is the mind's duty to search them out diligently and to apply them earnestly. Obedience has oppressive connotations for many people because it has been interpreted to mean compliance with authority, right or wrong. This is tragic, because obedience to the laws of God always results in personal fulfillment and empowerment. False obedience is usually held in place with force and punishment, and typically results in low self-esteem for those who are subjugated to it."

"How do we respond to, or reform, such false authority?" I inquired.

With complete simplicity, He replied, *"Demonstrate your devotion to workability, and challenge authority to do the same."*

As he spoke about ethics and morality, there seemed to be both a difference and a sameness in His use of the words. So I asked, "What is the difference between ethics and morality?"

He quickly responded, *"Ethics is the ongoing process of applying principles of higher intelligence to the problems of collective existence, and endowing life with values that support the well-being of all. Ethics is the care we show in affecting the lives of others as well as a sense for where one's greatest value lies in relation to others. Ethics might be summarized as cause and effect in balance, and applied for the greatest good.*

"Morality is essentially the devotion which is shown to bring about change for the better.

Morality involves a responsibility for the situations that arise in life and the willingness to confront them honestly and deal with them directly to cause an improvement. Part of this involves the personal hygiene of body, mind, emotions, thought, and spirit. Cleanliness is indeed next to Godliness. Morality, however, is a personal attainment. It cannot be enforced externally without weakening the 'I Am' presence of an individual.

"Ethics is imperative for social decency and a workable civilization. Morality is imperative for personal clarity, strength, and virtue. The simplicity of it all, though, is that both are rooted in love."

"Everything you have said is so affirmative of consciousness and responsibility in making life better. How does this relate to the Law of Moses and other rules of conduct which are essentially edicts against wrongful conduct?"

"First, it would be helpful to understand the history and circumstance of Moses' journey upon the Earth. Although the human heart is eternally similar, the nature of external reality was very different then than it is now. This was especially true regarding the special destiny of the Hebrew people at that time. Through Divine guidance, and by Moses' efforts, the Hebrews had been delivered from their long period of Egyptian enslavement. Even so, that was only a technicality concerning enforced bondage. How liberated is anyone who has no place to go? Moses had enough responsibility and wisdom to know that a man is not free until he has a place to be and a purpose in being there. This is why he kept the Hebrews in the desert for forty years. It was necessary for them to pass through two generations and

to acquire a whole new rank of elders who knew nothing of slavery. Only a free people could build a new nation. If they had proceeded straight from slavery to their former homeland all would have been lost. Hundreds of years of slavery erased any sense of personal responsibility, self-determination, and ethics. Slaves are not educated and are denied the privilege of making decisions, determinations, and dis-cernments. Thinking is disallowed. A slave must take orders only. The wisdom and greatness of their ancestors mattered little, for the continuity of the forefathers had been virtually lost. Moses had a giant cultural problem on his hands, and a massive responsibility for restoring the integrity of his people."

The Master's profound love and respect for Moses were obvious. As He spoke, it became clearly evident that those of us today who enjoy the benefits of western civilization owe an immense debt of gratitude to this man. Highlighting some of the critical decisions that this great leader had to make, Jesus explained how Moses instilled in the Hebrew people a new sense of ethics, pride, self-determination, and understanding of individual and collective rights. How can a civilization be rebuilt without accomplishing that first? Consequently, the law of Moses included references to structure as well as to principles of universal truth. There were also necessary elements of restriction, because the need to establish discipline and responsibility was essential for a self-governing nation. At the same time, each one of the commandments was also rooted in love. These commandments come from God in divine inspiration. Moses also had a profound understanding of love that comes only when a person is in deep communion with his own heart. It was interesting to me that one of the metaphors Jesus had used when describing the soul's entry into the Sacred Heart was the appearance of a burning bush beside its passageway. In the moment when He said that, I thought of Moses and knew surely that he had passed through the heart's portal before God spoke to him on the mountain where the Ten Commandments were delivered.[14] The Ten Commandments are the result of many tributaries of wisdom. First, there was the accumulated wisdom of human experience in social and ethical conduct through which there existed a foundation of readiness for new refinements. The second contributing factor was the profound enlightenment of Moses' own heart and his understanding of higher intelligence. Finally, there is the greater element of Divine guidance concerning fundamental laws of the universe. Nevertheless, true comprehension of those laws can be attained only by acknowledging love's role in their creation.

By respecting law at the source of its power, we are given both insight and freedom. Jesus stated, *"The laws which serve God are revealing and transformative, always in an upward direction. Law is to support life, and correct it where necessary. A society which uses law only as a platform for judgment will fall into peril. Law has no validity in itself except through the love in which it is rooted. Love's power does not replace nor override the workable laws of conduct. Love exposes the reasons for law, replacing enforcement with true enlightenment."*

I felt compelled to ask Him, "Would you care to explain the root of love in each one of the Ten Commandments?"

Without hesitation, He began to explain, *"The first law of Moses states,* **'You shall have no other gods before me.'** *This is the commandment which exalts our One Source and creates unity for all.*

"There is but one God, and the knowable presence of our One Source is Love. Divine Love **is prior cause***, and nothing preceded it. From love all was created. As a child, or an aspect of God, you have no prior cause except your Father. Therefore 'Love' is your name, and love stands as prior cause in your life for anything you ever seek to accomplish. By honoring the Father as love and first cause, you also strengthen the love in yourself to be the true cause of action. You are away from your point of power in any action not generated by love. Remember, love commands the adamantine particles, and the one spirit resonates to love. Where there is love, there is potential, there is hope, there is God. This is the primary reality and consideration for all creation. Nothing precedes it in importance, in power, or in truth. Our One Source is the basis of all unity.*

"Unity is the instrument of all goodness. Division is the instrument of all evil. You would be wise to observe this truth in all your ways. In the course of a lifetime, through many passages of growth and change, there will be moments of chaos when you are challenged to release old patterns and build new concepts of unity. New elements will be added and old ones will be removed. At such times it would be well for you to know that unity is of God and not of the world. Unity is dynamic and is forever forming itself into greater potential. As this happens, many structures may collapse and dissolve. This is different, however, from destructive divisions which are inserted into the harmonies of life. Division may be noted by its resistance to growth and by its use of judgment and conflict to retard the power of unity. Perpetrators of division regard change as threatening, and therefore, will infuse into the elements of change as much hostility or perversion as the

situation will bear. Division is easily observed in war and in criminal aggressions, although, most influences of division are more subtle than that. What you need to know about the world in which you live is that its stagnancy is not due to complexity or even chaos—those conditions can actually hold dynamic potential. Its sluggishness is actually due to many aspects of division held in passive equilibrium. That is counterfeit unity."

The second law of Moses states, **"You shall not make unto yourself any graven image or any likeness of anything that is in heaven above or in Earth beneath or that is in the water that is under the Earth."** I have to admit that this one worried me a bit, for as an artist, this is what it appears that I am doing. I asked, "Does this mean that artistic replication is wrong?"

"Not at all, because artistic replication is a form of admiration expressed about the essence of reality. Art is an attempt to enhance reality, not supplant it."

"Then can you explain how this commandment pertains to love?"

"God is love, and that means honoring love in all its forms as the real power of the universe. Do not weaken that power in any way by misrepresenting it, subverting it, denying it, or replacing it with structures which counterfeit the presence of love. Moses was telling his people not to counterfeit God with any form of invented concepts, substances, or structures. There is no dimension of structure that is capable of representing God. If you try, you will be deluded about the source of your strength. Structures are necessary for order and to serve as guidelines for living, but structure is not an aspect of divinity. Structure is merely a servant, a building block of existence, and nothing more. Do not symbolize or conceptualize the presence of God in any way that is transitory or mortal. Do not counterfeit the presence of the Holy Father in any form. Do not assign the power of God to any illusion and do not consider anything of God to be as frail as illusion. A positive way of saying the same thing is this: Honor and know always the power of love, while recognizing at the same time, the fleeting nature of illusion. To know the difference is the beginning of wisdom."

"You appeared to use the terms 'counterfeit' and 'illusion' interchangeably. Is there a difference in your usage of these two words?"

"Yes, there is a significant difference between an illusion and a counterfeit reality. When you dress in different ways to meet the needs of various occasions, you project different illusions of yourself. When you conceptualize the details of a project before it has a tangible

*reality, that is a kind of preparatory illusion. When you escape into a good book, in order to find a different dimension of feeling within yourself, you orchestrate the journey with believable illusions. On the other hand, if you were to dress like another in order to impersonate him and usurp his rights, that would be a counterfeit creation. If you live an illusion as a **substitute** for living a life, that is a counterfeit presence. Illusions are neither good nor bad, except for how they are used. When illusions have been confused with reality and given its authority, that is counterfeit existence. The world is full of counterfeit possibilities. If you give your life and passions to them, you will be left in a depleted condition. None of that needs to happen, however, if you would only remember to never counterfeit love or even consider it to be an illusion. Love is the basis of all reality. If you honor that truth in every way, and if you also refrain from counterfeiting a relationship with God through hollow concepts and rituals, you will never confuse reality with illusion. When a person is confident of reality, he then may interact safely with illusions for creative expression."*

The essence of this commandment is to know clearly and honor the power of love above all else that would seek to subvert or replace it. In realizing this, I was reminded of the immortal and beautiful words of Saint Paul. "Though I speak with the tongues of men and of angels, but have not love, I have become sounding brass or a clanging symbol. And though I have the gift of prophesy, and understand all mysteries and all knowledge, and though I have all faith, so that I could remove mountains, but have not love, I am nothing. And though I bestow all my goods to feed the poor, and though I give my body to be burned, but have not love, it profits me nothing."[15]

*"The third commandment states, '**You shall not take the name of God in vain.**' Love is the name of God. Love enacted upon existence generates life. Without love, there would be no life, for life is love in action. Do not devalue love, or use it falsely. If you deny the power or workability of love, or misuse love in any way, or tarnish its honor through misrepresentation, disbelief, or dishonesty, your life will suffer greatly. The power of God works through love . . . know this! If you pretend love in order to manipulate life, or if you invoke the sanction of God for anything less than the support of life, your influence over life will be diminished. This is the commandment which teaches you how to strengthen your connection to life and the living.*

"The fourth law of Moses states, 'You shall remember the Sabbath and keep it holy.' The Sabbath is a day of grace which follows six days of work or creation. It represents a rest from the labors of structure and a return to the love that you are. Your inner rightness can be appreciated more fully through a celebration of Divinity from which your love has come. Keep this day holy by entering the heart and experiencing the sacred bond between Father and child. Experience the love of peace and the joy which wholeness can bring. In this sacred time, love also the one spirit and celebrate its wholeness.

"The keynote and higher intelligence of the Sabbath is 'respect.' That begins with respect of the Father and extends to respect of all life and to the patterns of creation and the universe. There is a universal rhythm which comprises the melody of divine order. That rhythm is played out as six beats and one pause, six points and one center, six planes and one surface, six men and one leader, six factors and one purpose, six actions and one rest. Observing these rhythms is part of respect for divine order. It is no accident that man's appearance in the universe is expressed as the sixth major event of creation. The love, faith, and consciousness, which compose the true essence of man, represent the culminating glory of the universe. You are children of the Father set in the midst of and in command of life. Only in recognizing the resting interval can you savor that which has been given to you and release that which has no further purpose in your life. In the resting intervals the power of wholeness works its miracles, and Divinity brings forth its greater blessings. By respecting the intervals, you demonstrate your reverence for a greater power and a higher will than any you can possibly envision or manipulate. Through observing the Sabbath you learn the true meaning of surrender, which is nothing less than faith in divine providence, the principles of higher intelligence, and the power of non-action. Without these points of rest, life becomes an endless pattern of linear progressions, obligatory actions, and eternal drudgeries as cycles of six follow cycles of six, follow cycles of six, with no moments for rest, peace, or restoration. When the true principles represented by the Sabbath are disregarded within a society, it will fall into oppression. This follows as surely as day becomes the night. Our Father instituted intervals between cycles of action that the fruits of creation might be counted and appreciated. Without a pause for blessing, how can the soul be in receivership? How can the soul be at peace?"

At this point I asked Him whether it mattered which day of the week is considered to be the seventh day. He answered, *"That does not really matter as long as it can be agreed upon by a large enough sector of people for it to represent a suspension of work and effort **among** the people. The Sabbath is a holistic celebration of the one spirit."*

He reminded me again about the words of Moses, where he had requested that the Sabbath also include the manservant, the maidservant, and the beast of burden. This is a day of relaxation and introspection in which every member of the community is embraced in love and the wholeness of one spirit. A man may privately honor this day and experience it subjectively in his own way, although he cannot experience its full power without extending its blessing to others. This is a day of grace in which everyone is unconditionally loved and forgiven their obligations to structure. The Sabbath is the heart's day—a time for prayer, contemplation, spontaneous gifts, kind words, and simple respect for the holy. In this practice, we cultivate an abiding respect for the one spirit and its power to invoke divine order.

"The fifth commandment states, 'Honor your father and your mother, that your days may be long and prosperous upon the Earth.'"

I immediately thought about the difficulties we are facing today between parents and children. Many children are distracted and disturbed by negative influences outside the home which present unique and challenging problems for their parents. At the same time, other children are being neglected or abused by parents who are lost within dysfunctional relationships and situations. These children desperately need to recover their self-esteem from such influences.

He pointed out, *"This commandment encompasses a great deal more than just the protocol of respect between children and their Earthly parents. In the days of Moses the family unit was completely autocratic, populations were small, and tribal orientations were centered around family function. Therefore, the law could be stated narrowly and still embrace its fullest meaning. Today there are many more factors influencing the lives of children. Much more diversity and complexity now exists in society and the family unit. So, to appreciate the deeper significance of this law, a greater breadth of its application must first be considered.*

"The love that empowers this commandment is actually the love of everyone who has come before you. By respecting the bringers and givers of what has come before, you are able to receive with nourishment all that is

offered. You cannot stand on the shoulders of someone for whom you have no respect. History is part of each person's collective advantage. Surely there is something in each person's history which is acceptable and worthy of receiving with love. When I told you to bless the food that you receive into your body, it was to help you understand more fully that it is love, more than food, which nourishes you. The same is true of your personal and cultural heritage. You will make no progress in life without the love and respect for that which preceded your arrival on the Earth. Denial of the past causes a man to spend his life reinventing the wheel. Such a man will tend to break continuity on the misguided assumption that 'starting from scratch' brings more personal fulfillment. Or he will break that which he has been given in order to prove that he can fix it in a better way. How will your days be long and prosperous if you do not honor that upon which you are building? Living and working together is the key to brotherhood and prosperity. In honoring that upon which you are building, you create the foundation to move forward. Then your attention will be entirely upon moving ahead, rather than trying to replace that which you refuse to respect."

I thought about His statement in relation to my artistic career. As early as three years of age, I knew that my life would be spent as an artist. Before I was old enough to write, I would passionately pore over the pages of a wonderful book of old master painters that belonged to my mother. As she noticed the love I had for those pictures, she gave me the book. Although I have to admit that by the time I was four years old the book was beginning to look a little worse for wear. The images on those pages were my inspiration and the artists were my heroes. Even at that young age, I knew upon whose shoulders I wanted to stand. Because of that realization, I received generous support from everyone in my life, and enjoyed a fine head start in my career. Through the years, I was strengthened by the fact that I always could draw upon a reservoir of prior artistic achievement.

I expressed my appreciation for the value of that principle and discussed with Jesus the confidence I had derived from it. He responded with the following comment, *"Everything exists within a context and draws its nourishment as well as its honesty from acknowledging its context. Faithfully reporting facts and intentions is only part of honesty. The power of honesty comes from honor, and that involves an acknowledgment and appreciation of context. There is no fact, issue, or person that cannot be misrepresented by changing, hiding, or distorting a context. The pursuit of an honest life begins with honoring the relevance of context in all things. A person's first* *context is the family. There may be problems and hardships which need to be healed or left behind. Sometimes that is the case. Although, a context that is not understood and handled is a context which **cannot be left behind**.*

"Unfortunately, many children begin their lives by denying their context, choosing not to build upon their innocent beginnings. Instead, such statements are made as, 'I will begin my life after I'm out of this place!' Or perhaps they will protest the lives of Mom and Dad or other family members, promising never to be like them. With great resistance, objections are formulated and forceful proclamations are made about not repeating the mistakes of others. All of life is a stream of energy, experiences, and love. Learning from the perils and shortfalls of others is a mark of wisdom. However, when a person rejects the flow of life which brought his experiences to him, he destroys the context for future understanding and resolution.

"Also by denying a context, one is attempting to create a vacuum. The universe will tolerate many illusions, but not the existence of a vacuum. Such a thing would be a violation of the one spirit and its unbroken integrity. No sooner is a vacuum created than it is filled with the very thing which would have caused it to happen. The thought you formulated to create a vacuum will become the thing which is manifested. One of the surest ways to become like that which you judge, is to separate yourself from it and create an emptiness. History repeats itself generation after generation because of judgment and denial which create ruptures in the flow of life. The universe fills the ruptures quickly with the very thing your objections denied. Cycle after tragic cycle, unwanted elements are brought forth again for re-examination. It would profit mankind greatly to understand the heart's power to accept, process, purify, and allow the things which are less than perfect to serve their purpose and move on. Life is an ever progressing stream of love, creation, consciousness, and action. As the flow progresses though your heart and life, you will add to it from your own efforts and love, and gain from it the experiences you need for your own growth. Whenever we attempt to stop the flow, it will double back and repeat itself. Allowing the good things to pass through your life is easy enough. Admiration brings harmony and resolution. With things of lesser pleasure, forgiveness and tolerance are necessary if a flow is to move gracefully on to another place where it more appropriately belongs. As life progresses, it is refined and purified by its own change of context. Have you ever noticed that an action which may seem wrong in one context is very beneficial in another? The Sacred Heart is the

vehicle and conduit for perfecting and refining the fire of life as it moves
through your life. Life is not to be stopped. Life is for living, participation,
experience, and enjoyment. As a child of God you are part of the continuing
creation. Therefore, to move forward with growth and prosperity, you need
to acknowledge with love and respect the patterns of generation which
brought your life to you. This is part of divine order."

The sixth commandment states, **"You shall not kill."** The threat of
physical violence still clearly exists in many parts of the world today as well
as within certain sectors of our own society. Nevertheless, I rarely thought
about that commandment, and I assumed that anyone I knew never gave it
much thought either. The simple reason being that most of us would rather
lose our own lives than to destroy that of another. In a world of growing
global brotherhood and protective public institutions, we have relaxed into
a premature conclusion that life is now respected above all else and murder
belongs only to the world of barbarity. Yet, there is more to this subject than
meets the eye. As the threat of murder has become less prevalent, we have
also become less conscious of the intellectual depths invoked by Moses'
admonition. Contemplation of the sanctity of life is never wasted time.

The Master brilliantly and clearly led me to understand that there was
a great deal more to this commandment than simply a restriction against
homicide. *"The fundamental power of justice is a universal abundance
capable of rectifying and balancing any problem or inequity. Just consider,
for example, how many seeds one stalk of wheat produces, or how many eggs
a flea lays. Everything in nature multiplies itself richly in an ever-expanding
phenomena of life. Whenever an assault has been made against life, it
multiplies its production. The second power of justice is exchange. Because
primary essence is the same in all things, there is an infinite possibility for
exchange among elements and circumstances to provide for balance and
adjustment whenever needed. The third power of justice is the adaptability
of life to continue beyond all opposition, above all odds. It is futile to oppose.
It is senseless and wasteful to annihilate. Life will continue beyond all
judgments, beyond all resistance, beyond all attempts to obliterate it.
Therefore, when a man adopts a destructive approach to life, he becomes a
lethal virus to everything, including himself.*

*"When you behold expansion with love, you empower your life with
richness. If you think of life in terms of conflict, scarcity, and destruction,
you will sanction a denial of your own higher power. Expansion is life's way,
yet that way is frightening to a person who sees himself as separate from the*

greater whole of existence. To such a person, expansion for another means deprivation for self. Thus he will attack. For most people, the actual killing of a human being is unthinkable. All the while, a purpose, a talent, a dream, an idea, or a love may be killed without flinching. To invalidate, with the intent of stopping the life force of another, is to kill! The motivation for doing so might be nothing more than to hold ground or to gain a personal advantage. Because of fear, there is an urge to kill that which encroaches upon personal interests. The better approach would be to study how expansion could best serve the interests of all concerned. Often two businesses compete for the same public, when cooperation might provide a greater outreach for both into more diverse markets. Frequently, technology stifles collective advancement through withholding knowledge from competitors, when a sharing of science would open up more possibilities than either team could service. To the higher dimensions of the heart, the whole purpose of life is expansion. When we embrace the love of that expansion, there is no limit to how far your influence and awareness may extend. Religions and philosophies are serving the wrong end when they become the basis for conflict. The fact is, most wars have been waged over religious or philosophical issues. The founders of your nation realized this and set forth protections and freedoms to prevent internal conflict. Thus, you have freedom of communication, the right to pursue your life as you see fit, and to pursue happiness within an environment which grants the same rights to everyone else. Our Father's universe is supported by those rights and more."

By surrendering to Divine Order, by accepting and integrating life's many possibilities, we begin to understand the deeper meaning of the commandment, "You shall not kill." With its roots in love, we see that this commandment is the law of respecting life as an expanding phenomenon. Destruction is a futile and desperate attempt enacted to reverse expansion when we feel that our lives are displaced or threatened by patterns of growth which do not seem to serve our personal interests. When I asked Jesus about the apparent inequities of growth which occur, He explained, *"All of life has its cycles. The tide cannot be in and out at the same time. A tree does not put forth new leaves and new limbs simultaneously. Respect for divine order means sharing and often waiting. It can require tolerance and forgiveness along with a spirit of submission to prevailing forces which must first be allowed to complete their growth. "Countries go to war because they do not know how to expand without conflict. Destroying life, however, is not a solution to the conflicts of coexistence. Life will continue, no matter what, and one's frustration with conflict will continue until life is understood as an unfolding of the Father's will. The abundance and goodness of life is the foundation of all justice. In knowing that, you bring justice to life. Many solutions other than violence and hostility are available to a man who has that understanding. In the frontier, for example, if two brothers disagreed, one could go west and other could go east into new lands which absorbed their differences. Work together to expand the possibilities for all, and annihilation will become a thing of the past.*

*"The seventh commandment states, '**You shall not commit adultery.**' It is the Father's will that the institution of marriage be a holy bond, not entered into lightly or broken lightly. The holiness of marriage does not draw its power from the Earthly plane. The coming together of a man and a woman to create a life of devotion to each other is a symbol for the sacred marriage between the Father and His faithfulness to mankind, between the immortal soul and its beloved heart, and between all aspects of creation which are bonded together to work in love.*

"The marriage of a man and woman honors and recognizes the marriage of all other things. When a marriage is loving and pure, it is also the greatest expression of kindness and tenderness to be found on Earth. Compassion is the Father's will for all of life. Wherever kindness is held in loving sanctuary, there is hope and a basis for it to be extended throughout the rest of existence.

"Whenever two or more come together in love, for any purpose, whatever the relationship, whatever the bond, a union is created within the one spirit. Under the governance of love, a very close interchange of adamantine particles will occur. Such a deep and meaningful bond as marriage should be pure and free from irrelevant, debased, or dishonest ingredients. Every problem that occurs later on can be traced back to basic adulterations of love. If the commitment is weak and the motivations were less than honorable, there may not be enough strength and sincerity to produce an enduring marriage. When the bond is not pure, a relationship will fail. This happens because adulteration is already part of the relationship. Unity was formed for any number of external motivations, insincere reasons, or perhaps in an inappropriate way. If a marriage occurs only for money, convenience, or social advantage, adultery has already been programmed into the relationship. Is there any wonder that adulteration will later manifest as infidelity?"

"Marital instability and divorce are widespread problems today. Are there circumstances and conditions under which a marriage should be deliberately ended?"

"The real core of unity is the love of two people honoring their bond to each other with respect, sincerity, and depth of commitment. If this does not exist in sufficient measure to be cultivated, or if the adulteration of love is greater than the couple's ability to resolve, then it would be better to discontinue the marriage than to dishonor love. Even so, the dissolving of marriage should not be taken lightly or for reasons stemming from momentary stress and pressure, for this is a union instituted by God. All marriages belong to the Father, to be empowered or dispensed according to His will. This is necessary to ensure that human life never be owned by another, even through the bonds of matrimony. By the Father's will, even where the marriage has been a good one, there are times when a greater covenant will be established with the individuals to serve in separate ways. Therefore, structure is not endowed with the authority to imprison love beyond its service, merely to perpetuate the stability of vested interests or outward signs of solidarity.

"The union of a man and woman is the most pure and perfect symbol for the marriage of any two things. Therefore, its fullest significance can be seen as it brings depth of meaning to other relationships as well. The principles of marriage are symbolic for all relationships. When you commit your life in faith to a career or vocation, is that not a marriage? What about your relationship to brotherhood, to friends, to family, and the one spirit? Are these not also marriages?"

"What is the greatest marriage?"

"The union of God and man. That is the power behind all other marriages. When mankind responds to the will of God as a bride does to her groom, there will be Heaven on Earth."

After that powerful statement there was silence in the room. I expected Him to continue, but He said nothing else for almost an hour. During that time I painted and reflected upon His words. Then, as I reviewed my notes, a powerful insight washed over my consciousness. Each one of the first seven commandments had reflected and progressively developed the seven higher dimensions of intelligence within the heart. The reasons behind each of these laws could be seen as unity, love, life, respect, honesty, justice, and kindness, and within each law were those same propelling forces of higher intelligence. As that realization dawned upon me, our eyes joined again and

He began to speak. His statement rang like a benediction to my newly acquired understanding. *"You have now seen the greater truth behind these laws. They are instruments of the heart's command!"*

"What about the remaining three commandments?" I inquired. I was particularly curious, because I knew that in divine order there was no such thing as a "leftover."

He obliged, *"The last three commandments pertain to the heart's covenants. Through its magnetic power, the heart's first covenant is to unfold your life as an extension of the love that you are. That which you shall do and have is a direct result of the heart's balance between inner and outer potentials of life. The second covenant of the heart is to perceive life innocently. This is your right to be present as a witness of creation and to perceive the truth in all things. The third covenant of the heart is to hold and empower the life purpose which exists between you and your holy Source."*

The eighth law states, **"You shall not steal."** In all sectors of society, theft is becoming a major source of economic duress and societal danger. Many people feel that this is a sign of widespread moral decay, while a few more forgiving souls regard it as a desperate attempt to re-circulate wealth in a world that is quickly losing its economic mobility. Even so, most observations and conclusions about theft fall under the heading of judgment. Man has focused so intensely on the laws prohibiting and providing punishment for theft, that he has ignored the underlying reasons why ownership should be honored. From my early childhood training, I came to believe that each person had a moral decision to make about whether or not to steal. Once the choice was made, further thoughts were unnecessary–only the need to behave accordingly. Such a narrow viewpoint of the commandment's meaning left little for the intellect to ponder or for the soul to savor in the form of understanding. Therefore, I sought to approach the subject from a different perspective that would lead to more depth of understanding. I began by asking, "What is the nature of rightful ownership?"

"There is a right relationship between a person's love and that which truly belongs to him. Respect of property is a matter of honoring rights and honoring an individual. This commandment centers upon respect for the individual and the right of each individual to have his own appointed place and time, and to be supplied with that which is rightfully his. Regardless of whether property is intangible or material, it is attracted by love through the heart's power. From the beginning until the end, all things belong to the

Father. For purposes of living, responsibility, and pleasure, custody is extended to the children. Property is acquired in many ways ranging from earning to gifting, although the most important factor in attainment and acquisition is the love within your heart which allows you to receive and to use. Respect of property is just a symbol for honoring the love of one another and each other's rights."

After He mentioned that, I thought back to an incident many years ago with a young woman I had employed. I had no doubts about her basic honesty. Nevertheless, one time after being gone for a day, I noticed some notes were missing from my private filing cabinet. These were some research notes on my color theory which were irreplaceable to me, though of little value to anyone else. The loss was both disturbing and puzzling. With a certain amount of reluctance to accuse her, I continued my search and waited for more clues to emerge. Two days later I found that the notes had been returned to their original filing jacket. Nothing was missing, but I was obsessed with the mystery. I also did not want to hold negative thoughts about my employee, so I decided to clear the air. She freely admitted to taking the papers out of sheer curiosity, but then adding quickly, "I didn't steal anything."

I looked at her calmly and replied, "Yes, you did. You stole my privacy and my rights over this information." This was a new concept for both of us and a lesson to be mutually learned. She apologized, and I forgave. After that, there was more respect between the two of us. Ironically, there was also more sharing.

Jesus commented, *"Sharing is a natural outgrowth of respecting each other's rights to have that which is needed to fulfill and serve life. For lack of respect, material property has become a barricade which separates the lives of people. One man may have too much and another too little, and neither have enough trust to break the log jam, or enough wisdom to know how or why it should be done."*

"What if a man is really poor and desperately hungry. Is it wrong for him to take some food if there is no one to ask for charity or work?"

With immense compassion in His eyes, He replied, *"There is a wrongness, although it is a mutual transgression which can be resolved only from the Father's greater perspective. The crime will need to be corrected and adjustments will need to be made in the life of the desperate man, otherwise such actions may become an indelible part of his character. At the same time the deprivations which made his actions necessary will also have to be addressed. Hoarding and greed, which helped to create scarcity for him, will also be accountable. Greed is just another form of stealing. Scarcity and excess are both the result of losing a sense of true ownership. Knowledge of what is rightfully yours, from an inner certainty within the heart, is something money cannot buy. Without that certainty, ownership is reinforced with boundaries and restrictive covenants."*

The more He spoke, the more I realized that deeds of possession always bring responsibility, though not necessarily true ownership. There is also collective ownership, which is the pride we share in communities, activities, professions, schools, and groups. Such things are jointly loved and shared by many. Often I have prepared my lectures in the Fort Worth Botanical Garden, which I fondly call "my other office." I do not possess a deed to that garden, yet I feel it has been specially provided as a space in which I may find centering within the one spirit. As we expand our concept of ownership we have to include more than just what can be purchased and held privately. Some people are city people, and that space is shared by their souls. Others are ocean people, and there are people who favor the mountains. Whenever I heard John Denver sing about the Rocky Mountains, I liked to think those were his mountains.

*"There is an ebb and flow of creation which can be observed in all of existence. All things come from God and to that Source they return. Still, it may be said that during the course of existing, everything belongs to itself. This reflects the **supremacy of being** which sustains creation. **The deepest understanding you can have about the law of property is give unto everything that which is its own.** Give unto God that which is His, to the Earth that which is hers, to your brother that which is his, and to yourself that which is yours. This is both a sublime truth and a completely practical formula. The most common theft in the world is to steal from one part of your life to support another which is unproductive. For example, budgets go askew when rent money is used for something else. There is a kind of 'fund accounting' in the universe which causes the need for balance between that which magnetizes a flow of energy and that which receives it. When correct allotment is observed, there will be a magnification of energy, and when it is disregarded there will be a loss of support. It is love which commands and attracts. When love is honored, there is no end of wealth. Love is true ownership. When you fully understand this, thieves can no longer break in and steal that which is yours."* The ninth law of Moses states, **"You shall not bear false witness."** The obvious meaning of this commandment is not to

lie, and especially about your fellow man, or what you have witnessed or seen.

From a more positive perspective, the Master said, *"Love reality with such clarity and depth that you have no need to see it falsely or misrepresent it to anyone. Love of reality is the core of honesty and the essence of innocent perception. To practice deception is a treacherous thing, for it will take you away from yourself and from God. Yet the full meaning of honesty is the love of reality, to be present and to perceive what is in front of you. There are many who would refrain from lying and still go through life wearing rose colored glasses."*

Often we put on blinders, and deny what is in front of us. When He spoke about innocent perception, He was referring to the ability to see life as it is, and to accept it for what it is. Innocent perception is the heart's passion for discovery, enlightenment, and compassionate living. He noted that, *"Honesty is not just an act of morality. It is the foundation of wisdom and intelligence."*

"Many people think the truth hurts and therefore avoid it whenever possible. Why is that so?"

"The reason is that a great confusion exists between frankness and honesty. Some people are so frank their every word stings, yet they cannot see the moon rising. These people go out of their way to speak their minds even though their minds have no clear perceptions. Frankness can hurt and often does. Honesty always refers back to reality, and so there is an element of comfort, support, and resolution contained within it.

*"Truth is a universal constant. All one needs for conveying truth is respect for reality. The revealing of truth can be very gentle and kind, with tolerance and compassion for the other person's understanding. I often use parables to speak of truth. The benevolent aspect of parables and metaphors is their adaptability to the hearts, minds, and expectations of the listener. That way, one truth can be heard by many people and be understood on different levels of awareness, according to each person's receptivity and readiness. The truth lies in **what** is spoken and **what** is heard, and not so much in how it is conveyed!"*

The last law of Moses states, **"You shall not covet."** Coveting is an enormous problem in the world today. With so much competition and peer pressure, there is a fear of not living up to external standards. Products are advertised by super-stars and, of course, the idea is that we can acquire their successful image by consuming the same merchandise.

Jesus said, *"Do not seek your fulfillment in the external. An endowment of love and ability has been given to each child by the Father. This cannot be discovered by cultivating external advantages or by comparing your gains and your difficulties with those of another. The love behind this commandment is the love of being one with your purpose, which results in the love of inner accomplishment, and the full harvest of your own reason for being. When you truly are being yourself, you know that you are a child of God. There is nothing greater to be. You are here to forward His creation, and there is nothing greater to do. Therefore, you have a purpose, and the process of living will unfold it. To covet is to replace your sacred purpose with purely external motivation.*

"External motivation will eventually destroy a person's ability to recognize or honor his own purposes. This leads to jealousy over the accomplishments of others and a sense of self-defeat in the presence of another's triumph. To pursue a life propelled by jealousy, is to lead a life of counterfeit purpose. A sense of true purpose can be rekindled, however, by respecting the beauty of accomplishment and the true process by which it occurs. The real process of achieving is like building a house one brick at a time. First, one brick is set into mortar and then another is placed beside it. As the work continues, attention is given to each and every brick to ensure its level plane and proper joining. The true mason knows that in every line of bricks is the true character of the mansion. Eventually, he will stand back and see the wall complete and ultimately behold the entire edifice. In the meantime, what is needed is faith and dedication to the process of building. Without that inner confidence, the big picture will be lost and denial of personal importance will overtake the joy of dedicated work.

"Submitting love to the process of living is a powerful thing. When you look only to external achievement and forget to honor the process, you become like Icarus, the figure in Greek mythology. Icarus wanted to fly to the sun, and so he constructed a pair of giant wings, which he molded out of wax. These were enormous and beautiful wings which he strapped to his arms. Like a modern hang glider, he sailed from a cliff and seized the wind currents until he came closer and closer to the sun. He was ill-prepared to realize that in approaching the sun, it would melt his wings. Suddenly, Icarus fell into the ocean, from which he would be washed to shore. What Icarus forgot was that we make it to the sun, or to any destination, by taking one step at a time in a process which is appropriate to the goal. Icarus was so focused upon the desire to dazzle others with his finished achievement, that

*he devalued the process. When you love the process of achieving, you will be less tempted to compare your accomplishment with others. Each person is working on a different schedule, just as there are young and old in a society. There are those finishing projects and those who are just beginning. You start a project, follow it through to completion, and then start another. The fact that some people are arriving at their fulfillment ahead of you is just part of the cycle of life. The person laying the last brick in his masterpiece will surely experience pride in himself and elicit admiration from others. In the same neighborhood there may be someone else laying the first brick in his future building. He feels vulnerable and insecure as he hides his meager beginning from public exposure. The two are no different, however, for they each have laid **just one brick** in an ongoing process of purposeful living. The act of coveting externalizes a person's motivation and removes him from this deeper understanding. Loving the process of achievement and appreciating one's own purpose is the real foundation of the last commandment, for love and life are never ending processes."*

Chapter 10
Your Rights and Freedoms

The information in this chapter was first revealed by the Master on a late February morning in 1992, when I arrived for work in a distracted, downcast mood. My discomfort had been caused by the news of some illness in my family, and it seemed as though I would need to be away from the studio for a while to care for a family member. Actually, I felt sympathetic toward the problem and eager to help. Nevertheless, I was also a bit annoyed with the mandatory interruption.

Jesus saw that I was wrestling with that issue and trying to deal with it privately, so He broke my nervous silence by saying, *"You have the right to take a little time off if you have other things pressing for your attention."*

It was reassuring to feel His unsolicited compassion and to witness the depth of His perception without need of spoken information. Even so, the phrase which startled me the most and captured my lingering attention was, "You have the right." This meant, of course, that I had the right **to choose where I wanted to be**. Even being with the Master was not a compulsory thing! The minute He indicated that I had the right to decide, my dilemma seemed to vanish, and within an hour, I received a call from another relative saying that circumstances had improved. I would be able to stay and paint, after all.

After savoring my feelings in silence for a while, we began our discussion of human rights. He began by saying, *"When you know that you have rights, you know that you can change your life."*

I realized that was the core belief which made America different from every other country in the world at the time of her founding. People came here expressly to assert and defend their rights, in the total conviction that by doing so life would be better. Of course, that quest did not begin in 1776. The declaration and respect of human rights had been progressing within the consciousness of humankind throughout its history. We are today experiencing a growing sense of political, spiritual, and personal rights as we move into more fluid contexts for living. That morning when I saw the clarity in His eyes and the concern in His voice that I should be aware of my rights, I was deeply moved to ask for more understanding. I wanted to know, "What are these rights, and how may I implement them in my life?" He obliged in great length that day. Prior to discussing our rights and freedoms, however, He delivered a preamble on the very important and highly relevant subject of free will. With a clear understanding of what constitutes free will, the comprehension of personal rights is virtually self-evident. Without the existence of free will, there would be no basis for consideration of rights at all. A corollary to that subject, upon which He also touched, is the issue of human equality. All other freedoms seem to revolve around the two fundamental principles of free will and human equality.

*"Free will is the foundation right given by the Holy Father to all of His children. It is the right to be who you really are and to make choices in life which give evidence to that truth. Life is full of movement, with varying possibilities and options for change. Through the choices you make, you give support to your life, your love, and your truth. In and of itself, a context or environment may or may not honor or sustain the essence of who you are. The reason is that you are a child of God and **not** a child of circumstance. The very fact of having free will is what liberates you from the imprisonment of circumstance. You may initiate changes to make a situation compatible with your love, and you can choose not to support those situations which deny your love. Even if none of the choices available to you is ideal, the **very act of making choices** will give you an assertive power over external conditions and a way of moving through them.*

"Free will is not a sanction for destructive, deviant, or irrational behavior which might be stimulated independently of a person's character, life needs, or the laws of God. Free will is not a senseless free-for-all. Free will is essentially the right to be yourself, to know yourself, and to select the elements and companions of your life according to how appropriately they extend and serve the nature of your being. Free will is given equally to all in order that each person might have the right to express his love as it truly is, and to protect himself from the ravages of circumstance.

"All the children of God are equal in relation to their Holy Father.

There are none who have a preferred relationship to the Father or special advantages in fulfilling it. None are above experiencing the transitory hardships of mortal existence, and none are beneath the Father's eternal love and capacity for forgiveness. Every person was created in the loving image of the Father, and a loving core essence remains unsullied by even the most desperate circumstances. Within each individual is a Sacred Center wherein his covenant with the Father is purposefully sustained. Every individual is an immortal soul with a meaningful place in the whole of existence. These sacred equalities have a direct bearing upon your rights and freedoms.

*"There are also **inequalities** which directly affect your rights and freedoms. The reason is that an individual has a right to be respected in his inequality as well as his equality. Not everyone has made equal progress toward fulfilling his potential. Not everyone has been born into equal circumstances, with equal health, wealth, or intelligence. All of these considerations, and more, are part of each individual's life situation. Such conditions are very real, even though they are all changeable with a change of heart and application of effort. Regardless of the reasons for his circumstance, every person has a right to experience self-esteem within his existing realities. Nothing undermines equality of rights more surely than attempting to relegate them to sameness of condition. It is the person, **not** the condition, that has rights!*

*"When you offer charity, do so to lift up another, not to dishonor him with embarrassment. What is the point of helping your brothers or sisters if you only set yourself above them? Inequality of circumstance is part of reality. Even so, it is the power of brotherhood to acknowledge the differences while transcending them with love. **The highest unity is one which respects difference as well as sameness and regards both with equal respect.** Otherwise, the very concept of equality would become a yoke of conformity that would repress the advantaged and lay unkind demands upon the disadvantaged. Every individual should have the right to experience his worth, within whatever condition he might find himself. He also should have the right to enjoy emotional and life support from those who share his conditions. Enjoyment of peerage is an extension of self-esteem which generates strength for collective well-being.*

"In return for these fundamental rights, it is asked of you only that you refrain from judgment. You cannot know what is in another man's heart, and often outward signs are misleading. If you would attain and

protect the first two of your founding rights, you must clearly understand a third right. Your third fundamental right is to know, to experience, and to honor the spirit of innocence, and most importantly, to know where innocence can be found. Nothing will destroy your capacity for that understanding more thoroughly than judgment. Innocence belongs to the Father, to the sacred center of each person's heart, and to a quality of perception which is free from judgment and pre-conception. Through the exercise of innocent perception, all misconceptions may be exposed and released from one's life. Through the innocent heart, purposefulness with God may be restored to life. These are the only three aspects of innocence to be found in the realm of action and living. If you expect there to be any others, you will endlessly judge out of frustration and disappointment, and deny yourself the pleasure and fulfillment of tolerant living. The surest sign that a man has gained the wisdom of knowing where to find wisdom is that he has a sense of humor!

"Life is a flow. Within that flow, there are seasons. There are winter and spring, sunshine and rain, sickness and health. All of these potentialities bring experiences which are valuable to your consciousness. Some of them challenge your patience; some reward your devotion. Within all the choices available, some will support your life more than others, yet none will be externally flawless. For example, a man cannot pluck a carrot from the Earth for his dinner without depriving the carrot of its own life. With the best of intentions, parents may enroll their son in voice lessons, when his afternoons might otherwise be spent developing a greater athletic ability. On the other hand, there have been malicious actions which resulted in good, as in one case, where a man was unjustly terminated from his employment. Though untimely in the financial sense, it allowed him to find the career of his true calling.

*"I have said to you many times that a man who judges is in peril of losing his way in life. Judgment obliterates respect for innocence and a comprehension of where it may or may not be found. **Innocence does not belong to the external world**. With a loss of that understanding, an individual will become intolerant and vengeful toward others. In his own life he will be like a ship without a rudder, imprisoned within life-consuming formulas. This is why I once made the challenge to any man who is without sin to cast the first stone! To draw any correlation whatsoever between innocence and external action invalidates the meaning*

of innocence itself. Is the mountain lion less innocent for devouring the rabbit than he would be if he denied himself the food and starved?

"This is not to imply that in the arena of human conduct, all actions are equally supportive of life and personal fulfillment. For certainly, a man may virtually make or break his life based upon the choices he makes. Even so, there is a greater point to be grasped, and that is, goodness cannot be determined by outward appearance, and certainly not by the judgment of another. The goodness of a man lies within the innocence of his heart. All the while, his actions may sometimes fall short of the demands and expectations made upon him. In making the many choices which life will bring to a person, it is well to know that perfection lies in correlating your actions with the will of God, and the love that you are, rather than seeking for external approbation and admiration, which is fleeting at best. Anyone who loses sight of this will soon lose sight of his own salvation and deprive himself of the very rights and freedoms which could fulfill his life."

He did not number the other rights, nor did He ever imply that our rights were solely limited to the ones which we discussed that day. Nevertheless, the remaining rights and freedoms which He highlighted seemed to add up to twelve . Apparently free will, equality of humankind, and eternal innocence within the Sacred Heart comprise the foundation of all our other rights, and provide the elements of constancy which give meaning and direction to our other freedoms. My perception is that the primary rights pertain to the endowment of life itself, and the remaining twelve rights support us in the conducting of our lives.

The most important of these remaining rights is to have a relationship with our Creator. *"The connection with your Father is never broken, no matter how far you have detached yourself through living a life apart from the sacred. Your core connection is always sustained, despite your efforts to empower separation. In pursuing a life apart from God, the vacuum created will become filled with ideas, structures, institutions and relationships which dominate you mercilessly. You may feel that you are a prisoner of everything which has come between you and God; for, indeed, all those things which have come between you and your Creator have assumed the power of God over you. This leads to the unfortunate conclusion that if you would return to your Source, you first must seek permission from everything which has intervened and exploited your separation. This is not true, for your relationship with the Creator is immediate and everlasting. It is a relationship which is not dependent upon*

the consent of anyone else, nor is it controlled by conformity of beliefs. All
you have to do is act upon your immortal right to be restored in a
relationship with your Holy Father. No matter what condition in which you
might find yourself, the tie has never been lost.

"**You have a right to know yourself as love, and to manifest that
personal truth in your own unique and meaningful way.** You are love.
The world would have you believe that you are merely *from* love, and that
your life is justified by the love that you *do*. It may persuade you to believe
everything else about love, except for the fact that you *are* love. The very
essence of your worth, your purposefulness, your immortality, and your
freedom, however, lie in the certainty that you are love.

"In being the love that you are, you radiate the energy of your life.
You attract from the center core of your beingness that which your life
requires, and you join with that which your life needs to complete itself. As
love, you have a right to acknowledge the companions, activities, purposes,
and things which you love. It is your right to love, and to choose that which
you love. Prejudice, judgment, and conformity are strong in the world. The
pressure of these influences can weaken a person's desire or confidence to
express an unpopular love. However, nothing external can diminish the
power of your love. It is a matter of integrity to honor that which you are,
and to seek ways of nurturing your life so that your love is truly expressed.
Love is your eternal right; it is who you are.

"**You also have a right to be in communion with that which you love.**
Your love is your only enduring treasure. Of all the things which you own,
experience, generate, or cultivate, love alone will remain with you beyond
this life. All the love that you have, and know, is yours to keep. To be
separated from it is to be separated from your wealth. Is there any wonder
that so many people are having difficulties with prosperity, when they have
repressed, forgotten, or denied that which they love. You were created as
love to be joined with that which extends and completes your love. It is
your right to know that joy, fulfillment, and wealth.

"Your love, and your sustainment of that which you love, is an
enduring reality, because there is but one spirit which is part of everything.
The whole is undivided, and **you have a right to know that you are an
essential part of it.** Everyone's life is woven into the tapestry. No one can
judge you out of it, bully you out of it, or turn you away, for the spirit is
simple and unbroken. Only lies and delusions have imparted the suggestion
that spirit is divided or torn. The reason you have been persuaded to

believe in spiritual division is that you must first subscribe to such beliefs before they can be used to isolate and control you. Do not accept isolation as the condition of your life. You are part of the family, regardless of judgments which others may have placed against you. Let judgments be the problem of those who make them!"

Once more, it was quite apparent that He had more patience with human error than human judgment.

"You have the right to know and to profit by your connection with all of life and to be healed by your surrender to wholeness. Through the one spirit you can receive inspirations from across the universe, provided they are relevant to your life. You simply will not hear those messages which are not meant for you. The one spirit is a living intelligence beyond all comprehension, which retains all memory and holds all potential. Through prayer and meditation, in which you acknowledge the oneness of spirit, you can receive great ideas and wondrous messages about your life and your future. All you have to do is ask."

"It seems that some people are afraid of entering the spirit because of the potential for negative effects . . . after all, as you also have said, the spirit contains **everything**."

*"In communing with the one spirit, the key is **to surrender and to listen**. In that mode of receptivity the Holiness of the Spirit will descend upon you to give you nourishment and guidance. Those who have gotten into trouble spiritually are those who have attempted to assert themselves aggressively into the spirit, to manipulate or direct it according to their private desires. Remember, as I have already told you, anyone who disrupts or divides the spirit or violates its simple oneness, especially for selfish motives, will have the assault visited upon himself!*

"Most people decline to exercise spiritual awareness because they have come to believe they are separate from the spiritual kingdom. Well, I tell you this . . . the spiritual kingdom is not elsewhere, a place to be entered externally. It is within you. The spiritual kingdom dwells within all beings, things, times, and places. The one spirit is forever and everywhere. It is within you, and it is your right to know that you are a part of it. In knowing that, you can receive much wisdom and insight to make your life more whole.

"You have the right to enter your heart consciously and to know the higher intelligence which it is providing for your life. In order to do this you must understand and accept your basic innocence. To enter the heart,

*you do not have to ask permission. It is a right, although there is one requirement. You must enter as your true self, as the love that you are. Within the core of your own beingness, your innocence will not recognize anything else. Perhaps this seems impossible when your life is full of trouble, hardship, and difficulty, where it is difficult to determine the true from the false externally, much less in yourself. You may ask, 'How can I be innocent and perfect at the core of my being when I am immersed in Earthly predicaments?' This right does not exist as a point of logic connected to the world of conditions. Surrendering to the true self that you are and to the eternal connection which exists with your Father **does not have to make sense**. It is a right you may assume under any condition. Through your return to the heart's intelligence, you will find the answers you truly need.*

*"**You have a right to experience infinity from your own viewpoint and to appreciate within its vast potential the values and meanings which support your reason for being.** As part of this, you have a right to look above and beyond all structures, to disagree with common assumptions which you sincerely believe to be wrong, and to say no to prospects and proposals which do not exist in harmony with your life and values. You have the right to exceed any structure that would try to contain you. You have the right to reach into the unknown, and dare to dream. You have a right to imagination, and to the fruits of its creation. In that pursuit, it is your right to experience infinity and establish a viewpoint about your hopes and dreams.*

*"**You also have a right to know that you are immortal.**"*

To many of you it may seem shocking that something so obvious needs to be presented as a right. Yet the more shocking fact is that a large number of people in the western world have no greater concept of self than what can be derived from their biological origins and social contexts. To these people, when death comes, all is over. To an even larger number, comprising a majority perhaps, immortality does exist; yet, it is delegated only by permission and reward.

"There are those in the world who would reduce you to living with the concept of mortality in order that your life might be defined by the laws of limitation and structure. The idea is, 'Live now or not at all . . . submit to the program . . . what you do not get now, you won't get later.' When you know you are immortal, you simply are too free to control, and can jump any fence the agendas of man may erect. Therefore, the true understanding

of immortal life has been greatly suppressed. In some cases it has been blatantly denied; and in other cases, especially in the Eastern world, it has been misdirected to imply that mankind is trapped within an ever ascending wheel of life. The truth is, you have only one life, and it is forever. How your eternal life unfolds is entirely according to your love. Where your love is, there will you be also. *I do not say this casually. It is the law. As your love is, so will you be.* When your love has refined itself to prefer and enjoy Heavenly pleasures, then you will be there. For those who love the seamier side of life, there will be a domain where that aspect of life is made available to you. Wherever your love is, there you will be. Your love cannot be stopped, and you will be with it. Love brings your lessons, friends, blessings, and opportunities. All of your patterns of growth, and all of the changes in your life have occurred because something changed in the pattern of your love. It is through developing patterns of love that change unfolds in your life. You are not going to have your love in one place and be somewhere else!

"Your love walks hand in hand with your immortality. In knowing this you will have confidence that fulfillment is truly possible. It begins by realizing that your life extends well beyond any structures that would bind you . . . even to the point of immortality. This is your right. *"You have a right to live in fullness and to seek all the blessings of life.* No man has a covenant to suffer. Suffering may be a part of life from time to time. It may even be a necessary part of your unfolding lessons. However, suffering is no man's covenant. Whenever hardship appears, consider the greater purpose to which it may belong. Your Father wants to bless you with abundance and joy. Every covenant was etched in joy; therefore, if a man is suffering, it is not by the will of the Father. Often, suffering is an ingredient of life which brings joy upon completion, much like giving birth. Sometimes suffering occurs through collective abuse and ignorance, or a person's own willingness to participate in suffering. There are some who mistakenly believe that suffering is a punishment from God. As a consequence of cause and effect, there is some truth to that, although our Father does not intentionally punish. Tragically, many people suffer because they have more faith in the prospect of pain than in the reality of blessing. Those who have experienced a life of suffering feel that, at least, hardship is one thing on which to rely. Any prediction is better than none. Their father suffered, and their grandfather suffered before that, which bestows a kind of love upon that painful tradition. Some people have *actually come to love their suffering, for it is the strongest bond to be shared with those who are dear to them. For some, survival of misfortune has created a person's basis for accomplishment and self-esteem. The point is, when there is an attachment between love and suffering, the bond is self-perpetuating. **As you love, so you are!** To the contrary, some people suffer reciprocally, because they have contributed to an environment in which the threat of suffering is part of control and dominance. They have created the kind of environment which expects and utilizes suffering for leverage. Eventually, they will fall prey to their own designs and intentions, and receive their own full measure of suffering.*

*"**Most suffering occurs because humankind does not know that it has a right to the blessings of life.** You do not have to settle for hurting, disappointment, pain, confusion, or depression. Moreover, when you seek blessings, the rest of your covenant with the Father will unfold. As I told you, the Father has written your covenant in joy. Those who are obsessed with suffering do not easily find their covenant. It is when you seek blessings that you find the covenant. Seek blessings and expect them; be grateful and know they are yours for the asking.*

*"**You have the right to make your own decisions in life.** A decision involves not only what you choose to have, but also what you intentionally decline. No one else can do that for you."* In many ways, this is the right through which we exercise our **other** rights. In a world suffering from programmed conformity, we are being constantly pressured with demands from peers, business routines, and social protocol. Even so, we must always remember that we have the right to do the right thing, although it may involve saying "no." Sometimes we think it is dangerous to go against the flow—to disagree. Jesus helped me to see, however, that it is far more dangerous to forfeit our rights. When we forfeit our rights, someone else may assume them.

The right of personal choice is much more than a morality issue. It encompasses the whole of life. For instance, when I paint, I could easily make ten thousand decisions just in the creation of one painting. We make countless decisions every hour of our lives. Most of them are operational decisions, and many of them are decisions regarding priorities. In some ways, it might be said that success is just the result of making a lot of right choices. Failure, if there is such a thing, may be viewed as the result of making a lot of wrong choices. Unfortunately, many people have declined to make their **own** decisions, which may account for the uncertainty and confusion which surround their lives. Difficult as it may be at times to make a decision, a greater complication may arise from the consequences of not doing so. Seeking counsel from others often brings wisdom to the process. Nevertheless, in the end, we each have to live with the results of the decisions we have made or declined to make.

According to Jesus, *"Your life is the culmination of all the choices you have made regarding your many experiences, your origins, covenants, and abilities. By choosing, you exercise the core responsibility of being yourself and of unfolding your love into external manifestation. Choosing is an opportunity to influence the direction of your life. Saying 'no' is often the right choice. You have the right to disallow or defend against anything that is wrong for you or harmful to your well being. 'No' is not a popular word, but then making the right decision is not about popular consent."*

His teaching evoked a question I had about a belief which is prevalent today that, in order for a person's understanding to be full and complete, he would need to have **experienced** everything. Such beliefs go so far as to imply that before our eternal existence is fulfilled we **will** have experienced everything. I wanted to know what truth, if any, was pertinent to that idea.

The Master replied, *"You have to experience only that which gives fulfillment to the love that you are. You do not have to do it all, see it all, hear it all, think it all, believe it all, and feel it all. Each person is an individual, unique and like no other. You are complete when your love is complete, not when you are like everyone else in the world. Conformity is not part of your purpose in living."*

From a very deep heart level I was prompted to contribute a viewpoint on that subject before we moved on. "I think that beliefs of that nature are striving to give hope to the 'underdog,' by presenting the possibility that with a simple twist of circumstance the beggar might be king and the king might be a beggar."

With gentle support, He partially agreed, *"Yes, you are correct about the motivation of such ideas. However, the hopes which they generate are frequently unsupported by reality. Similarity of experience and conformity do not always result in tolerance and compassion. When your love is complete, you will be innately compassionate. When your love is complete, you will see that the beggar is already as great as the king!*

***"You have the right to an honest and correct understanding of life as it affects you.** You have the right to look at life with innocent perception* *and to seek an honest answer to whatever you might question. You do not have to settle for shallow, superstitious, politically correct, or conventional explanations of life. You can ask until you get an answer. You can ask further, until the answer is an honest one. When plagues swept through medieval Europe, some people felt it was a curse of evil; others believed that it was God's punishment, and not to be countermanded. As another example, scientists like Louis Pasteur looked for answers, and one day after careful study, he proclaimed, 'I think there is something wrong with the milk.' You do not have to accept conventional explanations which are empowered by ignorance and control agendas. You can open your eyes and see, open your ears and hear. You have a right to have an inquisitive, logical, and scientific approach to life which does not settle for unworkable explanations.*

"Too often in human history, the Holy mysteries have been used to sanction ignorance about practical affairs. There are most certainly dimensions of awareness above man's capacity to define. However, to use the realms of Divinity to suppress the growth of human consciousness is a desecration of honesty. Respect of mystery and mysticism in relation to God is an honest outlook, for it represents true estimation of your ability to comprehend the subject. Yet, in all other things, mystery should be replaced with every measure of consciousness available. Mystical truths were never meant to occlude your honest access to areas of practical knowledge and responsibility.

"A crucial part of honesty is the truth you admit to yourself about your subjective feelings and perceptions. Your subjective perceptions do not have to agree with external reality in order to be valid for you. That is part of the miracle of who you are, and the wonderment of your place in life. You are an amazement of internal realities and you have a right to view them honestly. Just because you look outwardly and see something which disagrees with the way you feel, does not mean you have to disavow your feelings and dishonestly adapt."

As He spoke, I was recalling times when I found myself humming a tune in the midst of a situation that might have appeared distressing to others. When I was a teenager, I rode my horse every day and looked forward to the onset of winter and the first "blue norther." Everyone else dreaded the shocking drop in temperature, and shivered with complaints. I loved my horse's excitement, and we both gained a certain kind of energy from the drastic change in weather. While others were putting logs in their fireplaces, I was out having the time of my life!

As a college girl, I had been cautioned that New York City was a dangerous place. I was told that people did not look each other in the eye and were generally unfriendly. I'm so glad I did not assume other people's beliefs, because when I visited that city, I found the people to be among the friendliest I had ever met. Perhaps other people had experienced it differently, but the fact is, on two different occasions when I entered a restaurant alone, couples invited me to join them. On one occasion I stood in a theater line a block long, and by the time I reached the box office, everyone within twelve persons knew each other on a first-name basis. Almost daily I visited the Metropolitan Museum and came to form friendships with other "regulars" who would join me on a bench to discuss the merits of great painting. If I had visited New York City with borrowed opinions and prejudice, I would not have been so open to such pleasant experiences. The fact that I was honest with myself about the positive nature of my feelings and perceptions, allowed me to be blessed with matching experiences.

There were other times when being true to my own feelings protected me from potentially harmful experiences. On another occasion in New York City, I was waiting for an elevator when a young man approached and asked if I wanted to buy some coke. I said, "No, thank you. I do not drink it!" It never occurred to me that he was talking about cocaine. I was so completely in touch with my own feelings that I didn't play into his game. He looked confused and walked away. On other occasions I have been offered business "opportunities" with a promise of great profits. Whenever I have listened to my feelings, I have done the right thing.

After a time of private reminiscing, I returned from my personal reverie, to hear Him repeat, *"You have a right to be honest with yourself about your feelings. No matter what other people may have conditioned you to believe, you have a right to be true to yourself.*

"You have a right to experience personal growth and to pursue your life with decency. Those who pursue change for the better are more moral and decent—regardless of their starting point—than those who change nothing. Morality is change for the better. This is the mechanism by which the first shall become last and the last shall become first. In this universe, love is the constant, and everything else is changing, either through growth or decay. Often those who are protecting their vested interests and their status quo are actually camouflaging a life that is tending toward decay.

This is what I often exposed as a wrongful tendency within the Pharisees of ancient Israel. They needed to change, all the while they clung to status quo and glorified it with their judgments. It is always better to unmask a cycle of decay than to permit its continuance. Until decay is exposed, there cannot be an improvement for the better. Many people spend their lives, their resources, and their energies to maintain images of propriety even though their 'feet of clay' are disintegrating by the year. Such people govern their lives with philosophies of judgment, not with principles of decency. A person who governs life with judgment, will be dishonest with himself, and therefore become a prisoner of his own fences.

"Love always seeks for betterment, for ways of making life more workable, joyful, whole, and beautiful. Love examines every option available to bring about an improvement in life. This kind of discernment is an act of decency, not an act of judgment. Rigid philosophies of judgment will seek to establish structure as a substitute for decency, control as a substitute for trust, and the mind as a substitute for higher awareness. Those who empower judgment in their lives generally live within dualistic formulas, where everything is labeled good or bad—usually bad. Judgment is a mockery of goodness and decency, for the sole intent of judgment is control. The worst thing about judgment is the deadly disease called irresponsibility. The most insidious intent of judgment is to assign control to those in a dominant position, and responsibility to those who are dominated. This is an unstable arrangement, for it is based on dishonesty. Eventually those in control will declare there to be no such thing as right and wrong, lest responsibility be forced upon them."

His comment reminded me of some current popular philosophies which propose to undo the harm of judgment by simply declaring, "No right, no wrong." I wanted to know if this was just a radical reaction or if such reversals of thinking were part of the process of developing consciousness.

He replied, *"The motives are sincere enough, but unfortunately it is often more destructive to disempower judgment utterly than it is just to let it run its course to self-consumption. You may compare such naive 'solutions' to the closing down of a toxic mining operation, while leaving the mining shafts open for unsuspecting children to fall to their death. True reversal demands an understanding of the true problem. The problem developed as man left the innocent heart and transferred his higher intelligence to the mechanics of the mind. When humankind left its home, it entered the world of judgment and hardship. The mind is interested only in control, and has no interest in right and wrong for purposes of bringing decency to life. Only the heart cares about decency, and only the heart pursues it with earnest concern for the outcome of human endeavor. Only by returning to the heart will you find the direction of true growth, creation, production, and innocence. This was the story of Adam and Eve and the tree of knowledge of right and wrong. In order to gain more control over life, they chose the world of mind-centered judgment and left the garden of heart-centered innocence. Adam and Eve are merely representatives for all your ancestors who made that choice, who then created an involvement with sin by accepting and forwarding the powers of judgment. Now the consequences of judgment have to run full course until judgment self-consumes, and the error of judgment is universally exposed.*

"Once you have conquered in yourself the tendency to separate and be separated, at last you will be able to apply wisdom to the process of discernment. Loving allowance and loving disallowance are not the same thing as labels of right and wrong. Consider, for example, a rattlesnake. Could you allow it to live in the desert, where it may serve its place in nature, and yet disallow it to take up residence in your back yard? There is a time and place for all things, and discernment is the act of loving allowance or loving disallowance.

"The long era of judgment has been man's darkest night, but that will end soon when the last judgment has been made. The last judgment will be the judgment against judgment itself. *At that time, human consciousness at last will rise in splendor like a valiant bridegroom to join his bride, the Sacred Heart. This is the Holy Wedding which has been the dream of prophets. After this marriage occurs, there will be peace on Earth. In the meantime, it is your right to seek a betterment of life in all the ways that are available to you. Enjoy every opportunity for positive change. Make the most of every day.*

"Last of all, you have a right to your own beliefs. *What you believe is your most sincere prayer."*

Everything became still, and for a while there was only silence. Then He gently uttered these poignant and simple words. *"As a man loves, so he is. As he believes, so he becomes."*

Chapter 11
God and Reality

"Our Father's love is revealed by His endless yearning to be known. Through all that is, He lovingly makes His presence available to the heart, the soul, and every sense of man." With such enormity of respect, the Master repeated many times that ***"God is one with reality."*** While affirming God's supremacy **over** reality, He nevertheless assured me that there is no separation between the Creator and the created, for Love is in flawless command.

This brings to mind an incident recorded in the Book of Mark where Jesus reprimanded the Pharisees' judgment against His disciples for harvesting on the Sabbath. Jesus said, *"The Sabbath was made for man, not man for the Sabbath."* His response on that occasion is rather typical of the priorities I observed Him to uphold in all matters. To Him, a protocol which does not respect God in **the reality of His creation** is less than sacred.

Everything He spoke of or shared with me was always anchored deeply within reality. Most of what He said I understood readily and applied easily to my life. Much of it was food for thought and growth, and some smaller part of what He taught me was beyond my comprehension at the time. Still, it is significant of His regard for both reality and the Giver of it that He offered treasures of insight which stimulated my greater yearning to know, toward which I could only marvel.

The messages relayed in this chapter and the next were transcribed with the greatest attention for detail, due to the fact that sometimes a deeper comprehension of their meaning or practical applications might have eluded me. In certain cases, that might be true even to this day. All of reality—indeed, even a greater part of it—cannot be understood by any one person. Therefore, it is with profound respect for the varieties of human interest and expertise that I present the contents of the next two chapters with the faith and expectation that persons with preparation and readiness in special fields of endeavor will provide a more fertile ground for understanding and exploring than I happen to possess.

The value of any message or idea is ultimately determined by its ability to perform. In the course of a lifetime we have many ideas—some are great and some are patently ineffective. Jesus said that, *"Any idea which is integrated with reality is worth pursuing and the others are futile. One rule of thumb in determining whether an idea is from God is the reality test. Is it real, and does it amplify the meanings of reality to higher levels of consciousness and application? All ideas from God are one with reality."* One of the things that made Jesus' words so alive was His conviction in reality. To Him, God is not only real, but the source of reality and the highest reality.

Western philosophy has taught us to believe that God is somewhere else, in a state of passive watchfulness over creation, and that Heaven and Earth are on two different planes. The unfortunate by-product of that kind of thinking is the legacy of philosophical dualism—up/down, dark/light, and so forth. The other loss comes from a presumption that science represents the summation of practical and workable knowledge, and that religion only represents beliefs about an infinite and unknowable God. Thus, the two most vital areas of human concern have been segregated into opposite corners of a boxing ring, with proponents of one field knocking the daylights out of the other.

Jesus laid before me a banquet of reality, and most especially He made God real. All too often we view reality as a harsh set of conditions from which we seek deliverance by the power of God. We judge reality as being hurtful and adversarial, while praying for miracles through a belief that God dwells in a far off place inhabited by angels, blissful souls, and sacred music.

"Even now, God is not separate from His creation. You have permitted reality to be harsh by leaving God out. People are finding their problems difficult to understand and confront because they work only within the prevailing structures, and then think that God has abandoned them to suffer whatever trials may inevitably result. Ignorance, judgment, and confusion mount up when you believe that God is somewhere else. When you leave God out, reality just boils down to structure, opinion, illusion, and chaos—nothing more. Reality is a living miracle if you

would only behold it!"

His assurance compelled me to express my inner feelings and reservations. "I appreciate your explanation that our predicaments are magnified by considering that God is somewhere else. If this is a miraculous universe, why do we need to have hardships in the first place? Why must we endure pain and suffering? "

His eyes became deep, compassionate pools as He answered. *"You are here to build faith and consciousness. These are two strong aspects of character that a child of God must have. And they must be forged simultaneously at a level of reality which is capable of presenting many varieties of conflicting experience and feeling. Consciousness is the product of compressing and integrating eons of experience and awareness full of every variety of perception. Consciousness grows in proportion to the richness, depth, and completeness of your experiences. For example, consciousness is greater today than it was two thousand years ago, and therefore, insights are available today that were unattainable at that time. Faith correlates with consciousness, for it is the certainty a soul has in the fruits of right action. In order for faith to be forged, however, there has to be a profound threat to one's certainty through great compressions of conflicting situations. If you knew where you were going, where would be the faith? If everything were provided without effort or risk, what would motivate you to become fully conscious?*

"Interestingly, faith and consciousness are both forged under similar circumstances. Like the finest steel, they emerge strong and true. Once a soul has achieved both faith and consciousness, there is no further need to remain in the confusion of conflicting reality. Until then, it is necessary for you to live at the level of many varied experiences, feelings, and challenges where both your faith and your consciousness may be awakened and fulfilled. Within this struggle, you will discover the power of truth.

"The presence of God as pure and innocent manifestation is available to be experienced in all reality. From this, consciousness is born. Within your perception of reality, you will find many harmonies, patterns of perfection, and universal constants. These are the truths which allow greater, simpler, and more meaningful integrations of life to be built. By such truths you are lifted above the drudgeries of unconscious living, and are able to enjoy life with greater clarity, purpose, and effectiveness. As your experience of truth is heightened and perfected, it will confirm the reality of God. To this your faith will bear witness."

According to Jesus, truth is not an archetypal formula or concept from which reality was replicated—as in the relationship between a blueprint and a building. Such concepts consign the truth to historical perspectives and to idealized concepts. Moreover, ideologies can be greatly manipulated to support assertions of human rather than Godly authority. *"The primal constants of the universe are free of time and space, and therefore reveal the height and depth of consciousness. Truth transcends reality and distills it into simple understanding! It is truth which sets you free from the limiting aspects of dependencies and conditions.*

*"**Truth is the power of constancy**. Without constancy there would be no correlation between the blueprint and the building, or between consciousness and reality. Truth is neither the building nor the blueprint, but rather the power of constancy which allows the marriage and the miracle of cause and effect to occur. Without constancy, there could be no truth; without truth, there could be no consciousness, and faith would have no purpose.*

"Honesty is a very important character trait, for it means that one honors the truth. Yet, truth is more than the faithful reporting of facts. How many times have you reported the facts conscientiously only to find that the facts had changed or were beyond your grasp?

*"Through the **revelation of constants**, a person is freed from the oppressions of changing reality and made whole again within himself. Within each person or situation there is an element of constancy which prevails, despite the variations of external form. There is healing whenever a constant is revealed. Even within irrationality, there are constant factors to be pleasantly discovered. This is the power of humor and its healing effect upon the human spirit!*

*"In the presence of truth, equilibrium is restored. And with it comes the vertical extension of God and higher consciousness which intersects and stabilizes an infinite horizon of existential reality. Reality is extending horizontally in an infinity of ways **as existence**. This is so, whether or not you are aware of it. Infinite reality does not require your consent or knowledge in order to perform its duties or to support life. Know what you can and honor the rest as your unfolding future. Through daily living you are increasing your awareness of what God has put before you."*

Jesus was always careful to point out that we are collectively building our consciousness of reality. In relation to reality we are all like "blind men" touching some part of the proverbial elephant, and then attempting to construct the whole by comparing observations. The merciful aspect of reality, however, is that when we compare our experiences, if they are honestly reported, they will provide us with the knowledge we seek. The greater blessing is that reality is not limited to the extent of our awareness. Even though each person brings his own perceptions of reality, the fabric of existence is consistent, measurable, unbiased, and uniformly predictable in the way it performs its ceaseless tasks without respect of special interests or even knowledge.

In the simplest terms, reality is the continuing presence of God in existence. Truth unveils the constants by which that Presence is known. *"Truth brings clarity and certainty to your understanding of reality, thereby giving it a predictable and manageable nature. The miracle of truth is that its constancy appears with equal grace in fluid as well as stable conditions. Truth need not be attached to fixed ideas or formulas. As a matter of fact, the truth will just as likely shatter a fixed idea as surely as any other structure."*

Many times He explained that we fend off the miraculous potential within reality because we are not prepared to accept the illusional nature of the structures in which we have placed our faith. It's quite a shock when predictable order is completely dismantled—even if it brings great blessing! When structure reveals its illusional nature we are shaken to the core—especially if we have more confidence in structure than in God.

*"Miracles come to those who appreciate the miraculous nature of life and surrender to the experience of it. The Creator will dazzle you every now and then, **but only to get your attention**. Never will He dazzle you in order to separate you from the miraculous potential of reality. This is because miracles bring **fulfillment to reality**—not a diminishment of it."*

Nevertheless, the miraculous cannot be "figured out" in the normal way, **because the logic we use to explain reality is itself structured,** and endlessly conditioned by predictable patterns of cause and effect. Such thinking could never comprehend a miracle, much less explain one.

*"God is waiting to greet you with a miracle, if you would only receive the Presence that is with you and before you. Man is blocking the path to miracles primarily with two obsessions. **One is dependency upon structure. The other is trying to recreate existence to match his every illusion**. All the children of God are most surely co-creators within the shared reality, and you do indeed manifest your lives through patterns of creation. However, there is a matrix of common reality which is greater*

than anything you alone could create. There must be a point where your confidence in the foundation of existence is greater than your anxiety and removes your dependency on limited sources of supply.

"Without this confidence, I promise you that you will set more faith in structure than God. There is nothing that impairs a miracle more than the fear of releasing the predictable and limited control of structure." He constantly reminded me that love commands the universe. ***"Love is who God is and who you are, as well.*** *The seed of everything you need is already within you. If you would receive a miracle, be still and receive the manifestations of love. The fact is, you take most miracles for granted. Life is full of them and never without them.* ***Love is the source of all miracles—it invokes their presence."***

Eventually, I came to understand that miracles are just the power of growth as love and life push through the veils of illusion holding them back. If one focuses on the impact of love and its capacity to bring about miracles, then miracles become an expected part of life. If one focuses on the structures that would deny the greater power of love and life, then an emerging miracle may erupt with startling surprise—even shock or duress!

"If you would behold a miracle, you must also behold the miracle of reality—that its wholeness is unbroken—that it can provide a different experience for each, and yet be consistent for all. There is but one reality, and that is the very essence and presence of existence itself. To this you bring your own perceptions, experiences, contributions, hopes, and dreams."

As He spoke, reality seemed so fluid and welcoming that the volley of cause and effect subsided for a moment. That peacefulness actually precipitated one of my earliest scientific questions, which was about the place of cause and effect in a dynamic, holistic pattern of existence.

His answer involved the use of communication as a metaphor. He explained, *"The Holy Now is the presence of God from which everything takes shape. This is a state of perfect synchronicity where all potential resides in* **perfect communion***. That is the eternal beginning and ending of existence. Although, for purposes of creation, communion must expand from there* **as dialogue***. Dialogue is brought into existence by various parts of the whole recognizing and interacting with each other. Communication proceeds as parts of the whole begin to interact in mutual support.*

"Incongruities and disharmonies will eventually appear in the patterns of interaction. Therefore, densities will accumulate, and more time

*and space will be necessary to provide margins for harmony. As distance becomes necessary for positive interaction, **cause and effect will become the basis of communication**. Therefore, as a progression, what began as perfect synchronicity becomes harmonious dialogue, and eventually will arrive at the function of cause and effect.*

"You can see a similar pattern in human relations. Tribal societies live in simple communion. As populations grow and cities develop, their densities and conflicts can pose many problems. People then return to rural areas to gain more distance between neighbors. Should circumstances force them to remain in crowded cities, their only hope is to seek more harmony through mutuality."

As the metaphor unfolded, I began to realize that the law of cause and effect governed the state of separation and separatist thinking. Realizing where my thoughts were focusing, the Master was quick to point out, ***"All three levels of communication exist concurrently in the universe.*** *In perfect synchronicity, there is total communion. At the other extreme of separation, the law of cause and effect prevails. Cause and effect are the universal means of communicating and rebalancing across distances of time and space—especially where there has been conflict. If a man or even a particle would have any peace or purpose at all in a state of separation, there must be an abiding respect for the law of cause and effect. Yet, **between these two extremes**, mutuality is the law of communication. That is the Law of Grace: harmony of existence, mutuality of brotherhood, synchronicity with God.*

*"**Most of the universe, with which science has concerned itself until recently, is the domain of separate particles and masses, and that domain is governed by the law of cause and effect.** However, the transitional distance between that domain and the other domains of perfect stasis and mutuality is very short. Those distances are being crossed at this time. The forthcoming accelerations of understanding will be major! Scientific thinking already includes a number of perceptions about mutuality. **Soon it will enter the domain of perfect synchronicity.** This is an infinity of pure, undesignated potential, which supplies all other levels of interaction and communication with life energy.*

*"The whole universe is implicitly and explicitly of one piece, and from the point of perfect synchronicity there is a never-ending rhythm of compression and expansion. Compression and expansion are the **great breath of the universe**! The perfect compressions which gave birth to universal*

order eventually gave way to expansion. These pulsating rhythms alternate between silence and percussion, providing the origin of sound. The successive intervals of silence and percussion exist in all things as the unique tone and energy of each respective life force. Thus, everything has its own song, its own sound imprint." This was His only reference in our conversations to the role that sound played in our well-being. I concluded from His comments, however, that music must draw its power from those wondrous pulsating rhythms of universal song.

The subject of compression was of vital interest to Him, and He spent the better part of several days explaining its many influences in life. He said, *"the ultimate expression of compression is simultaneity."* Simultaneity is the "zero point" of perfect balance where all potential is in simple coexistence. Even though we are far removed from the historical origins of the universe, we still feel that original stasis every time we experience simultaneity—every time we feel ourselves able to be in "two places at once"—every time we experience true empathy for another—every time the miracle of coincidence disrobes the power of time and space. Through the power of simultaneity, God is able to be with both the bird and the breeze, the fish and the ocean, you and me.

Clearly, simultaneity and synchronicity do not represent the bone-crushing experience of compression that we associate with a trash compactor. He emphasized that **perfect compression** never results in conflict, pain, or destruction, but rather in a state of transparent co-existence of infinite potential. Compression is with us on all levels of existence. Therefore, if we do not seek the harmony of God and respect the consequences of cause and effect, then we may indeed experience life in a "crash and bang" way. Jesus said that within each of us, and in all things, there is a magnetic center which invokes compression. How we relate to this reality is very important to our overall well-being.

Apparently, the miracle of creation in the universe corresponds to the patterns of compression. It appears to me that in the microcosm of atomic particles, compression is magnetically activated. This compression subsequently attracts and holds many other compressions in the form of molecular density. Like a wheel with many concentric rings, compression pulls to itself more of the same. Considerable density can accumulate without the loss of coordination, although as coordination is lost, thermal energy results. Compression piles density upon density. Random and discordant elements begin to enter the formula and are shaped into specialized arrangements of structure. At this level of compression, organization replaces synchronicity, and force begets energy. This is the level of material density and the 'garden variety' of force we know all too well. There is a natural progression from perfect synchronicity, to harmony, to organization. At each level there is greater density and a more complex structural patterning. These progressions parallel the three progressions of communication.

He said the entire universe was built on compression and that is the law of energy. Compression generates energy. Expansion releases it. He also said that every compression yields new energy. So I asked, "What about the law of conservation of energy? We were taught in school that there is a fixed amount of energy in the universe. You just said that energy is being continuously created."

He kindly remarked that He meant exactly what He said. That did not imply, however, that the law of conservation is not valid for certain levels of understanding. "*It is a valid explanation of the field of separating and interacting particles. Indeed, that law has its limits and will be reassessed as more is learned about the greater power of magnetism and the ultimate power of love, which provides a constant supply of energy to the universe.*"

Then He added, "*From that love, there is a constant potential, although there are no limits to its net production. The yield that can come from love is literally unlimited and every new compression creates more of it. It is through that power that the universe continues expanding even though thermonuclear forces proceed without end to consume structure.*" He made it very clear that thermonuclear forces consume only structure—not primal essence!

The reference to thermonuclear forces piqued my curiosity about the laws of thermodynamics. He responded, "*Like the laws of conservation, which are part of it, thermodynamic forces are relevant to fields of density capable of generating and responding to thermal energy. In regard to those fields of density, these laws are accurate for all practical purposes. Even so, there is a fatal disability of thermodynamics which prevents it from logically integrating the whole of existence. It defines energy as a function of matter existing within a macroscopic system, which is isolated against a backdrop of infinite unperturbable 'unknown.' In other words, infinity is a left-over! This is indicative of proprietary motivation . . . what cannot be controlled is disregarded.*"

"What, then, creates compression?"

"Love . . . first, foremost and always! Love creates compression, because love calls everything into assembly. Love ignites union. Love unites particles and formulates relationships. The physical agent is magnetism. That power applied to physical existence is compression."

His use of magnetism in that way clearly indicated the existence of primary magnetic properties in the universe which precondition the derivative action of magnetic attraction that we observe to be true in the world of particles and structure. "Does this greater knowledge of creation support current scientific observations that the universe is still in the momentum of some enormous explosion that supposedly started it all?" I was referring to the 'Big Bang' theory.

"Well, before there can be an explosion, there first has to be compression! The amount of compression necessary to bring about such a critical event would be unfathomable to the imagination. What science has observed is the result of that compression. Such intense compression will inevitably result in an equally powerful release. You might say that the great explosion was a 'wall of fire' which marked a transition between infinite and finite supply. As of yet, logic and instrumentation cannot penetrate it, but that will not be the case forever."

I wanted to know more. There are many explanations of creation. In the *Book of Genesis,* we are told, "In the beginning God created Heaven and Earth. And the Earth was without form and void. And darkness was on the face of the deep. And the spirit of God moved upon the face of the water and said, let there be light. And there was light."[16]

Now that passage puzzled me more than ever. If there is but one spirit, pervasive in all, and as all, then there could be no such thing as a vacuum. "What was the void, and what was compressed? Also, how could there be any substance as complex as water before there was light?"

He replied, *"The void was a magnetic vortex created within the One Spirit, through which the adamantine particles were called into assembly."* Then He proceeded to explain that in ancient symbology, **water represented magnetic influence and response**, not necessarily the liquid substance itself. *"Often, in the symbology of biblical times, 'water' was a symbol for magnetics."* At last, the first words of Genesis made sense to me! Today we still associate the magnetic pull of the moon with high tides, and associate the element of water with magnetic fields or properties.

"The adamantine particles are the living body of God. As they were called into assembly and compressed, particularly designated elements

were created. *The first and primary compression of adamantine particles resulted in the creation of light. That, however, was **first light**. It is visible to the conscious soul and is present always on the higher dimensions of what is often called Heaven. This light is a long way from the compression necessary to produce sunlight. What you receive from the sun is a complex result of many levels of compression. With the great explosion, which reversed compression, came the release of **photons, which are second density light.***

"*Before the great explosion, all matter and energy were in first density compression and there was only continuous light. From that explosion came an unbridled force of expanding particles which manifested the phenomenon of energy and space as you know it. And so there could be designations of difference among elements. Thus, at that point, there was night and day. Therefore, the second day was complete.*"

According to Jesus, moreover, each day was a quintessential act of creation unto itself. "*After the great explosion, compression continued and that eventually resulted in the creation of suns. Before the creation of suns could occur, the third act of creation had to be accomplished, which was the separation of the waters, the establishment of ground, and the production of vegetation.*"

Again it was written that there was water before there was even a sun. Jesus reminded me that the separation of the waters was in reference to the expansion of magnetic fields and activation of separate vortexes. "*The third act of creation was the multiplication of magnetic vortexes. There had to be more than one for compression to continue, because now the universe was in an expansion mode. Thus there were vortexes in solid matter, vortexes in the heavens, and vortexes assigned to generate the forms of organic life. On the third day, differentiated potential developed within the rapidly multiplying magnetic vortexes. Thereby compression could be extended into specialized realms of manifestation.*"

If, like me, you ever wondered how trees and plants were supposed to thrive on the third day of creation when the sun was not yet created, the answer is that the basis for their eventual appearance had been established. All potential was developed through multiplication of magnetic vortexes.

"*Every plant and every animal has within it a magnetic center. This is the signatory assignment of purpose which life bears even to this day.*"

At that moment I realized another implication of what Jesus had said. I had previously assumed the sun was a molten mass of iron, burning and exploding. He just stated that our sun is a powerful magnet! As I inquired further, He explained that it began that way and, by progressions of half-life, it always will be that way to some degree.

"Your sun began with a magnetic vortex which drew to itself uncountable masses of hydrogen gas. It attracted the atoms of hydrogen one after another until they compressed. As hydrogen was compressed, great heat was generated. Thermal energy set off a transmutation which turned hydrogen into helium. That happened between five to ten million degrees Kelvin. Every new level of compression generated more heat and more transmutation of energy. Helium turned into carbon 12, then into oxygen, neon, magnesium, silicon, sulfur, argon, and calcium. Each transmutation brought more density, building a solid ring around the magnetic center. At that point in time, the sun was still hollow and the magnet was beginning to be even more powerful. The final result of energetic heating, which was more than fifty million degrees Kelvin, caused the formation of iron. Iron came as a result of transmuting the preceding elements. In other words, the sun did not begin with solid substance. The preceding elements compressed from hydrogen and eventually became iron.

"There is a critical point in the life of a young star. The transmutation to iron can happen in a matter of only seconds. If it does, indeed, happen that rapidly and if the star is a giant, then the entire core could fill with iron. Whenever this happens, a tremendous implosion will cause the star to explode. This is a supernova. It only happens with young giants, and it is not a frequent occurrence."

I was specifically concerned about the future of our sun, and He responded.

"There are two other things that can happen. The transmutation to iron can occur at a rather slower pace and fill the entire void, at which time the sun is no longer a living magnet. From that point it has a finite history, a finite life span. This is a dying white dwarf.

"Now there are also living white dwarfs. These are suns where the transmutation of iron is still occurring and the core is still actively magnetic. Yours is one of these. Your sun is a living magnetic force, and that is necessary to support the development of organic life in a solar system." I suddenly had a thought that perhaps His recommendation to contemplate and enjoy the sun's beauty at the beginning and ending of each day was because our physical well-being resonates in harmony with its

magnetic core.

As Jesus said, *"In all living forms there is a magnetic center and that is relevant not only to the planet, trees, animals, and human bodies, but also your thought forms, emotions, and consciousness. All are products of compression and hopefully proceed under the guidance of love."*

As He spoke, it became obvious to me that compression was not an incidental part of creation, but rather a pivotal activity within it. It now seems to me that compression is a subject we cannot afford to avoid any longer if we hope to understand how the oneness of spirit connects the randomness of physical manifestation. Perhaps the randomness we perceive is only an illusion!

"The Sacred Heart is your magnetic center as well as your source of higher intelligence and your very life force. The very center of your life is a great and powerful magnet. Would it not be a mistake to look for your purpose outside yourself? Is this not one of the greatest fallacies in the world that people are looking for their purpose outside themselves? They are traveling from place to place to find a purpose. They are studying every conceivable kind of manuscript or talking to every teacher along the way to find a purpose outside themselves.

"If you are to extend the Father's creations, you are going to have to do it in harmony with the very principles on which the universe was created, and of course, the first principle of creation is love. You are love. As love, you have the power to attract to yourself everything you need. As love, you have the power to ignite into compression every form of energy and every form of supply that your life requires."

In response to my musings about how God can be everywhere at once, He said, *"From God's viewpoint, the ultimate expression of compression is simultaneity. The Holy Source compresses all time, all space, all energy, all manifestation. Pure and perfect simultaneity of presence, awareness, and manifestation is the unique and omnipotent power of God."* This is the ultimate state of compression. This is where it all began. It began with the "zero point," the **point of perfect equilibrium where everything exists in unison, in simultaneous communication, and simultaneous understanding**. Thus, He can be here with me, with someone in China, and literally throughout the universe! He can be attentive to a particle and also be mindful of the cosmos. The birds do not escape His awareness, nor does the air through which they fly. This is perfect and complete simultaneity—the unique and omnipotent power of God.

As I contemplated that ideal state of compression, it became clear that there is no pain associated with it. To the contrary, there is release of pain, duress, and oppressive density. Simultaneous performance, by extension, also belongs to us as the children of love which we truly are. Even now, we live and function on many levels simultaneously. For an obvious example, we are breathing and our hearts are beating even though we may be deeply absorbed in thought. Our soul touches heaven as we speak, although our bodies are anchored to the Earth. Is that not simultaneity in its purest form? Anyone who has ever felt sad and joyful, or felt a loss and a gain at the same time, knows the grace of simultaneity. As the Master summarized it, *"Simultaneously, you are everything you have ever been, and also with you is the seed of everything you will ever be. Is there any conflict in that? With just the tiniest shift of attention you can go from yesterday to tomorrow. With another tiny shift of attention you can go from awake to asleep. Does the sleeping state change the nature of who you are? It is still utterly and totally you. Are you not a being who has all faculties simultaneously functioning?"*

This is easily comprehended once our attention is focused on it. In the course of our linear lives we have adapted to specializations, and these adaptations have led us to believe that the patterns of cause and effect provide the only explanation for how life works.

"Not everyone's petition for understanding can be supplied by the explanations of cause and effect. It is very important to understand the consequences of cause and effect, although it is equally important to understand mutuality and synchronicity. All three levels of understanding should be sought and applied to life wherever they are relevant."

I felt a sad sense of irony in realizing that man conveniently ignores the laws of cause and effect whenever his rationalizations "require" it, yet he fails to look beyond the narrow framework of linear consequence to the larger perspectives which would give him true answers. For the first time, it became obvious to me how much better life would be if we took all three types of interaction into our understanding.

"That's mostly because of specialization, and partly because man's quest for knowledge about physical existence drives him to look for prime cause as a physical factor.

*"From time immemorial, man has been looking for prime cause within the physical universe. Such a thing does not exist. The entire phenomenon of cause and effect is a derivative one. There is **Prime Source**, and that is*

God. However, in the heart of Divine Consciousness there is only perfect intention in harmony with perfect manifestation. **You might regard this as cause-cause.**

"The search for prime physical cause could go on endlessly, never arriving at a fruitful harvest. The desire to deify cause as lord of effect has written the script for immeasurable human suffering, hardship, and mental anguish. In addition to that, it has handicapped certain avenues of scientific progress. Cause and effect are part of a **much greater whole**. The fact is, in one phase of life a chicken precedes the egg. In another, the egg precedes the chicken. However, neither phase can be understood without a larger comprehension which takes into consideration the mutual interactions of all life."

"Why then, has man persisted in deifying cause as lord of effect?"

"The motive was a strong one. If man could succeed in sanctifying cause and effect, then he would have also achieved unimpeachable sanction for his own 'control by punishment' agenda. This is why I ask you to forgive, to release, and to observe the greater power of grace in order to end your long separation from God, which has made you a captive to the lowest level of reality.

"Within the full spectrum of possibility for any situation, there are patterns of cause and effect, rhythms of mutual involvement, and perfect synchronicity. That upon which you focus is your choice, and in many cases the choice made is a reflection of your own wisdom. It is unwise to avoid the consequences of cause and effect where it is most relevant. However, it is equally unwise to disallow grace and tolerance in areas of mutual support. It is most unwise not to know the power of God.

"This is an infinitely workable universe, with all possibilities for creation working concurrently. Whatever is most workable for you is a revelation of your purpose in life and your path of service and fulfillment. As you reach the limits of your ability, you will seek the support of others. It is my hope for you that it occurs with mutual respect."

To understand this is to grasp our sense of totality. Specializations have cut us off from the greater whole that we are. As a result, we have a limited perception of existence and its many dimensions. Compression, expressed in its many forms, is an indelible part of the life we live. Compression is part of the entirety of existence, although it manifests in different ways, according to the different degrees of conflict or harmony that may be involved.

Jesus recommended that we consider these varying levels of compressions in our own lives. *"You can take charge of your life again by reviewing the states of compression in which you find yourself. Wherever there are dark and heavy densities, you have many incompatible elements compressed. **Just change something, release something, or move something around."***

He emphasized, *"Perfect compression never results in conflict, but in a state of transparent overlay,"* which is perfectly compatible with the magnetic core that attracts and holds its many compressions in place. These are the various layers of transparency in our lives. From that perfect state of compression, we can observe all other manifestations. *"Acknowledge where there is much transparent overlay of simultaneous awareness. In that realm of life there is much rightness of purpose and oneness with God. You will find that these areas are very rich with meaning for you. Strengthen these things that all your life may expand with multi-layered simplicity."*

The next level of compression is coordination and interaction. Although it is orderly, there is more resistance and therefore it results in the generation of thermal energy. Such compressions, which are invigorating and productive, may be compared to athletic prowess. When an Olympic runner breaks a world record, what has he done? He has achieved more in less time. Is that not compression? Such compressions are stimulating, productive, and passionate. In our work, we have all experienced exhilaration in getting more done in less time. We attempt to excel, and we enjoy the challenge. Frankly, it is invigorating to exceed in production the amount of energy being consumed!

The Master voiced one precaution, however, about spending too much of our lives at this level. *"Where there is much fire and energy, you have many coordinated forces working together. Perhaps there is a dynamic activity which you really enjoy. Before the fire consumes you, find your place within it and discover the meaning and purpose it holds for you—that you may eventually move on to other activities. This is not where you are meant to live forever."*

The third level of compression focuses on organized enforcement of random and discordant elements which form special aggregates of structure. This is the level of material density and the familiar varieties of organization, conflict, and force. This particular level is the one that causes us so much frustration. If this were our only experience with compression, it is doubtful that we would ever associate that process with God.

I like to think that the painting of *The Lamb and the Lion* was in many ways an example of the highest level of compression. Every day as I worked, the oil paint would be dry, even though its normal drying time was three days. Time, at least, had been compressed. Also, everything I needed was provided immediately without effort, and there were no problems. Clearly, I was in the presence of someone who was commanding the highest level of compression. I believe this is how the Master can be with many at the same time. That state of perfect compression permits Him to be utterly transparent, thereby allowing Him literally to be in our midst, only to be seen by mutual consent. This is also the transparency of God.

The miracles which have happened around the painting are, perhaps, due partly to the high degree of compression under which it was produced. Perhaps the anatomy of a miracle is to erase the conflicts of structure and facilitate a surrender to the perfect compressions of simple existence. In the last week of Jesus' life there was tremendous compression and the highest level of passion. In only a few days, the entire history of mankind and the world was changed. **That is compression!**

The whole subject of compression has great potential for the world of healing. At times in my life when I was very whole, when I was engaged in high levels of compression and living, my immunity to disease was enormously high. I could be in the presence of people with colds or flu, and experience no vulnerability. When wholeness leaves no room for invasion, I suspect one could walk safely through a den of rattlesnakes! Perhaps this is one of the great secrets of healing—to be in such a state of wholeness that invasive elements have no welcome.

There are several extremely important reasons to become practical about compression. Our involvement with compression is unavoidable, and compression reveals a great deal about a person's life when viewed objectively. Jesus said, *"Whenever you combine elements which do not belong together, the result is pain and suffering. A common example of that is the use of alcohol, narcotics, or even unnatural food obsessions which are nonsupportive of bodily functions. The point is, some combinations of elements, ideas, actions or human relations simply do not work in terms of actual reality. To persist in forcing or manipulating an unworkable assortment of elements will only cause pain, hardship, unhappiness, loss of energy, and eventually poverty.*

"On the other hand, failure to integrate and compress at all results in

a life that is dispersed, unfocused, and lacking in energy. We must each ask, 'What can we compress? What can we put together and make work?' A very interesting thing about compression is the way it brings purpose, priorities, and values into view."

How do we get started? How do we make it happen?

"With great simplicity. The greatest compression of time is NOW! Just be here now. Do it. The greatest compression of perception is innocence. Do not put additives on life. You do not need to alter it. Do not add conditions that are not necessary. Do not invent realities. Do not fix things which are not broken. Get to the point. Use what you have, including all your available tools, awareness, and talents. Do not procrastinate. LIVE! That is compression right here and now. It will take you back to the center of yourself—your own 'zero point.'"

The concept of compression seemed strangely new and yet deeply familiar. Why, I wondered, was I feeling so poorly educated in regard to it? I had nineteen years of excellent formal education. But where was "Compression 101"?

He answered, *"One of the greatest obstructions to practical understanding of compression is job specialization and specialized thinking which are so prevalent in the world today. The dominance of structure is another important factor. Compressing structures is often a difficult pursuit, requiring heavy applications of force. If it is done wrongly, there can be pain and misfortune. Above and beyond that is the element of illusion. The world is driven by many illusions, and there is a significant difference between the way illusion and reality respond to compression. Reality can be compressed and decompressed infinitely. Actually, reality builds strength through compression, while compression crumbles illusion! The reason compression is so unfamiliar to your ears is that a discussion of it would be highly repressed by a world which relies so heavily on structure, specialization, and illusion.*

"The reality of human brotherhood is the strength of all men. In times of trauma and disaster, the compressions of that reality make this truth even more powerful. In times of achievement the joy is shared by all. By comparison, the illusions and structures of human agenda fall aside as irrelevant and useless. Remember always that human brotherhood exists as a reality, and is the reality of your common support. It matters little what system of administration is empowered, as long as it is fair to all and supportive of human needs.

*"Reality is the best economy there is—actually, reality is the **soul** of economy. If you did not have to finance illusion, just think how rich you would be! If structures were limited only to those that were needful, just think how much free time you would have to pursue the joys of life! Much energy is spent in creating illusions and supporting structures, which would be better spent on personal health and productive living. **Illusions and structure can steal your life if you let them.**"*

"How can we know the difference between illusion and reality? Sometimes the veil between them is very thin."

*"I realize that. In approaching the subject, do not begin with fear, or treat illusion and reality as adversaries. Illusions are part of each individual's **personal reality**. If you correctly understand and use your illusions, they can be a blessing. They are detrimental to the common reality only if you misuse them. Illusions are creative interfacings with reality, which your mind, heart, and soul use for approaching, learning, tasting, and evaluating potentials within reality **from a point outside the realm of involvement**. Illusion is to reality what a road map is to the highway system, or what theater is to the drama of life.*

"The problem arises when illusions acquire a life of their own and become an escape from reality, or even worse, a misrepresentation of reality. The difference can be observed by involvement and discernment. If there is any doubt, you might try this: consider what would happen if a situation in question were no longer being created. You see, reality does not go away when you no longer create it. Illusions do. If all else fails, consider what would happen if compressions were accelerated in the situation. What would crash and what would endure?"

His explanation reminded me of the years when Brian and I had owned a vineyard in Paradise, Texas. It was an illusion of paradise, yet we still enjoyed a wonderful, romantic experience. It was a beautiful vineyard and, actually, we were the first producers in Texas to sell table grapes to the Kroger food chain. We also grew a large variety of wine grapes which we sold to a nearby winery. In relation to climate, however, there was a coordination discrepancy between illusion and reality. The climate of central Texas is far from suitable for producing fruit of the vine. We had to use chemical intervention for a myriad of problems, and then there were late freezes every spring. One time we stayed up all night, burning every disposable item of substance, trying to force a reversal of the plummeting thermometer. Year by year we were losing energy, and the vineyard was losing production. Improbable combinations of reality had clearly exposed our discordant illusion. Moreover, if we had stopped our compensations, and ceased creating momentary "solutions," the vineyard would have failed altogether. On the other hand, if our vineyard had been located in northern California, the situation would have been entirely different. We would have had wonderful grapes and a great deal of profit. Eventually, it was necessary to admit the obvious: that vineyard could flourish only in the romantic misconceptions of illusion. Sometimes it is worth enjoying our fantasies anyway, despite the risk, although eventually we have to confront what really is before us.

"All children build sand castles of one sort or another. This is good, because it gives them a way of examining their expectations about reality before taking the plunge. The mistake comes in expecting to **live** *in the sand castle. Adversity arises, however, through misconceiving God's relationship to your sand castle. The sand castle is* **yours alone**. *It is the core of human folly to build a sand castle, expecting God to make it real or to salvage it when the tides wash it away. Your covenant with God is* **in regard to reality**. *In regard to that covenant, you could have no more loving, compassionate Sustainer. Every prayer asked through the heart, with respect to reality, will be answered. The great tragedy is that most prayers are asked on behalf of threatened or broken illusions. The great thief and heartbreaker is illusion, for it has given man the false idea that God does not care about the human condition.*

"God is one with reality, and man has been chosen as the heir and extender of that reality. Do you not think that He cares whether you attain that fulfillment? As you demonstrate your **zest for reality**, *you will be met more than half way with love, support, and assistance that will seem nothing short of miraculous to you.*

"Your life on Earth is to build faith and consciousness. As you do that, you will find that reality is both a comfort and a miracle. Until you have settled into that simple process, you will mistakenly seek your comfort through structure, your miracles through illusion, and your competence through specialization. This is the state of separation that most men experience."

"How does one communicate to another that he is living an illusion without falling into patterns of judgment?"

"You do not. Every man must learn for himself the difference between illusion and reality through the pursuit of faith and consciousness. It is the

nature of immature perception to see all experience as an illusion of reality. Then with maturity comes the realization that there is both illusion and reality. Once you know the difference yourself, you will know when and how to disallow the effects of another's illusions on your own life.

"As you gain that understanding, I suggest you use moderation in all things. There is an inherent grace in moderation that will provide a great deal of discernment and protection for you without the pitfalls of judgment."

Specialization makes it particularly difficult to discern between illusion and reality. Specialization builds linear lives strung out in time, while the great tragedy is our shortness of time. Jesus explained that the two greatest causes of stress in the American workplace were specialization and the decline of value-based understanding. Instead of having one job that works very well, with many layers of potential, a person could very well end up with two or three specialized jobs that eat up the day and the night, and still not pay the bills.

Value-based understanding builds from experience a greater certainty of what can effectively be compressed or put together and what the outcome will be. On the other hand, specialization destroys this awareness because the integrational options are so limited. It has long been demonstrated through careful study that assembly line workers doing specialized work are the most exhausted at the end of the day. The job itself may be fine, although endless attention to details will leave the worker depleted of energy. Jesus said the entire universe was built on compression, and that is the law of energy. **Specialization causes depletion.** Every time we limit our activities to single-dimension performance we are going to lose energy. He revealed this as one of the reasons people in America are so tired. Their lives are becoming very mono-dimensional.

"A long day of tedious work, followed by chores and duties at home and a restless night of sleep hardly prepares one for a new day with energy and vigor. The last thing anyone wants under such conditions is more work, and the answer is not to do more. The point is to take what you are doing and make it richer. Express more dimensions of yourself or put more dimensions of yourself into the workplace. Make friends. Explore a learning curve that could enrich life on other levels. Practice memory, concentration, or social skills. You say this takes energy you do not have. Actually, this will give you the energy you have lost. Apply more dimensions of yourself to whatever you do. This recommendation is not for adding to the length of your agenda. It is for enriching it with more transparent

overlays of all the things that you are, compressed into the same period of time."

He warned, however, that only compressions supervised by love yield energy that is valuable to the soul. Therefore, as we create and generate compressions, it would be wise to do so with love. *"Compressions generated with love represent your profit in living. This is also your profit in the workplace. The concept of profit is often accompanied by feelings of guilt or jealousy because its nature is misunderstood. In many situations there is no true profit—only dollars are being shuffled. Where new energy has not been created, dollars tend to be stuffed into the pockets of those with the greatest leverage. For that reason, profit has come to have a bad name, and people do not understand the principles of prosperity.*

"As mankind moves toward the use of higher compression under the direction of love and value, profit will become a word of accomplishment and not a signal for guilt. Instead of being taken from another man's plate, profit will be seen to yield value and prosperity for other people as well. The very existence of profit will generate new values and energies in which others may partake. Good profit lowers prices and inflation and increases joy and morale. Maximum effect for minimum effort does not lead to laziness, but rather, it restores a willingness to work.

"What produces laziness is worn out bodies and rebellious attitudes deploring force-based business and production where there is no true profit and no reward. Good profit is the investment of love to move advantages into the lead. You might learn from the geese. In a 'V' of migrating geese, you will notice one goose has the lead, although he doesn't take the lead to dominate. He takes the lead to break the wind and make the flight easier for others. This is what good profit does for everyone. Good profit has actually created energy, and so it enlivens and enriches the totality of an economy in which everyone participates. In the presence of effective compression, there is never any serious or widespread poverty."

The power of compression is love. The agency is magnetism. The full technical manifestation of that truth has not yet presented itself on the Earth. We have been living in a world of friction-resistive energy from the first time man rubbed two sticks together to make a campfire. Friction-resistive energy is the basis of electrical force. On this we have built our technologies and our thinking. Most of the difficulties in production now come from the use of electrical power which is friction-based force. The electrical mode generates high pressure specialization which can support only dense compressions which in turn degenerate all higher compressions. In the last fifty years, high pressure growth of force and specialization has wiped out most independent enterprise in the industrial nations. According to Jesus, the giant companies will only survive if they can move to a wiser use of compression. As they do, there will be a major reversal into re-evaluating satellite support companies and individuals who manage their lives and industry with multi-dimensional compressions. It may not happen overnight, although it is definitely the wave of the future.

He gave me an example from the agriculture sector. High pressure takeovers have driven small farmers and ranchers off the land. This has been a long term tendency that reached a crescendo about ten years ago. Now the over-extended responsibilities of production management are forcing a critical reassessment of profits and liabilities. Many conglomerates are beginning to face the fact that effective field management and production are difficult from a marble-top desk. There is probably no business in the world that demands more aspects of compression than agriculture or horticulture. In that business, one has to manage many factors simultaneously on location. On the other hand, only very large companies, through brokering and distribution, can actually get food to the homes of people around the world. Each player's role will be ultimately determined by effectiveness of compression. Illusions can be maintained only for so long, behind the mask of structure, until the power of necessity and compression bring the walls tumbling down.

"This is true of nations as well as businesses and individuals. Watch for signs that over-extension and specialization are reversing to compression. There is still hope that the transition will be made successfully. If it is not, there will be economic collapse. This is what happened to Rome. She over extended her force-based economy. Then there were too many breaches of morality, philosophy, and human organization to reverse her over-extension back into compression. Compression and expansion are the breath of the universe. When health is lacking, one or both aspects of the cycle will fail. Rome had lost her basis for compression, and so she died of over-extension."

The closest example of such a calamity in our time is the fall of the Soviet Union. Over-extension depleted the nation, and then there was nothing left to finance and sustain the necessary return to compression. The only workable compressions that could be implemented were those of regional management, common heritage, and factory production. At least, those compressions and certain others are allowing the people to rebuild their lives. This is a dramatic example to which all of humanity should pay heed with compassion and assistance.

Jesus said, *"It is the mark of true civilization to expand and contract with equal grace, cycle after cycle, with neither expansion nor compression dominating the inevitable rhythm. This is reality. However, it is the mark of structure and illusion to generate the misconception that expansion is the only route to power and glory. When a nation or society has centered its power primarily on structure and illusion, it will be driven compulsively to continue expansion at all costs. Opportunities for natural cycles of compression will be missed or shunned for fear that it would expose and collapse some needless structures and false illusions. Then, as expansion accelerates, the fear is that a reversal to compression would be traumatic, which it possibly will be. Nevertheless, such a reversal is inevitable."*

He said, *"Remember, in knowing God, your ideas become more real, and reality becomes more relevant to your dreams and your ideas. You can always tell if an idea comes from God because it will work more effectively with reality and will carry reality to a higher plane. As a person or society moves away from God, the ideas generated lose application to reality, unless a great deal of force is applied. The great misconception is that with enough force and manipulation, any idea can be made to work. That is a God-separated concept, and will result in a world of force and manipulation. When you are living in a world where unreal ideas prevail, I assure you force and manipulation will enter and attempt to make up the difference.*

"As you know God, your understanding of reality will increase." It is important to note, He did not say your reality will increase as you know theology. *"Theology is just a broad summarization of beliefs **about** God. There is no substitute for the real thing, and you **can** know God. It is one of your divine and immortal rights to know your Creator. You do not need a facilitator, and you do not need someone else's opinion of God to know rightly. For God is in your heart. As you know God, your ideas will work better. You will also be able to concentrate and generate higher levels of compression which will leave you healthy, wealthy and wise. Thus you will know **what to put together** and how to do it. The many layers of your life will unfold simultaneously, with great richness."*

It was after that teaching that He graciously contributed another dimension of understanding to the great triangle which designate Love,

Spirit, and Adamantine Particles as the pillars of creation. He suggested that
I take my pen and impose on that equilateral triangle another triangle
pointing in the opposite direction so that the two, together, formed a six-
pointed star. *"This second triangle indicates the elements of enduring
reality. On its corners write, Life, Purpose, and Existence."*

That made six elements altogether. Jesus said, "*All that is was created
out of these six elements. Love is the originating point, and existence is the
culminating point of all creation. Thus existence is the one that touches
Earth and sustains a universal reality. Love activates spirit and commands
the adamantine particles. Then love directs life with purpose, and through
purposeful living existence is fulfilled.*"

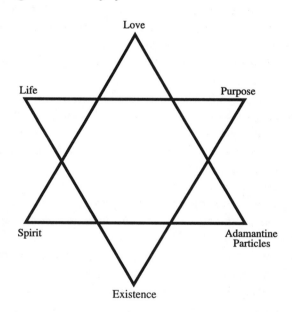

According to Jesus, this was the original meaning of the Star of David.

After days of discussion with Him and years of private reflection, I have
come to see that the three points of each triangle reveal a great deal more
than the obvious meanings of their simple construction. You can also use two
points of one triangle to explain the intersecting point of another. For
instance, life is revealed to be the midpoint between love and spirit. Existence
is the manifestation resulting from spirit's interaction with adamantine

particles. Purpose is the midpoint between love and adamantine particles. Love is the uppermost point of causation, while existence is the culminating point where all is revealed. Purpose and spirit provide complementary forces of guidance, while life and adamantine particles complement each other with energy and empowerment. Contained within this symbol is a code for knowing reality as a manifestation of God. This is the power contained within the ancient symbol of Israel.

Even with all the wisdom of the ages, knowing God is still the greatest personal challenge any man or woman will face in life. Therefore, I asked Jesus what the greatest difficulty was in knowing God. *"It is the feeling of unworthiness. That is why most people choose to know theories about God instead of knowing their loving Father directly. It is unfortunate that many theological agendas enforce the idea of unworthiness. Thus, people are trapped. God is a power and love greater than words, greater than anything that could ever be put into words or formulas. Yet, what Father would not welcome the presence of His own child?"*

I could respond only by applying His words to myself. "I think I am no longer affected by false unworthiness, imposed by human judgment. Still, there is an awesomeness and wonder about the Creator which reduces me to mere insignificance by comparison. As you have said, the Definer is beyond comprehension by the defined.

"All of this is true, Glenda. However, you have been given contexts of reality in which you may grasp what you need to know. There are approximately eight contexts of awareness upon which you may focus to strengthen your knowledge of God.

"1. To know yourself as Love, and therefore as a child of God.

"2. To know the grace, health, and truth of equilibrium. To pursue this knowledge, you have been given the masculine and feminine aspects of life as well as other complementary aspects of balance. Male and female relationships provide an opportunity for furthering this knowledge, along with the total concept of family, wherein a variety of interests and needs are brought into balance and mutual support.

"3. To know the power of purpose as it reveals reality and binds the hearts of many into groups of common endeavor.

"4. To know service through human brotherhood.

"5. To know the holistic patterns of life through observing the tendencies of nature.

"6. To know consciousness through innocent perception and through

objective comprehension of universal principles.

"7. To know the power of faith as the sustainment of our one spirit, and the power of love as the will of God.

"8. To know the Infinite as exceeding all structure. The Ultimate Reality is God."

Chapter 12
Jesus on Science

Few people would ever associate the name of Jesus with science. And quite possibly those who would seek practical answers from Him would expect Him to respond in a religious rather than scientific way. However, one of the most amazing revelations I had in His presence was the privilege of observing His love of reality and His command over it.

Over the many days that we spoke, He never segregated reality into separate classes. He did not place theology in one corner and science in another. It was **all reality** to Him. Like a gymnast who could be in the air one moment and on the floor the next, His grace was fluid and always of one piece. There are references to both God and spirit in this chapter which might seem unscientific to some readers. To Him, however, science is the study of workability innate to all reality, a study which cannot be complete until its Source has been taken into consideration. Other readers will be surprised to find how easily He makes Himself at home in the area of pure physics. Prior to writing this manuscript, I had the privilege of presenting some parts of it to scientists in various fields. Uniformly, there has been a response of amazement coupled with such statements as, "I expected to be hearing spiritual truth, but **this** is pure science!"

Throughout our conversations, there were many explicit references to the way life works. Most of these explanations need to remain in their original contexts, where they have more relevance to His other messages. Therefore, what I have assembled in this chapter is not the totality of what He had to say about the components of existence. Rather, I have brought together those revelations which shed light on the future of scientific understanding as well as the priorities and developments that will bring it to us. For me, the greatest value of speaking with Him on science was in receiving His viewpoint on the subject.

"Science is a dialogue between truth and reality," He said. *"You have the whole universe in front of you, but until you understand the crucial relationship between truth and reality, you do not have science."*

Of all the things which Jesus taught me, there is perhaps none more relevant to all areas of life than the subject of truth, itself. Because of its attachment to proprietary issues, the history of truth has flowed in a trail of bloodshed and warfare. Yet, it has been promised by the Master that, *"You shall know the truth, and the truth shall set you free."* When this profound revelation comes, is it to be in the form of scientific discoveries? Will it be found in the dissertations of law or some surprising new phenomena? Or will it to be in the form of a final clarification *"on the nature of truth itself?"* I like to believe that the latter option is more likely. My preference is reinforced by the Master's own instruction about the nature of truth set against the cosmic background of existential reality. He said quite emphatically, *"There is but one reality, and that is the very essence and presence of God manifested* **through existence itself."** This reality is perceivable to all senses, internal and external, by all emotions, and by every instrumentation known to science. The salient characteristic of reality is that its integrated consistency permits verification from all the many perceptual approaches. For example, our eyes, nose, and palate all confirm the delectable presence of a cherry pie. This is no less true in science, for the comparison of data from several sources of retrieval, confirmed mathematically, is the very nature of what we call "proof." *"For reality is the consistent, measurable, unbiased, and uniformly predictable nature of existence which performs its ceaseless tasks without respect of special interests. Your only duty toward reality is to experience, perceive, and report it honestly. There is but one reality, and it is available to anyone who would behold and interact with it honestly. Reality is not owned by the intellectually elite or privileged, nor controlled by them. It is ascertainable only by experience, observation, comparison, integration, and honesty. One's grasp of reality grows as his outreach into life increases.* **Reality is the Creator's democratic gift to all of life and to mankind. If so much as one person could change reality to match his own private viewpoint, then that gift would be undone.**

"Truth, on the other hand, is the breadth and depth of consciousness **which transcends reality** *and distills it into simple understanding! It is truth which sets you free from the limiting aspects of external dependencies and conditions. Though truth is constant, its constancy must be confirmed*

through experience. Therefore, every man's path to transcendent awareness will be unique. Truth has its roots in a common reality, yet it is not archetypal. You see, truth is not separate from the reality it serves. It is indigenous to it. God is not separate from sacred truth, nor the universe from its own, nor I from mine, nor you from yours. Respecting that principle of ultimate integrity **is respect for truth**. *It is the long practice of human dishonesty that has made you think that truth is somewhere else, or enshrined in a prior domain of perfect order. Truth is a living part of existence, the constant reminder of meaning, certainty, and purpose which is your compass for navigating. If one would seek to gain freedom from truth, perhaps it would first be wise to grant freedom to it!*

"Liberate truth from the ivory tower. Truth does not precede reality, formulate it, or replace God as Source." Jesus said that nothing has detached us more from reality or distracted us more from the genuine pursuit of truth than the philosophical misconception that truth is archetypal. The anatomy of this mistake is that fixed ideas become "appointed truths" through which new aspects of reality are then examined. Where's the innocent perception?

Regarding scientific procedure, He said, *"Reality is where you start. Truth is what you distill through observing patterns of constancy. Truth is the consummation of understanding which has proven to be workable, useful, and progressive toward life."*

Establishing these priorities is a necessary preamble to the Master's discussion on science because, according to Him, *"Misconceptions of truth or misapplications of it have done more to subterfuge the progress of science than all the other reasons put together."* He made that statement in reference to the Greek philosopher Plato, to whom he referred as a pillar of influence in formulating the logics of separation. This was accomplished by postulating the "ideal" to be archetypal and reality to be a frail, imperfect substitute. Despite the artful beauty of Plato's reasoning, and the intellectual depth of his mystical insight, the destructive impact that Plato's philosophy has had on the history of western science is immeasurable. It also provided intellectual reinforcement for certain misguided assumptions that the Creator who resides in perfection is alienated from "the created" through great densities of imperfect reality. Ideas that are generated independently of reality are of little value. Ideas formulated without respect for reality will have a negative and stagnating effect upon progress and true workability. Jesus said, *"The problem with idealistic philosophy is that it considers truth to be an archetypal idea, from which reality, in a somewhat imperfect form, is derived.*" According to that viewpoint, reality matches the ideal only randomly, approximately, and imperfectly. Intellectual idealism postulates truth to be primal and perfect, reality to be derivative and imperfect.

From a scientific viewpoint, such an approach to the universe has two fatal flaws. First, it will nullify objectivity by preconceptions of the universe. Second, the expected imperfections in reality become an excuse for careless observations, dishonest reports, and self-serving justifications. This especially becomes apparent when discrepancies can be disregarded as predictable margins of error concerning the "fixed idea" which is being upheld.

From a historical and social perspective, most wars have been fought because of insoluble conflicts existing between two or more fixed ideas. Excessive amounts of energy, intelligence, and time have also been spent on "wild goose chases" to discover a truth that could dominate all others. *"In such pursuit, one has left the pathway of truth altogether, for truth is the element of constancy which brings meaning to life and equilibrium where once there was only conflict. Learning will never end, and its path is one of fulfillment in both Heaven and Earth. However, the slippery high ledges of glorified knowledge can bring forth only a perilous fall into separation.*

"Truth is not archetypal. **God is archetypal! Reality is fundamental! Truth is the fulfillment of understanding substantiated by its constancy in experience and the power of equilibrium it brings to life.**

"This is the equation which integrates God and science. For it is also correct scientific procedure to approach reality with objectivity and to distill truth from it."

Then He added, *"It is incorrect scientific procedure to postulate a truth or theory as an idealized concept and then proceed to extract from reality patterns of evidence which are suitable to substantiating the theory.* **The purpose of science is to verify reality, not to prove theory!** *In the vastness of reality, you can always find a match to theory if you leave out enough evidence and tolerate a wide enough margin of error."* He added that science dominated by theory would inevitably result in atheistic concepts coupled with toxic waste industry. As He said that, it also occurred to me that possibly there may be control motives impelling science to spend its efforts confirming theory instead of reality. Theory represents "intellectual property." Therefore, any activity deriving from that also has proprietary rights! If reality is God's democratic gift to all of life, then confirmations of reality would be a contribution to our **common property**.

Faulty procedure can still be observed in science today, although it is vanishing. For more than a century, Platonic idealism has been dropping away as scientific minds are now confronting reality directly. None of the monumental breakthroughs of the twentieth century would have been possible had not a new paradigm been formulated around direct confrontations with **reality as primal existence**. However, this did not begin in the twentieth century. Parallel with the philosophy of Platonic idealism was the Aristotelian philosophy of nature as **"the mother of truth."** According to the ancient Greek philosopher, Aristotle, truth is distilled from primary unbiased experience with reality. Reality is our basis for understanding and careful study of it provides a more accurate description of nature. In the past, experimental scientists drew their methods from Aristotle, while theoretical scientists tended to draw their methods from Plato.

After Einstein's Theory of Relativity, the theoretical and the experimental branches of science saw their boundaries virtually disappear. Platonic Idealism was weeded out with vigilance, as objectivity and scientific intelligence were being advanced. Consequently, as idealism was eliminated, an important point of logic for including God in science was also removed. There was deadly silence about the Divine, and atheism ruled supremely in the academic community. Yet, by the marvelous nature of paradox, after counterfeit idealism was removed, the reality of God could then be seen more clearly. By 1965, science had penetrated to the thresholds of infinity—both minutely in particle physics, and cosmically in galactic outreach. **There could be no further sublimation of the vast, uncontainable presence of reality as existence!** From 1965 on, there began to appear small trickles, then noticeable flows, and now small streams of serious scientific literature with metaphysical overtones. In scientific literature there were even occasional references to the concept of God. That, of course, would be the God of order, for the God of miracles is still unacknowledged within the scientific domain. Jesus helped me understand this developing trend by explaining that it is the function of truth to take us back to God, and we may know the truth by whether or not it does just that.

His explanation was not an invitation to interject theology back into the scientific process. That would be as great a mistake as Platonic Idealism. The central point to understand is that God is inseparable **from** reality, and if reality is honestly observed, the truths distilled will eventually enhance our understanding of both God and the universe. These same truths can be used to build a better world. As we direct these truths back to the world we can then combine them with ideals for shaping better qualities of life. The following diagram shows the application of truth to the practicalities of life. In regard to this chart, He explained that the truths which take us back to God are sacred, and those which allow us to build a better world represent practical applications of understanding.

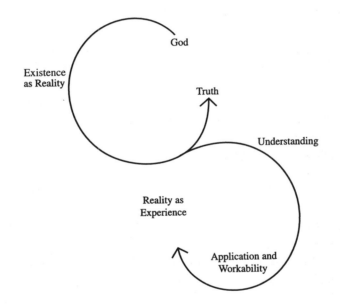

Being an artist, I wanted to know how ideals and beauty fit into the scheme of things. He explained that ideals and beauty were aspects of truth perceived by the senses and focused by the heart into harmonies and patterns for enhancing life. Truth belongs to every area of life—not just science.

"*Science properly fits along a line from primary reality to functional truths, then proceeding to practical application. The introduction of idealizations into the world of science is often beneficial, but only in the* *sense of **perfecting applications** and defining their innate quality. The work of Buckminster Fuller is a wonderful example of taking the principles of classical engineering and perfecting them through idealistic refinement.*

"There is one other condition under which "the ideal" is relevant to science. Although when I say this, I hope you will understand that I am most certainly not referring to the imposition of ideals **upon science**. That would be as stultifying and retrogressive as the quest for archetypal truths.

"At this point in time, science is still externally oriented and driven by standards of objectivity. This is both correct and necessary for the current level of scientific procedure. Science is on the threshold of leaping into the greater definition of what truth is. At that time, ideals will take on a new meaning for science, and there will be no danger of those ideals aborting reality."*

With a bit of hesitation, I asked, "If you told me about that greater truth, would I understand it?"

"Yes, I think so, because you are using it already in your work as an artist. As a matter of fact, this greater truth will first be perceived and utilized outside the sciences by people such as yourself who will demonstrate the power of it."

"Then, what is it?" I pleaded.

*"The ultimate condition of truth is the point where the inner and the outer are one. No matter how completely you have studied and observed the external factors of a situation, until you have located the internally motivating forces, and their relation to the external, you do not know the complete truth. By corollary, no matter how well you understand the internal, you do not have the complete truth until you also understand its impact upon the external. The universe is implicitly and explicitly of one piece. At the point of perfect stasis between the implicit and the explicit, there is a condition of hypersynchronicity, where matter, energy, space, and time move into a 'no-resistance' mode of infinite potential. This is not the collapsing of matter. This is the **synchronizing** of it to a 'zero point' of perfect stasis.* (Stasis, He explained, is the perfect repose of hypersynchronicity.) *Understand that 'zero point' is not about 'nothingness.' It's a designation of infinity. Having this knowledge will do for physical science what the zero did for mathematics—expanding its potential beyond all boundaries. Hypersynchronicity is the ultimate source of patterns, rhythms, ratios, and harmonies which you regard as ideal. Knowledge of this will give new value and meaning to the concept of ideals,*

*but at that point you will also understand that ideals are **implicit** to the universe, not applied upon it as an external prototype generated by the mind."*

Then He looked at me firmly and said, *"The mind cannot create true ideals. The mind is derivative, not causative. It was **derived from** the same ideal state that it would have you think it created. The reason for such confusion is, in the state of hypersynchronicity, cause and effect are the same. As awareness departs from that sacred point, cause and effect are observed to be complementary. The mind in its typical polarity, records the effects while choosing to remember itself only as a causative factor."*

He had already anticipated my next question, for He gracefully responded, *"Yes, there is a universal mind which retains all memory of original cause and monitors its infinite potential. It does not operate with any confusion of cause and effect, as individual minds can do, for it never left the state of hypersynchronicity."* In our many conversations, this was His only reference to a universal or cosmic mind. Perhaps everything that needed to be said was contained in that single sentence. I prefer to imagine that He was deflecting my attention away from a subject which my own mind would have used to empower itself. He was forever nudging my attention back to the Sacred Heart's greater intelligence. As a matter of fact, He concluded that part of our conversation by reminding me that the Sacred Heart is the point within each person where the inner and the outer are one. *"This is your personal point of truth. There is more intelligence within the Sacred Heart than any mind could ever comprehend."*

His message that morning had been ripe with scientific implications which I chose to ponder as I quietly painted. Later that day, we returned to the subject of universal reality, and I was eager to explore the subject in greater depth. I wanted to clarify and explore why cause and effect were not fundamental to the universe, but were instead derivative manifestations of expanding phenomena. If there is perfect stasis at the "zero point" of hypersynchronicity, then under what conditions do cause and effect happen?

He explained that, *"**Perfect stasis is perfect equilibrium**: the Holy Now, from which everything takes shape. Interchange is then brought into existence by various parts of the whole recognizing and responding to each other. In this state, the possibilities for interaction can range from simple harmony, with all parts in mutual support, to the development of incongruities and disharmonies from which densities can accumulate. As that happens, more time and space become necessary to maintain harmony.*

This generates cause and effect, *for that is the universal means of interacting and rebalancing across distances of time and space. All three modes of interaction exist concurrently in the universe. In perfect stasis, there is perfect synchronicity. At the extreme of separation, the law of cause and effect prevails.* ***Between these two extremes,*** *mutuality is the tendency of existence."*

As He spoke, I was remembering the Great Triangle which consisted of Love, Adamantine Particles, and Spirit, and I began to envision the perfect and wonderful integration which He had articulated. He explained that love is the source—**the power which supplies all beingness with its life and energy**. The adamantine particles are the truly uncuttable particles (the original meaning of atom), and He sometimes referred to them as particles of infinity. **These comprise the generic, universal body of all existence**. In reference to the Spirit, He had stated, *"There is but one spirit, the continuous and unbroken matrix of all existence."* Spirit is in all things, around all things, with all things and of all things. All things are inseparable and indivisible and there is no place that spirit is not. It is the ultimate connection, the truly unified field. The discoveries and hypotheses of twentieth century science have led to a vision of the inherent orderliness of the universe, of creative processes, and dynamic continuous change that still maintains order. Existence is now seen essentially as a flow of continuous potential which unfolds into discrete physical manifestation only under certain conditions. The concept of a unified field theory is much debated in scientific circles and so, I asked Jesus, "Is singularity a valid concept?"

"Due to the one spirit and the highly integrated, synchronous nature of all existence, there is ***an aspect*** *of singularity, although it is not a particle or a point. It is the* ***function of hypersynchronicity*** *which can compress any or every part of existence to a singular state of infinite potential. Thus, 'singularity' as an aspect of separation does not exist.* ***Separation is not honored to that degree."***

It was now easy to see how we could enter the field of relativity by dispensing with our ideas about separation. Clearly the concept of one spirit is the key interfacing link between divinity and practicality. Yet, the question which continued to haunt me was the one about love. How did the power of love extend to the realm of particle physics?

Many times He repeated, *"Love is first, foremost, and always, because love calls everything into assembly. Love ignites union. Love unites particles and formulates relationships. The physical agent is magnetism.*

That power applied to physical existence is compression."

Whatever the nature of primal magnetism may possibly be, it was clear that He connected it intimately with the power of love. It was not until some days and many conversations later that He was willing to reveal the nature of love as a physical power, a source of creation, and a sustainer of it. He frequently reminded me that the force He was referring to was not the sweetness of affectionate bonding, the "chocolate and roses" variety of feeling the world most commonly regards as love. This is not to say such emotions do not have their roots in the actual power of love, yet were that all we knew of the subject, we would be helpless to explain our lives, much less fulfill them. Jesus always spoke about the power of love in an extremely holy and reverent way. Nevertheless, there is a scientific component to the power of love which is most appropriate to be shared in this context. It is with deepest respect and gratitude that I now share this wondrous information.

"If you would think upon the function of love scientifically, think of it as a reversal transference—a point of function where two complementary forces, in the presence of a third stabilizing factor, exchange modes and one becomes the other. This is primary magnetism and compression. It is an ongoing function among all primary particles and energies. In organic life, DNA is constructed to conduct this complex and mysterious function. This is also the mystery of paradox which precedes, supersedes, exceeds, and reconciles all patterns of structure into simple fluidity."

Later He explained this in greater detail. *"This primal power of love has within it a function of 'self-awareness,' 'self-acknowledgment,' and 'self dialogue.' This is true regardless of whether you are referring to love as beingness or as energy. You might call it the 'I AM' force. Through internalized communion, the whole becomes aware of its variable possibilities. Differences of potential are established and activation of them begins. Simultaneously, there is a holding and a releasing action which isolates the presence of a static field, a constant existing in neutrality toward the activating variables. This field can be seen to functionally operate as the 'zero point' for compressing and expanding energy. The outer perimeter of a whole can never be determined for there is no point at which one element does not connect with yet another. A whole is designated by its character and quality—not by its boundaries! Its center, however, can be marked by '0.' The forces expanding from that point exponentially multiply the energy released. Simultaneously, through the aspect of energetic tension, energy is transferred from one extreme of expansion to another. By these reversals, torque is generated, and that sets in motion a spring wheel of magnetism."*

The awesomeness and significance of those thoughts are beyond my comprehension to this day. His explanation, however, adds a depth of richness to the other aspects of creation which I find easier to understand. One dazzling thought which has proven to be useful in various ways is this: *"Magnetism is native to primal energy. Since you are part of that energy, you do not have to generate or manipulate it mechanically. What you have to do is stabilize your connection with it through self-awareness and acknowledgment."* This statement reinforced again the reason why **love must be acknowledged as the basis of our self-awareness**!

Love, magnetism, and compression—the primal causes of energy — continue to supply our lives on the distant shores of created manifestation. Yet the ability to access these fountains of potential directly through effective technical interfacing is still beyond our reach. The structures of thought and function which define our existence at the moment do not extend into that frontier. I was particularly intrigued by His explanation that the entire universe was built on compression and that is the law of energy. Simply stated, compression generates energy, expansion releases it. He further emphasized that every compression yields **new** energy. This brought up a question about the law of conservation of energy. "How can new energy be created when there is a fixed amount?"

*"The energies of the universe were built up through immeasurable degrees of compression, which were then released in the great explosion commonly called 'The Big Bang.' From that great explosion came the release of photons—which represent light as the constant of motion within the thermodynamic field which was being created. Through this release of compression also came the observable distances you regard as space and the formulation of elemental patterns you know as matter. Thus you have matter, energy, space, and time. This was a critical point in creation. The energy released through explosion was actually **a reversal** of the basic way it was formulated. From then on, **that** energy released has maintained itself as a 'fixed quantum' conditioned to regenerate itself through similar reversals. Thus all structure shall be limited and be constructed upon reversals of the original quantum of energy. This is the law of conservation.*

"The largest structure in existence is the unified field of conservational energy. That field is comprised of a fixed quantum of energy because it is

derivative and is stably suspended in perpetuity. The structures which comprise it are exact and finite. However, this is not the end of energy or the only supply of it. The free and infinite field of adamantine particles, activated by love, represents the greater supply of energy, and it is available for unlimited current and future compressions." He often referred to these particles as "particles of infinity," and He maintained that science must first address the nature and integrated wholeness of infinity before it can truly understand the nature of adamantine particles.

"Magnetism is electrically generated within the conservational field. Moreover, for any specified amount of magnetic attraction, an equal motion of charged particles is required. Therefore, within this construction, there is no direct access to magnetic potential as a **source of energy**. *The answers to magnetism will not be found within this limited structure. Electromagnetism occurs within the conservational field, but there is another function of magnetism which supersedes those polarized arrangements, and is pure energy. In the larger spectrum, magnetism is activated by alignments of infinity.*

"The mind tends to prefer the explanations which conservation provides, even with all its restrictions. For the mind also is essentially electrical and structural. The same is true of all your instruments of computing, experimentation, and data collection. All of them have a natural preference for electrical priority and polarity. I would suggest you begin with a change of viewpoint. You might call it 'the Copernicus insight.' You see, as long as man's viewpoint was geocentric, it was inconceivable that the Earth could revolve around the sun. After a change of viewpoint which exposed heliocentric motion, the doors to a galaxy were opened.

"Like the laws of conservation, the laws of thermodynamics are relevant to fields of density capable of generating and responding to thermal energy. In regard to those fields of density, these laws are accurate for all practical purposes. However, there is a fatal disability of thermodynamics to logically integrate the whole of existence. It defines energy as a function of matter existing within a macroscopic system, isolated against a backdrop of the infinite unperturbable 'unknown.' Its primary regard for infinity—if it has any at all—is as a 'catch-all' for leftover existence which cannot otherwise be explained. This is usually labeled 'dark matter.'

"Science is not the only discipline guilty of assigning the unknown to separate quarters. Many religions have confined God to the distant past

and the eternal future, leaving the present to be dominated by other issues. That's quite a 'sandbag' against God, considering that the Creator dwells in the Holy Now!" This made it easier to understand why so many people appear to know so much about religion and so little about God.

"*Defining the universe as a macroscopic system of matter and energy isolated against an impenetrable field of raw potential creates the same kind of 'sandbag' against infinity. Furthermore, it eliminates synchronicity and hypersynchronicity as scientific principles while confining the subject of compression to the 'crash and bang' formulas of thermodynamics.*"

"What about numbers?" I asked. "Science, as we practice it, operates by numbers."

"*The mathematics needed to designate infinite and primal energy is angular and proportional in nature, for only proportions and ratios can penetrate the nature of infinity and transpose quality into probable quantities. Angular proportions will resolve to '0,' allowing for the isolation of a static center which retains indeterminate potential.*

"*You must understand that the functional power of true static can never be defined by structure or absolute quantities, for it is outside the realm of structure. Nevertheless, its potential can be understood and accessed. In accessing particles and energy within the conservational field, absolute numerical values can be assigned to constants. **Outside this field, 'static' is the constant**. Stasis provides a basis for fluctuating potentials and for the compression or propulsion of potentialities. Such potentials activate vortexes which may be located, predicted, and affected by angles and proportions. These are not, however, macroscopic systems floating in isolation within a larger indefinable field. They are simplistic. As particles and other elements coordinate with them, there is an increasing simplification in the direction of zero, and an increasing complexity with distance from zero.*

"*There are no singularities in the dimension of matter. The interesting thing about static is that, being indefinable, it can serve the singularity function as a unifying force without having to be a raw singularity in the isolated sense. The most marvelous thing about the indefinable is its ability to adapt to circumstantial needs while being unconditioned by them. A good beginning may be to realize almost everything is space. . . .*"

Before He could continue, I interjected. "What is the most pivotal viewpoint which needs changing in the disciplines of physical science?"

"*That energy=mass. Actually, energy is potential. The perfection of*

*Einstein's equation lies in the fact that it is written $E=mc^2$, not $E=M$ (conditioned by the constant of light squared). You may think this difference is too subtle to matter. Yet, I promise you it is equal to the difference between geocentric and heliocentric explanations of your solar system! Potential is composed of a quantity, a constant, and a quality. In his formula, Einstein isolated the bottom line factors of energy in the conservational field. Mass provides the quantity, light provides the constant, and the square designates the quality. In a conservational field, replication and containment is 'the quality.' $E=mc^2$ is universally relevant because it gives **equal weight** to **all three factors**.*

*"You see, energy is a potential which is inter-dimensional and inter-positional. Many extrapolations which have been made from Einstein's theory tend to reinforce the limited assumption that energy is equivalent to mass and mass exerts gravitational force. The primary drive behind such thinking is to develop the broadest, most workable, definitions of the universe which can yield the maximum **proprietary control within a conservational field.***

"This was also the case for Copernicus. The Earth was believed to be the center of the universe. Therefore, whoever controlled the Earth expected also to rule the universe. Proprietary control was the driving motivation behind every ancient conqueror. Galileo was persecuted for his ideas because they nullified such visions of grandeur. This is also why so much liberation of human potential resulted from them.

"Once it is understood that energy is a potential comprised of a quantity, a constant, and a quality, then a formula will be developed which can be applied to many situations within and beyond the conservational field. With that understanding, conditions of infinity will be comprehensible."

Before this revelation, I had been hesitant to express my confusions between space and infinity. Now it seemed imperative to ask, "Is infinity explainable in terms of matter, energy, time, and space?"

"Not definable, but explainable," He replied. *"In addition to relevant magnitudes, infinity is also simultaneous and qualitative. It exists in space, but is not determined by it."* His answer had all the simplicity I would have expected, yet I still did not understand infinity within the physical world of particles.

*"Well, consider this. Two particles are traveling at the speed of light **in opposite directions**. If you regard their embarkation position as a fixed*

*'geocentric' mass, the particles will prove to be traveling at the speed of light, which is the constant of motion **in relation to mass**. However, you might perceive an alternate connection between the departing two particles, which is a point of equilibrium ascribed not by their point of origin, but rather by their **collective impulse to perform**. This can be designated as a **zero point**, from which they can then be observed as expanding at **twice the speed of light**. These two original particles can then 'bump' and activate more particles into a many-fold multiplication of this process. This is done through the agency of qualitative transmission and replication, interdependently with any quantitative factors or constants. The key is the '0' point which is a true static, from which can be extended angles of infinity. Because of this, the universe was created very quickly!"*

When He said this, something about it reminded me of the chaos theory. *"Yes, that theory represents progress in regard to recognition of simultaneity and qualitative replication, because infinity is **the simultaneous transmission of potential through similarities of quality**. Nevertheless, the search for a single numerical constant for every instance of chaos will not prove fruitful."*

These are two examples of infinity which He offered. "Angularity expresses the quality of infinity, for by implication, do not angles extend infinitely? Infinite quantity progresses proportionately, in the way that progressions of 'half-life' approach but never reach '0.'"

"Is the constant a numerical absolute?"

*"No, not in the ultimate sense. A constant is a factor, dimension, potential, or point which is unchanging within a particular context. Every constant is an index of equilibrium—the point from which all variations and accelerations in that context depart and by which they may be measured. Take, for example, the speed of light. The brilliance of Einstein's observation about the constant of light is that he was the first to demonstrate equilibrium **in motion** as a constant of energy. Actually, the whole galaxy is equilibrium in motion. Locate the factors of equilibrium and you've located the constant.*

*"Simple as that realization may seem, many discoveries dependent on it are currently being inhibited or overlooked by the mistaken association of equilibrium with inert, motionless, 'dead-points' where action, life, and function are relatively suspended. This comes from observing equilibrium **in structure**—like the fulcrum of a see-saw, the hub of a wheel, or the inertia of a resting object.*

"True equilibrium is vital, reciprocal, and synchronistic. It generates the utmost in potential even though its constancy represents a 'still-point' for surrounding variables." (He cracked a smile, and reminded me that I was going to have to get used to paradoxes like that in order to be comfortable outside the domain of linear structure.) *"It is the function of a constant to stabilize variables, therefore it would be a mistake to view it as a frozen absolute. Occasionally, the function of a constant is so obvious that it may be indicated, measured, and assigned a numerical value, as is the case with light (deductive reasoning). Normally, however, the constant must be isolated through reciprocal factors within a field of variables (inductive reasoning)."*

I needed a little clarification about the "0" point, so I asked Him, "Is a vacuum an aspect of energy and space, or just a hypothetical position?"

"Any of the above. It could be a vacuum, a field of energy with indiscernible fluctuations, an embarkation point within a field of expanding potential, or a point of manifest equilibrium. The crux of the matter is that '0' point is a designated reference to the master constant which is the perfect stasis of hypersynchronicity (ultimate equilibrium). The '0' point factor underwrites the power of all other constants such as the speed of light which are assigned specific quantities. If the supreme constant were not '0,' then constants which have been assigned a quantitative value would not hold true when introduced into variable situations."

I must have looked a little bewildered, because He graciously added, *"It is not important at this time that you understand how this works. What is important is that you equate energy with potential, and know that potential is comprised of a quantity, a constant, and a quality. Regardless of what value is assigned to the constant, it draws its stability and equilibrium from the '0' point of hypersynchronicity which is present in all phenomena."*

"Why is this so hard to see?" He grinned from ear to ear as if He anticipated the pleasure of sharing a Divine secret. Almost in a whisper He confided, ***"Because hypersynchronicity cloaks itself. Like the truth, you must be in it to see it!"*** Withdrawing into my own silence, I returned to painting.

On another day, late in the afternoon, I was feeling a bit tired, and He suggested that I step out in the backyard and have a brief look toward the sun. It was low in the sky, and conditions were such that I could almost look into it. Even though I could only glance toward it quickly, there was a very relaxing effect. After returning to the studio, He asked how I enjoyed my trip to infinity and remarked that my concentration should be stronger now that I was re-magnetized. **"You mean that the sun is magnetic?"**

"It began as a powerful compression vortex, and is today a magnetic force throughout the solar system. The sun was built up electron by electron from compressions of hydrogen gas. The heat generated by those compressions ignited a chain of thermonuclear reactions which eventually resulted in what you see today." [I was delighted recently to receive some pleasant reinforcement on this explanation. A friend forwarded me a newspaper clipping, with a Washington 'date line.' **Astronomers say sun's 'blanket' magnetic.**" "Astronomers announced yesterday (11/5/97) that they have solved a 55-year-old puzzle: Why is it hundreds of times hotter outside the sun than inside? The answer, they said, is that the sun is surrounded by the equivalent of an electric blanket to keep it cozy from the bitter cold of space. The blanket is heated **by magnetism,** however, not by electricity. Alan Title, director of the Stanford-Lockheed Institute for Space Research and leader of the international research team called it "the Sun's Magnetic Carpet." About 50,000 magnetic spots sprinkled across the sun's surface pump a continuous flow of heat and energy from the **interior** up into the corona, the outermost reaches of the sun's atmosphere." I look forward to the day when many other confirmations come forth.]

Intrigued by His explanation of the sun's magnetic nature, I wondered if the magnetic process was also relevant to black holes. I was curious as to whether a black hole was a point where matter and energy had completely collapsed and disappeared into infinite density with a ravenous appetite! He grinned and said that totally collapsed matter was impossible. With a big smile He added, *"These vortexes are not instruments of death. Most of them are instruments of birth which will eventually gain enough mass to transmute into new suns or other configurations of cosmic matter. Actually, what science is now generally referring to as black holes are* **three different phenomena.** *As infinity and 'true static' are better understood, these different forms will stand out more clearly.*

*"**First**, there are ruptures in the energy grid, which expose the phenomenal power of true stasis and its ability to generate magnetic attraction. These are the birthing fields and may become future suns.*

*"**Second**, there are the gigantic mature vortexes which grew so rapidly as to transmute into colossal energy fountains without ever becoming completely solid. These are the mighty quasars which exert an influence*

upon everything around them **across distances as great as a galaxy**.

"**Third**, there are collapsed energy fields where an aging star lost its ability to keep the matter, energy, time, and space in a system of balanced motion around it. This is not the same as thermonuclear collapse of a young giant that goes super nova. Because in this case the magnetic field continues to generate a powerful influence upon nearby energy and matter—but without a balancing system which its own planets once provided. This is not collapsed matter. It is a **collapsed system** approaching infinite density."

As He spoke, it all seemed so simple and so grand that I just marveled at the amazing potential of the cosmos. Through His eyes, it was so easy to see the never-ending pattern of expansion and contraction in all existence. Never was it more poignantly highlighted than in the last detailed discussion we had about physical properties. He had made the subject of black holes so easy to confront that I couldn't resist asking about the other intriguing element of the universe—antimatter. Antimatter is unstable stuff. Whenever antimatter and matter collide, they annihilate each other. Scientists say that a particle of antimatter is the exact opposite of a particle of matter.

"**Antimatter and matter were both created simultaneously out of pure energy.** The crucial aspect of their relationship is that antimatter represents the noncompressible aspect of energy. In high compression fields, matter accumulates into densities and antimatter falls away. It is necessary for them to separate in order that matter can persist through accumulations of mass. Only when the two meet again can all energy be released from the mass. When the two valences of energy make contact, all compressions of matter are released into pure energy.

"**As it is created, pure energy splits into two lines of potential**—one line of potential responds to compression and the other does not. This is not a perfect symmetry in the sense of structure, because matter contains both positive and negative charges, and antimatter will form minute, occasional accumulations of mass. Their complementary function is a dynamic equilibrium. Normally, these two lines of potential are not actively involved with each other. Actually, they are protected by intrinsic disregard for each other until a condition arises where compressions are so dense as to produce a conservational field that is repellent to antimatter. The attempted expulsion of antimatter is the very trigger which attracts it, for antimatter is the primal corollary which permitted the formation of matter in the first

place. Attempted expulsion begets attraction. Attraction begets release of
compression. Occasionally this could be a very big bang. That is the eternal
rhythm of the cosmos!"

His eyes twinkled as He paused for a moment, and allowed me to
behold the simplicity of universal creation.

The purpose of science, He said, *"is to expand understanding of life*
and to make life work." I doubt He would have shared any of this technical
and scientific data if He had not observed how my awareness and
consciousness were expanding. In all conversations He was careful to
weave patterns of integrated meaning and to find ways of applying the
information to practical living. One of the most relevant summarizations He
made about the subject of energy in our world is its relationship to scarcity
and force.

"Because man is dealing with energy defined by the principles of
conservation, he understands it only as a scarcity. This is reinforced by the
fact that the primary source of energy he can perceive and understand is
solar supply. This supply is suffused through the whole planetary system
and works its way up through all the patterns of life. Because there is
limitation and dependency within this system, there is also competition.
Thus the strong, the aggressive, and the highly conservative forces
dominate. As long as man's primary supply of energy is subject to such
scarcity, there will be no system of social democracy that can last long
upon the Earth. It is imperative that man change his viewpoint and look
toward physical infinity and the reality of God if he would bring forth upon
the Earth a brotherhood of peace and prosperity. Within this change of
viewpoint he will find both the physical and the spiritual answers for which
he has been looking."

He clearly emphasized that *"Science is the pursuit of workability,*
developing consciousness about how life works, and applying that
consciousness toward solving the problems of living. Any activity which
employs that attitude and process is science. In recent decades, because of
the overwhelming dominance of high technology and military competition,
science has succumbed to the glamour of elaborate machinery and
intellectual elitism. This is not the true measure of science. Such
investments have given the false impression that mental elitism has greater
value than practical service. Actually, the opposite is true. It is from service
to life that all true science springs, after which the mind may express its
servitude *by summarizing the brilliance of our natural inclinations.*

"There is a key to the universe. All the answers are right in front of you. It is your job to formulate the questions. Without the right question, the answer is invisible. Therefore, approach reality with a humble, inquiring mind, open in heart and perception, and free of judgment. If you will ask the right questions, all will be revealed!

"True intelligence is innately humble—not in a self-effacing way—but in the way of innocent perception and workable discernments of reality. The issues of life are like broken points in a circle of wholeness. They are very specific in nature and can be repaired only with correct assessment.

*"From the beginning of consciousness, man has searched for the 'Grand Plan,' in hopes that he would discover some holistic imprint for all existence and then learn to administer it as a technology. If such could be done, then man would have the ultimate panacea—the cure for all ills. The idea is to 'just impose the Grand Plan like a golden blanket upon the Earth, and **no more problems**'! If such a thing existed, it surely would be the most valuable commodity upon the Earth!*

*"There **is** a holistic imprint, but it cannot be summarized in a blueprint, nor monopolized by technology. **That imprint is love.** There is no matrix, gridwork, or blueprint large enough to catch it all!*

*"**Still there are no panaceas. Even love must be given and nurtured with respect for particulars of reality and restored at the points where it has been broken.** It is the nature of holistic reality that any fracture or disruption of order is very particular in kind and occurrence, yet the contributing factors may be many or varied. The very idea of a panacea is a misconception of workability.*

*"It is characteristic of the naive, the desperate, or the mercenary to gravitate toward archetypal concepts which can be represented as panaceas. The hope is to cover all bases with a generality that promises to correct hidden ills without ever acknowledging or delving into them. When I said long ago that a man cannot be redeemed from his ills without confessing them, I was not being accusative or invasive. Actually that was a very scientific statement for those days and times. **It means that you must be subject specific in your handling of life!** You may break a circle at any place you choose, but I assure you that it can be rejoined only at the very place of the fracture. There are no magic circles which descend in polite generalities and repair problems without exposure and clarification of them. Nor can you handle one problem by polishing something else which was not broken. If the foundation of a house is cracked, you are **not** going*

*to fix it with a new roof or camouflage it with landscaping. The same is true of broken relationships, broken plans, and broken hearts. Find out where the break **really** occurred. Fix it there.*

"*Discernment, acknowledgment, and workability are humbling attitudes, but without them you do not have science. Through them, you have the love connection—the caring for particulars which moves life forward, and the devotion to workability which is a primary impulse of love.*

"*It is the job of science to address the workability of particulars and to strive for explanations and understanding within categories of common probability. This is an unassuming pursuit, but a very noble one, for it will take man to the threshold of infinity. Such attitudes generate respect for life, for infinity, and all particulars of existence.*"

Once again the concept of infinity appeared. Now it had expanded to include particulars and common reality. "Are you implying that infinity is here and among us, like spirit?" I trembled a bit to consider that infinity was not so far away after all, that perhaps I had conveniently misunderstood the subject in order to avoid its potential first hand!

"*Infinity is the universal factor which allows quantities to be translated to quality and qualities to be translated to quantity. Therefore, it relates to the transmission of potential in every dimension of reality. It is through this function that adamantine particles* (particles of infinity) *synchronize with the power of love. Perhaps this is why man gravitates toward panaceas, because he instinctively seeks for contexts of commonalty and predictability. The instinct is healthy, but the mistake lies in man's reliance upon archetypal formulas which have been artificially imposed **upon** life instead of being distilled from life's intrinsic nature and true tendency.*

"*The critical mass today in all technologies is not with the science itself, but in human expectations about it. For example, the field of high-tech medicine has brought countless blessings to mankind—answers about which we only dreamed a hundred years ago. Its accomplishments, however, have been so dazzling as to suggest a new panacea for all human ills. This is a more dangerous illusion than you might think, because whenever anything is regarded as a panacea **then unrelated injuries will transfer their symptoms to that domain.** Let's consider, for example, a man who has suffered financial failure. Instead of confronting and handling it in a subject-specific way, he **may** have a heart attack. **That way a panacea in which he believes—medicine—might come to the rescue and give him the new lease on life he needs.** Chemical medication, in general, has come* to be regarded as a panacea, even though many human ailments are not chemical in nature. Now a world full of distress is transferring its symptoms into chemical dependency.

   *"It is the nature of all panaceas to illicit transference. Eventually, they fail to provide all the solutions promised, but in the meantime they become a magnet for ills that need to be dealt with in other ways. **You should be careful to understand that any problem will transfer its symptoms to whatever it believes contains the solution, but the eternal truth is that solutions will be found only in relation to actual causes.** Respect for this should be ingrained in any scientific procedure. This is an infinitely workable universe, but you cannot make it work by avoiding its issues or by hiding behind generalities which promise you a rainbow for breakfast.*

   "These phenomena are not limited to physical health. Any panacea is a dangerous illusion. Eventually all panaceas will self-destruct. Education, for example, is very beneficial, but general education enforced by public regulation is not the panacea for social ills that it was believed to be. Now all the ills which it cannot handle have transferred their symptoms into the public school system.

   "The best example I can give you on the perils of panacea is that of money. Money is a marvelous lubricant for life. It keeps the wheels turning, but the hope that it can cure the ills of the world has brought all the evils of the world into its domain.

   "This is a subject-specific universe which honors the presence of its Creator in all things."

   His explanation about how life works was a model of simplicity. As I absorbed it, a question rose from the deeper recesses of my consciousness and with the careful respect, I gently inquired, "Can the idea of God not also be perceived as a panacea—a cure all?" I could tell by the twinkle in His eyes and the expectancy in his smile that He had been waiting for that question. With beaming pleasure, He sweetly replied, *"That all depends on whether they're referring to God as **an idea** or as **a reality**! In reality, God is subject-specific, a guiding force in all that is. When one knows God in reality, he has all the answers potentially in front of him. **Where is there not God?"***

   His answer left me speechless, and suddenly as if a locked door had been opened, I perceived a new depth of feeling and understanding which was previously unavailable. I began to comprehend the problem of knowing "about God" only through ideas rather than "knowing God directly through experience." Through ideas, one can know God only as a generality. Suddenly, the history of generalities unfolded before my eyes with its fostering panaceas which had drawn to themselves all the dysfunctions of the world. I no longer wondered why science and theology had embroiled themselves historically in such contradictory viewpoints. Most importantly, I saw that it does not have to remain that way.

Chapter 13
Pathways to Success

Sunlight was pouring through the large floor-to-ceiling window in my studio on one particularly brilliant February morning, as if to give external acknowledgment of the Great Light already present in the room. It was warmer than usual that day, and the birds were fluttering above the ground looking for seeds while my dear cat Gunnar watched in fascination all the activity from a sunny spot on the windowsill. Outside the window, a flowering quince gave evidence to the promise of spring. Altogether, it was a picture of happiness and beauty that prompted me to ask the Master, "Do we have to go to a higher dimension to fulfill our love and purpose, to do our work, and to be all that our Father created us to be?"

With a gentle touch of humor, He replied, *"The higher dimensions are in fine shape as they are. You are here to further God's creation in this one."*

"Then, are we to make this dimension a different place?"

"You are here to learn the process through which sacred transformation occurs in all times and places. The raw material of Planet Earth is fertile ground for demonstrating to the children of God an eternal truth: as the internal is fulfilled, the external is brought into alignment and manifestation. Likewise, as the external is created according to the will of God, the internal reclaims its original perfection. You were created in the likeness of God to extend the creative powers of our Father into all the dimensions in which you dwell, seek and create. Where you are is where your work unfolds. You are where you were meant to be."

That statement was both comforting and challenging. When I thought about the difficulties in our world and the obstacles that can arise with even unassuming tasks, I was confronted with the distinct probability that I needed a better approach to living successfully. In the simplest way I knew, I asked, "Then, how can we have more success in living?"

In His typically lucid way, He gave me four principles for achieving success, which represent a simple and focused application of much that had already been explained. Nevertheless, the uncomplicated power of His delivery deserves a presentation in its own right.

*"**The first principle is: Be the love that you are.** You see, when you are being the love that you are, you are also being the child of God that you are. You are being the likeness of God, present here upon the Earth to forward the creations of your Father in whatever situations you find yourself. This causes immediate changes in your outlook and performance. The first thing that happens is that you rise above the problems facing you. This is critical to success, because no problem is solved at the level on which it was created. The solution to every problem is to be found on a level which is slightly, or even greatly, above the conflicting perceptions. As long as you are eye to eye with the difficulty, you will fight the problem rather than resolve it. When you are being the love that you are, you realize that the secret of success already exists in the nature of your beingness. Solutions to problems, answers to prayers, and revelations of purpose already exist. It is your duty and challenge to make yourself available to receive them.*

"Love commands the universe. Man resorts to control only when love is missing. Control is a very shabby substitute for command, and it is an enormously exhausting pursuit! One of the most refreshing realizations that you may have in being the love that you are is the greater feeling of restfulness. In a world obsessed with control, it is difficult to find even a moment's rest. In many ways, control is a competition for dominance of time and timing. As you command with love, you will notice that the timing of your life will be much more consonant with your own purposes and true nature. When you command, you can rest. This is the importance of acknowledging our Father's rest on the Sabbath.

*"**The second principle of success is: Do the right thing.** Then do it consistently with momentum until you are doing one right thing after another in the process of living. Make 'doing the right thing' the freight train of your life. Now, be clear with this, I am **not** referring to **judgments** of right versus wrong in conformity with a backdrop of structured morality. Morality is subject to constant revision, according to changing protocol and beliefs. What you consider moral today might have been thoroughly*

shunned in the seventeenth century. Only a few decades ago in your country it was considered wrong to dance and for women to wear slacks! Today you understand both as very enjoyable and expressive liberties. Concepts of morality are constantly in a flux, which is due to the greater truth that morality is change for the better. There is some rightness in anything which you change for the better. By just doing the right thing, you are in harmony with life without having to confine yourself to some limiting formula of what others might consider to be proper behavior. The truest guideline for determining a right action is contained within the seven principles of the heart: Unity, love, life, respect, honesty, justice, and kindness. Whenever you practice those seven principles of the heart, you are instinctively doing the right thing in any given situation.

"There is still another way to determine rightness. Ask these questions: What brings out the best in you? What brings out the best in a situation? What brings out the best in other people?"

His statement reminded me of a situation I had recently experienced with a friend. She had been ill for several years and her health was continuing to degenerate. To compound her problem, she would not consent to medical procedures. I asked one day, "Why not?" Her answer was that she wanted to be healed in a way that would give God all the glory. I agreed that her desire was worthy, although I had some serious questions about her understanding of the concept. So, I asked, "What makes you think that God couldn't work through a physician, or through a medical procedure? Did it ever occur to you that God just simply wants the best for you? Don't you think that it is the will of God for you to get well and to do whatever is required to make that happen?" Shortly after that she relented and agreed to receive medical assistance. Her recovery was slow, but during her convalescence she experienced an inner growth that arises from having faith in someone else. It brought out her best to trust in human care as well as that of God.

There is a little anecdote which makes much the same point. A man named Jim arrived in Heaven and walked up to the pearly gates. He saw Saint Peter, who said, "I am glad to see you. Come on inside and meet the Lord." Jim met Jesus, who gave him a hug. Then Jesus said, "I am glad you are here, but why did you choose to come right now? You did not have to die in that flood. Was there some reason you thought you did?" Jim looked bewildered and reflected back on the events which took his life. As flood waters swelled over the river banks, inundating his house, Jim took refuge in his boat. Then after the boat capsized in the raging river, he washed upon a roof top. A helicopter arrived and attempted a rescue, but he waved it away. "Why didn't you take that ladder"? Jesus asked. Jim replied, "I thought you were going to bring down the waters and save me in that way." Jesus answered, "I sent all the help I could." With one last attempt at defending his limited expectations, Jim mumbled, "I wanted to give you all the credit." Jesus consoled Jim with a hug as He corrected his misconceptions, "You would have made me happy enough just by doing the right thing."

Jesus pointed out that we can sometimes get 'hung up' on even noble agendas which keep us from doing the right thing. Through contemplating His teaching, I have come to believe that all other agendas and preconceptions have to be suspended in pursuit of doing the right thing. At times, doing the right thing means reaching for the stars, at other times it means being practical. At times, it means speaking up, and at other times, being quiet. Sometimes it requires courage, and often humility. There are occasions when it is right to stand up for oneself, and at other times the greater rightness lies in service to others. Working with life as it **really is** seems to be the recurring theme in doing the right thing.

"The third principle of success is so integral to life that most people overlook it as a basis for achievement and fulfillment: Simply follow life and the living! The whole universe is built around a priority for life and the living. Therefore, you cannot afford to ignore this principle. Do not follow the dead and the dying. By this, I mean do not adapt to ways of life, structures, ideas, concepts, or businesses which are becoming ineffective and obsolete. Look for new alignments, opportunities, and understandings which refresh your life."* Jesus said long ago, *"Let the dead bury their own dead."*[17] He explained to me that those words were spoken in reference to this very principle. As we follow life and the living, we move forward. Life is being created anew each day, and consciousness is expanding with every new burst of life. This is not to say that our heritage should not be studied and honored. However, we cannot effectively navigate our lives through a rear-view mirror. We cultivate a true competency for living by adopting a forward approach to life while learning to value its potential for change and growth.

Jesus discussed human suffering with me only on three occasions. This was one of them. He mentioned that people are unnecessarily suffering and hurting in life because they are struggling to preserve the dead and the dying instead of following life and the living. This would include dead and dying attitudes, businesses, situations, structures, and ways of life. He stated that, *"Our Father created this universe to celebrate life and to go on forever. In order to ensure this would always be true, He gave priority to the living. Newborn children entering the world are your future. If you do not honor these children and take care of them, your future will have a regrettable absence of meaning and quality. New and abundant animal and plant life is bursting upon the Earth. If you do not honor this gift of life, there will be no harvest in your old age. If you serve only the dead and the dying that is what you will have for your company.*

"Respect of prior creation is a pillar of wisdom. Nevertheless, it is important that you do not confuse such respect with ancestor worship. Even above money, the most prevalent false god upon the Earth always has been ancestor worship. People are dependent upon the old ways, and the old paths of the dead and the dying. Such ways and paths once represented life and the living. Now you are the life and the living. The most important reason to study the past and to honor those who have come before is to give new life to their work and service by applying it to the future. Just as children bring new blood, new life, new energy, new ideas, and new visions to a family, so too, can new creation bring vitality and regeneration to all that has come before. If you want to be successful, give your full and uncompromised support to life and the living.

"When decisions arise, all you have to ask yourself is, 'Does it support the living or the dying?' Many situations are mixed with both potentials of living and dying. This is especially true in the workplace. When confronted with that discernment, simply focus on the living, or apply the power of life to regenerate the dying.

"As you follow life and the living, you will instinctively do the right thing. When you do the right thing, you are being the love that you are. Logic is inherent to this process. All of these principles flow together: one, two, three."

"But what about number four?" I asked. "You said there were four principles to success. When we are doing all three of these things, what could possibly be left to do?"

*"There is nothing left to do except to forgive those effects which did not constructively apply to your life, and then continue forgiving as an ongoing process of 'keeping your temple clean.' **Forgiveness is the fourth principle of success.** One of the miracles about forgiving is that you cut away*

anything from the past that did not work for you. Most people are stuck with the dead and the dying, because they won't forgive. People hang onto grudges as if they were sacred treasures. The tragedy of a grudge, however, is that it keeps you connected to something that did not work for you, failed you, betrayed you, or let you down. Grudges weigh upon you, and distract you from focusing toward success. Resentments make life into a cluttered disarray that never makes sense. If souls were compared to moving vehicles, an unforgiving soul could be seen as a dump truck with tin cans dragging off the back side. Clatter, clatter, clang, clang!! If you listen, you can hear them coming."

Ever since I heard that metaphor, I cannot walk through a shopping mall without noticing the "dump trucks" and the "Porsches." Life is easy to observe by its lightness, freedom, and action. The "Porsche" is almost always a kid. He's supporting life and the living, instinctively doing the right thing, even though he may not think about it. Most of the time he is being the love that he is. The "dump truck," representing the other line of possibility, is so tied to the dead and the dying, that a real future is almost out of reach. *"Such a person is preoccupied with making up his damages in the stock market or other businesses that failed for him. He may be consulting an attorney every few months for one thing or another until accumulations of stress require medical attention. He does not get along with the neighbors because of his argument over their dogs. This is a typical situation for many people. This man's life is so consumed with regret and difficulty, there is no longer a focus toward the future. Then he wonders, 'Why can I never come up with a good idea anymore? When I was twenty years old I had the world in front of me and more ideas than I could use.'*

"It would be easier for a person to move through such difficulties and to forgive the accumulating offenses and disappointments of life if one crucial aspect of forgiveness were better understood—that is the harmony between intelligence and forgiveness. Forgiveness is made complete, not by forgetting, but rather by understanding what went wrong and how it happened. Usually things go wrong because an understanding, ability, capacity, or readiness for an opportunity was incomplete in the first place. You will not make it right by forgetting, and then doing the same thing again. Besides, you cannot fully release your grievances against others until you understand your own participation in them.

"Though I ask you to forgive without ceasing, there is focus and

*intelligence to that also. The act of forgiving should not be a sacrifice of consciousness in which a person submits passively to repeated abuse. The purpose of forgiveness is to release negative attachments so that true enlightenment may be attained and constructive justice may be applied to a situation. For instance, repeated forgiveness of a destructive child, without corrective intercession, would imply consent or permission for him to continue in the same way. The reason to forgive is to restore love, not to continue an unworkable or unconstructive situation. Forgiveness is eminently practical. You will benefit more from forgiving a neighbor who has accidentally blocked your driveway than to forgive an act of terrorism on the other side of the Earth. **The closer an offender is to your life, the more important it is to forgive.** By this same measure of truth, **I hope you realize that the most crucial person to forgive is yourself.** If everyone forgave himself and those close to him, the world would take care of itself!!*

"When you forgive, it gives you a new lease on life, as well as those you have forgiven. Instinctively, you will then be drawn towards life and the living. In responding to that impulse, you will do the right thing instinctively. When you do the right thing, you become more and more the love that you are. These four principles of success constitute an endless cycle of life-giving support. No matter where one enters the cycle, every other part of it is strengthened. Application of these principles can put love back in command of your life."

I began to wonder, "Is this the way God's will works in our lives? When I was young and receiving religious instruction, God's will was usually presented more as a dictatorial fact than a gentle force which permeated the potentials and harmonies of life." I asked Jesus if He could respond to this and assist me in understanding the subject of will, and most especially the will of God, with more clarity and perception.

He graciously proceeded to say, *"The first thing you need to understand is that God's will is already at work. It is not a detached potential, sitting on the sidelines of life waiting to be invited to play. All of life is God's will. The will of God is intrinsic to reality, and is no way arbitrary to it. When you think that it is somewhere else, you are missing the point, and most likely, you will begin to think that you need to be somewhere else yourself. Your life is unfolding where it is for a very good reason. Find out what that reason is. There is no better way to confirm the rightness of where you are than to view its relationship with the Sacred Heart, the one innocent place within yourself. In that place, the will of God is made known. Your proper place is exactly where you are, at least for the moment. Whenever you do not feel a rightness in that, it is because you are not empowering life with a synchronicity between yourself and the will of God. You are seeing God somewhere else, instead of within your own reality.*

    "There is another thing that will help you understand the will of God. God's will abides in truth. Know the truth and you will know the will of God."

    That statement sharpened my senses and peaked my desire to know more about the truth. "There is probably nothing which has been more debated—or fought over—than the truth. You said that a person who knew the truth would be set free. Isn't it curious that the very source of our liberation is the very thing over which we are fighting?"

    He smiled and responded, *"The reason for the apparent conflict is that only part of any truth is ever seen externally. Complete truth is found only at the point where inner awareness and outer reality are one. As part of your replication of the Father, you possess the ability to know perfect synchronicity. This power is preserved in the Sacred Heart, the center of innocent stillness where your inner life is joined with your outer life. An interesting thing about truth is that no matter how much external information you may possess, if you have not determined what it means for you, what you have is less than truth. You could measure every rock on the planet, survey every country on Earth, or weigh and measure every molecule, but if you do not know what that information means in your life, you have no way of using it or unburdening yourself from its influence. There is a correlation to that, which relates to other people who spend much of their days in prayer and meditation, yet never examine the outer world. All they know is the inner. No matter how well you know the inner, if you do not know the realities which envelop and surround your life, you also do not know the greater truth.*

    *"A more complete understanding of this will help you negotiate the issues of life more effectively. There is a common reality that binds us all, yet every individual has a right to his own relationship with that reality and to honor both perceptions as his complete truth. As you respect reality, you have a common ground for working with others, but as you respect the truth of another person, you learn to respect your own truth as well. It is not so much a factual truth that will set you free, as it is the realization of **what truth really is**. Once you learn what truth is, you have a meaningful basis*

for communicating with others with confidence and certainty. As you regard the truth of others, you understand how God works within the same reality to bring a different focus for each person, for different meanings, and different covenants. As you honor that balance you will look for it in yourself as well.

*"The miracle of truth is that it is unique for each and yet constant for all. This relates to another principle which is crucial to alignment with our Father's will, and that is the law of mutuality. Mutuality allows expansion and differences to occur in the universe or among humankind without loss of harmony. All communication is based upon this law of mutuality. If there were no mutuality between two people, there would be no sense in talking. Neither person could understand the other. However, without different experiences or viewpoints to share, what would be the point of communicating? On the very obvious level, having a common language is mutuality. Through a common language, differences may be compared and overcome, if necessary. Through mutual understanding you are set free from another's viewpoint. You do not have to serve the dreams of another. All you have to do is honor the other man's **right to dream**, for in honoring his right, you honor your own. This is the blessing of mutuality.*

"The law of mutuality is perhaps the finest guideline to the will of God, for the Creator does not violate His own laws. It is the will of God that you grow and challenge yourself in relation to realistic possibilities, and that you apply your efforts to that which will be mutually beneficial to all concerned. What you are led to do may seem difficult in relation to your confidence or self-esteem, but such considerations are often denials of reality. It will never be impossible in relation to what truly is."

This truth was clearly illustrated by my own experience of painting *The Lamb and The Lion.* The calling was most definitely beyond my level of confidence, and the likelihood of being able to produce such a painting seemed almost out of reach. Nevertheless, the reality was that I had actually spent the whole of my life preparing for that challenge. It's just that, until 1991, my covenant and my preparation had not coincided in a meaningful or revealing way.

As He progressed in His teaching of will, He compared it with intention. It was through this corollary concept that I came to realize why will is not an external force imposed on life. From the instructions of my childhood I had come to believe that the will of God and my parent's will were external forces shaping my life. For reasons of such belief, we often strike back at influences imposed upon us. Even so, we have to take orders at work, at school, and in other situations where compliance with directions and leadership is mandatory. Sometimes we accept orders with grace, and sometimes we push back. In considering these things, I realized that I still had lingering issues related to a confusion about will and control. To expedite a higher understanding, He suggested that we change words temporarily.

"Instead of using the word 'will', may we refer to it as 'intent'?"

Quick to agree, I said, "Okay. We can use intent."

"How old were you when you decided or intended to become an artist?"

"I was just three years old."

He replied, *"All right. That is an example of intent."*

I thought for a moment, and then agreed, "Yes, I guess so." That made sense. I had never thought of it as will, only intent.

He persisted by asking, *"Did you think about it and apply that intent every day of your life from that moment on?"*

"Oh, no. I was just a little girl, painting in my coloring books. As a matter of fact, I never even asked for art classes. My mother saw to it that I received them."

He added, *"Yes, she responded to your intent."*

"When I was in school I made my best grades in art, so I was always given projects that gave me more experience."

He urged me to continue by affirming, *"So even your teachers were responding to your intent. As you entered high school, were you thinking about painting as a career?"*

"I never actually planned a career in my teens, because horses were my passion in those years. I was just being a girl growing up, although in my senior year I was awarded a university scholarship in painting."

He seized that opportunity to complete His objective, *"Was that the universe responding to your intent?"*

At that point, He must have observed my readiness to receive a deeper explanation. *"Glenda, what you need to understand is that intent is a seed planted at some point in your life. All you have to do every so often is acknowledge it, water it, and fertilize it. You do not have to think about it all the time. Consider the lilies of the field that volunteer for life and grow wild. You see, your Father created a universe that will honor the intentions of every heart. If you plant the intentions of your heart like a seed, they will grow. Other people will recognize them. Your intentions will burst forth from the ground as little sprouts, and will set forth leaves, flowers, and fruit. You planted a little seed when you were only three years old, and now we are here together, painting this painting.*

"This is the way intent works. Our Father created a universe that honors every seed planted. The seeds that you plant are your intentions. You do not have to apply external force, although it would help to take stock of their directions of growth. Unfortunately, some intentions could be more accurately compared with weeds. When you decided to be an artist, another child might have decided to leave home. Another child might have responded to a negative situation, an abuse, or a destructive emotion. Another child might have decided to enter the field of medicine in response to a serious family illness. Whatever seeds were planted will continue to grow and bear fruit.

*"The universe is built upon **four levels of intent. First**, is the intent of God. You can summarize the intent of God very sweetly and simply this way. **It is LOVE**. Love is the will of God. This is why I gave you love as **my only commandment**. For love shall triumph in all things **as** the will of God. No matter what illusions seem to subvert the process, love will triumph in the end. The will of God is that the best will happen to you. The will of God is that the best will happen in life. The will of God is that by the power of grace, each one shall be lifted above the delusions of separation and taken home. You shall never be left in any situation that shall have the power to destroy your soul. Love and only love is the will of God. Divine will is very easy to know, once you understand that.*

*"**The second level** of intent was placed by the Creator into the physical functions of our universe. This level of intent performs under the power of basically two principles. One is that life and the living shall prevail over the dead and the dying. That is the will of God, so whenever you support life and the living, you are in harmony with the will of God for this universe. The other principle which resides under this intent for physical well-being is the law of cause and effect. The Creator intends for the universe to return always to a state of balance. No matter how far a state of existence might swing to 'the left,' it will always be rebalanced to 'the right' and eventually back to center. He has placed this law of balance into the physical universe so that what you sow, you shall also reap. What you do unto others will be done unto you. What you have planted is exactly what you will harvest. This is a fundamental justice system which requires*

everything to balance in the end. *If you live in such a way that you do not expect this to happen, you are going to be very surprised by the outcome in your life. For your life will become the reciprocal force to balance any imbalances you have caused. All the books will balance, and life and the living shall prevail over the dead and the dying. That is all you have to remember about how the universe works. If you will understand those two principles, you know the intent of God in the realm of physical existence.*

"The only thing which complicates or obscures your perception of how perfectly this balance performs is that the universe is an enormous place. When Job was suffering so badly in his state of despair, he cried to God and he pleaded, 'Why, why?' God answered, 'Where were you when I created the sun, moon, and stars? Where were you when I created the whales? Where were you when I created the vast array of existence'? In other words, 'Job, there is a very big picture that also has to restore its balance. The whole universe cannot accommodate your personal needs for balance in every moment of your life'! Sometimes you are asked to serve the bigger picture by being tolerant and patient with your small one. The larger design has to integrate and balance first in order for the affairs of your own life to be lasting and meaningful, and for you to reap an enduring prosperity and happiness. The best way to work with the larger alignments of life is to follow the four principles of success.*

"Your life will be affected by many things you did not cause. Therefore, it is important to have a sense of tolerance and forgiveness. It is a mark of wisdom to be responsible for that which you did cause, but it is also a mark of wisdom to study the larger pattern and let it release you from responsibilities that are not yours. There are some people who burn themselves out trying to be responsible for too much. You cannot be responsible for everything, although you can work toward greater responsibility for the things you did cause. The surest way to make progress in that is to follow life and the living, respecting always the laws of cause and effect.*

"**The third** aspect of intent relates to the subject of respect and justice within the brotherhood of man. You do not live alone. You live within a family, a brotherhood, and the plan is that someday it will be a wonderful brotherhood. Right now, it is a rather mixed picture. Nevertheless, wonderful or not, you still have to live together. The only way you will be able to live together is to recognize and respect the other person's intentions as well as your own. Sometimes this may be as simple as asking

'*What part of this situation is mine and what part of it is yours? Let's deal with this. This is our situation.*'

"*Then last, though by no means least, are your own intentions. If you would direct your life in a purposeful way, you must be cognizant of your own intentions and understand what you have set in motion. These seeds you planted, possibly a long time ago, are still growing. This is not something you have to inventory every day, yet the more fully you understand what you set forth, the greater wisdom you will have in managing your life.*

"*If you would be successful in your life, you need to work with all four levels of intent. You need to work with the will of God in all things, to understand and respect the universal imperative for balance and for favoring life and the living. You need to observe and recognize the intentions of others around you and either honor them or deal with them. All too often one person blames another as being the source of a problem when there is usually a shared responsibility in any situation. Finally, you need to acknowledge your own intentions by bringing them forth into conscious understanding. Nurture them, care for them, or change them if necessary. In the final analysis, get back to yourself. When you do that, you are addressing something that you actually can change.*"

In this regard, He made a very crucial instruction—**that we can change only our own intentions!** "*You may be able to persuade another to redirect intention, but you cannot do it for him. Intentions are sealed in the heart, and this is why you must change your heart if you would change your life. You can change your mind a thousand times, and you will never touch your intent. If you never enter your heart, you will forget what you have placed there and lose command over it.*

"*You are not going to change the will of God. You are not going to circumvent the two principles of intent placed into the universe. And you are not going to change the other person's intent. However, it would be wise to negotiate with those who do not support you and to align with those who do. You can change only your own intentions. This is where you begin.*

"*The most typical human mistake in situations of distress or crisis, where there is need of some change, is to try and change the things over which one can have no effect. For example, a woman who is unhappy with her employment situation may try changing departments, programs, assignments, or locations. She may apply for a transfer from Milwaukee to Denver, or attempt to change any number of things that have nothing to do with her own intent. The one thing that she needs to do is take stock of her own original intentions and see how they have progressed or stagnated. In doing that, she can regain command of her situation, and regain a sense of certainty on why she is there and what to do next.*

"These four aspects of intention exist in any situation. For example, let's suppose you became ill with the flu. Perhaps you will rest, retreat within yourself, meditate, and restore your sense of balance. Sometimes that is all that it takes. But typically, this is not enough. You may ask, 'Why is it not enough?' Let me explain. The first reason is that you did not intend to get sick. Therefore, other factors are at work with which you need to deal outside yourself.

"The first thing you may do is pray that the love and grace of God, which override all things, will enter into the situation and work its miracles. The second thing you may do is study the situation in terms of the universe's own tendency. Perhaps you have been working too hard, and the universe is willing to balance your life with a bit of rest. Ask for intercession from anyone qualified to help, such as a physician, spiritual counselor, or friend. And then, last of all, contemplate how your own intentions may have affected this situation. What did you intend that may have resulted in this? Clearly, you did not intend to become ill, but perhaps you really did not want to go to work. You do have an intention buried somewhere in the circumstance. With a conscious awareness of all these ingredients, you can sort out the difficulties of any situation. Some people have suffered financial disasters and surfaced with a whole new lease on life. Being forced out of a business that was a part of the dead and the dying freed up their attention to enter a new dimension of life and living. Very little money is required to cultivate genuine capacity for growth. The reason businesses typically require such an outlay of capital to start and support is that most of them are complying with the demands of structure. It takes a lot of money to keep a conservative or dying potential in forward momentum, while very little money is required to develop a living resource. You may be surprised how little it takes to start a whole new life, if you are really backing life and the living!

"Regardless of whether your difficulty is health, business, financial, or family, consider the four aspects of intent. Apply this understanding to the four principles of success, and you will have a masterful command of life.

"There is one other possibility which needs to be considered from time to time. This is something which many people are reluctant to do. That is

to give or receive intercession. Intercession means for another to step into the situation and render assistance. The value of this principle is appreciated and widely used in the case of emotional disturbances and substance addictions. Intercession is often used and helpful in cases of family abuse, and it is frequently the only effective course of action. However, there are other less dramatic situations where help may be offered in the way of consolation, greater clarity, or assistance in acquiring professional guidance. Therefore, it is important for you to know why you can and should ask for help at times. The central reason is that there are many intentions in any situation which may exceed any one person's ability to identify and resolve. What a person did not cause will require assistance from some other quarter. It would be in order to ask for the first intercession from your Heavenly Father. Ask that love prevail in the situation and that by grace you be lifted above it. Then, if it is a medical situation, consult a physician or some other practitioner. Depending on the nature of your problem, ask for support from your family, a friend, a financial advisor, or a counselor. Where there are complex possibilities, it is wise to seek help from those who can expand your understanding."

Through the years of observing and practicing the Master's wonderful instructions, I would certainly attest to the fact that we find the will of God manifesting in the way love works through a situation. Sometimes it is enough for us to simply forgive, so that we can get on with living. The four principles of successful living have become easier with conscious application. Be the love that you are. Do the right thing. Follow life and the living . . . and forgive. He was careful to remind me that in any situation it is as important to recognize the limits of personal responsibility as it is to fulfill responsibility where it exists. Some predicaments are simply beyond us, and we need to humble ourselves and ask for help. I have been surprised with the way sincere and needful requests have brought out the best in others and myself. When we give people a chance to help, we do not struggle alone. Working through the problems of life together builds faith, trust, and brotherhood. Working in unison illuminates the outer world as well as the inner. As Jesus said, *"You will never know the truth of any situation if you are not in touch with both the inner and the outer."*

The last important guideline for success and for working within the will of God has to do with knowing that which we humans can and cannot create. Being an artist, that is a critical consideration for me. I like to think of myself as a creative person, although I am well aware that everything has already been created. Everything we behold has always been. It is just represented, recreated, and reformulated into new patterns and new functions and for new purposes.

Therefore, I wanted to know, "What do we create? Obviously the Creator has already given us everything with which to work. Where do we go from here, and what do we do with what we have been given?"

He very graciously replied, *"The first thing to understand is that you cannot create reality. Fundamental reality, like the one spirit, is universal to existence. Reality was created by the Father and is one with the Father. It is given equally and democratically to all."*

He looked at me with very piercing, serene eyes and emphasized, *"If anyone other than the Holy Source could change even so much as one fragment of existence, the democracy and fairness of the universe would be broken. You cannot change reality. What you are invited to do is shape it, build it, process it, and redesign it to meet your needs, pleasures, and purposes. That is your dimension of creation and expression. Through this invitation, all the fruits of your labor and all the creations of your life are brought forth. This is what you do when you paint. You didn't create the molecules of the paint, create the colors, grow the flax that made the linen, or weave the canvas. You have taken what is made available to you, and you have shaped the fruits of your labor according to the purposes of your life.*

"You also create viewpoints of reality. With those viewpoints, you unfold your life, shape your values, and direct your intentions. The nature of your viewpoint and what you do with it is crucial to your life. You need to ask yourself, 'What is my viewpoint upon the world? What is my viewpoint in life?' Never underestimate the value and the power of the viewpoints you have established. It is equally important to understand the fundamental nature of reality. How could you ever change your viewpoint of reality, if reality itself were not a constant? You would have no freedom of change whatsoever if there were not a basis for default. It is very important that you know both those things. You could not be honored in your uniqueness were it not for a background of oneness!"

He looked directly into my eyes and asked, *"How many times have you changed your viewpoint in this one life?"*

I admitted with almost a tone of embarrassment, "More times than I could probably count." His answer was full of strength and affirmation.

"You have an inalienable right to create and change your viewpoints

. . . *for through this, you experience, participate, and grow with reality. The concept of human constancy and loyalty must not be manipulated into stagnant denials of the right to change.*

"*Perhaps the most important thing you create is space in which to dwell. Like its Creator, humankind is also a creator of places. You too have the ability and the right to create places in which you and others may dwell. In doing this you are most like your Father, for it is His pleasure for you to forward His gracious creation through all your generations as you create a place in which to be together. You create even a place for the Father. Whenever you pray, you create a place for your Father. Whenever you express gratitude and appreciation, you create a place for your Father. Whenever you express wonderment for the beauties around you, you create a place for your Father. There are times also to be alone, to be in your heart, and to dwell in peace. In those times, you are creating a place for yourself. It is very important that you create a place where you can simply be yourself, unconditionally, without judgment, without restraint, to simply dwell in peace and be the love that you are. Last, but not least, when you live in brotherhood, you create a place for each other.*

"*In creating a place for each other, for God, and for yourself, you are perfectly fulfilling my commandment that you love God with all your heart and your neighbor as yourself. By loving, you are creating places. In being the love that you are, you are centered in your immortal place. In knowing the Source of your love, you are creating your place with God. Through extending the benefits of that love, you have created your place in brotherhood. These are the things you create . . . the places in which to be, your viewpoints of reality, and the fruits of your labor. However, there is no better way of forwarding creation than simply to love God with all your heart and your neighbor as yourself.*"

Chapter 14
The Beloved

When this wonderful child was born two thousand years ago, Joseph was told to call Him Jeshua. This was His Hebrew name so cherished by family, friends, and disciples. The name Jeshua has been subsequently translated into every language known to man. In the English language we call Him Jesus, but there is a universal name which is precious above all the rest. As a result of our personal conversations, I was granted the higher awareness and privilege of knowing this holy name which is simply "The Beloved."

To appreciate the meaning of this name more fully, we must remember that we are also love, and as the descendants of Divine Mystery, we are also our Father's beloved children. It's just that, relative to our current condition, we do not remember ourselves within that holy context. We have drifted so far away from the Source of our being that we think of ourselves as different from Jesus and separate from love. One of the main causes for this unfortunate occurrence is that we try to know our lives through mirrored images. We seek to gain self understanding through feedback, evaluation, and opinion. He called this "reflectance." If one fully comprehends why a flame cannot step aside to see itself burn, and why water cannot see itself flow, then one can also appreciate his own eternal mystery. Surrendering to that mystery will yield more wisdom than any reflection full of illusion could ever reveal. Once this is accepted in faith, there will be no further need for external formulations of self worth.

He stated, *"You seek to know love by your own efforts and the efforts of others in turn, so you have learned to think of love as a commodity. You have learned to think of love as an action or an external thing. Such ideas of viewing love externally have led you to judgment and separation. Most significantly, it has led to separation from yourself.*

"The truest way to know your love is not by reflectance but by the joy you feel in its presence. That joy is the soul's pleasure in the presence of love. Whatever you experience as joy is the cup of your love overflowing. By your joy you shall know your love, and the nature of your soul, as it casts your love upon the waters of life."

In His presence there was love overflowing. Glowing with an aura of contentment and happiness, His face radiated joy, and He often smiled from ear to ear. I was fascinated, however, by the fact that I never saw Him laugh. What I found intriguing was that most people consider me a naturally humorous person, able to make people laugh easily. Yet, this did not happen with Him. I did not consciously focus upon this aspect of His demeanor until months later when I was recollecting our visit. Coincidentally, I was reading two different documents which professed to be ancient descriptions of the Master. One was by the historian Josephus and the other was by a Roman governor named Publius Lentulus. What was particularly interesting about these documents was that they were extremely synchronous in their description of the Master, and even though both quotations were brief, they each made a point of mentioning that He was never seen to laugh. These passages revived a memory of what it was like in His presence. Then I began to wonder how He could spark a burst of laughter from me, and yet have no apparent need of it Himself.

Finally, in a moment of inspiration, it dawned upon me. Joy is the outpouring of love, while laughter is what we feel when we release the **blockages** to our love! We laugh as part of our processing of love. Laughter enables us look at something that we could not face before. It allows us to accept something we previously rejected—to generate a flow where before there was a blockage of energy. The release makes us laugh, and the freedom makes us happy. **Jesus has no blockages to love.** This is how He could be so humorous, causing me to laugh frequently, while maintaining a spirit of calmness within Himself. This may seem like a trivial point, yet I assure you that it was incredibly indicative of a monumental truth which surrounds His being, and that is **His Divinity.**

I have been reluctant to reveal my thoughts about His Divinity, because in doing so, I sense that I might be entering the realm of theology. I do not consider it my place upon this Earth, or my life purpose, to be a formulator of beliefs. So, for that reason I have not wanted to divulge these higher feelings and perceptions.

Towering as His Divinity was, it was revealed to me in the gentlest of ways. The only incident I experienced of being completely overwhelmed by His presence was on the day of the first appearance, November 23, 1991. After that, I experienced His mastery as a kind, human, and courteous way of considering my needs above any desire to impress me. He wanted me to be happy and comfortable in my work, and He expressed no reservation about descending to my level of reality. In His own wonderful and gracious way, His presence exemplified contentment. He was the consummate gentleman. Warm, compassionate, and often humorous, He spoke with me in terms that I could understand, and there was nothing too unimportant for His attention.

My whole experience was within the scope of familiar realities, yet from the very first day we were together, I detected a new and higher dimension of awareness unfolding within myself. I felt on that higher level a rare emotion which is still difficult to describe. I can only call this feeling adoration. It was more complete than any love I had known, and it was love so pure as to have a sound and a fragrance. Adoration is a feeling not easily experienced upon this Earthly domain. Even worship fails to encompass or convey its depth of feeling, joy, and peace.

If you could imagine an ascending scale of emotions, beginning with enthusiasm for life, leading upward to exhilaration, and moving even higher toward the peace and serenity that passes all human understanding, it will become clear that we are climbing an emotional mountain. Finally, in our ascension we arrive at the ultimate point of sacred passion, and there resides adoration. Adoration is exceptional, like nothing else. It is the king of emotions, for it is the love of one soul recognizing and honoring the love of another. It is so easy to overlook this feeling on the material plane, where we focus upon the physical human form and fail to look into each other's hearts with eyes of love. Being with Him, this higher perception was unavoidable. There was nothing there but purest love. Saint Paul frequently referred to Jesus in his writings as "The Beloved," and clearly understood the meaning of this emotion. Yet this emotion is a great deal more than a feeling or expression. It is **a Power!** "The Beloved" is the consummation of **Love as Beingness!** The great "I AM" Presence, which is the Source of all existence, could fulfill itself with nothing less than the great Power of existence we know as Love.

That the Apostle John understood this higher concept of Love is revealed in his writings and by the fact that Jesus gave him charge of His Mother. The Gospels also give evidence that Mary Magdelene knew this higher love and, because of that level of devotion, was cursed by slander and resentment. There is actually no explicit reference in the Bible that she might have been a prostitute, yet her virtue has been questioned throughout history. Some people have even speculated that she was the Master's wife, but I doubt that was true either. What I believe is that her consciousness and passion for "The Beloved" was so strong that it warranted total devotion, similar to the bond between a husband and wife. Her special love ignited great jealousy and accusations of lost virtue which are probably utterly unfounded. Her courage and understanding of the truth were so great there was no stopping her dedication, for she had beheld "The Beloved." In the streets of Calcutta, Mother Theresa worked with equal courage to bring "The Beloved" into the lives of desperately poor and hopeless people. How did she do it? By looking in their eyes and seeing "The Beloved" in them. That is **the process** of human miracles!

Jesus came to Earth to ignite the living fire of "The Beloved" within each of us. Saint Paul was the first to comprehend the profundity of that concept, and with this understanding he formulated a message which changed the world. He saw that worship without love is a meaningless formality devoid of any intrinsic purpose or value. Worship is often misdirected. Our primitive ancestors habitually worshiped the forces of nature as they were unable to comprehend natural phenomena. Today, man's obsession with money, material status, and celebrity achievement comes dangerously close to worship. True worship is a valid exaltation of all that is Holy, as it represents a sublimation of the self to a Higher Power. Even so, worship can also be a practice in which the ego positions itself **with** Higher Power. Ego is utterly baffled, however, in the presence of "The Beloved." Ego cannot begin to comprehend that state of perfection. Adoration cannot reside with illusion. Man may worship money, but I can assure you he will not adore it. Man may worship fame, but I can assure you he will not adore it. Whenever we contemplate that incomparable emotion, it will take us straight to the face of God, straight to the face of "The Beloved." Adoration is so hard to describe, yet it can be experienced easily and wonderfully through total surrender.

King Solomon was a prolific writer and literary genius in his day, but he, too, was at a loss for words on how to describe love. Jesus recommended that I read Solomon's "Song of Songs" because of its marvelous expressions of adoration. On those pages, the beauty and splendor of love is extolled in its many forms. Solomon used the parable of a bride and groom to communicate adoration. One of the purest and most tender experiences of adoration to be shared on this Earth is the passionate love of a newly married couple. The adoration of a bride and groom for each other is also a very special bond with God who has created and blessed the relationship.

There has been extensive speculation as to whether the "Song of Songs" was written to celebrate Solomon's own marriage or whether it was purely an allegory which he used to evoke and describe the passions of Higher Love. Perhaps it does not matter, since the story unfolds like a parable with multiple meanings on a variety of levels. Jesus explained to me that its highest meaning is in reference to the love which joins the immortal soul with the Sacred Heart. This is a yearning deep within the soul of each being, a seeking for its fulfillment, quite like that of searching for one's life mate. In hopes that your true love is somewhere, you seek with all your heart to find this special person. After finding each other and falling in love, the agony of separation can be simply overwhelming. At last there is recognition, but no lasting attainment until there is marriage. Even then, from time to time the two are apart and experience the yearning for blessed reunion. What a wonderful way of declaring the true love between the Sacred Heart and the soul! Jesus described the Sacred Heart as the Daughter of God and the soul as the Son of God, as sacred brother and sister, each loving the other forever as bride and groom, each seeking to know the other's passion throughout eternity. In Solomon's "Song of Songs," his soul is personified as the one who tells of his love for the heart. He writes,

> "How delightful is your love, my sister, my bride. How much more pleasing is your love than wine and the fragrance of your perfume than any spice. Your lips drop with sweetness as the honeycomb, my bride. Milk and honey are under your tongue. The fragrance of your garments is like that of Lebanon and you are a garden locked up, my sister, my bride."[18]

Jesus referred to the Sacred Heart several times as a garden, saying, *"This is the garden for which you yearn."* Interestingly, almost everything in Solomon's story happens in a garden or a vineyard. Is this not reminiscent of the Garden of Eden?

"Your plants are an orchard of pomegranates, with choice fruits, with henna and nard. Nard and saffron, calumus and cinnamon, with every kind of incense tree. With myrrh and aloe, and all the finest spices, you are a garden fountain, a well of flowing water streaming down from Lebanon. You are beautiful my darling as Tirzah, lovely as Jerusalem, majestic as troops with banners. Turn your eyes from me, they overwhelm me. You hair is like a flock of goats descending from Gilead, your teeth are like a flock of sheep coming up from the washing. Each has its twin, not one of them is alone. Your temples behind your veil are like the halves of a pomegranate. Sixty queens there may be and eighty concubines and virgins beyond number, but my dove, my perfect one, is unique. The only daughter of her mother. The favorite of the one who bore her, the maidens saw her and called her blessed. The queens and concubines praised her. Who is this that appears like the dawn, fair as the moon, bright as the sun, majestic as the stars in procession?"[19]

He could not answer his own question because the Sacred Heart is an eternal mystery. One can only behold it and cherish it with love. Then the heart sang her song to the soul.

"My lover is radiant and ruddy, outstanding among ten thousand. His head is purest gold, his hair is wavy and black as a raven. His eyes are like doves by the water streams, washed in milk mounted like jewels. His cheeks are like beds of spice, yielding perfume. His lips are like lilies dripping with myrrh. His arms are like rods of gold, set with crysolite, his body is like polished ivory, decorated with sapphires, his legs are pillars of marble, set on bases of purest gold. His appearance is like Lebanon, choice as its cedars. His mouth is sweetness itself. He is altogether lovely. This is my lover, my friend."[20]

Such is the love between the soul and the Sacred Heart. The joining of these two essences is the love of purest adoration. There are the beautiful times of togetherness and the deep yearnings for reunion after being apart. Have we not experienced these feelings within ourselves as well as with others? Are there not times when our oneness is bliss, only to be followed by moments of distress when the self feels divided to its very core? We ask, "Where is the completeness of all that I am?" This timeless drama was exquisitely revealed by Solomon as the parable of love between a man and a woman.

One of the choruses that Solomon repeats many times is very important to the Master's overall message. "Daughters of Jerusalem, I charge you, do not arouse or awaken love until it so desires."

Love is not something that can be forced or manipulated. It is not something to be frivolously called forth, except by the very will of love itself. Love is a power beyond our ability to control, although by understanding the power of love we are given command of life. In love's presence we experience true humility, and stand in awe to honor its power. Love's expressions can never be fully predicted, yet it is important to accept love as it unfolds—even when it is taken away from us for a while.

I asked Jesus, "Why is love given and then taken away?"

"So that you will search for the Beloved within yourself and within the hearts of your other brothers and sisters. If all you knew of The Beloved was one person, then where would there be a place for anyone else? Even if your only love were God, everyone else would fall so short that you would do nothing but judge. You will be given a taste of love, and then allowed to hunger for a while so that you will seek for love within yourself and within greater and greater stretches of reality. It is not the will of God that you should live within a tiny little self-possessed bubble, but rather that you have all of reality for your playground."

"Why do we create such powerful protective bubbles? And why do we cling to those illusions with such determination, to the detriment of our life's purposes?"

"Because they are built around the fictions of ego."

"Would you care to elaborate on that?" I asked.

"Ego is composed of all the fictions you have used to replace the love that you are. In today's jargon, there is a misconception of ego as pride and self empowerment. However, ego is the vanity of building your life around fantasies about yourself. Like a sand castle that cannot stand up to the tides of eternity, it has no real power. Ironically, most personal fantasies have nothing to do with self-esteem, but are usually great destroyers of self esteem—such as the fantasy of unworthiness, or the

fantasy of martyrdom when really there are hidden agendas, or the fantasy of compliance when really there is only fear. The hub of most egos has little to do with self-esteem, but what they all have in common is a fantasy with which love has been replaced.

    "The love that you are is your real self-glory. Consequently, your knowledge of true self is being destroyed by the dominance of ego. When I said 'a man must give his life to find it,' I was referring to the unfortunate fact that the only life known to most people is built around ego. That false life must be slain if you would know the love that you are. Until you know what ego is, however, you will continue suppressing your love and slay the wrong thing."

    "Some people feel that we need to live a life of sacrifice in order to purify and fulfill the potential of love. Is sacrifice required to slay the ego?"

    He stated, *"Creating an ego is the greatest sacrifice you ever made! How could more sacrifice undo that? How can you love life and also deny it or deny yourself!? I have asked always that you grant mercy, not make sacrifices!* **To grant mercy is the ego's sacrifice!!** *When you can release all desire for vengeance, when you can release all desire for self-justification, when you can cease playing games with justice, when you can accept that it is not in your power to make yourself right and another wrong, when you can cease opposing another simply to dominate a situation, then you will understand mercy. Your ego cannot survive the power of mercy.*

    "Remember, the ego is the personal fiction that attempts to subvert and replace the love that you are. One of the most common fictions is unworthiness. Such ideas of self will never take you to God, and any religion which employs unworthiness as a pillar of belief will just foster ego development with a self-replenishing nature. Love is who you are! To that you may add personal viewpoints, enrichments, dreams, desires, and unique abilities.

    "In contrast with love, the ego feeds upon fear and is driven by all the mechanisms of fear. Because the ego is an invented thing, it is very perishable. In the light of reality, it feels eminently threatened. Therefore, it needs to be encased within a fantasy existence, secured and protected by structure and agendas.

    "Moreover, your ego is very angry with God, for God is one with reality and the Source of your true beingness as love. When I said that

upon my return I would separate the sheep from the goats, I was referring to a manifest exposure of the ego apart from the true self! That statement has been falsely interpreted to mean that I will select some people and not others. That is patently incorrect, for my love, my truth, and my gift have been given to everyone. Through my presence, I will strengthen the true self in each person, and the willful goat-like egos will be dismissed."

The power of love within us is greater than anything we can currently comprehend. There are countless stories of heroic accomplishments and miraculous feats which have demonstrated the power of love in everyday living. One of my favorite stories involved an automobile accident in which the mother was hurled out the driver's door as the car rolled over and trapped her child inside. The door was jammed and the child was screaming in pain. Even though she was a small woman, her strength was magnified by her loving intention to save her child's life. With a feat of Herculean strength she rolled the car over and freed her son. Similarly, during World War II, there was an incredible story about a group of nuns who took some orphans through the most horrible terrain in order to shelter them from gunfire. It is **just** amazing that any one of them survived, and yet they all arrived in good health. Such is the power of love. It is unfortunate that in the process of normal living, we do not access this power more frequently and, indeed, apply it or even trust it. In dire circumstances, it is love that vanquishes our doubts and hesitations. We all are much more powerful than we yet know.

Jesus said, *"All these things that I do, you shall do and more. That is the greatness of love. Although in making that statement, I want to caution you that I am not referring to your fictional self. I am not inviting you to believe that the goat-like part of human willfulness and invention has any real power at all. It may employ force, contrivance, and clever manipulations of circumstance, but those things are all self-consuming. It is the power of love which will allow you to do as I have done."*

At that moment my consciousness was flooded by an intense desire to ask a question that would have been unthinkable without His preface about ego. "It is mentioned several times in the scriptures that you cast out demons from a person's body or soul. Exorcism has been a practice within the Catholic Church for centuries, and many credible therapies today recognize the presence of forces within the human psyche which create a split personality. Are demons part of the ego? Are demons real and specific entities in their own right, or are they illusions of being which personify dysfunctions within the person?"

*"It could be viewed in either way, Glenda. However, please know this: There is nothing in existence except for Being and beingness. Everything which you cannot be **as yourself** surrounds and envelops your life with the remainder of whatever is needed to complete your context and reason for living. **Problems arise because not all of the remainder is in harmonious alignment within itself or with you.***

*"Everything was created as **BEING** and beingness. As beingness multiplied itself into **many beings**, there came to be diversified awareness of expanded potential. From the many powers of beingness, all existence is manifested.*

"At the heart of every aspect of existence is beingness, and it is pure in its alignment to the Source of all Being. Whenever beingness declares itself to be autonomous, and turns away from its Source, then disharmony and misalignments begin to occur. Degrees of separation begin to appear, along with an accumulation of physical barriers and material densities. Possibilities for fluid interaction and adjustment are lost except through the linear progressions of time. Thus, the illusion of past and future begin to dominate a being's desire for change. In truth, there is only BEING, only Love, only alignment with Source, and that is a being's only HOME!

"A being who is far from his awareness of Home, whose perceptions are conditioned by layers of substance, rivers of time, and boundaries of control will feel plagued and trapped by seen and unseen beingness which permeate his existence and threatens his free will. A being who is far from home will attract others who are equally detached or lost. Most often these attachments are unconscious. At times, such misaligned connections are simply destructive, and need to be cut with intercession. This is what I did when I cast out demons. Demons are only lost souls who have drifted so far from their own true being that they will not easily respond to loving alignments which attempt to influence them. Instead, they attempt to subvert the positive alignments that might otherwise give them support.

*"If any soul—no matter how lost—would simply turn and face his Source and the light of Home, he would experience a marvelous realignment of everything in his life. This is because everything has the **same Source**. Any person who faces away from Source will experience disharmony. All attempts to make himself into a new source of alignment for others will fail dismally. Eventually, such misguided efforts will result in personal entrapment, pain, and further estrangement from the true*

Source. *Any being's original covenant is written in the patterns of alignment with its Source. Beingness does not evolve into something other than its intrinsic nature. It merely expands its reason for being through involvement with other beings and life. History is real in so far as it is the repository of experience, although you would be operating under a very strained illusion to believe that your personal history is the cause of who you are. This is why a person can reveal himself, in the quickness of a heart beat, to be quite different than his personal history might suggest. Such startling manifestations are most likely to occur in the presence of rekindled purpose or the restoration of one's true state of love. To the contrary, as estrangement progresses through the time stream, irresponsibility and unconsciousness begin to mark a person's character. A being in this condition can no longer shape reality to meet his needs, and so he will invent it to match his delusions. For this reason, history only repeats its lessons, challenges, and difficulties. The successes, victories, and achievements scattered throughout history are not the product **of** history, but rather are the result of elevating consciousness and actions* **above** *history!*

"*History is simply the repository of completed experiences which are retained in memory, along with your partially completed experiences, held in suspension until appropriate conditions exist for reintegrating them with life. Either way, history is that part of your life which pertains* **the least** *to where you are now! It is that which—for the moment—you have released.*

"*Now consider this new perspective. It is vital that you reverse the world's view of time if you would recover your true nature of being. The world considers history and the momentum of time to be a* **potent force** *which generated the present and established its foundation of power. By that reasoning, you would certainly be what the past has made you. By contrast, the viewpoint of true being sees the past as panorama of experience, education, goals, and desires which have finally been reduced to relative* **impotence**. *It is you who* **reduce** *the past—not the past which* **produces** *you! Considering the timelessness of being, how could it be any other way?*"

"Then what is the future?" I asked with soaring curiosity.

"*Future is the promise of completion which you remember and seek again. In that pursuit, infinite potential will supply your needs, yearnings, lessons, and alignments until at last you realize that* **true completion has always been**, *and is reattained through liberation of* *desire as well as attachment."*

As I sat quietly and absorbed that amazing answer into my heart and consciousness, I was awestruck by how effortlessly He had described the whole subject of beingness . . . and how simple it was! I was overwhelmed with an emotion that I could barely express. Mostly, what I felt was adoration as my awareness overflowed through the expanse of infinite spirit. What I saw is that IN OUR UNITY, WE ARE THE BELOVED. In this perfect state of Being, no words or concepts are necessary to expedite its empowerment, for it is simply PERFECTION.

I knew that our highest quest for understanding was directed toward returning to this state. Eventually, my thoughts returned to this present state of existence which is where my lessons and challenges awaited. Within that practical context, I wanted to know more about the fictional self.

"Your fictional self has little power, because it is terrified of reality. In fact, it is so easily shattered by the light of truth that it can only endure within the shelter of a comfort zone, a bubble of support, and constant affirmation. Reality is a living, responsive flow of life which continues forever on many levels of existence. Reality honors each being, and responds to its love. You are invited and encouraged always to shape reality to your needs and purposes. However, there is a significant difference between shaping reality and inventing it. You would be wise to learn the difference and to know that the fictional self is the creator of fictional realities which have undone you."

This was His second reference to the difference between shaping reality and inventing it, so I asked further, "Can you explain the difference between these two concepts?"

He continued, *"The process of shaping reality can be compared to the life story of a fifty-year-old house that has been owned by eight families. In the beginning it was a farm house. The next family spruced it up with Victorian decor. Following that were six more stylistic transformations leading eventually back to the original farm house motif. At every point it was the same house, simply redesigned to meet the preferences, joys, pleasures and needs of eight different families. Shaping reality is easy and beneficial. Reality responds to her beloved with honor and support, just as surely as she will shun and disregard fictional reality. Invented reality would be like leasing a house in a neighborhood above one's means, in order to pretend a level of success which has not been attained. If you do manage to achieve fictional success, you will not be happy.*

"Any prayer asked in love, or honoring love will be answered, although your Father has no covenant to answer the prayers of your ego, to solve its self-made problems, or to make its fictions result in happiness. Your Creator is one with reality, so how can He answer a prayer that seeks further separation from the love and the reality that He is? Even if He were willing, how could He? When you pray to be strengthened in your understanding of reality and your competence with it, your every prayer will be answered and often dramatically.

"God will be patient with your illusions, just as a parent is tolerant and often amused with a child's inventions. If a child is building a sand castle by the sea, his dad may take pride in the display of dexterity and imagination. Except, when the fragile creation is washed away, it would be the father's more important duty to help the child understand how it was only a passing fancy, a play experience for what is to come later. It is no different with your Heavenly Father.

"Sadly, most prayers sound something like this. 'Please, Father, rescue my sand castle.' All He can say is, 'My child, you must learn the difference between sand castles and houses of mortar and wood built on a true foundation. If I rescued your sand castle, what would impel you to learn the difference?'"

Responding to His emphasis upon God and reality, it occurred to me to ask about something in the Bible which has troubled me since childhood. "The passage in Psalms 11 which reads, 'The fear of God is the beginning of wisdom' is discomforting to me. Everything you have said about God is Love, and I cannot think about Divinity in any way motivated by fear."

"God is Love, and your heart is right for seeing Him that way. In the Bible, 'fear' in relation to God means 'respect.' If you consider that God is one with reality, you will see that there is a very pragmatic meaning to that teaching. The message will be magnified if you consider it to mean, 'Respect of reality is the beginning of wisdom and knowledge.' Can you relate to that more easily?"

"Yes, I can."

"Once you have accepted God as being one with reality, then reality becomes a source of comfort and enlightenment. Reality becomes the servant of your love, rather than an agent of disappointment, as it can be if you respond to it with fear."

I asked Him, "How can we know the difference between reality and invention so that we may practice discernment? Should we not be alert to danger or treachery?"

"*Yes, always be alert, and especially know that your ego is your greatest magnet for attracting danger and treachery. Anything sent forth to deceive you will be directed exactly to your ego, or to your mind. The reason is that a person's ego considers anything to be true which supports its survival, just as the mind considers anything to be true which supports the supremacy of logic. As a matter of fact, the mind cannot discern fact from fiction* **if both are presented with equal logic!**

"*The practice of discernment is part of higher consciousness. Discernment is not just a step up from judgment. In life's curriculum, it is the opposite of judgment. Through judgment, a man reveals what he still needs to confront and to learn. Through discernment, one reveals what he has mastered!*

"*Your heart will always know what is true, although the process of living is required to learn the details! Reality responds by instinct to love. You do not have to use force to implement reality. Have courage, for reality exists to work. You do not have to use persuasion, or know influential people to invoke reality's potential. Reality belongs equally to everyone. Therefore, licensed permission, special education, and originality are not required. Reality represents the utmost in honesty, innocence, and approachability, even to the smallest and most innocent child. You simply have to know that reality is one with God and have the courage to accept it. The heart knows truth as that which sets it free.*

"*Your heart is one with the love of God, and God is one with reality. You might define truth as a triangle of God, love, and reality. Truth is the point where love and reality are one in God. This is why truth is the universal solvent for all blockages, limitations, conflicts, and problems of mortal existence. Some say the truth hurts, but it only hurts the ego, never the loving self that you are. Truth is the highest consciousness, and the ever abiding presence of God in reality. In knowing that, you know the truth which is consonant with love.*

"*Truth is revealed only in the presence of love. Have you ever known an angry person to be honest? The truths that are occluded from you are the ones smothered by your breaches with love. This is the great value of a true friend or a true love. In his or her presence, truth is a shining revelation. That is the truth which will set you free.*

"*If you would know the truth about any soul, look in his eyes with love and accept the reality which infuses his life. There is but one spirit, one God, and one basis in which all reality resides. It is our Father's pleasure to grant freedom of perception and consideration about reality. Nevertheless, one should not forget that the purpose of special viewpoints is to enhance and personalize reality, not to replace it."*

Today, society's psychological and social vernacular is permeated with concepts and ideas about an individual's right to create his own reality. When I asked Jesus about that belief, He explicitly stated that there is one great universal reality, against which our own viewpoints of reality create subtle and important differences. *"Do not underestimate the power of your viewpoint of reality, because your viewpoint of reality will bring to you the things which you see and desire. Your viewpoint of reality is a very important key to managing your life, yet it is wise to remember that a viewpoint of reality is not a replacement for the universal matrix of common existence."*

You might compare this to the different results achieved by ten artists, congregated in the same location to paint a particular landscape. In viewing their artistic creations, an observer may conclude they were portraying ten dissimilar places, because of each painter's unique interpretation. The renditions would be distinct and rich with personal perceptions, yet if you looked beyond the expressive strokes and focused closely upon the various items portrayed, you would discover a common reality.

"The people of Israel found early favor with God because of their profound understanding of reality and its Creator. There is but one God, one spirit, and one coherent basis for reality. This gave the people of Israel much wisdom and an unshakable influence over the history of the world.

"By the time I was born, religious doctrine was beginning to serve as structure more than spiritual guidance. Israel was true to God in her faith, in so far as she would not resort to treachery or force to save herself. Nevertheless, she had lost touch with reality, and the hardships which that brought upon her began to turn hearts away from love. This is true of many Christians today. They observe their doctrines and the word of God, though in all too many cases they have applied their beliefs to establish comfort zones apart from reality. In so doing, the hardships of life mount up and hearts turn away from love. Thus the greater understanding is lost. Love commands reality, and reality responds to love like a new bride. You are the Beloved of God, no less than I am. If you would receive this blessing you must step outside your protective shell and allow your fictional self to shatter in the light of reality. You must be strong in the love that you are

if you would inherit the power of God lying dormant within you.

"Fear not, for you are the Beloved of God. You will not be set to fly and then be allowed to fall to Earth. Only the fictional self and the embellishments you have used to support it will perish. This is the only need that ever existed for death. Therefore, when you choose, of your own volition, to kill your fictional self, you have taken the first step toward the recovery of your conscious immortality. By the love and grace of God, you will then be led to your next step until your full and complete Sonship is recovered. For some people, the process will be complete within the twinkling of an eye, and for others a little more patience will be required. This is no different than the way some children arrive at adulthood overnight and other children take years. Such developments are not the result of preference, hierarchy, or status. Growth has its own curve which is unique for each individual."

I asked Him at that point if He could summarize one more time what the fictional self was. He accommodated by saying, *"The fictional self is who you thought you were when you forgot that you were love. You may also include every invented reality you used to embellish those misconceptions. Everything must have a context, even the ego. When a fictional aspect of personality is confounded with true existence, such questions arise as: 'Who am I? How can this invention be integrated with reality? How can these unknown factors be made real?' Existence exposes truth, and it can be a great defender of your own truth if you allow it to shatter that which is not really you. However, if you persist beyond your challenges and revelations to enforce your invented reality with intentional deception, you will enter the world of sin. Sin is a much simpler thing than you may think it is. It is just the force and mischief used to instill and empower invented realities. To the degree that you have made such investments, you have moved away from God.*

"The world spends a great deal of energy on judgment, which is nothing less than a competition for invented realities. Love does not judge. Judgment is a cruel, childish game of egos, competing for position. The sly, unspoken intent is that he who succeeds in sustaining a judgment is above judgment. That is not true. The fact is, the ego cannot and will not forgive. Withholding forgiveness is the ego's assault against life. Only the ego judges, and through judgment it will perish. The love that you are will sustain your immortality, for love knows nothing of judgment.

"Man's original sin was judgment. That is the only sin which a pure and innocent soul can commit. The immediate, inevitable, and unavoidable consequence of judgment is separation from the object of your judgment, and from God to the degree that the Creator is also part of that which you have judged. Judgments have a way of expanding and multiplying until separation from God becomes a real and monumental problem. A being in separation is unconscious of his Source, and therefore he will endlessly pursue the task of creating himself.

*"Without the long forgetfulness of separation, and the many densities of useless identity which result from it, a soul could never be led astray and would never conceive of misdeeds. What the world calls sin is the long term, tragic derivation of the real sin—which is judgment and its resulting separation from God, reality, and brotherhood. All misdeeds are a sad occurrence. However, to consider them to be the **real sin** only furthers the problem. If man is to live together in brotherhood, immorality cannot be condoned. Yet, to condemn immorality only feeds into the vicious cycle of judgment. This has been man's dilemma. If all judgment had ceased and the spirit of forgiveness had prevailed, man would have returned to his innocence by grace, and my intercession would not have been necessary.*

"When I came to the Earth two thousand years ago, I was not essentially different from you in potential, except that I had never known separation from My Father and I had never known myself as anything but the love that I am, nor had I ever created fictions about myself. It was necessary that I be conceived by a virgin, not that I would shun the normal way of human conception, but the fact is, there was a problem which had to be overcome. In organic life, DNA is constructed to conduct the complex and mysterious functions of love. Human DNA is constructed to handle and to conduct very high levels of love function. As you accelerate those love functions, your DNA will change accordingly. In my case, using human DNA produced in a state of separation would have been like putting rocket fuel into a Volkswagen. I simply could not have been joined with such a body, and my time to experience separation had not yet come. From the time of my conception, to the cross, I prepared myself for the separation which I had agreed to experience. Thus, my mother's pregnancy was a normal one, and my development from childhood through adolescence proceeded in the usual way.

*"You see, the point of my sacrifice on the cross does not lie so much in the fact that I died for you as that I **separated for you**. Death means*

*nothing to me, for I am utterly assured of my immortality and the pain of death could have been canceled in a moment by my love. My gift to mankind was the separation that I **chose** to experience. Uniformly without exception, the separations of man have occurred because man **drifted away** from God, the Source of love and reality, through his devotion to private fiction and ego projections. Man's headlong pursuit of personal agendas and invented realities caused him to forget the love that he really is.*

*"**I separated as an act of love**, so that love could then be united even with the state of separation. The long estrangement from God could then be ended. Many have died for you. Many have given their lives for a brother, for freedom, or for mankind in honor of cherished principles. Many saints have died for you. Countless people have suffered for you. **But no one else separated for you!** I separated in the spirit of love, that love might be joined even with separation, and thereby the fact of separation would be reduced to mere illusion. The event of my separation was the most extreme grief I have ever known in my entire existence. While on the cross, I momentarily experienced full release from my Father as I received unto myself all the separations of the world. Now, by the law of grace, all you have to do is accept the fact that you are love and return to the Father. This is an enduring miracle which I gave unconditionally to all mankind. It is for the receiving by anyone who would choose to accept. Separation—though essentially an illusion—was once a very real problem. Now it is only an illusion which anyone may end by picking up the sword of truth and ripping the veil.*

*"The miracle evoked by my death was the cancellation of separation by **equating it with love instead of judgment**. The miracle of my resurrection is not so much that my body was made whole **as that man was made whole with God,** and separation was transmuted to an illusion. This transfiguration is now available to anyone who accepts the love that he is. You may perpetuate the illusion if you choose, or you may accept the gift. This was my Father's gift and mine, given freely to anyone who wishes to regard the change of potential which now exists for mankind.*

"I would much rather the gift be promoted than the giver. In savoring the blessing of the gift, the receiver will eventually seek out the giver. That point is difficult for many of my friends and followers to accept, for they are protective of my glory. It is sad that the gift has been shunned by so many, simply because it was poorly understood, or because the giver was thrust upon them. I would rather have it be the other way around—that

the gift be understood and be received by all universally. It was freely and unconditionally given.

"Personal salvation, in the way it is often regarded today, was not claimed by me nor taught by my disciples. A man is saved by his own return, not by the fact that I made it possible! *Free will is always a critical point of redemption or peril. It was man's choice to judge, to separate, and to miscreate himself. Now, it is for each one to seek his own return. As I have told you many times, you are not bound by the laws of cause and effect in the same way that it holds sway over structure and material existence. There is a single-minded equilibrium which governs all physical form and results in immediate and just reactions without consent. There are consequences to human behavior as well. However, by the Father's love and wisdom, His children have been given free will over the nature of their consequences. Your redemption is always by grace and by choice.*

"What I did for humankind was, indeed, a gift like no other. I made it possible for you to go HOME, to return to a knowledge of the love that you are and to restore a personal relationship with your Father. Separation is now a shark without teeth—an illusion that can be penetrated by anyone who seeks to know the truth. Nevertheless, the shark might as well have teeth for anyone who remains frightened on the shore and imprisoned by his own judgment and self-creation. Such a person will continue to fear spiritual reconnection through his own hatred.

"The problem with the human condition which provoked the necessity of my gift is that free will had been virtually destroyed by the dysfunctional cycle of judgment into which man had fallen. In every generation, there were a few devoted and virtuous souls who returned in full consciousness to God, though alas this was not possible for most of humankind. Those who returned to their Sacred Home left a legacy of greater clarity and compassion to human consciousness. Even so, the perilous condition prevailed."

It was at that point when I came to a startling realization, which He promptly confirmed. No one can **evolve** to perfection! Perfection is the **original state**, to which we must return! With penetrating clarity, I saw the trap of believing in personal evolution. Only illusions can evolve, for truth is a constant, always! Combining this personal realization with His explanations about the meaning and purpose of His life, it suddenly became clear that He did not evolve spiritually and personally to the point of accomplishing transcendence. He fully understood from the beginning that He was striving for intentional separation in the name of Love, in order that the greater power of innocence may be revealed as man's native and intrinsic state of being. I did not have the inclination or opportunity to ask Him if He had ever walked before on the Earth in another life. Most surely, He has been with us forever, and there are some who believe that He has appeared from time to time and influenced the course of human events. Perhaps this is true, and perhaps it is not an issue at all. The greater revelation is that regardless of **how** He has been with us, it has always been in the spirit of innocence. By returning to that same spirit of innocence within ourselves, the power of our love is restored.

"The realization of love restored can come in a thousand ways . . . a peaceful heart, a dance step in your walk, a child's kiss, or a glistening spring morning. What it universally means is that the love of God is present. If love appears to vanish for a while do not worry; it only seems that way, so that you will seek it again. Love is a mystery — the greatest mystery of the universe. Love is your true self, which springs forth from God, the indefinable everlasting fountain of existence. There is no explaining what or who will ignite the fire of love within you. There is also no explaining how you, in turn, may light the fire of another. How many times in a group of three travelers did you start out preferring the company of one, and then discover that the other was your true friend?

"Love is a gift, a miracle, a mystery. You are led to its threshold by your affinities, by your inclinations, and by the yearnings of your heart, although its power and presentation is by grace, not by expectation, demand or requirement. Love is the ultimate paradox, for it is the lamb that is also the lion. Love is the ultimate power which resides in surrender.

"The power of love is that it commands the zero point where time and space become one, in the eternity of divine energy and divine awareness. At this holy zero point, God is both the bird and the breeze, the trees and the land, the boat and the river, the lamb and the lion. Whenever you live within the power of your own love, you also experience that zero point, and resistance falls away. There, in the Holy Now, all duality is resolved into the miracle of paradox. By giving, you receive. By releasing, you attain. By forgiving, you are forgiven. By doing nothing, all is done. By surrendering, all is conquered. This only works in the presence of love. That is why, if you give without love, you have wasted the gift. For the mystery and miracle of love is that it can turn any set of opposites into a living dynamic

paradox. For example, an illness of the body can bring a healing to the soul. Or financial loss could become a catalyst for new life and vision.

"Be grateful for love whenever it flowers for you. Behold, and see The Beloved. Those people and those situations are your friends and your points of joy. When you do not see love, do not infer that there is an enemy or a hostile situation. Everything and everyone belong. Bless them, respect them, forgive if necessary. Above all, do not force love or instill guilt that it is not there, or make accusations for why it is absent.

"Love cannot be forced. The absence of love must be accepted with equal grace and humility, for it is also part of God's will unfolding. Many conflicts could have been averted by a mutual understanding that the absence of love only means the time to work together is not yet at hand, or perhaps it may have passed. Instead, bless each other in your separate pursuits. For when love is not present, it should be accepted with humility and release. You cannot make someone love you. Love is a mystery in all its ways.

"You cannot define love with even the largest definition, for your understanding is not external to it. Because love is who you are, you will never fully comprehend its mysteries. Because love is who God is, love is the Divine Mystery. Love cannot be controlled. It cannot be predicted. It cannot be enforced. It cannot be enslaved. It cannot be killed. It cannot be defined. If you would speak of the depth, the power, the mystery, and the infinite capacity of love, think upon its capacity to end all duality. Love has no opposites. It cannot be captured, and yet it willingly serves. It is infinitely free, and yet it abides in captivity. It cannot be enforced, and yet it is the basis of all law. It is the bringer of truth, and yet it never judges. It is the seer of all things, and yet it never condemns. It conquers by surrendering. It rules by lifting up. Through its mysterious capacity for paradox, love ends all duality.

"If you would think upon love's function scientifically, think upon it as reversal transference—a point of function where two complementary forces in the presence of a third stabilizing factor, exchange modes and one becomes the other. This is why experimenters have not yet found the ultimate particle. At the point of love, and by its power, one is always becoming the other. This is an ongoing function among all primary particles and energy . . . and among all beings engaged in love. Once the functions of love are better understood, the mystery will be solved."

He explicitly stated, "It is love that causes change s in our DNA, not *the other way around. It could be a vicious trap to consider that by scientifically engineering a DNA change, humankind would be elevated to a higher plane. Love IS the engineer which causes DNA to change. The main blockage to this acceleration is your ego, which is the containment structure of your personal defenses. Ego is preventing love's energy from bringing about the healing and the miracles that could happen in your life.*

"The ego must always be in control, for deep within its nature are feelings of unworthiness and failure, often enveloped within a mystique of privacy. Even though failure and unworthiness are both lies, they can be made to look quite real if enhanced with enough creation. In the end, one's ego is the source of all failure, because it will bring about its own demise through resistance. This is why an ego cannot tolerate the anxieties of paradox and reversal. Once you know who you are, however, both ego and anxiety will vanish as you are restored to the infinite potential of love."

That was said on March 12, 1992, as was much of the message in this chapter. On that day, the painting was so near to completion, I spent most of my time looking for something to perfect. I spent extra time conversing with the Master, and nursed a quiet anxiety about some impending change which was about to occur. As I looked at the clock, I noticed that it was already 4:30, and the best of the day's light would soon be gone. Therefore, I moved quickly to mix some paint and fully intended to add a few more strands to His gently blowing hair. When I looked up from my palette, however, the thread of energy which had connected the vision to my eyes was gone! I saw Jesus standing in front of me, although His image was growing dim. The visual presence was fading, and I knew this great passage in my life was ending. The painting was complete, yet He continued to speak with uninterrupted clarity.

"I am the lion who came as a lamb and the lamb who roared as a lion. I am the living paradox of love unleashed upon the Earth . . . a force to end its duality." As a smile spread across His face He focused upon me with burning, yet peaceful, eyes and spoke these last words. These were not for me alone, but for you and all mankind. *"And you are My Beloved."*

Footnotes

[1] T. S. Eliott, "Little Gidding," in *The Norton Anthology of Modern Poetry*, ed. by Richard Ellman and Robert O'Clair (New York, 1973), p. 472

[2] Words reminiscent of these were spoken by the Master numerous times in the Gospels. Two particularly close references would be Matthew 10:26 and Mark 8:18.

[3] T. S. Eliott, op. cit., p. 472

[4] T. S. Eliott, op. cit., p. 473

[5] T. S. Eliott, op. cit., p. 473

[6] Christ Truth League is a non-denominational Christian Fellowship with an international outreach. Its chapel and office are located at 2409 Canton Dr., Fort Worth, Texas 76112. While the directors and associates with Christ Truth League have been generous and unreserved in their support of these messages, I feel obliged to add that the foundation of their own beliefs both precede and exist independently of these writings.

[7] Jeffrey Furst, *Edgar Cayce's Story of Jesus*, (New York, 1969), p. 212. This is one of numerous reproductions of that quotation. However, I chose to cite this particular source, because in the same manuscript is Edgar Cayce's own visualization of the master, p. 213. "A picture of Jesus that might be put on canvas . . . would be entirely different from all those that have depicted the face, the body, the eyes, the cut of the chin, and the lack entirely of the Jewish or Aryan profile. For these were clear, lean, ruddy. Hair almost like that of David's, a golden brown, yellow red."

[8] T. S. Eliott, op. cit., p. 478

[9] Job 38-40

[10] Matthew 6:9-13

[11] John 10:30

[12] Matthew 5:3-10

[13] Matthew 22:37-40

[14] Exodus 20:1-18

[15] 1 Corinthians 13:1

[16] Genesis 1:1ff

[17] Matthew 8:22

[18] Song of Songs 4:10-12

[19] Ibid, 6:4-10

[20] Ibid, 5:10-16

About the Author

With paintings in such important collections as the Smithsonian Institution, the Museum of the City of New York, and Williams College Museum of Art, Texas-born Glenda Green has for many years been considered one of America's finest realist oil painters. Her thriving and extensive career began in 1967 when she graduated *magna cum laude* with honors in painting from Texas Christian University. Continuing in her academic preparation, she obtained an M.A. in art history from Tulane University in 1970. There she held a three-year Kress fellowship, taught art history on the faculty, and was curator of collections for the Newcomb College art department. During a portion of this period (1968-69) she worked at Fort Worth's Kimbell Art Museum as Research Assistant to the institution's first director. These extra dimensions of preparation and competency would prove invaluable to her painting career, which began to seriously flower by 1971. By the time she joined the art department of the University of Oklahoma in 1972, she had established herself—among many of the nation's leading scholars, critics, and museum officials—as one of the world's foremost portrait painters.

As her creative style emerged into full character, it was marked by intuitive spirituality, profound subjective feeling, evocative color, and exquisite craftsmanship. Starting in 1980, her prints were published and distributed by Bruce McGaw Graphics of NYC, through which they were established in the national and international marketplace.   Today her original paintings are housed in major collections throughout the United States.

Much of her time in recent years has been devoted to public speaking, where her warm, witty, and confident manner evokes in the listener an inner certainty of one's own. With a clean, energetic style, and masterful comprehension of the most critical spiritual issues, she offers the listener an exceptional opportunity to acquire a truer, more complete understanding of the universe and one's own place in it.

Biographical references include, *North American Women Artists of The Twentieth Century: a Biographical Dictionary,* edited by Jules Heller and Nancy G. Heller; *Angels A to Z,* by James R. Lewis and Evelyn Oliver, 1996; *Who's Who in American Art* (15th and 16th Editions); *Who's Who in the South and Southwest* (17th and 18th Editions); *Who's Who of American Women* (12th, 13th, and 14th Editions); *Dictionary of International Biography, Vol. 16.*

Visual images of her art may be viewed at *glendagreen.com*

Spiritis

Love Without End has evolved into a rapidly expanding ministry, which we have chosen to call Spiritis in honor of the one spirit that unites us. Spiritis is an all-denominational assembly of friends, growing as did the original church, through local study groups and evangelistic messengers. We are dedicated to:

Promoting Jesus Christ as the physical embodiment and Master of Divine Love.

Promoting that love is the most important power for mankind to know and master.

Promoting the ending of duality, separation, and conflict.

Helping others to find and serve their covenant with God.

Helping others make their way back Home, to knowing themselves again as The Beloved.

For information on forming study groups, or to find out more about activities, seminars, workshops, and speaking tours you may write to: Spiritis, P.O. Box 239, Sedona AZ 86339, *info@lovewithoutend.com*

Spiritis Book Store
offers the following items for direct purchasing:

Books: *"Love Without End: Jesus Speaks."* $18.95+$4 S/H
Tapes: *"Conversations With Jesus"* by Glenda Green.
Each tape is a full 90 minutes of power-packed information about the impact of Divinity in direct communion with a thoughtful and well-educated woman of our generation. Even though the book is a close transcription of these tapes, the recorded lectures provide an invaluable expression of human warmth, candor, and vulnerability that cannot be conveyed through the written word. They communicate to the heart with authenticity and immediacy. Truly a course in life!

14 Tape album...$112 + $5.50 S/H

Art Prints: All prints are beautifully reproduced on conservation paper.

The Lamb and The Lion, 18" x 18"..$25
The Flame of Love (the infant Jesus with His Mother), 20" x 16".......$25
First Light (a spiritual portrait of Jesus--front cover), 20" x 16".........$25
Mary Magdalene, 20" x 15"...$25

    Shipping and handling $4.50

Canvas Transfers: *The Lamb and The Lion,* and *The Flame of Love* are also available on canvas. These provide the closest likeness to the original paintings. Sizes are the same as the prints. Unframed, $100, framed exquisitely in a 3" gold frame with liner, $225. Shipping and handling, unframed $10, framed $15.

Iris-Giclee: This is the most advanced and perfect form of replication ever developed for painting. Vivid in detail and faithful in color, these replications are on canvas and are exquisitely framed to enhance the beauty and reverence of the work of art. These replications have been technically produced under the artist's close supervision, and each one is made individually. This edition is limited to only 950, and each is signed and numbered by the artist. The finished framed size is 38"x 38," although they are also available unframed. Framed: $950, unframed: $700. Shipping and handling will be quoted with the order.

Ordering information: Make checks or money orders payable to: **Spiritis, P.O. Box 239, Sedona AZ 86339**

To place an order by phone or for credit card orders: **1-888-453-6324**

Wholesale orders may be placed with Spiritis Publishing at **1-888-453-6324,** or e-mail: *info@lovewithoutend.com*

If you would like to be added to our mailing list, please send your name and address to Spiritis, P.O. Box 239, Sedona, AZ 86339 or e-mail it to *info@lovewithoutend.com*

Visit our web site at *www.lovewithoutend.com.*